QUE VIVA MEXICO!

The two names in this turbulent moment of modern Mexico's history are Pancho Villa and Zapata.

Villa began his revolutionary career at the age of sixteen by killing the son of the local landlord who had raped Villa's sister: then he fled to the sierra.

Zapata's career began on his discharge from the army when he found that his little village's common land had been enclosed by the local landowner. Zapata immediately went guerrilla. (His stirring call to arms, by the way—'It is better to die on one's feet than live on one's knees'—was, a quarter of a century later and some thousands of miles distant, to rally the republican militia during the Spanish Civil War.)

These two moments of revolutionary gesture were to trigger off almost a decade of unmitigated violence and blood-curdling cruelty. The reasons for the mindless, practically medieval cruelty, are made abundantly clear in this tense book. Among the numerous examples the author quotes is that of one rancher who locked his workers up at night in rooms so small that they had to sleep one on top of the other. Mr Atkin coldly comments that a day came when they crucified the rancher on the beautifully carved door of his *hacienda*.

Revolution! Mexico 1910–20, tautly told and tensely structured though it is, may seem of peripheral interest to most of us. We would be wrong to think so. As the bloody events during the last Olympic Games in Mexico City told us—the revolution of Villa and Zapata has yet to achieve its terrible apotheosis.

Ronald Atkin, born 1931, has spent most of his life as a newspaperman. It was while he was on a tour of duty in Bermuda that his interest in Mexico was aroused. Subsequently he travelled widely there gathering the material for this book.

Ronald Atkin

Revolution!
Mexico 1910–20

Panther

Granada Publishing Limited
Published in 1972 by Panther Books Limited
3 Upper James Street, London W1R 4BP

First published in Great Britain by Macmillan & Co
Limited 1969
Copyright © Ronald Atkin 1969
Made and printed in Great Britain by
Richard Clay (The Chaucer Press), Ltd.,
Bungay, Suffolk
Set in Linotype Times

Contents

List of Illustrations

The author and publishers are grateful to Jose Andow and El Paso Public Library (south-west reference department) for permission to reproduce those illustrations marked EPPL; and to Senora Y. C. de Casasola for those marked (CS).

Maps (drawn by Edgar Holloway)

'City streets and country lanes have flowed with the blood of thousands. . . . The whole land is bathed in blood.'

Randolph Wellford Smith: *Benighted Mexico*

for Brenda

Brief Chronological Table

1910	July	Porfirio Díaz re-elected President
	November	Plan of San Luis Potosí. Revolution launched under leadership of Francisco I. Madero, supported by Pancho Villa and Emiliano Zapata
1911	May	Capture of Ciudad Juárez by Madero's forces Díaz flees
	June	Madero enters Mexico City
	September	Madero elected President
1913	February	The Tragic Ten Days of heavy fighting in Mexico City Madero falls and Victoriano Huerta comes to power
1914	April	American occupation of Veracruz
	July	Huerta resigns in the face of opposition from the Constitutionalists led by Venustiano Carranza (the 'First Chief'), Alvaro Obregón and Pancho Villa
	October	Convention of Aguascalientes
1915	February	Obregón's Army of Operations occupies Mexico City
1916	March	'Columbus raid' Villa attacks the small town of Columbus, New Mexico. The U.S. Government retaliates by sending General John J. Pershing's Punitive Expedition
1917	March	Carranza elected President
1919	April	Death of Zapata
	May	Fall and death of Carranza
	November	Obregón elected President
1923	July	Death of Pancho Villa

Preface

The Mexican Revolution, which began in 1910, was the first social upheaval of the twentieth century. Although Mexico's powerful northern neighbour, the United States, was several times embroiled in the troubles, the Revolution (always accorded a capital R by Mexicans to distinguish it from the myriad minor rebellions and barrack uprisings which plagued the country for years) was essentially a Mexican affair, a civil war unmatched for bitterness and cruelty until the Spanish Civil War twenty-five years later. For the Mexicans, the Revolution was a bloody ten years of wearisome trial and incredible suffering which forged a modern nation from a feudal society, but at a crushing price in terms of prosperity and progress for many years.

The Revolution struggled officially into being, in a fashion which was bizarre even for Mexico, on 20 November 1910. That date is enshrined in the names of streets and squares in almost every Mexican city. What is a good deal less clear is the date that the Revolution *ended*. On my two visits to Mexico I was told many times, 'The Revolution still goes on'. In the sense that its sweeping aims and Utopian objectives remain incomplete, this is certainly true.

However, for many people the Revolution as such ended with the publication of Mexico's historic Constitution of February 1917. But I have chosen to take my story of the Revolution a further three years, to 1920. There are two reasons for this. The first is that Mexico's last successful uprising, against the presidency of Venustiano Carranza, took place in that year. The second is that Carranza's rule was replaced by what came to be known as the Northern Dynasty, a circle of military men from the north-western state of Sonora headed, until his assassination in 1928, by Alvaro Obregón and afterwards by Plutarco Elías Calles. Though the country continued to be plagued by unrest and uprisings for some time, Mexico's era of reconstruction and consolidation began with Obregón in 1920, and the rule of the Northern Dynasty continued until the fall of Calles in 1935.

The Revolution was achieved only at a tremendous cost

in suffering (the population between 1910 and 1920 went down from fifteen million to twelve million), but hardship and death are accepted as everyday factors in a land in which men have always survived against long odds.

Mexico's history and Mexico's earth are red with blood. It is a nation dominated by death: the people have even dedicated one of their fiestas to it. On 2 November, the Day of the Dead, candlelight meals are eaten on the graves of departed ones, and skeletons and grisly skulls of candy and confectionery are on sale in much the same way as hot cross buns are sold in Britain.

The Mexican Revolution was a complicated decade in the violent history of an emerging nation. The Revolution, its history and its treatment by the Mexicans, has been neatly summed up as 'folklore with footnotes'. For this reason, and also because of the deep passions which the Revolution aroused, I had to tread with caution when I came to write this book. Many Mexican, and indeed some American, writers on the subject had an axe to grind, an axe which they plunged into the skull of their chosen victim. For instance, Pancho Villa was neither the hearty Robin Hood nor the leering, evil sadist he has been made out to be, though he was certainly a figure much larger than life—a bandit-turned-revolutionary, who, though a teetotaller and non-smoker, had an enormous appetite for ice-cream, women and war, and whose compassion was exceeded only by his cruelty.

I have attempted to streamline and simplify the vast, sprawling story of the Revolution without distorting it or consciously presenting a view biased in any way. Only the long-dead participants will know for certain whether the story is an accurate assessment. I hope they would agree, for this book is a tribute to them.

RONALD ATKIN
Chislehurst, Kent
August 1968

Part One: Díaz

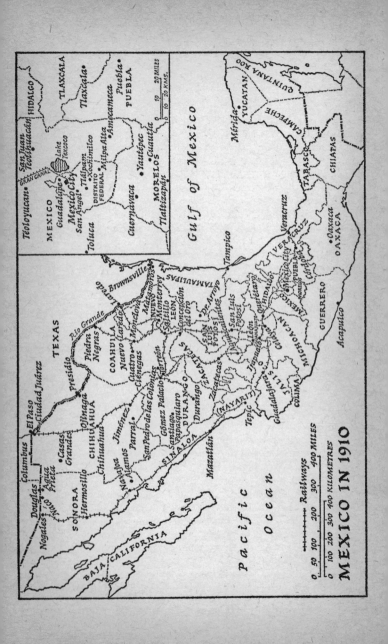

MEXICO IN 1910

1 : Dancing on a Volcano

In September 1910, Mexico celebrated its 100th year of independence. September, too, brought the eightieth birthday of the nation's dictator, Porfirio Díaz, who had ruled for thirty years. To mark the double event, the whole month was set aside as a holiday and two million pounds, more than the year's budget for education, was lavished on the festivities.

The dazzling month of celebrations began on an ironic note with the inauguration of a mental hospital, followed two days later by a stone-laying ceremony at a new jail. There were other, more appropriate ceremonies. The National University was re-opened, a gilded angel was set on a pedestal high over Mexico City, a monument was unveiled to Mexican military cadets killed resisting the American invasion of 1848. And on a practical note, the capital's water and street lighting systems were improved.

Distinguished guests were invited to the celebrations, all expenses paid, from every important nation in the world, and elaborate preparations were made to ensure that the foreign delegations would be impressed by what they saw. Mexico City's hordes of beggars were driven out of the paved section of the capital, and soldiers and police turned away ragged peasants if they attempted to approach the city centre.

Flowered arches in the national colours of red, white and green decorated the main streets. Flags and bunting hung everywhere. At night the words 'Progress' and 'Liberty' shone from the towers of the magnificent old Spanish cathedral in the main square, the Zócalo.

Beautiful women were gathered from all over Mexico and 'distributed like a thousand sweet blossoms to grace the entertainments'. European waiters were imported to serve at the most important banquets. Mexican hospitality even extended to the provision of proper clothing for certain shabby ministers from Central American countries.

The guest nations responded with equal enthusiasm and ostentation: Germany's Kaiser Wilhelm conferred the Collar of the Grand Cross of the Order of the Red Eagle on

President Díaz and sent a life-size portrait of himself; Italy gave a statue of Garibaldi, America one of George Washington; France returned the keys of Mexico City, taken away during the French intervention in Mexico in 1862; and Spain sent back the uniform and other revered relics of José María Morelos, the priest-turned-general who was captured and shot by the Spanish in the War of Independence. It was a time of forgiveness all round.

A huge delegation of senators, congressmen, businessmen and journalists descended from the United States. Among them was General Harrison Gray Otis, owner of the *Los Angeles Times*, who was quite frank about his intentions. 'I'm out for a good time,' he told an *El Paso Times* reporter. 'All I've got to do, according to instructions, is to extend the hand to the president of Mexico and all of his people.'

Even Japan was represented at the centenary. But Britain, mourning the death of King Edward VII, took no official part, though a congratulatory message was sent to President Díaz.

'There were banquets, celebrations, ceremonies in fatiguing succession,' wrote the newly appointed American Ambassador, Henry Lane Wilson, and gradually the festivities worked towards the mid-month climax, Díaz's birthday on 15 September and the independence centenary the following day. The birthday parade was worthy of Cecil B. De Mille; it depicted Mexico from Montezuma to independence, and ten thousand participants, including fifty pure-blooded Aztecs whose great temple had stood on that very spot 400 years ago, marched past the reviewing stand in the Zócalo.

That night sixty distinguished guests from the world's great nations sat down in the National Palace to a ten-course dinner; the first eight courses were served on silver plates, the last two on plates of solid gold. While Díaz's guests were being sumptuously fêted, the crowds outside were entertained by music from sixteen bands spread across the huge square, all blaring different tunes at the same time. Overhead whooshed the most elaborate fireworks display that even a pyrotechnically-minded nation like Mexico had ever seen.

At five minutes to eleven all was hushed and a spotlight focused on a velvet-draped balcony on the second floor of the Palace, where hung the Liberty Bell. It had been shortly before midnight on 15 September 1810 that Hidalgo, the parish priest of the little town of Dolores, in the state of Guanajuato, had rung the bell of his church calling on patriots to fight for freedom from Spain, thereby sparking off the War of Independence. In 1896 the bell had been brought to the capital, hung at the National Palace and rung every year since then to celebrate Mexico's freedom. The ceremony is still one of Mexico's most important annual occasions.

Precisely at eleven the erect, white-haired figure of President Díaz appeared on the balcony and, to the *vivas* of the crowd, struck Hidalgo's bell three times, as he had done for the past fourteen years.

On 23 September came another spectacular occasion, a grand ball in the Palace. The huge patio had been roofed over and hung with thousands of lights and roses. Two thousand guests danced to the music of a 150-piece orchestra and drank twenty wagonloads of champagne, poured by hundreds of costumed servants.

An American resident, Mrs Leone Moats, was quite carried away by the ball. 'The scene and music were so lovely that it all bore an air of enchantment; you simply floated, dancing, through the crowd,' she wrote, '... I often think back to that night. It celebrated so gorgeously the beginning of the end.'

The Palace privileged were dancing on a volcano.

There had already been rumbling warnings.... Five days before his birthday, a mob had thrown stones at the windows of the Díaz house in Calle Cadena and the old man had been anonymously promised a bullet as a birthday present. And even amid the gaiety of the Palace ball, the detested Vice-President Ramón Corral had been greeted by icy silence as he escorted Díaz's wife Carmen onto the floor.

Díaz seemed at the pinnacle of success. He was embarking on his eighth term as president, having ruled Mexico since 1876, apart from a four-year spell from 1880 to 1884. His power at home and prestige abroad had never seemed greater and he had been spectacularly successful in bringing stability and at least the outward signs of material prosperity to his country. After suffering more than three dozen dictators, presidents and assorted rulers in fifty-five years since Independence, Mexico had needed peace above all. And, since 1876, peace—at a price—was what Díaz had provided.

Yet within eight months of the great celebrations his dictatorship, seemingly indestructible, had crumbled and he had fled with most of his government into exile before the early-warning signs of the revolutionary hurricane.

What went wrong? Díaz had created a machine which he oiled with the blood of the underprivileged. He rewarded all except the people, and in the end he paid the price.

Though he still appeared alert and vigorous, Díaz's hand had weakened after thirty years of power. He was eighty and not one of his cabinet was under sixty. They were called 'a group of doddering mummies as respectable as they were useless'. It had become a government of old men and decrepitude extended right through the Díaz power structure. His judges and generals were fat, rich, relaxed—and old. A random choice of some of his state governors gives an idea of the dictatorship's ominous brittleness.

In Tlaxcala, Próspero Cahuantzi was 77; in Querétaro General Francisco González Cosío was 68. In Tabasco General Abraham Bandalia, 78, 'an amorous old man given to raping', had ruled for 2 years. In Puebla the tyrannical General Mucio Martínez was 75, in Michoacan Aristeo Mercado was 77. Aguascalientes had been run for 24 years by the 72-year-old Alejandro Vázquez del Mercado. Guanajuato's governor J. Obregón González was 70 and had ruled for 18 years.

The longevity of these politicians was testimony to their careful self-preservation in a nation in which the average life expectancy was 27 years.

A new generation had grown up during the years that Mexico lay quiet in her straitjacket, and the younger men who were excluded from the benevolence of Díaz formed an inexorably mounting opposition—not overt, perhaps, but real enough. The Revolution was conceived, controlled and fought by young men. A new generation displaced an older one.

Young intellectuals like Francisco Madero, son of a rich northern Mexico landowner, went abroad for their education and learned something of democracy. When they returned home they naturally wanted to see such ideas promulgated in their homeland. When the Díaz régime melted away before Madero the Redeemer it was ironic that the rallying cry of the new freedom-seekers was 'Universal Suffrage and No Re-election'. Porfirio Díaz had ridden into power thirty-five years earlier with exactly the same slogan.

Díaz had shown strength from birth—and had needed to. A cholera epidemic was raging when he was born, of mixed Indian and Spanish blood, in the southern town of Oaxaca in 1830, and his parents had him christened as quickly as possible in case he should fall victim. But Porfirio survived that crisis, and many more too.

After first studying for the priesthood and then for the law, Díaz found his true vocation when he joined another native of Oaxaca, Benito Juárez, in fighting the French imposition of the Austrian, Maximilian, on the Mexican people. Díaz was twice wounded, three times imprisoned and three times he escaped. In addition to recognition of his bravery, he also gained a reputation for honesty. After the fight against the French was won, Díaz returned to the National Treasury 87,000 pesos (about £8500) of unused campaign funds, a thing unheard of in the grab and graft of those days.

In 1871 Juárez, Mexico's greatest president, stirred up opposition by seeking re-election for a fourth term. He was opposed by Díaz and by Sebastian Lerdo de Tejada, who for eight years had been the faithful subordinate of Juárez. In the election no candidate received a clear majority, so the choice devolved upon Congress. They elected Juárez, while Lerdo became President of the Supreme Court. Díaz rebelled but he was crushed and fled into hiding in the north, disguised as a priest. By spring of the following year Juárez was in full control of a country apparently headed at long last for a spell of peace and prosperity. Then, on 18 July 1872, Juárez died suddenly of a heart attack. With him was buried the last hope for at least half a century of combining peace with freedom.

Lerdo succeeded to the presidency (in those days there was no vice-presidential office) but when he too sought re-election in 1876 Díaz rallied the malcontents under the banner of 'effective suffrage and no re-election' and rebelled again. After initial reverses, Díaz triumphed and on 21 November 1876 he rode into Mexico City and up to the National Palace, in which he was to reign for so long.

The historian Henry Bamford Parkes has summed up Díaz's aims: 'He set himself to enforce peace by making himself the national *cacique* [chief], binding together the various discordant elements in the Mexican population through a common bond of loyalty to himself. Only a dictator, it was argued, could enforce peace....'

That the Díaz government was a dictatorship no one denied. Since Mexicans had known precious little liberty or democracy since independence, it was merely a question of whether Díaz proved a good or bad dictator.

Díaz's first term as President was relatively uneventful and he used it mainly to consolidate his political position by playing off his enemies against one another and by the judicious distribution of favours. When in 1880 he had, under the new amendment to the constitution, to hand over power, Díaz was able to engineer the election of Manuel González, his Minister of War and a friend on whom he could count to retire obediently after four years. González's term of office was distinguished by corruption on a scandalous scale, with the Minister of Public Works, Carlos Pacheco (who resembled President González not only in dishonesty, but also in the lack of an arm, lost fighting the French), as one of the chief offenders. His ministry embarked on a frenzied attempt to boost the economy and it was during the González régime that the era of vast railway expansion began. The government recklessly pledged itself to pay up to £900 to American companies for every kilometre of railway built. The flow of American capital and business was encouraged and public lands were given away with scant regard for the consequences. Mines and other concessions were granted lavishly. González also tried to win favour abroad by grandly recognising the debt of £9 million, which Mexico had owed England for twenty years.

Inevitably, the government ran itself into a state of financial collapse, aggravated by the rampant graft and by the unrealistic subsidies to railways and other developers. 'Few governments have furnished a more conspicuous example of administrative prostitution and corruption,' wrote the Mexican historian Luis Lara Pardo. 'The looting of the exchequer was never more complete and shameless. All the revenues went to fill the coffers of González and his favourites ... the wages of civil servants were suspended; the army alone received its pay—otherwise revolution would have broken out afresh.'

As Díaz had foreseen, the cry of 'no re-election' was generally forgotten in the thankfulness with which the country welcomed him back as president in 1884. The González régime ended in a welter of riots, looting and threats of Congressional investigation of the government's finances. González, whose wife had left him and was publishing pamphlets attacking his private life, relinquished office in the grand manner. Mrs Leone Moats, who had been so enchanted by the centenary ball, thought González 'not much of a manager, but instinctively acquisitive. He left but one place clean, the National Treasury, and on his last day in office he was not able to resist removing the furniture from the National Palace.' Perhaps as a souvenir of four memorable and profitable years.

Díaz permitted a Congressional investigation to go on just long enough to ruin González's reputation, then he quashed its findings and presented the former president with the State governorship of Guanajuato, where González reigned until his death, boasting that the government had killed all the bandits in Guanajuato but himself.

Now Díaz was back in office and he meant to stay....

Before detailing the accomplishments of the Díaz régime and the iniquities and failings which led to its overthrow, it is essential to describe something of the country itself; its geography, its racial structure and its backwardness. Mexico is a land of paradox and stark contrast—between rich and poor, between desert where years may pass without a drop of rain and tropical jungle, where the rainfall can exceed 100 inches a year.

The eighth largest country in the world, it has an area of more than 760,000 square miles. It is three and a half times the size of France and in shape resembles a vast horn of plenty. Mexicans wryly point out that the open end of this cornucopia is pouring out its treasure across the 2000 miles of border with the United States. Díaz himself once neatly summed up his country's problem : 'Poor Mexico—so far from God and so near the United States.'

Generally speaking, Mexico is a mountainous country. Only about a third of its area is below 1600 feet and more than half is above 3000. When Hernán Cortés was asked by the Emperor Charles V of Spain what the newly-won land of Mexico was like, the Conquistador crumpled a piece of paper in his fist and dropped it on the table in front of the king.

The nation's rocky backbone, the Sierra Madre, thrusts aloft several notable peaks, all of volcanic origin. The highest is Orizaba (18,700 feet), third among North American mountains. Its snow-capped peak can be seen two days out in the Gulf of Mexico by ships approaching Veracruz. The two next highest are the spectacular volcanoes which stand guard over Mexico City, the active Popocatapetl (Smoking Mountain), 17,887 feet, and the extinct Ixtaccíhuatl (Woman in White), 17,343 feet.

The distance from Mexico City's 7350 feet altitude to the sea at Veracruz is no more than 265 miles, but the change in height and climate has been likened to the equivalent of motoring from Scotland to Nigeria in five or six hours.

Mexico has been justifiably called a three-storeyed land : the tropical hot lands, which border the Pacific and the Gulf of Mexico; the temperate lands, which comprise the seaward slopes of the mountain ranges and the depressions in the central plateau of the country, at a height of about 4000 feet; and the so-called cold lands, the higher parts of the central plateau and the surrounding mountains.

But in European terms, these arbitrary divisions have little relevance. The hot lands can sometimes prove quite temperate, while the winter temperature in sections of the 'cold lands' is often warmer than that of the French Riviera. The climates crowd in upon each other; it is possible to stand in the snow on a Sierra Madre ridge and look down into a valley where orange trees are in fruit.

Despite its horn of plenty appearance, two-thirds of Mexico is desert or mountain and lacks two essentials: rivers and a generous rainfall. It is a thirsty land.

This diversity of climate and terrain was, and in some cases remains, an obstacle to transportation and communication; this, in turn, was one of the most formidable hindrances to progress. Despite three centuries of Spanish occupation and nearly a century and a half of independence, strong elements of regionalism still exist. Mexicans prefer to identify themselves in terms of their home community (or *patria chica*, little homeland). In the early days of the Díaz régime, with paved roads non-existent, railways in their infancy and many centres accessible only on muleback, these feelings were markedly stronger.

Mexicans consider taking a racial census undemocratic, not to say impossible. But, according to statistics published in 1965, about thirty per cent of the present population is Indian and about sixty per cent *mestizo*, mixed blood, though technically more than ninety per cent are mixed bloods, tailing off to Indians at one end and whites at the other. About nine per cent of the population is white and one per cent has marked Negroid characteristics.

The white Spanish blood was, for the most part, disseminated among the Indian stock shortly after the Conquest. At no time during the Colonial period were there more than a few thousand whites in Mexico, and most of these were males who were either unmarried or had left their wives behind. In fact there were more Negroes than whites in Mexico during most of the sixteenth, seventeenth and eighteenth centuries, although by the end of the 1800s the bulk of the Negro population had also been absorbed into the mushrooming *mestizo* population.

During the colonial period there developed a terminology for sixteen kinds of mixed-blood Indian, though the three most common were *mestizo,* mixture of white and Indian, *zambo* or *pardo,* mixture of Negro and Indian, and *mulato,* mixture of Negro, Indian and white. Some parishes kept three books to record baptisms of Negroids, Indians and whites and *mestizos.*

When Díaz seized power in 1876 the Indians made up about thirty-five per cent of the population. In spite of this number, they were a negligible political factor because of their lowly social and economic standing; and because of this, Díaz never considered it necessary to make any special concessions to them. From the beginning he tended to believe that the Indians were a hindrance to progress and should be kept in perpetual subjugation.

The *mestizos,* who according to one observer 'have inherited the vices of both Spaniard and Indian without any of their virtues', made up about half the population—Díaz himself was a *mestizo*—while at the very top of the social heap were the creoles, people of pure European stock. Eighty per cent of the population were illiterate.

These barriers of geography, race and education fragmented would-be opposition to Díaz, enabling him gradually to dominate every aspect of Mexican society and life.

Installed once more in the National Palace, Díaz set about bringing the country to heel. Because he had fought valiantly for the liberals, and because after the excesses of the González period any change was seen as a change for the better, many people gave him enthusiastic support when he took office. Indeed, for the first decade of his rule, the régime was perhaps the most popular in the short history of independent Mexico. But eventually the hopeful smiles died on the faces of a betrayed nation. This 'liberal' was to hang on to power for a third of a century, though he cleverly covered his iron fist with a variety of velvet gloves. But his control was absolute. Democratic principles were discarded and everything staked on economic development and peace.

Peace was what Mexico needed above all. And a period of peace was what Díaz provided, for the first time since 1810. That achievement alone, in a nation as trigger-conscious as Mexico, serves as some mitigation for the fact that individual liberties and lawful processes were abandoned for thirty years. No matter how bitter the price, peace was the prerequisite of any hopes of betterment and development.

Díaz offered Mexicans the alternative of *pan ó palo*, bread or the club. A dog with a bone in its mouth neither kills nor steals, he philosophised, offering the bone of power and prestige to all the dissatisfied elements. He bought the loyalty of some by gifts of *haciendas* (large estates), concessions or cash. If they refused the *pan*, the *palo* was wielded mercilessly. All possible instigators of opposition—landowners, clergy, army, intelligentsia and even the bandit chiefs—were converted into followers of Don Porfirio. He did not amass a personal fortune but he spent untold millions on keeping what he wanted, the dictatorship. He gave away the country's wealth in the form of privileges, monopolies and concessions to all those who might be able to help him towards this end.

Parkes has written: 'The meaning of the Porfirian dictatorship was that the bands of wolves, instead of fighting each other as they had been doing ever since the establishment of independence, were now invited to join each other in an attack on the sheepfolds.'

In other words, peace was achieved in Mexico by making the bandit the symbol of authority.

Petty tyrants were granted formal sanction. Bandits were hunted down and given their own version of *pan ó palo*: join us or die. Those who chose amnesty were recruited into the *Guardia Rural*, a Mexican version of the Mounties. Those who did not surrender were pursued and killed by the very men who had accepted the government's pardon. The move was brilliantly successful and Díaz was soon boasting to a British journalist that the Mexican countryside was safer than Hyde Park, and that the burglar and brigand had gone out of business. Mexico was indeed one of the safest lands in the world—for all except Mexicans.

The *rurales* were happy. They got a good—and legal— living off the countryside and Díaz ensured pride in their work by dressing and equipping them lavishly. They wore suits of grey or brown suede, with silver embroidery on the jacket and trousers. Silver also glinted on their saddles, sombreros and spurs, and the red blankets they carried over one shoulder were flaming badges of authority. The officers' hats, loaded with silver braid, cost hundreds of pesos. With their Mauser rifles, knives, revolvers and lassos, they were mobile arsenals.

Mrs Moats, after conceding that they were mostly bandits, found them 'the world's most picturesque policemen.... To see them on parade ... was a sight to thrill the most apathetic. They rode proudly on fine horses with silver trappings.... And their martial music—there was none other as stirring. I can hear their bugles now!'

The *rurales* may have been picturesque but they were also licensed robbers and killers, the tools of the *jefes políticos* (district political bosses), and their brutality went almost unchecked. In the state of Hidalgo a group of Indians who resisted the appropriation of their lands were buried up to their necks in the ground they had attempted to defend, and the *rurales* galloped over them. Enemies and critics of Díaz became victims of the *ley fuga*, the law of flight, by which *rurales* and the army were permitted to shoot prisoners, afterwards explaining that they had been killed while attempting to escape. Though Mrs Alec Tweedie, a Díaz biographer, called it 'a law which allows any man running away from justice to be shot—a simple method which saves much trouble', obviously not all the victims were 'running away from justice'. There were more than ten thousand instances of *ley fuga* during Díaz's rule.

Gradually the dictator's grip tightened.... By 1887 Díaz had pushed into law a new amendment to the constitution authorising a second presidential term and in 1880 a further amendment made possible indefinite re-election.

The Press was bribed or bludgeoned into submission. Soon after his re-election in 1884, Díaz summoned the country's leading journalists for an 'interview'. Towards the end of his talk, Díaz turned the conversation to the new methods being introduced of capital punishment by electricity. Most of them took the hint.

Newspapermen and newspapers, except for the brave few

in precarious and intermittent opposition, were subsidised. The puppet press helped to keep bureaucracy and army in order by ruining the reputations of the over-ambitious. Those editors who were still bold enough to attack the régime were imprisoned and sometimes assassinated by the *bravi*, a group of hardened criminals who smashed up opposition newspaper offices and provoked duels with anti-Díaz editors and politicians. One unrepentant editor, Filomeno Mata, went to prison thirty-four times.

The dictator's control over the judiciary was an even more potent weapon. Díaz removed and appointed Supreme Court judges at will, heavily bribed judges and magistrates freed the *bravi* and imprisoned the outspoken. Only official lawyers won their cases, whatever the merits.... For the ordinary people, justice did not exist.

Favourites rarely needed to fear the law. It was popularly said that generals, bullfighters and foreigners were assured of favourable court decisions. One matador was arrested and charged with the murder of a woman but, in the face of public clamour, was released for a bullfight that weekend. He promptly fled to the United States, whereupon his brother was arrested, tried for the murder and acquitted.

There was so little justice that, as late as 1923 one American, long resident of Mexico, could write: 'Justice is really much more satisfactory in Mexico than in the United States. There you never know how your case is coming out. Here you know to a peso the price of each judge, and if the matter under litigation is worth the price, you pay it.'

Congress was controlled in the same arbitrary manner as the judiciary. The legislature became a mockery, retained to add the flavour of legality to the dictator's acts. Díaz cynically referred to his lawmakers as *mi caballada*, 'my herd of tame horses'.

The names of victorious candidates often became known before the elections and one state, trying to maintain the semblance of democratic principles, set the prisoners in the penitentiary the task of applying crosses to an impressive number of ballot papers. Díaz received many letters soliciting Congressional seats and used painstakingly to compile a list of those he wished to reward. Relatives came top of the list; about a dozen seats were allocated to his son Porfirito,

sons-in-law and nephews. Next in order of priority were old
military associates or their sons. Then came the relatives of
generals, governors and cabinet ministers.

Some owed their seats in Congress to the fact that they
were natives of Díaz's home town of Oaxaca. Don Porfirio
even found places for his dentist, Ramón Reynoso, and his
doctor, Angel Gutiérrez. Occasionally mistakes occurred in
the list of 'candidates' and the names of dead persons were
put forward for election. The loyalty of the Army, so vital
to a dictatorship, was ensured by allowing the generals
unlimited opportunities for graft. They were given *haciendas,* granted concessions for gaming houses and brothels
and collected pay for regimental companies where nothing
more than platoons existed.

So Díaz ruled Mexico with what was called at the time
'the most perfect one-man system on earth'. He appointed
the governors of the twenty-seven states and gave them
licence to tyrannise in return for their loyalty. These men in
turn appointed the *jefes políticos.* So the staircase of power
was built: minor officials answerable to the detested *jefes,*
who were in turn answerable to the governors. And they
answered to their master, Díaz. In the midst of such blatant
misdealing Díaz was careful to maintain an air of scrupulous honesty and integrity. In contrast the operations of the
state governors reeked of graft and these very misdemean-
ours helped to anchor Díaz even more firmly in power. No
one wanted to see such a patently honest and loyal man as
Díaz replaced by one of the state governors.

Now Díaz required the backing of one further vital institution, the Church. The foundations for this had been laid
when, in November 1881 while he was temporarily out of
power, he remarried. Díaz was then fifty-one and had been
a widower for a year and a half. He had three children,
Porfirito (little Porfirio), then fourteen, and two daughters,
Amada, eight, and Luz, six. His bride was Carmen Romero
Rubio, eighteen-year-old daughter of one of the most
powerful conservative politicians of the time and a member
of an ardent Catholic family.

The marriage was the making of Díaz; it converted him
from a rough chieftain into a gentleman and, when he resumed office in 1884, a president acceptable in the eyes of

the world. Carmen, educated in the United States, was
fluent in English and French, whereas her new husband
spoke neither language. She had poise, intelligence and
glamour, and her influence on a man old enough to be her
father was extraordinary. On their return from honeymoon
in the United States Díaz was a new man.

His mane of white hair, once so unruly, was neatly
brushed; his moustache, which formerly drooped on either
side of his mouth, Indian style, had taken on a civilised and
martial appearance. Now his shoes were always shined;
collar, cuffs and shirt front were white and starched; his
clothes well-pressed. He used gloves without embarrassment
and his steps had become measured, his gestures grave. He
conducted himself properly at the table and no longer used a
toothpick in public.

The most important achievement of the marriage, however, was to unite Díaz and the Church. The Conquest of
1520 had brought to Mexico not only a new race but a new
religion. For 300 years of colonial rule, the Catholic
Church's strong and universal influence with the Indian
population and the government gave it an important place,
and it acquired great wealth and power. A conservative
Mexican historian, Lucas Alamán, estimated that by the
end of the colonial period 'not less than half of the property
and capital of the country belonged to the Church. Most of
the remainder was controlled by the Church through mortgages. The Church was the landlord, the banker, and the
trustee of the period.' This wealth, in stark contrast to the
poverty of the struggling new state, made the Church un-
popular with progressives, and its position was further
weakened when the revolutionary priests Hidalgo and
Morelos were excommunicated and handed over to the
secular authorities for execution.

In 1859 President Juárez instigated sweeping reforms.
Monastic orders were suppressed and church property was
nationalised. Bitter religious feelings, both for and against,
brought outbreaks of violence, which culminated in the
French intervention and the setting-up of the Austrian
Maximilian, as Mexico's Emperor. The Church, seeking a
new champion, backed Maximilian, but with his defeat and

execution by Juárez, its last hopes of retaining significant
power were gone.

Díaz, however, needing the support of all factions,
allowed his new wife to arrange a meeting with high
Church officials, at which it was secretly agreed that clerical
appointments should be submitted to the dictator for approval, much in the manner of Congressional appointments,
while in return the Reform Laws of 1859 would not be
enforced. Monasteries and convents were again established
and there was a progressive decline in the implementation
of the repressive laws. The grateful clergy used their influence to preach obedience to Díaz, and since the decline
in the popularity of the Church as such had not been
matched by any lessening of religious fervour among the
masses, this was a highly significant source of pro-Díaz
propaganda.

The foundations had thus been laid for Mexico's economic development. Only a treasury surplus could finally
guarantee the stability of the dictatorship, however, and
since the government was heavily in debt after the fiasco of
the four years of González administration, Díaz decided to
encourage the flow of foreign capital in a more prudent
way but still on terms highly advantageous to the investor.
In the 1880s and 1890s cash poured into the country.
Plantations, factories and railways sprouted all over Mexico.

The railways expansion scheme, started under González,
was a prime example of the economic scramble. Mexico's
first eight miles of track were laid in 1850 and twenty years
later had only been extended to cover the British-financed
route between the capital and Veracruz, 265 miles away.
But by 1892 there were 6873 miles of track and by 1910 the
total was more than 12,000 miles. Graft operated on an
equally grandiose scale . . . £5 million vanished into receptive
pockets; contractors were paid for miles of supposedly
completed track that were non-existent; in some areas steel
bridges purchased abroad lay in the jungle while the timber
operators kept replacing the wooden bridges—short-lived in
the tropics.

Don Porfirio's railway programme was one of the most
highly-praised accomplishments of his régime. Tributes
poured in from abroad. But the American builders had laid

the lines with more regard for their own convenience than Mexico's economic needs. The great trunk lines paralleled each other across the desolate, sparsely settled north, ending up at the American border, while the wealthier agricultural areas, notably the state of Oaxaca and the lands to the south of it, were left without a railway.

Exports and imports increased tenfold. Then at the end of the nineteenth century the discovery of oil along the Gulf coast strengthened the boom, and, apparently, Mexico's prosperity. Commercial production of petroleum commenced in 1901 and within that year Mexico had already become the world's twelfth largest producer. Between 1911 and 1917, despite the interruptions and destructions of the Revolution, Mexico rose to third-ranking producer and from 1918 to 1926 was second only to the United States.

Many quick-thinking foreigners cashed in on oil, but two in particular, the American Edward L. Doheny and the British Weetman Pearson (later Lord Cowdray) made vast profits. In 1900 Doheny acquired enormous stakes of oil-rich land near Tampico for less than five shillings an acre.

Lord Cowdray's firm, Pearson and Son, had built the Blackwall tunnel under the Thames, the East River tunnels in New York and had undertaken a series of spectacular construction projects in Mexico which had made Díaz and Lord Cowdray firm friends, enhancing the status of the Mexican and enriching the Englishman. And now his oil company, Mexican Eagle, struck it rich near Tuxpan in 1909.

Weetman Pearson was, until he was raised to the peerage in 1910, Liberal MP for Colchester, but he spent so much of his time pursuing his business interests abroad that he became known in Parliament as the Member for Mexico; and the figure of a Mexican peon on the Cowdray coat of arms bears mute testimony to the part played by the underprivileged of that country in his business success.

Lord Cowdray's influence and interest in Mexico aroused jealousy and mistrust in the United States, particularly when the Republican and pro-business president, William Howard Taft, was succeeded in 1913 by the Democrat Woodrow Wilson. In March 1914 the American Ambassador in London, Walter Hines Page, wrote to Wilson: 'I

believe that if Taft had had another four years Cowdray
would have owned Mexico, Ecuador and Colombia. . . .'

He was accused of taking more money out of Mexico
than anyone since Cortés, but his detractors failed to point
out that the public works undertaken by his company had
also benefited Mexico. Not quite all the money went out of
Mexico. In 1918 the Cowdray Hospital was founded and
endowed at a cost of £130,000. Built in spacious grounds on
the outskirts of Chapultepec Park in Mexico City, it was
opened in 1923. Now known as the British-American Cowdray Hospital, it is still in use, though in a new building and
a new location.

Lord Cowdray's attempts to obtain further large concessions in Ecuador, Colombia and Costa Rica were frustrated
by the invoking of the Monroe Doctrine (which postulated
that non-American powers should not intervene in the
political affairs of the American continent). The Monroe
Doctrine, however, did not prevent Americans from cash-
ing in on the boom south of the border. The American
Ambassador Henry Lane Wilson estimated that by 1910
there were 75,000 Americans living in Mexico and that U.S.
capital investment amounted to more than 1000 million
dollars, forty per cent of America's total foreign investment
and greater than the capital stock owned by Mexicans
themselves.

U.S. interests accounted for more than half the oilfield
concessions and three-quarters of the mining interests.
Americans also owned great sugar, coffee and maguey
plantations, as well as vast cattle ranches. The Hearst newspaper family owned a tract 'about the size of Maryland and
Delaware combined'.

British interests were by no means negligible, being estimated at nearly £100 million, but the overwhelming influence was American. 'Mexico is rapidly becoming a land
of large American estates', wrote one American observer.
Naturally American businessmen thought a lot of Don
Porfirio and his reputation soon spread further. Before
Díaz took power, Mexico was pitied or despised in Europe
as one of the world's most backward nations. But as Mexico
gradually took a place in the sun the tributes began to pour
in. And they were all aimed at Díaz. Few rulers have been

so extravagantly praised and honoured.

Elihu Root, a former United States Secretary of State, said of Díaz: 'If I were a poet I should write eulogies; if I were a musician I should compose triumphal marches; if I were a Mexican I should feel that the steadfast loyalty of a lifetime would not be too much to give in return for the blessings he has brought to my country.

'But as I am neither poet, musician, nor Mexican, but only an American who loves justice and liberty, and hopes to see their reign among mankind progress and strengthen and become perpetual, I look to Porfirio Díaz, the President of Mexico, as one of the great men to be held up for the hero-worship of mankind.'

To Tolstoy, Díaz was the greatest political genius of the age and his government 'unique in history'. Andrew Carnegie called him 'the Moses and Joshua of his people ... who guided them for the first time along the road of civilisation'. Cecil Rhodes thought Díaz was the leading worker for civilisation in the nineteenth century; for Theodore Roosevelt there was no greater contemporary statesman; the Empress of China awarded him the Order of the Dragon; Britain made him a member of the Order of the Bath; and he was decorated by France, Japan, Russia, Italy, Portugal and Austria.

And, eulogy of eulogies, Marie Robinson Wright dedicated her book *Picturesque Mexico* 'To Señor General Don Porfirio Díaz, The Illustrious President Of Mexico, Whose Intrepid Moral Character, Distinguished Statesmanship And Devoted Patriotism Make Him The Pride And Glory Of His Country, Is Dedicated This Volume, Describing A Beautiful And Prosperous Land, Whose Free Flag Never Waved Over A Slave, And Whose Importance As A Nation Is Due To The Patriot Under Whose Administration Mexico Now Flourishes And Now Holds Its Proud Position Among The Republics Of The World'. Mrs Wright appeared to be suffering from a surfeit of enthusiasm and capital letters, as well as a shortage of facts.

The praise rolled in.... American businessmen even began to say that a man like Díaz was needed in Washington. He might have a brown skin, but he had the soul of a white man, they said—the highest praise at their disposal.

An American newspaperman living in Mexico City felt that 'Díaz was no less deceived than the outside world by the incessant chorus of flattery which had so long sounded in his ears.

'The spectacle of a ruler surrounded by sycophants is hardly an unfamiliar one, but the courtiers of Díaz possessed the immense advantage of modern business methods; they were in effect a corporation, a trust ... and for a long time fortunate in the weakness and incoherence of the opposition. To exalt Porfirio Díaz was a business policy, which had been carried out with such ability and persistency that it deceived all nations, including the one which was being exploited, and the man who sat upon its throne.'

Díaz's indulgent attitude towards foreigners was typified by the experience of an English widow, Rosa King, who in 1905 opened a tea room in the resort town of Cuernavaca, where, then as now, people came down from Mexico City for a change of air and for holidays. 'The prices I charged for my tea and buns were high but no one ever disputed them,' wrote Mrs King. 'Under Porfirio Díaz, foreigners were able to make so much money in Mexico that prices did not matter to them.'

In disputes between Mexicans and foreigners, the Díaz administration—and therefore the law—invariably took the side of the foreigner. An American was generally above the law, whatever his rank and whatever his offence. Even Ambassador Wilson, a great admirer of Díaz, was moved to criticise 'the lame, incompetent, corrupt judiciary'.

Foreigners were treated with the deference due to invited guests. Mining laws were changed to conform with foreign concepts and practices, and enormous tracts of land were sold very cheaply to them.

The government's proportion of the rich mining dividends was negligible; apart from a trifling stamp duty the oil developers paid no taxes and were free to export Mexico's wealth for their own profit. Finally, the preference shown to foreigners was humiliating to a people as proud and as touchy as the Mexicans. They complained that their country was 'the mother of foreigners and the step-mother of Mexicans'.

But it never occurred to the outside world to inquire into

the moral consequences of Díaz's régime, or even whether the famed railways had been intelligently or economically laid out; to marvel at the mileage was sufficient.

While foreign capital poured in to develop Mexico, the great mass of the people continued to live in appalling squalor. Though most had never known anything else, the emphasis on development and industrialisation widened the already vast gulf between rich and poor, and the contrast between the splendour of the few and the wretchedness of the many became even more marked.

In many ways Díaz was a great man, with many tangible achievements to his credit. He did much to develop his country. *But he did nothing to develop his people.* He could have helped them towards literacy, he could have created a nucleus of skilled workers, he could have raised a new generation of enlightened citizens. Instead, he tightened upon a nation of serfs the shackles of political and economic servitude.

The historian Gruening writes: 'What use was it to the peons that Mexico could borrow all the money it wanted at four per cent when they could not borrow or earn the few pesos necessary to release themselves from peonage? What use was it that 200 million pieces of mail flowed through the national post office every year when they could neither read nor write?'

The resentment against exploitation by foreigners was the thin edge of the wedge of disconcent. The misery of the peons and the theft of their lands was a far bigger reason for the Díaz régime's loss of support.

Throughout the colonial period Mexico's millions of Indians had lived in virtual independence, cultivating their *ejidos*, the common lands of a town or village. These *ejidos* were divided into portions for each peasant, the size depending on the number in his family and the quality of the soil. And with this portion went a share in the common grazing ground and water supply.

The separation of the Indian from his land started twenty years before Díaz became president. In 1856 a law called the *Ley Lerdo* was passed, dividing the *ejido* lands in fee simple among the peasants, rather than leaving them as communal holdings. In theory it was a just piece of legislation, but in practice the Indians, unused to private ownership, fell easy victims to land developers. Some unscrupulous officials appointed to parcel out the land sold it to companies or *hacienda* owners.

Under Díaz this robbery gained new impetus and incentive. The construction of railways and the influx of capital gave land a new value. In 1883 President González ordered the surveying of the vast areas of undeveloped lands, *terrenos baldíos*, mostly lying in the northern deserts or southern jungles. Almost unbelievably the surveying companies, largely foreign-owned, were given *one third* of the territory surveyed, in return for their work. As a result 125 million acres were surveyed in the next ten years, and some forty million acres went into private hands. By 1906 this had grown to fifty million acres. Even so, the move might have proved of eventual benefit to the nation had the surveyors stuck to undeveloped land. But surveying companies and government officials took advantage of the vagueness of boundaries and titles to include as *terrenos baldíos* much land that already belonged to other people.

Many villages which had managed to hang onto their *ejidos* after the *Ley Lerdo* were now robbed of them. Bewildered Indians who had held their land since pre-Conquest days were asked to prove legal title to it.

When they could not, the land was put up for sale. Legally the property owner had first chance to buy but in effect hardly ever had the money to do so.

In the rare cases where the Indians did possess deeds, they were often persuaded to part with these in exchange for a few bottles of the local brandy, *aguardiente* (literally 'fiery water'). When villagers still proved intractable, corrupt government officials granted water and irrigation rights to developing companies and the owners of the huge *haciendas*, and the village water supplies were cut off. After the dusty acres had been abandoned they could be legally 'denounced' and taken over. If the peasant still refused to knuckle under, the villages were often destroyed.

As the productive lands passed to the wealthy landlords, *ejidos* became so pitifully small that many family allotments were reduced to a couple of furrows and the Indians were driven onto the rocky mountain slopes to scavenge a living. The peasants did not always give up meekly; but they had no chance against the combined forces mobilised against them. Local judges and *jefes políticos* would sentence an obdurate villager to army conscription or to slavery on a distant plantation. These men rarely saw their families again. And those who gave up their lands quietly drifted into serfdom on the *haciendas*.

This epoch of land grabbing produced effects similar to the enclosure of the English commons. Both processes created a destitute and economically-uprooted population. But while England's new unemployed force fed a booming textile and mining industry, the destruction of communal lands in Mexico dispossessed peasants far more rapidly than the country's new-born industries could absorb them.

By 1910 almost half of Mexico belonged to fewer than 3000 families. Most of the remaining half was virtually uninhabitable, being either waterless desert or dense jungle. The historian Francisco Bulnes compiled a list of seventeen families who between them owned 150,000 square miles of territory, about a fifth of Mexico's total area, and a combined kingdom larger than Ireland, Italy or Japan. The estate in Chihuahua belonging to the state governor Luis Terrazas covered more than seven million acres. Many owners of these vast *haciendas* did not even know the real extent of their estates.

Had the *hacendados* been efficient and the lands they acquired been profitably used, this colossal looting might have proved less disastrous. But the *haciendas* were less productive than the smallholdings and were a dead weight on the economy of the country. Their feudal self-sufficiency —they imported nothing and exported next to nothing— meant that they promoted little commerce; cheap labour kept the need for modern machinery to a minimum. In 1892 Mexico, a country whose economy was then overwhelmingly agricultural, was forced to import £500,000 worth of grain. By 1909 this import figure had doubled—a sad commentary on the *haciendas'* productivity.

The *hacienda* system was the most characteristic, the most unyielding, of the institutions planted by the Spanish Conquest, and was the root of the political, social and economic structure of Mexico. In the hundred years since independence most of the other Spanish influences had been weakened or destroyed, but not the *hacienda*. The *hacienda* was Mexico. It paid negligible taxes, and in Guanajuato, for example, the land tax levied on all the *haciendas* produced less revenue than the tax imposed on the state's street pedlars!

Ownership of such vast areas, which might equal the size of a small European state, vested a man with power, prestige and the nearest social equivalent to a title, but rarely carried with it a love of the soil. Some of the newly-created land barons—the cattle kings in the north, sugar growers in Morelos, coffee and rubber cultivators in Chiapas—operated their lands efficiently, but the old creole *hacienda*-owning families of the central plateau, on whom the country depended for its food supplies, left great areas of their estates uncultivated, yet denied the use of these areas to others.

The tendency of these *hacendados* was to use their political powers to enlarge their estates rather than make them more productive, to exploit labour more and the soil less. The typical *hacendado* rarely lived on his estate, leaving its administration to managers while he spent the estate profits on high living in Mexico City or more frequently, London, Paris or the Riviera. His sons were often educated at the English Jesuit college at Stonyhurst, and his daughters went to French convents.

Parkes describes this luxuried class as 'courteous, sensual and decadent, with nothing to live for except pleasure'. The sons were invariably frivolous idlers and early adepts at every form of dissipation. One young member of the Terrazas family, Alberto, was said to have been so dissolute that he seduced his own niece. He was given the governorship of the state of Chihuahua 'to steady him'.

As the Díaz régime drew to a close the plantation system was at its height. A measure of the *hacienda*'s durability was that even in 1923, after thirteen years of revolution, 2682 owners out of a rural population of about eleven million still owned more than half of all lands in private hands. And of these, 115 held a quarter of all Mexico's private lands. In succeeding years, however, a vengeful people and a hostile government drastically reduced the number of *haciendas*. Nowadays many of the buildings still standing have been converted to other uses: schools, restaurants, hotels, even night clubs.

The British writer Mrs Tweedie visited the *hacienda* of San Gabriel, in the state of Morelos, in 1901. The owners, the Amor family, were a rarity in Mexico—they believed in treating their workers with compassion—but her description (if inaccurate in some respects) gives a vivid picture of life on a feudal estate before the Revolution.

'In all probability it was built for a monastery; the enormous thickness of the walls, which keep out the heat in the summer and cold in winter, the extraordinary solidity of everything, and the vast space it covers, bespeak a religious house. At the back is a fine stone swimming bath; indeed, it is well supplied not only with necessities but luxuries.

'With its long corridors, numerous chambers, strange balconies, its church, shop, great yards and outbuildings, it forms a veritable town in itself. . . .

'The village, containing nearly 3000 souls, belongs to the *hacienda*. The people pay no rent and the owners of the *hacienda* hold the right to turn them out. The peasants are lent the ground on which they build their own houses—such as they are—merely bamboo walls roofed with a palm leaf sort of thatch. They are all obliged to work for the *hacienda*, truly feudal style, whenever called upon to do so. Each man as a rule has an allotted number of days on which he is bound to render service. . . .

'The priest comes from the next village to celebrate Mass on Sundays, holidays and "days of obligation" . . . the proprietors of the *hacienda* pay the priest and the doctor . . . practically, however, the landowner has to look after the spiritual and bodily needs of his people. He is in fact, a small king with many responsibilities. . . .

'Each *hacienda* is obliged to keep its shop (the *tienda de raya*) and there all the purchases of the villagers are made, the owner of the *hacienda* taking the risk of profit or loss. . . . As a rule all the employees are paid in cash each Saturday night and a little on account every Wednesday; no bills are allowed at the store which is conducted on ready-money principles . . . unfortunately at some *haciendas*, the peons are not paid in money at all but have to take out their wages in goods from the store, a bad principle which renders the people little more than slaves.

'A man and his family live on six or eight cents a day (a cent is about a farthing) and men earn 50 cents a week on average; this is quite sufficient; they sit rent free, they have no fires to pay for, little clothing is required, and if so minded they can get *pulque* or *aguardiente* for a couple of cents. . . .

'In the evening about sundown all the hands come up from the fields and pass before the book-keeper, who sits behind a large table on the balcony at the bottom of the house stairs, and as he calls out the names each man answers in his turn. It naturally takes some time to register one thousand or more names . . . they were all respectful and nice, standing hat in hand and bowing civilly as they passed the office desk. . . .'

(The Amors' relatively fair treatment of peons saved their lives when Emiliano Zapata swept through Morelos early in the Revolution. The bandit chief provided them with horses, food and a safe conduct pass. They escaped with nothing more than their lives, but this was something more than Zapata generally granted to *hacendados*.)

In spite of seeing it in such favourable circumstances,

even Mrs Tweedie exclaimed at the 'magnitude' of peonage,
and slavery would be an apter description of the condition
of the Mexican farm labourers, who made up over half the
nation's population. The peon's life was enmeshed in a web
of rules, regulations, prerogatives and laws. He was usually
born into debt because children inherited their parents'
obligations; if not, he promptly acquired a debt of his own
at baptism to cover the cost of the fiesta it required, for the
priest, for the liquor. His first clothes were purchased from
the *tienda de raya* against his future wage. When he was old
enough to marry, the money was again borrowed. When
children were born the dreary process was repeated.

The *tienda de raya* was the chain which bound the peon
to the *hacienda*. He was usually paid in metal discs which
could be exchanged nowhere else, rather than in hard
currency, or he was given credit against the commodities
which he needed to purchase to live. Even under an honest
administrator the debt could never be paid. The corrupt
administrators of the *haciendas* charged what they liked for
goods and generally the peon plunged ever deeper into
debt.

The peon had no rights, and a minimum of freedom. The
only justice he knew was dispensed by the landowner or his
foreman, backed up by the *rurales*. There were *haciendas*
where paternalism prevailed, like the Amors', but in the
main the peons were subjected to unspeakable brutality.
Many overseers treated them worse than animals, since
they were cheaper to replace, and if an overseer beat a peon
to death the local authorities took no action. In Yucatán,
the workers on the *henéquen* plantations (often deportees
from other parts of Mexico) worked in chains and were
flogged for trifling offences.

Everywhere the *hacendado* and his administrators enjoyed first right over the workers' women. Frequently a
young girl would be seduced, then handed over to a peon
with the remark 'This is your wife.' Since a marriage cost six
pesos (60p) and was usually considered in any case an
optional extra by the couple themselves, this was often the
only marriage ceremony the unfortunate pair would ever
experience.

One Spanish *hacendado* locked his workers up at night in

a room so small that they had to sleep on top of one another. When the Revolution came, the workers crucified him to the beautifully carved door of his house.

John Reed, an American journalist, wrote: 'It is impossible to imagine how close to nature the peons live on the great *haciendas*. Their very houses are built of the earth upon which they stand, baked by the sun. Their food is the corn they grow; their drink the water from the dwindled river, carried painfully upon their heads. The clothes they wear are spun from the wool and their sandals cut from the hide of a newly-slaughtered steer. The animals are their constant companions, familiars of their house. . . .'

Beans and corn formed the basis of their diet. Since the manner of preparation generally rendered these staples indigestible, the caustic chili was used to stimulate digestive juices. Then *pulque*, the fermented juice of the maguey cactus, was drunk to soothe the effects of the chili. It was a vicious and fatal circle.

One traveller thought it was not difficult to account for the Mexicans' lack of energy and to excuse their worldwide image of a small man in a big sombrero sleeping against a wall in the sun. 'No people whose diet consists chiefly of *tortillas* (thin pancakes made of corn meal), chili, black coffee and cigarettes are ever going to be lashed by the desire to accomplish. . . . It is not surprising that a population perpetually in the throes of intestinal disorder should be somewhat lacking in energy.'

He went on: 'One marvels . . . not that they are dirty but that under the circumstances they are as clean as they are; not that so many of them are continually sick, but that any of them are ever well; not that they love to get drunk, but that they can bear to remain sober.'

Mrs Moats felt that the countryside 'gave one an overwhelming, sinking feeling of hopelessness. A people born without hope, dying without hope. Death seems always to be lurking. A country of death.'

Parkes writes: 'Liquor and fiestas were their only escape from misery; and whenever a village celebrated a religious holiday with ceremonial dances and the exploding of firecrackers, the whole population, from young children upwards, would drink itself into a blissful intoxication.'

The very accessibility of alcohol to the poorest, who
needed only to tap a cactus, made inevitable the universal
use of a drink which had been known to the Indians from
the earliest days. In their ignorance, mothers weaned their
babies on *pulque,* whose only resemblance to milk was its
whitish colour. Since the rest of a baby's weaning diet
consisted of *tortillas,* beans, chilis and bananas, the infant
mortality rate of twenty-five per cent can readily be understood. Those children who survived this cripplingly inadequate diet entered adult life handicapped beyond repair.

When the Revolutionary politician Alberto J. Pani examined the living conditions of the Mexican labourers he
discovered that the caloric content of their food barely
furnished the energy required by an individual 'at absolute
rest'.

Coupled with an almost total lack of knowledge of the
principles of hygiene, a factor detrimental to health was the
chili added to all meals. Mexicans developed not only a
tolerance to but a craving for highly-spiced foods, and paid
the price in the high number of gastro-intestinal ailments.
Of the deaths from all causes in Mexico City from 1904 to
1912, thirty-two per cent were due to disorders of the digestive tract.

Generally the peasants were too apathetic or ill to attempt escape from this appalling way of life. Some, like the
famous Revolutionary figure, Pancho Villa, fled and became hunted outlaws, and some managed to get over the
border into the United States. Others were recruited as
railway labour, but the mass stayed silently on the land,
held in place by the *hacienda* priests and overseers, the *jefes
políticos* and the *rurales*. Those who escaped to Mexico
City fared little better in the appalling slum tenements of
the capital.

The Indians were constantly humiliated. In some towns
they were barred from the main streets and squares. Whenever men were needed for roadwork or building, Indians
were arrested on vague charges and put to work as forced
prison labour. In Guanajuato, Indians who wore the traditional, and practical, loose white cotton trousers, resembling
the lower part of pyjamas, were not even allowed to enter

the town. They had to hire a pair of European trousers for the day. An American author noted, 'It would be interesting to know who, in Guanajuato, owns the largest interest in the local trouser factory.'

But not all the Indians lay down while they were kicked. The Yaqui tribe of the north-western state of Sonora owned fertile lands which had been in their possession since pre-Conquest days. The Spanish were never able to subdue these fierce Indians and eventually the King of Spain signed a treaty acknowledging their right to the land. It was honoured by every ruler—until Díaz.

The Yaquis' land was assigned by the Díaz government to wealthy creoles, with the argument that the rich land-owners would make better use of it by establishing plantations. The Yaquis were harassed and finally goaded into war, though Díaz undoubtedly would have preferred to see them give up their lands peacefully, as others had done.

In 1880 the Governor of Sonora, Ramón Corral, who was even then gaining for himself an unpopularity which was to last until his days as vice-president, sent *rurales* to sack Yaqui settlements. The next year, under their chief Cajeme, the Yaquis rebelled because troops were again trying to force them off their lands.

The bitter war went on until Cajeme was captured and shot 'while trying to escape' in April 1887. Peace was signed the following year and the Yaquis were settled on unoccupied *ejido* land, a fraction of the size of their former territories. But after two more years of uneasy peace, more land concessions to the Sonora Irrigation Company had the Yaquis in rebellion once more.

The exasperated Díaz ordered that the Yaquis be subdued once and for all and later, as an incentive to slaughter, soldiers were given a bonus of £10 for producing the ears of a Yaqui warrior. Plenty of bonuses were claimed, since it often proved easier to kill an unarmed peasant, lop off his ears and gain the bounty. Federal troops and *rurales* were guilty of the most appalling atrocities. In May 1892, the whole population of the town of Navajoa was imprisoned and so many of them were hanged that the town's supply of rope was exhausted and each piece of rope had to be used five or six times over. In the same year, before the introduction of the bounty, 200 Yaqui prisoners were taken in a gunboat and thrown into the sea off the Pacific coast port of Guaymas.

In 1898 government troops, armed with the new Mauser rifle, exterminated a Yaqui army at Mazacoba. Thousands of dispirited Indians surrendered after this débâcle and were 'granted' lands in a waterless desert in the north of Sonora; but many took to the mountains and fought on. To end their resistance, wholesale deportation of their families was ordered. They were rounded up and sold into slavery at £7 a head to the plantation owners of Yucatán and the Valle Nacional.

The move was so successful in stamping out resistance and so profitable that in 1908 the government ordered the deportation of all Yaquis to Yucatán. This brought a horrified protest from the Sonora *hacendados*—not for humanitarian reasons but because they would be deprived of cheap labour to harvest their crops. They sent a strong protest note to President Díaz and the order was revoked.

Enslaved Yaquis, mostly elderly people, women and children, were shipped from Guaymas to San Blas, then herded on foot over mountains to San Marcos, a journey of about fifteen days. From there they went by train to Mexico City and Veracruz and then again by boat to Progreso. Between ten and twenty per cent usually died on the journey. Families were deliberately split up en route to break their spirit even further before they were sent to work on the *henequén* plantations.

One plantation owner told the American writer John Kenneth Turner: 'If the Yaquis last out the first year they generally get along all right and make good workers. But the trouble is, at least two-thirds of them die off in the first twelve months.'

In February 1908 one boatload of Yucatán-bound Yaquis committed mass suicide to avoid being sold into slavery. Colonel Francisco B. Cruz, in charge of the shipment, reported: 'Those Indians wanted to cheat us out of our commission money and so they threw their children into the sea and jumped in after them. We lowered boats but it was no use; they all went down before we got to them.'

To add to the peasants' miseries, inflation was rampant
during the later stages of the Díaz régime. The vastly
increased cost of buying the basic necessities of life was not
matched by any form of wage increase among agricultural
or industrial workers. In 1908 the average daily wage was
almost exactly what it had been a hundred years earlier, yet
the cost of living had gone up 400 per cent in that time.
Between 1893 and 1906 alone, the cost of corn went up fifty
per cent, and the cost of staple foods fluctuated violently
from day to day. Under the Spaniards the peons had at
least been able to live on what they earned; under Díaz they
were slowly starving.

Though sullen and hostile, the half-starved, apathetic Indians of the countryside were little threat to the dictatorship
as long as they lacked leaders. But the new industrial working class was different.

The employers' paradise, in which men worked unques-
tioningly for a pittance, could not continue indefinitely in
the face of fixed wages and inflation. Labour organisations
were unknown before 1900 and in most states strikes were
forbidden by law. But in the last decade of the dictatorship,
enterprising Mexicans who had worked in the United States
came back to preach workers' rights. Unions were formed,
wage demands were made—and turned down.

The first violence broke out at an American-owned copper mining company at Cananea, Sonora, where Mexicans
demanded equal pay for equal work with Americans. When
this was rejected, 2000 workers went on strike on 1 June
1906. The strikers approached the company's offices to ask
the American personnel to come out in sympathy but the
apprehensive Americans opened fire on the strikers, provok-
ing riots and destruction.

Martial law was declared; troops were rushed to the area.
A score of workers were killed and a similar number
condemned to a lingering death in the waterlogged, rat-
infested dungeons of San Juan de Ulúa, an old military
fortress in Veracruz harbour which had been converted into
a political prison.

The fierce repression of the Cananea strike did nothing to
muffle the discontent. Other strikes flared, and Díaz promised to investigate the workers' complaints. But when his

decision came, it supported the bosses all along the line: there were to be no changes in wages or in working hours.

On 7 January 1907, textile workers in Veracruz rioted when they heard of the president's decision, burning factories and employers' homes. Troops shot many of the rioters in the streets of the city. Another 200 were summarily executed by firing squads. Mexico might have been made safe for the traveller and the foreigner, but the humble Mexican might be excused for not appreciating what Díaz had done.

The Veracruz killings brought an end to strikes but Díaz paid the price. He lost the support of the only section of the working class who could materially damage his power structure. It was an indication of his diminishing political perception. Mexico was outgrowing Díaz.

The rise of a group known as the *científicos* (scientific ones) marked the final turning away of Díaz from his *mestizo* upbringing and feelings. It was the *científicos* who cut the last bonds of affinity between Díaz and the cause of the masses.

The group was formed in the last decade of the nineteenth century by Romero Rubio, Díaz's father-in-law, who had been granted many gambling concessions in the capital, and by others of the newly-moneyed class. The *científicos* were not a political party, since they possessed no popular support, but they came to exercise the functions and influence of one.

The *científicos* dismissed as naïve the talk of democracy, freedom and equality and maintained that Mexico's rudimentary social organism was not capable of absorbing freedom. They were the apostles of progress by science, and measured development by the output of mines and factories and the mileage of railways and telegraph lines. They discredited everything Indian and were the extreme proponents of control by the upper class, believing Mexico's salvation lay in complete white domination.

They considered the Díaz dictatorship the natural result of the inability of the people to govern themselves; further, they felt that the nation should be 'protected' against the

dangers of political action by the illiterate masses. As they
increased in strength and power, the *científicos*, successfully turning Díaz from his *mestizo* affinities and into the
arms of the creoles, openly advocated a dictatorship as a
permanent form of government, at the same time attempting to gain control as far as possible over the government
during Díaz's lifetime and to impose absolute control after
his death.

As their power and wealth spread, and as Díaz grew
older and less capable, this tightly-knit group—there were no
more than sixteen men in the central organisation—came to
dominate the government more fully than the dictator was
aware, and by 1910 at least seventy-five per cent of all
public employees, including Senators and Congressmen,
were *científico*-inspired appointees.

The *científico* business circle was an extremely tight one
and resented any intrusion. The central organisation, which
met fortnightly to plan business and consisted of politicians,
bankers, businessmen and editors, became known as The
Full Car, since there was never any room for would-be
hangers-on.

The real rise in the *científicos*' influence did not come
until after the death of Romero Rubio in 1895. The new
leader of the group was José Yves Limantour, who had
been appointed Treasury Minister two years earlier and had
made an immediate impact by converting Mexico's habitual
budget deficit into a surplus—for the first time since independence seventy-two years previously—in his first year in
office. Under Limantour's brilliance, Mexican prosperity, at
least on paper, continued to blossom astonishingly, and for
the final seventeen years of Díaz's rule Limantour's power
was second only to that of the dictator himself.

Limantour, polished and scholarly, was a thin, dapper
man with a skinny neck, a high broad forehead and the
habitual drooping moustache of the era. His 'lovely teeth'
captivated Mrs Tweedie.

Unlike the overwhelming majority, Limantour was not in
politics for profit, but for reputation and what he hoped
would be enduring fame. He was rich enough already.
Limantour's father, a French adventurer, had dug for gold
in the California rush of 1849 and had then gone to Mexico

and made a much easier fortune buying up cheaply church properties confiscated by the Juárez government.

For many years Díaz leaned heavily on the wisdom and fidelity of Limantour. Because of Díaz's jealousy and Limantour's realisation that the dictatorship was on its last legs, the ties which had united them were later considerably weakened, though they never reached the breaking point.

The treasury surplus which Limantour had provided for Mexico was invested mostly in costly, show-off improvements in the capital—broad avenues, and ornate public buildings.

'Those were the great days,' wrote Mrs Moats. 'Mexico City was at its zenith. Everywhere you turned you felt the wealth and grandeur of the place. The city was well-kept. Each house was compelled to keep its sidewalk and half the road in front of it clean and sprinkled twice a day.... I remember seeing a young woman of the Mexican aristocracy reprimanded by a policeman for having thoughtlessly thrown an empty box from her carriage....

'It could have been perfectly lovely if they had only continued to build the typical Spanish colonial house with a patio, instead of permitting José Limantour to impose upon it the horrible bourgeois French house that was later to be the pattern of taste.

'That great white elephant, the National Theatre, which was built after Limantour's idea, may have been one of the most legitimate reasons for the revolution against the Díaz government. This horror would have been better suited to some *nouveau riche* oil town in Texas....'

The National Theatre, an enormous pile of marble, was castigated as 'atrocious and absurd' and had begun to sink into Mexico City's marshy soil even before it was completed.

But bad taste or not, Mexico City began to pride itself on being the Paris of the Americas; and there was some justification for the claim, provided one did not check too closely on the areas in the east and north of the city where the working class and the poor were crowded in slum districts which wallowed in heaps of garbage and lacked drainage.

Patrick O'Hea, an Englishman who went to live in
Mexico City in 1905, describes it as

'a gridiron of avenues centred upon the great cathedral-
palace square ... The National Palace ... set the level of
height for the buildings ... this served to preserve the
harmonious Spanish colonial aspect of the city, the domes
and towers of churches here and there rising above the flat
roofs. ...

'Narrow, mostly cobbled streets carried the graceful
horse-drawn carriages of the period, the few motor cars of
European or United States origin also being limited to the
town and its suburbs by lack of paved highways beyond ...

'The worthy hotel where I first lodged ... was served
with water by porters who carried great cans slung, fore and
aft, from their leather-capped heads. Modernity had its
touch almost only in the tramways that served the city and
linked it with its suburbs. ...'

The arts followed the same imitative pattern as the
capital's new buildings, and had lost their affiliations with
native traditions. Painting copied the French salon style,
and Mexican art was at such a low ebb that a statue of
Juárez, the national hero, was imported from Italy, where it
had been carved by an Italian sculptor who had neither seen
Juárez nor visited Mexico.

Díaz re-elected himself in 1896 without dissent, the only
opposition coming from students who, recognising the election for the farce it was, put up as rival presidential candidate a harmless lunatic called Zuñiga y Miranda. He wan-
dered the streets of Mexico City wearing top hat and tails
and forecasting earthquakes, floods and other disasters.
Zuñiga took his rôle seriously, if no one else did, and afterwards he put himself forward at every election until his
death, long after the Madero Revolution.

The only untoward occurrence in the 1900 'elections'
came after the six-hour procession to celebrate another
Díaz triumph at the polls. It was discovered that the Queen
of the Parade, a buxom beauty, was dead of sunstroke. She
was still standing, however, having been tied into her place
on the float alongside a large plaster bust of Díaz.

By now Díaz was seventy and everyone was thinking in

terms of a successor to the ageing dictator, although they
had even ceased to count upon his death. One wit commented, 'Don Porfirio will simply pick up a pen and publish
a decree authorising him to live another twenty years.' The
científicos were anxious to see their leader, Limantour,
become Mexico's next president, but the most obvious candidate was General Bernardo Reyes, civil governor of the
northern state of Nuevo León and military commander of
north-east Mexico, who had flourished in the warmth of
Don Porfirio's benevolence. In addition to his double
salary as civil and military chief, Reyes also received a
'gratification' of £200 monthly out of War Department expenses and had charge of—and a share in—£18,000 military
funds.

This pompous, bearded sycophant, who loved to be
photographed in full military regalia and who wore bells on
his spurs, wrote a biography of Díaz which was so absurdly
eulogistic that the embarrassed president had all the copies
seized and grumbled, 'Oh, that I might be loved with intelligence.'

Reyes had cruelly suppressed anti-Díaz demonstrations
in the states under his jurisdiction but he had introduced
wise and popular reforms, too; the first workmen's compensation law in Mexico had been enacted under his administration. He also gains credit for the vigorous development
and industrialisation of the city of Monterrey. Reyes, who
had strong Army support, gained further encouragement
for his presidential aspirations when, in 1900, Díaz brought
him into the cabinet as Secretary of War.

But the *científicos* were opposed to Reyes. He was a
mestizo and a military man. They wanted a dictatorship run
by creole businessmen. The Reyes supporters were against
Limantour for the opposite reasons. Further, they pointed
out, Limantour, as the son of a French citizen, was legally
disqualified from becoming president.

Díaz watched these hopeful gyrations with grim amusement. Eventually having played one aspirant off against the
other, he decided to act. He distrusted Reyes and feared his
growing power, so the general was kicked out of the cabinet
and sent back to Nuevo León, and Díaz tied himself even
more closely to the jubilant *científicos*. It was typical of

Reyes' lack of courage that he meekly accepted the demotion when he might profitably have defied it.

For the 1904 election, however, Díaz consented to the appointment of a vice-president, though he insisted on choosing his own deputy. At the same time he extended the presidential term from four to six years. And as a further sign of the president's democratic ideals a National Liberal Party was formed—pro-Díaz, of course.

A party convention was called before the 1904 elections, at which Díaz promised to nominate his vice-president. The Limantour and Reyes factions gathered in force to hear which of their leaders was to be named—and both parties were flabbergasted when Díaz sent a messenger to the convention at the last minute to announce that his choice was Ramón Corral, the fifty-year-old, moon-faced Minister of the Interior, best remembered for his activities as a Yaqui slave trader, and now notorious in the capital for the lecherous life he was leading. There was a burst of incredulous laughter from the Reyes supporters at the announcement.

Though nominally a *científico* supporter, Corral was hated and distrusted by all political and public elements in Mexico. But he had proved an efficient and faithful Díaz henchman and Ambassador Wilson may have touched on the real reason for his appointment when he said that 'in character, Corral more closely resembled Díaz than any other man in public life'.

Corral's unpopularity delighted Díaz; now nobody would want to kill him to make such a man president. He also knew that Corral was ill (he had cancer) and confidently expected to outlive his deputy. Once installed, Corral, like all the other office holders, became nothing more than a sublimated secretary, whose main function was to attend as government showpiece at ceremonies which Díaz found too fatiguing or boring. Even Corral himself shared the public's amusement at his humiliation. 'Porfirio remembers me only when he wants me to attend some official ceremony not convenient for him. The day is hot ... raining ... cold ... let Ramón go.'

The next four years were marked by yet another Díaz about-face. Alarmed by the over-abundance of American

interests in Mexico, Díaz again practised his old game of
playing off one group against another by encouraging the
flow of European business to counter-balance American
investments. In October 1909 a meeting was arranged between Díaz and the new American president, William
Howard Taft, on the international bridge over the Rio
Grande separating the border towns of El Paso, Texas and
Ciudad Juárez (now more commonly known as Juárez).
Taft travelled to the meeting full of goodwill and wrote to
his wife from the presidential train 'I am glad to aid him for
the reason that we have two billions of American capital in
Mexico that will be greatly endangered if Díaz were to die
and his government go to pieces.... I can only hope and
pray that his demise does not come until I am out of
office.'

The presidents met in the centre of the international
bridge, Taft wearing the voluminous frock coat required by
State Department protocol, while Díaz glittered in a superb
uniform, a dozen medals spread across his chest. Taft confessed that he felt 'quite outshone'. He was soon to feel
even worse. When the two men met for talks in El Paso's
Chamber of Commerce building, Taft, conscious of his
country's unease over the rising Yellow Peril from Japan,
requested a renewal by Mexico of the lease of Magdalena
Bay on the coast of Baja California for use by the American
Pacific Fleet. Díaz shocked the American president by
refusing, and shortly after the meeting rubbed it in by
arranging an enthusiastic welcome for a party of Japanese
marines visiting Mexico.

There were wild cheers at a banquet when Admiral
Yashiro, Grand Admiral of the Japanese Fleet, made a
speech loaded with hints of common action by Japan and
Mexico against a certain common enemy. He pointed out
that both countries had 'terrible and untamable volcanoes
which, though now quiescent, can erupt and make the
world tremble in their fury', and when he added 'both are
building up their armies and navies to resist insults to their
national honour', there were cries from the audience of
'Down with the *gringos*.'

Now even the Americans were beginning to notice that
their idol Díaz had clay feet.

Though he and his country knew it, Díaz was finely
balanced on the edge of disaster. Only one more nudge was
required. But before anyone had time to push him, Don
Porfirio stepped off the cliff.

Díaz announced that he had decided not to stand for re-election in 1910. He did so, not in a government bulletin or even in the Mexican Press, but instead in an interview which appeared, in February 1908, in the New York publication, *Pearson's Magazine*, which filled its front cover with the exclusive news. The story was written by James Creelman, whose interview was not short of purple prose. He described how Díaz 'brushed aside a curtain of scarlet trumpet flowers and vine-like pink geraniums, moved along the terrace ... the green landscape, the smoking city, the blue tumult of mountains, the thin, exhilarating, scented air ... stirred him. Colour came to his sun-touched face, he threw back his head, nostrils wide. . . .'

Then Creelman shattered the idyllic scene by asking a question no one in Mexico would have dared to put: What provision was Díaz making for Mexico's future? Díaz replied by affirming his 'strong belief in democratic principles', glossing over his thirty years of dictatorship by explaining that his retention of power had been necessary, both for the welfare and development of the country and as a duty which the public expected of him. He had been careful, he added, to preserve the *theory* of democracy during his presidency!

Now, however, after thirty years he felt his task was completed. Mexico had been set on the path of progress and he could retire happy. Díaz went on to explain the absence of opposition parties by saying that since his friends were in such an overwhelming majority, his handful of opponents did not wish to be identified with such a small dissenting group.

But now, he said, he welcomed and would support the formation of active political parties at the forthcoming election, and concluded: 'Regardless of the feelings and opinions of my friends and supporters I am determined to retire at the end of my present term and I will not accept re-election.'

The news did not break in Mexico until 3 March, when the daily paper *El Imparcial* published a translation. Filomeno Mata, the much-imprisoned editor of *El Diario del Hogar*, asked Díaz to repeat his statement to the Mexican people, but the President tried to brush him off by saying that any statement 'had been purely a personal desire' and that further discussion was inopportune.

Díaz's intentions in leaking the news to Creelman are debatable. It has been argued that he was trying to placate American opinion, that he was seeking to lure political opponents into the open, that he wanted to prove to the world how democratic his government was before accepting the country's anxious plea that he stay on.

Whatever his intention, the interview was a major mistake. Díaz sat back to await the mass protest against his retirement. It never came. Finally on 30 May, the awkward suspense was broken when Díaz allowed Limantour and Corral to 'convince' him of the necessity of standing for election once more in 1910, his eighth term of office. But Díaz had invited opposition, and opposition was what he got, though at first it was on an understandably timorous note from a people who had been subjugated for so long.

When Don Porfirio went back on his statement, all the would-be successors meekly accepted it. The bone of contention was going to be the vice-presidency, since no one expected the dictator to live through another six-year term.

Limantour and Reyes were still the most obvious candidates to replace either Corral or Díaz, and it was the Army man whom the president feared. As a usurper of power himself, he knew well enough that dictatorships are only overcome by violent methods, and his fear of Reyes and his large, well-armed following bordered on the neurotic. Reyes protested his undying loyalty but the ultra-suspicious Díaz smelled intrigue in his every move. As early as 1906 he had called in a secretary and shouted 'Tell Bernardo I'm not letting him out of my sight ... I know he is plotting ... he will feel my hand.' But Reyes, though ambitious, was a loyal Díaz man. The danger lay elsewhere.

The gradually coalescing opposition needed as leader a man from a respected family, well educated, relatively unknown politically, with liberal leanings but conservative ties and above all courage and colour to stimulate the imagination of the people. They found that man in Francisco Indalecio Madero, a young *hacendado* from Coahuila.

A more unlikely-looking threat could not have been imagined. Madero stood only five foot two inches tall. He was ill-shaped and delicate in health. A goatee beard hid a weak chin. He had a broad forehead, receding hair and a high-pitched voice that sometimes spiralled into falsetto during his speeches. He was a vegetarian and a follower of spiritualism. But his courage was as impressive as his appearance was unprepossessing. His obvious sincerity, enthusiasm and belief in what he was striving for overcame his lack of political experience.

Madero was born in 1873, the first child of one of the richest creole landowning families in northern Mexico. The Maderos, of Jewish and Portuguese origin, had never shown much interest in politics but had instead devoted their energies to increasing the fortune which had been founded by the patriarch of the family, Don Evaristo Madero, Francisco's grandfather. They owned vast areas of land as well as mines, factories and a wine and spirit industry. When Evaristo died on 6 April 1911 aged 82, leaving behind fourteen legitimate children, thirty-four grandchildren and fifty-six great-grandchildren, his own property added up to almost two million acres and the rest of the family between them held as much again.

Madero's early life was typical of an *hacienda* heir. Private tuition was followed by a Jesuit school in Saltillo and a year at a Catholic school in Baltimore. In 1887 Francisco and his younger brother Gustavo were sent to France, where they attended colleges in Paris and Versailles for five years. Francisco was tremendously impressed by the spirit of equality and democracy in France. It was during this time that his liberal views were formed, and he gave away most of his allowance to the poor of Paris, earning him the nickname among his classmates 'The Chocolate Fool'.

In 1892, after a summer holiday in Mexico, the brothers went to California, where they spent a year at university studying American agricultural methods.

Back home, instead of treading the *hacendado*'s accepted path of dissipation, Madero set to work to improve conditions on the family properties over which he was given

control. To the annoyance of wealthy neighbours, he established model estates, increased wages and improved the
living conditions of his peons. He was deeply interested in
the people who worked for him and particularly keen to
help any promising youngster to get an education. In the
face of official lethargy and even disapproval, Madero built
schools on his properties and paid for the teachers out of
his own pocket. He was firmly, and quite correctly, convinced that Mexico's only hope of progress lay in a massive
improvement in education.

Madero married Sara Perez, a small, frail woman. It was
perhaps appropriate that there were no children of the
marriage, for he had already decided by then to become
father to the oppressed millions of Mexico.

In 1904 Madero started a reform movement, the Club
Democratico Benito Juárez, but four years later, despite his
hard work, little had been accomplished. Then came the
bombshell of the Creelman interview, followed by Díaz's
decision to stand again. It was time for Madero to make his
move. He made it in unlikely fashion by writing a book. It
was called *The Presidential Succession of 1910* and, though
it was a work of mediocre merit, it changed the course of
Mexican history.

Madero spent the autumn of 1908 preparing the book,
most of which was a rather dry discussion of the country's
political situation and which ignored the economic maladies. But when he got around to the need for change and
improvement, the little northern *hacendado*'s sincerity
brought the work to life. He carefully avoided attacking
Díaz as a personality; indeed, he treated Don Porfirio with
courtesy. But the Díaz myth and the Díaz régime were
lashed mercilessly, and again and again Madero emphasised
the need for freedom of suffrage and the abolition of re-
election.

But he was careful to condemn revolution as a means of
bringing about change. The book, a curious mixture of
praise and criticism, ran into its biggest problems before it
was published. Out of respect for the elder members of his
family, Madero requested their permission to publish,
knowing that his outspokenness could affect the family
businesses.

Eventually, in January 1909, the seniors of the Madero clan gave reluctant permission and a few days later the first edition of 3000 had been printed. Madero sent Díaz a copy, asking him to read it carefully. Díaz's reaction is not recorded but there was no doubt about the reaction of the people—those who could read, at any rate. Here was a man who had the courage to castigate the dictatorship, if not the dictator. The first edition was quickly sold out and reprints were hurriedly ordered. The name of Madero was becoming known.

In the spring of 1909 Mexico was alive with a political activity which had not been seen for years and when, on 25 March, Díaz announced an unchanged team of himself and Corral for re-election it only served to spread the ripples of reaction.

In May Madero and a group of about 50 formed the Anti-Re-electionist Party with the slogan 'Effective Suffrage and No Re-election' as its main platform. Madero was an obvious choice as the party's spokesman, because of his leadership in organising the movement, because of the difficulty in persuading anyone of acknowledged political standing to speak in opposition to Díaz and also because his book had made the name of Madero relatively well known. As one Madero biographer, Charles Cumberland, points out, there was an even more important factor. 'He was the only man of independent means in the group ... the other qualified speakers had neither the time nor the money to devote themselves completely to politics.'

Since nobody was willing to risk disputing the presidency with Díaz, the election issue revolved around the vice-presidency. Limantour refused to be drawn into the race, so there were three main contestants: Corral, Reyes and the as-yet unnamed candidate of the Anti-Re-electionists.

Reyes was still the one Don Porfirio feared, and in the autumn of 1909 Díaz acted. The general was removed from his north-eastern military command and replaced by an old rival, General Jacinto B. Treviño. To the dismay of his supporters Reyes withdrew to the solitude of his *hacienda* to brood over the demotion and eventually sent word to his party workers that he backed Díaz unconditionally, intended to vote for Corral as vice-president and urged all his friends to do the same.

By way of thanks Díaz next ordered Reyes to turn over the governorship of Nuevo León to José María Mier and to report to Mexico City. When he got to the capital, Reyes was told he was being sent to Europe on a military mission—in other words, put out of the way until the election was safely over. He might profitably have disobeyed this order, launched his candidacy and perhaps started an uprising with a fair chance of success. But he left the country meekly in October 1909.

So, apart from the niggling challenge of the Anti-Re-election Party, Díaz and Corral had the field to themselves. The *científicos'* Re-election Party and a group of Díaz supporters known as The Circle of Friends set out to sell the candidacy of Corral to the country. They were stoned at Guadalajara and doused with water at Guanajuato but these were regarded as unimportant expressions of discontent!

In June 1909 Madero had started on the first opposition speaking tour of Mexico since the beginning of Díazpotism. He was given a tremendous welcome in the provincial towns and in Monterrey, the Reyes stronghold, he was carried from the speaker's stand on the shoulders of a jubilant crowd.

By sheer force of will rather than any oratorical skill, he managed to lift the mantle of political lethargy which blanketed the country. The elimination of Reyes brought many of his supporters over to Madero's side in opposition to Corral and the *científicos*.

Eventually the government ceased to regard Madero and his party with amused tolerance. Thugs were hired to break up Madero's meetings, hotels in the towns he was visiting were ordered to refuse rooms to his group and the authorities forced them to hold their meetings on the outskirts of populated areas. On 30 September 1909 the offices of their four-month-old newspaper *El Anti-Re-electionista* were raided and the staff arrested. These repressive methods scared away the party's timid supporters and during the winter it was in danger of disintegration. Madero, although suffering from a fever, worked desperately to rally support and spent most of the winter on speaking tours of the north and west, traditional areas of discontent with Mexican governments.

The Anti-Re-electionists arranged a convention for 15 April 1910 in Mexico City to choose a presidential candidate (by now the idea of trying to find a running mate acceptable to the old dictator had been sensibly dropped). In a desperate attempt to throw the convention into confusion Corral ordered Madero's arrest on a trumped-up charge but Madero defied the order and was acclaimed as the party's candidate with Dr Francisco Vázquez Gómez, who had once been Díaz's personal physician, as vice-presidential candidate.

Next day, Madero had an interview with Díaz, who promised a free and fair election. Madero spoke of his personal admiration for Don Porfirio but admitted he was working to overthrow the Díaz system. He told the dictator: 'The country is ready for democracy and we must have unbiased elections.... It is time you relinquished the power.'

'Into whose hands do you counsel me to give it?' Díaz asked.

'Into the hands of an honest man,' replied Madero.

'Señor, a man must be more than honest to govern Mexico,' answered the president, a comment which was to prove only too true in Madero's case.

Neither man seems to have been overly impressed by the other. After the interview Díaz told his friends that the crazy Zuñiga y Miranda now had a rival, while Madero reported to his followers that the president was 'no longer a fighting cock'.

No further mention was made of Corral's arrest order and for a while it looked as if Díaz intended to keep his word about fair treatment for Madero.

Madero and other Anti-Re-electionist speakers had enthusiastic welcomes in important centres like Puebla and Guadalajara at which the authorities did little to interfere. But the expected blow fell in June when Madero arrived with another member of his party, Roque Estrada, to make a speech in Monterrey.

A crowd which had assembled at the station to welcome

Madero was dispersed by troops and police. But when he got to his father's house in the city, Madero was permitted to make a short speech to the people waiting there. When Estrada tried to speak, too, he was ordered not to. He defied the police order but next morning, as he left the house with Madero, he was arrested. Madero insisted on seeing the arresting officer's credentials and in the argument which followed, Estrada escaped. This was the excuse the Monterrey officials were looking for: Madero was arrested and accused of having helped Estrada to get away.

Though Estrada, on hearing the news, immediately gave himself up, Madero was not released. On 21 June both men were transferred to the town of San Luis Potosí, charged with inciting rebellion and held safely out of the way until the elections on 26 June were over. On 10 July Díaz ordered the Electoral College to announce that he and Corral had received a majority of votes. Ten days later Madero and Estrada were released on bail but remained in San Luis Potosí under heavy police supervision. The Anti-Re-electionist Party complained to Congress about the election farce but their protest was rejected and Díaz and Corral were officially declared re-elected. Madero was allocated 196 votes from the entire republic!

Most of the mutterings of discontent were drowned in the fanfare with which Mexico prepared to celebrate September's centenary of independence. Madero, temporarily forgotten, now realised that Díaz could only be removed by force. All his hopes of a peaceful change of government had faded, so he decided to start an insurrection. But first he needed his freedom. So on 6 October Madero jumped bail and, disguised as a railway worker, fled to Texas.

There he set up headquarters at the unpretentious Hutchins Hotel in San Antonio, where he was joined by his brothers Gustavo, Raul, Alfonso and Julio, and by Estrada. As soon as there were enough followers to form a quorum Madero was proclaimed president of a revolutionary junta.

It was the custom of leaders of Mexican uprisings to publish a 'plan' on the lines of a political manifesto, announcing their intentions if the people would help them into power. Madero's manifesto was issued from San Antonio early in November but in order to avoid the possibility of objections that the United States was harbouring and encouraging a rebellion, it was backdated to 5 October, the last complete day Madero had spent in Mexico, and it was given the title of The Plan of San Luis Potosí.

Under the plan the recent Mexican elections were declared void, Madero was named provisional president and a free presidential election was promised as soon as the country was in the hands of 'the forces of the public'. Madero also promised a revision of all the laws and decrees adopted during the Díaz régime.

Copies of the plan were immediately distributed throughout Mexico and an uprising was planned for 20 November.

The Revolution was under way. . . .

The beginnings of the Revolution were ludicrous and tragic, even by Mexican standards. Many copies of the Plan of San Luis Potosí fell into Federal hands and, after urging Washington to throw out the San Antonio plotters, Díaz's troops began to make wholesale arrests in Mexico of suspected Madero sympathisers.

The first shots in the Revolution were fired in the town of Puebla, hundreds of miles from the Texas border. Here a Maderista named Aquiles Serdán had armed 500 followers. On 18 November the Puebla police chief, Miguel Cabrera, headed an attempted search of Serdán's home. Serdán opened fire, killing Cabrera, but he and most of his family met their deaths in the gunfight which followed. The other would-be rebels were disarmed and arrested. The Revolution had a martyr, but it was a depressing start.

Madero and his small band left San Antonio and crossed the Rio Grande into Mexico on 19 November, planning to rendezvous with a group of 300 rebels led by one of his uncles and to capture the border town of Piedras Negras. The Madero group lost their way and their chief spent the first night of his campaign in an Indian hut on the border. Next day, the official dawn of the Revolution, there was no sign either of the small army or of the supply of American arms and ammunition for which Madero had paid in advance.

Late that afternoon the uncle turned up, accompanied by an army of ten. Soon afterwards fifteen more men arrived. Disillusioned, the 'provisional president' splashed back across the Rio Grande into the safety of Texas without having fired a shot.

On 24 November Díaz issued the following statement: 'The political situation in Mexico does not present any danger, and the lives and interests of all foreigners are absolutely secure. All that has occurred to disturb order is a few mutinies of small importance in Puebla, Gómez Palacio, Parral and the city of Guerrero. These having been suppressed, at this moment order is complete in the whole of the Republic.'

But all mutinies had *not* been suppressed. Madero had chosen his ground well. The north, where Díaz himself had gathered power to overthrow Lerdo de Tejada's government in 1876, again bore the seeds of rebellion in its bleak, burned landscape. Madero drew his most effective support from a people impassioned by poverty, a people who had nothing to lose but their lives and for whom anything gained was bound to be a relief from a miserable existence. In the north, too, American influence was most conspicuous and there was convenient access to the border for supplies and, if necessary, escape.

From the barren north came the men who were to win the Revolution, dispute the spoils among themselves and eventually provide a succession of presidents for the next twenty years.

Men like Pascual Orozco, a tall, gaunt mountaineer with blue eyes and a freckled face, born of American and *mestizo* parents, who was to add the profession of general to his previous activities of freight porter, mule driver and storekeeper. It was Orozco who was to lead, and win, the hardest fighting of the revolt against Díaz.

Men like Doroteo Arango, a *mestizo* with a touch of Negro blood, born into peonage in the Durango village of Rio Grande the year after Díaz came to power. When he was sixteen Doroteo killed the *hacendado*'s son who had raped his sister, fled to join an outlaw band in the mountains and changed his name to the more virile-sounding Pancho Villa. When eventually he learned to write, Villa insisted on signing his letters with the flourishing 'Francisco Villa' but it was as Pancho that he became known, revered or hated by his fellow-countrymen and by the millions of Americans who were to read and hear for the next thirteen years about his escapades, achievements and brutalities.

In Villa, the common people of Mexico found the man to wreak vengeance on their despised overlords. He has been described as 'a twentieth-century compound of Attila, Robin Hood and Jesse James, with a flavouring of red-hot chili sauce'.

His daredevil deeds made him the idol of the masses and at times, like the legendary Robin Hood, he really did rob the rich to feed the poor. But if he was famed for his bravery, he was even better known for his short temper and outbursts of unspeakable cruelty.

An Englishman, Dr E. J. Dillon, thought Villa 'a creature of wild and contradictory impulses ... at times he would take a malignant pleasure in human suffering ... and then suddenly, overwhelmed by a wave of maudlin tenderness, would perform an act which, emanating from a normal individual, would be classed as magnanimous. He was a token and portent of the period, and his name the symbol under which all the delirium, the savagery, the disconcerting confusion of those troublous times were focused and epitomised.'

Villa was of medium height, powerfully built but with short, bowed legs which made him look awkward as he shambled along, pigeon-toed. But once on a horse, he was completely at home, master of the animal. He had brown, kinky hair and grew a droopy moustache to disguise the fact that adenoids prevented him from closing his mouth completely.

Orozco, Villa and others disenchanted with or already fighting against Díaz were recruited for the Revolution by Abraham González, a leading anti-re-electionist politician in Chihuahua State, who was busy gathering forces in readiness for Madero's uprising. Villa was living quite openly in the city of Chihuahua, despite having recently shot down in the streets a man he claimed had deserted from his band to become a government spy. Orozco and Villa were appointed officers in the revolutionary 'army'— as yet a non-existent one—and shortly before the date of the planned nation-wide rebellion Orozco and González headed north from Chihuahua City and Villa went south with fifteen men, both groups bent on recruiting armies.

As the rebels melted away into the deserts the government blandly assumed that Madero's revolution had been a wash-out. Henry Lane Wilson reported to Washington, 'The conspiracy lacks coherence and the government will easily suppress it,' and he criticised 'the lack of intelligent leadership' among the would-be revolutionaries.

James Creelman, whose exclusive interview with Díaz had supplied the spark which originally ignited the unrest, was busy preparing a biography of the Mexican dictator, in which he wrote: 'It is preposterous to talk about a reversion of the Mexican people to the old revolutionary habit. Díaz has done his work well. . . . All the thousand productive results of continued peace have made civil war unattractive to any important or numerous part of the nation. The Mexican people are too busy to fight each other now.'

When Creelman's book appeared it had been overtaken by events. The people who were 'too busy' to fight were on the brink of overthrowing Díaz. . . .

But Creelman's forecast came close, very close, to becoming history.

The rebels' limited finances were soon exhausted and the dejected members of the Madero junta in San Antonio were reduced to one meal a day. Madero himself was so hard up that he was darning his own socks and having his laundry done on credit, and it came as a relief to the overwhelming conservative element in his family when he and his brother Raul decided to give up the struggle, travel to New Orleans and sail to exile in Europe as soon as they had enough funds.

But their disillusion was premature. Villa, who had drummed up a force of 500 from the deserts, captured the small town of San Andres near Chihuahua, while the larger town of Guerrero in the south of the state fell to Orozco. Though the Chihuahua rebels were unable to hold any populated areas and were desperately short of guns and ammunition, their example encouraged further uprisings. In Sonora, José Maytorena started a rebellion which soon saw the whole state infested with rebel groups. In southern Chihuahua the *hacendado* Guillermo Maca and the mine labourer Maclovio Herrera joined in unlikely partnership to capture Parral after a bloody combat. In the cotton-growing Laguna area, scene of Madero's works of *hacienda* reform, there were, understandably, further signs of support for the rebellion.

By mid-December the unrest had moved to the sugar state of Morelos, uncomfortably close to Mexico City. Here the rebellion was headed by Emiliano Zapata with his cry of 'Land and Liberty', by the Figueroa brothers and by Margarita Neri, a red-headed dancer who had once been the mistress of a member of the Díaz cabinet.

La Neri, disenchanted with her former lover and the whole of the Porfirian régime, took to the hills, formed her own bandit group and swore she would decapitate Díaz personally.

But the outstanding figure of the southern rebellion—and possibly of the whole Revolution—was Zapata, a small, slender man with a sensuous Asiatic face, mandarin moustache and eyes as black and as hard as obsidian. Unlike the rough, rude Villa, Zapata was a dandy. He always wore symbolic, theatrical black—a fitted jacket and tight trousers with silver trimming down the seams. He wore enormous, silver-laden sombreros and his taste extended to fine horses and beautiful women.

Zapata was born in the Morelos village of Anenecuilco, where he became a *mediero*, a cultivator on a fifty-fifty basis on *hacienda*-owned land. It was one stage up from the labouring peon. Zapata raised melons, and the small profit gave him the nearest thing to independence possible for a low-born Mexican in those days. An expert horseman, he was befriended by the *hacendado*, Ignacio de la Torre y Mier, who had married Díaz's daughter Amada.

Don Ignacio made the mistake of inviting Zapata to Mexico City to look over his stables. Zapata never forgot the contrast between the magnificent accommodation provided for the *hacendado*'s horses and the miserable huts that passed as homes for most of his fellow-villagers. His outspokenness at the injustice of this soon landed him in trouble and he was sentenced to army service by the *jefe político* of his region.

Zapata spent several years in the army, rising to the rank of sergeant. He was released from service, along with hundreds of other conscripts, as an act of clemency by Díaz to celebrate the 1910 centennial, but showed his gratitude by becoming an outlaw and campaigning for the restoration of his village's lands, taken over by the Torre y Mier *hacienda*.

'Of all the figures produced by the Revolution, that of Zapata is the most clear-cut,' writes Frank Tannenbaum, an historian of Mexico. 'He was a man of no learning, of no broad social contacts, a simple, vigorous human being ... but who knew that his people had been robbed of their lands, and that it was his call to return these lands to them.'

Zapata rose against Díaz—and kept up the fight against successive presidents and dictators, including Madero himself, until his murder in 1919. In those nine bloody years the only government in Morelos, and later in neighbouring states, was that dispensed by Zapata and his Army of the South. A Communist who had never heard of Communism, he fought relentlessly and mercilessly for the rights of the poor. Peasants by the thousands rallied to his stirring cry, 'Men of the south, it is better to die on your feet than live on your knees!'

Zapata was up in arms, or rather in rebellion without arms, with the first news of Madero's pronouncement of the Plan of San Luis Protosí, and within nine months he was able to field an army of three thousand armed and mounted peasants with the boast, 'We have begged from the outside not one bullet, not one rifle, not one peso; we have taken it all from the enemy.'

And so, because it was timidly opposed, the Revolution slowly gained momentum. Had the government acted with promptness and authority it could have crushed the rebellion, though it would surely have been unable to fight off social reform for much longer. But the very first shots exposed the hollowness of the dictatorship. The army, the most solid prop of any authoritarian régime, had waxed fat and flabby during thirty-five years of peace. Nominally 30,000 strong, it contained only 18,000 men; the officers, resplendent in gold braid, had embezzled the pay of both the real and imagined soldiers. An American journalist living in Mexico City wrote: 'The Army was honeycombed with padded muster rolls and petty larceny. More than half the roster were men of straw who were clothed and armed at regular rates but from whom no bugler, not even Gabriel himself, could bring forth an answering "Here".'

The rank and file, sentenced to army service for trivial offences—and sometimes no offences at all—were hardly likely in any case to provide the sternest fighting material. Ill-fed, badly clothed and rarely paid, the ordinary soldier's chief ambition was to desert and get back to the family and *patria chica* from which he had been dragged. In order not to lose the services of an efficient housemaid, one influential Tampico family had arranged with the authorities to have

her lover conscripted. Little wonder that the maid's unfortunate boy friend, and thousands more like him, showed
no stomach for fighting against men with whom they had
every sympathy.

Still Díaz and his henchmen refused to acknowledge the
gathering clouds. Don Porfirio thought the uprising 'a thing
of no importance' and promised 'If they ever reach five
thousand I shall take the field myself, despite my years.'

Lord Cowdray, too, thought little of Madero's chances.
He told Henry Baerlein, *The Times* correspondent in
Mexico, 'This affair will be forgotten in a month.'

Madero himself was so pessimistic about the Revolution
that, although he had temporarily abandoned his plans to
go to Europe, he stayed safely on the American side of the
border while the Díaz government made repeated protests
to Washington about the situation. Madero was clearly
guilty of breaking the United States law which forbade
anyone starting a military expedition from American territory against a friendly power. The Americans hedged by
requesting proof of an open act of rebellion by Madero and
the San Antonio group basked in the sympathy of Washington and Texas. Díaz's intransigence over Magdalena Bay
had cost him much in popularity.

After Madero had been in Texas four months, U.S.
Federal officers were ordered to arrest him. Warned of his
danger well in advance, he fled from San Antonio to El
Paso and, receiving another warning, hurriedly crossed to
the Mexican side of the Rio Grande on 14 February, to be
met by women bearing armfuls of flowers.

Now that he had been forced into action, Madero decided
to capture some of the smaller towns in north-east Chihuahua in an attempt to isolate the important border point
of Cuidad Juárez. So on 6 March, accompanied by a force
of about 500 woefully ill-equipped troops, he launched an
attack on Casas Grandes.

Incredibly, it was decided to fall upon the town at 2 a.m.,
though by tradition Mexicans never fought at night and the
rebels were, in any case, exhausted after a hard day's
march. By dawn, however, the battle seemed won. The
Federals ran up a white flag and a bugler blew for an
armistice talk.

But as Madero's officers went forward to receive the surrender, another bugle blew, this time sounding the charge. A relief battalion of Federal troops, backed by artillery, was approaching Casas Grandes and, seeing this, the defenders ignored the white flag they had just run up and began firing again.

Madero's men began to give way all along the line and soon the retreat turned into a rout, every man for himself. A company of American volunteers, stranded by the disappearance of their allies, suffered heavy casualties extricating themselves. Madero himself was wounded in the wrist and his company suffered fifty-one killed, twelve captured and lost most of the scanty equipment it possessed. As was the Mexican custom, the jubilant victors made no attempt at pursuit, or else Madero's force would have been irretrievably crushed. Had the Federals been able to field 5000 men in Chihuahua at this stage, the northern part of the revolt could have been stamped out.

Madero's luck held. The day after the Casas Grandes débâcle, President Taft ordered 20,000 troops, a quarter of the American army, to the Mexican border on 'routine manoeuvres'. Actually Taft had become doubtful of Díaz's ability to control the rebellion and therefore to protect Americans and their huge property holdings. Díaz was further distressed and humiliated by the news that the U.S. Navy was planning to hold 'exercises' off the west coast of Mexico.

Taft intimated that, in the event of the death or overthrow of Díaz being followed by anarchy and wholesale destruction of American-owned property, U.S. troops would cross the border 'to restore order'. The American move brought nervous protests from the Mexican government. Among the complainants was Treasury Minister Limantour, who at that time was in New York.

Limantour had left Mexico City on 11 July 1910, in the middle of the presidential election storms, bound for Europe to negotiate a twenty million pound loan. Many politicians felt he was deliberately absenting himself from the country to avoid possible implication in any election double dealing. Whatever the reason, Limantour had never before been away from the country for so long. And never had Díaz more desperately needed his expert advice.

By the beginning of December Limantour had closed negotiations in Paris for the loan, which was taken by a syndicate of French, British and German banks. When Díaz heard the news he urged his Treasury Minister to come home. Díaz believed that Limantour was the one man who could tell him what was wrong and what he should do.

By February Limantour decided he was ready to return. He left Paris on 27 February and arrived in New York on 7 March, the very day that President Taft had ordered troops to the border. After registering his protest at the troop movements, Limantour received instructions from Díaz to start negotiations in New York with representatives of the rebels.

Limantour's arrival made the fifth in an oddly assorted company assembled in the American city to play out a game of cards with Mexico as the stake. In a suite on the fourth floor of the Hotel Astor were Francisco Madero senior and Gustavo Madero, the financial managers of a revolution that was rapidly going broke. In the same hotel was Francisco de la Barra, Mexican Ambassador to the United States. Dr Francisco Vázquez Gómez, head of the Madero junta in Washington, was at the Hotel Imperial, while Limantour's operations centre was the Hotel Plaza.

The Maderos, particularly Francisco senior, were desperate for a peace settlement. Only 1500 dollars remained in the revolutionary war chest out of a sum of 375,000 dollars which Gustavo Madero had extracted from a Spanish banking house on the promise to construct a railway in Mexico. Early in 1910 Gustavo, who held a concession to build a railway across the state of Zacatecas, linking the two main north-to-south lines, had interested a French–Spanish concern in the project and they had agreed to underwrite it.

In August of that year Gustavo went to New York to receive the first payment of 375,000 dollars. He loaned a third of it to his family to relieve hardship caused by a government embargo on the Madero businesses and devoted the rest to the revolutionary cause. He spent 55,000 dollars on badly-needed guns and ammunition, most of which was not delivered to the rebels until after peace was signed. The European consortium were wondering what had happened to their money and Gustavo Madero was anxious to see a settlement before criminal charges of embezzlement were laid against him.

On this anxious note the talks opened, though not before there had almost been a split between the Maderos and Dr Vázquez Gómez on 11 March. Vázquez Gómez complained that he was unable to pay his bills in Washington because the Maderos would not provide him with funds. He was also resentful because he felt the Maderos were attempting to usurp his functions as chief revolutionary representative in the United States. The Maderos gave way on both points. They agreed to cover his bills and to attempt to arrange for him to see Limantour.

The meeting took place in Ambassador de la Barra's room, on 12 March, and as a result of their talk Vázquez Gómez wrote Limantour an informal letter summarising the reforms for which the Revolution stood and demanding the resignation of Díaz.

Two days later it was the turn of the Maderos. They went to see Limantour in his suite at the Hotel Plaza, the elder Madero obviously in an extreme state of nervousness, Gustavo outwardly calm. They had the Mexican Revolution in their pockets and were about to be searched by Díaz's right-hand man. Limantour asked what so-called reforms they were seeking. Madero senior told him: 'Effective suffrage, no re-election to the presidency, abolition of *jefes políticos*, land for the poor, the opening up of public lands and cutting up of the great estates.' The last demand must have seemed startling to Limantour, since the Maderos were among the greatest land-owning families in the Republic.

The Maderos sat back, expecting a wordy harangue, but were astounded when Limantour told them he intended to give them 'every assistance' in effecting the reforms for which they were fighting. He was convinced, he said, that their views deserved consideration because their movement obviously had much support.

When the grey-haired Francisco Madero got over his surprise, he followed up by demanding Díaz's resignation, too. But here Limantour cut him short, though he did agree that, whatever his own feelings, 'a vacancy might occur in the presidency'. Madero then offered to support Limantour for the post, ignoring the fact that his son was already styling himself 'provisional president'. Limantour rejected the suggestion, however, and they all agreed that Ambassador de la Barra should become provisional president if Díaz stepped down.

On the surface the gains seemed entirely on the side of the Revolution. Limantour announced he would leave at once for Mexico City and use his influence to press the demanded reforms. The meeting ended hurriedly when Gustavo Madero received word that an application had been made in Washington to extradite him to France over the misuse of the railway funds. He went into hiding in New York and two weeks later he and his father turned up at the border to bring the good news of Limantour's co-operation.

During the New York talks, events on the border had also taken a turn for the better. At Cerro Prieto, although they were defeated, the rebels captured their first machine-gun and on 12 March there was a spectacular battle for the border town of Agua Prieta, watched by thousands of Americans from its twin border town of Douglas, Arizona, divided by a street's width from Mexico. After the rebels had ousted the Federals, American spectators crossed the border in their cars to render first aid to the wounded.

Next day Díaz issued another statement, which this time reflected his unease. 'There have been slight disturbances of public order,' it said. 'They are of no importance. The government with the means at its disposal, expects to re-establish complete order in a short time.'

The means at his disposal were fewer than Díaz realised. The country was aflame and the venerable fire engine had run out of water. The War Department was so hopelessly out of touch that it could not even provide military maps of the country for Don Porfirio to study. So instead, the dictator, his officer son Porfirito and Foreign Minister Creel pored over near-useless postal maps spread out on the National Palace billiard tables.

By now the rebels far exceeded 5000 but Díaz overlooked

his promise to take the field. Instead, he pathetically attempted to stem the tide by sticking little flags in the billiard table baize, sending irritable, confused telegrams to his generals and ordering every encounter with the rebels to be written up in the Press as a Federal victory.

And so the rotten army edifice began to crumble away. Díaz, realising too late that the Revolution was going to be won or lost in the north, hastily dispatched reinforcements by train, with officers standing at the carriage exits with loaded revolvers to discourage desertion among the press-gang conscripts. Small bands of soldiers still managed to get away, jumping from the troop trains, tearing off their regimental insignia and fleeing into the countryside.

In Ciudad Juáraz *The Times* correspondent saw soldiers pulling off their badges and stripes as they descended from a newly-arrived train. And when eighty men were sent to water horses on the outskirts of town, sixty of them failed to return. Incredibly, many of the abused soldiers stayed in line, though their dubious loyalty to Díaz must have been further strained when they found that in some battles they had been issued with faulty ammunition purchased at great discount—and at great profit to himself—by the Army chief, General Manuel Mondragón.

The clouds of gloom over Mexico City lifted slightly with the arrival, on the evening of 20 March, of Limantour. He was greeted like a saviour as his train pulled into Colonia Station. The police band struck up *La Paloma,* government officials lined up to shake his hand and soldiers formed an avenue of honour from the train steps to his car. He had never been so popular.

Limantour, however, intended to keep the promises he had made to the Maderos at the New York talks. He urged Díaz to concede some of the rebels' demands and before the end of the month the entire cabinet, including Limantour, sent in their resignations. Díaz accepted all except Limantour's. At Díaz's insistence he stayed on; but the new cabinet was a mediocre collection. The most important appointment was that of de la Barra as Minister of Foreign Relations, which placed him next to Corral in presidential succession.

More concessions followed quickly. On 1 April, escorted

by cavalry units and surrounded by a squad of plainclothes bodyguards, Díaz travelled to address the opening of Congress. His speech was a confession of government helplessness. The man who was beginning his eighth term as president stood up and solemnly declared for 'no re-election'. The far-reaching demands of Madero's group were put forward as long-contemplated government policies. Díaz's speech amounted to an indictment of his own administration. His sweeping concessions, instead of settling the crisis, merely spurred the revolutionaries to increased efforts. The speech was another blunder committed by an old man.

Madero's answer was prompt and to the point: his supporters demanded the resignation of Díaz. Nothing less would satisfy them. They could afford to be dictatorial now. Every day brought further successes and by early April a large part of the northern states was in the hands of rebels of varying shades of greed and ambition, but all proclaiming support for the Plan of San Luis Potosí.

As the realisation dawned that the yoke of Díazpotism was slowly being lifted, the long-subservient people of the capital also became bolder. Posters were stuck up at night demanding Díaz's resignation, *vivas* for Madero were heard on the streets, newspapers criticising the government were left unmolested. The signs were enough for the vice-president Corral. By now seriously ill with cancer, he fled to Paris on 12 April.

Still the government tried ... an appeal was issued for 'loyal subjects' to volunteer for six months' army service. There were few takers.

But the Federal commanders in the north fought on ruthlessly to preserve the dictatorship: all captured rebels were shot. The *insurrectos* were guilty of similar atrocities. In Guerrero, Orozco's men executed the town's judge, *jefe político*, postal inspector and other leading Díaz supporters. All captured Federal officers were shot, but soldiers were given the choice of the firing squad or enrolment with the rebel cause.

The slaughter sometimes extended to the innocents, too. Pancho Villa showed the first signs of his senseless and sporadic ferocity in the killing of 200 Chinese in the industrial town of Torreón. Most of the Chinese residents of

Mexico had drifted down from California after the Gold Rush days. Hard-working and thrifty, they had built up laundries, restaurants and other businesses. Villa despised them so much that his choicest way of insulting an American was to call him a *chino blanco*, a white Chinese. His hatred of the yellow race was shared by his followers.

The Torreón trouble started when a bunch of Villistas, who had drunk several bottles of dubious local brandy, followed this up with a meal at a Chinese restaurant. When some of them later died the Chinese were blamed and the pent-up ferocity of some of the worse rebel elements was loosed upon the unarmed Chinese. It was well known that the Chinese did not trust banks and usually carried their savings secreted about their persons or hidden at home. To facilitate their robbery, they were shot down wherever they were found.

'Some were cut to pieces, some beheaded, some tied to horses by their pigtails and dragged along the streets,' wrote Henry Baerlein. 'Others had their arms or legs attached to different horses and were torn asunder; some were stood up naked in the market gardens of the neighbourhood and given over as targets to drunken marksmen. Thirteen Chinese employees of Yee Hop's general store were hauled into the street and killed with knives; 200 Chinamen were sheltered in the city jail but all their money was appropriated. One brave girl had nine of them concealed and calmly she denied their presence, even when her father had gone out to argue with the mob and been shot for being on the Chinese side.'

Foreign property owners, too, suffered at the hands of rebel bands in need of money and supplies. The Hon. Claud Stanhope, brother of the Earl of Chesterfield and manager of an English salt company at Salinas, was one example. Rebels rode their horses into his house, wrecked the furniture and demanded £300. When he was unable to provide this, the fifty-four-year-old Stanhope was marched through the town at bayonet point and held prisoner under threat of execution until he managed to escape.

The most ready sources of both funds and equipment, however, were the Mormon colonies, which had been established in Chihuahua in the 1880s. The industrious and peaceful settlers, whose thrift had accumulated plentiful supplies of food, were plagued by rebel bands who demanded food, shelter and the Mormons' rifles.

Trains were also prime targets. The Englishman, Patrick O'Hea, was in one passenger train which was attacked by bandits near Torreón. He described how they 'charged, yelling and whooping, primitive, excited, unruly, ragged, dusty, bloodshot and some bandaged, all highly nervous and pretty well charged with "dutch courage". Carbines and rifles, of every age and type, pistols and shotguns, the rabble was as motley in its armament as in its other gear.... Smelling of sweat, offal and grease, grimy hands pawed us for concealed weapons and pillaged us of our cash.... No man was slain in cold blood among the passengers, though some were threatened when it was felt that they were resisting search.'

But for the time being the comic opera aspect of the uprising outweighed the grimmer side. 'Never was there such a colourful, romantic, noble and foolish period as the first Revolution in northern Mexico,' according to Timothy Turner, an El Paso newspaperman.

At El Paso, Douglas, and other American border towns, hostesses inaugurated novel social functions called 'battle teas'. Whenever a border skirmish was reported they gathered their friends on the flat roofs of their houses and supplied them with tea, cakes and field glasses with which to view the fighting.

On 13 April there was a battle which had the tea hostesses of Douglas ecstatic. A force of 300 rebels commanded by a former cattle rustler named 'Red' López made a surprise attack on Agua Prieta, steaming into town aboard a captured train. They took the Federal garrison by surprise and blew up its headquarters before taking up positions along the American border. Hundreds of Americans swarmed to the border to watch the battle; three were killed and eleven wounded as the Federals fired into the rebels' positions. Finally, Troop K of the U.S. 1st Cavalry galloped across the street which formed the border and ordered the Federal defenders to surrender. They eventually agreed, on the condition they would be interned in the United States.

'Guests at the battle tea parties, despite the fatalities

attending them, were delighted with the spectacle,' reported the *Daily Mail*.

The American casualties brought a warning from Washington that a recurrence would 'compel action by this country', and the 800-strong 6th Cavalry was ordered to Douglas. But the threat was unheeded. On 17 April fighting again broke out as a force of 1500 Federals moved in to recapture Agua Prieta. Huge crowds again jammed the battle areas; two Americans, one of them a newspaperman, were wounded. But this battle was a much shorter one. The rebels, leaderless and short of bullets, quickly abandoned the newly-won town. Shortly before the shooting started, 'Red' López had crossed into the United States to be fêted by saloon admirers. He got drunk, fell asleep and woke up with a hangover to find himself with no army and no town. Despite the new civilian casualties Washington still took no action.

Arms and ammunition were, at this time, the rebels' most serious problem. Many of the *insurrectos* had brought along their own guns to the war and this variety of weapons made it even more difficult to keep every man supplied with bullets.

Though the revolutionary cause was undoubtedly prospering, it was going to be a race between the success of the movement and its bankruptcy. Madero had even mortgaged his house and was sustaining his ragamuffin army on loans or contributions from friends, and by appropriating supplies from captured towns and *haciendas*.

Late in April, the rebels received an unexpected boost from sympathisers in El Paso. An American Civil War brass muzzle-loading cannon, which stood at the entrance to the town hall and which belonged to the city's Pioneer Club, was surreptitiously inspected by a group of Americans, pronounced still serviceable, moved off its blocks one dark night, attached to the back of a car and towed across a shallow part of the Rio Grande.

The cannon, for which shells had to be specially made in the United States and smuggled over the border, proved of great worth in the decisive battle of Ciudad Juárez. After the success of the Madero rebellion, Abraham González, the governor of Chihuahua, ordered the cannon returned to

El Paso. It remained on exhibition in Ciudad Juárez for a few days; then the four Americans who had originally stolen it drove over the international bridge into Mexico, attached the gun once more to their car and drove slowly past a Mexican guard of honour back into El Paso.

Dr Ira J. Bush, who accepted a commission as chief surgeon in the revolutionary army, felt that 'Americans on the border were almost to a man friendly to Madero and to the Revolution'. As the tempo of border battle increased, more and more Americans and other adventurers flocked to join Madero's ragged army. Among this group, which became known as 'The Foreign Legion', were Giuseppe Garibaldi, grandson of the liberator of Italy, Ben Viljoen, a Boer general who had fought the British and had after- wards become a farmer in the United States, A. W. Lewis, a Canadian machine-gunner who had also fought in the Boer War, but on the British side and Lou Carpentier, a French- man noted for his skill with cannons. Americans with Madero included Sam Dreben, known as 'The Fighting Jew', Oscar Creighton, a New Yorker who swapped a stockbroker's office job for the excitement of the Revolution and who gained the nickname 'The Dynamite Devil' be- cause of his prowess at blowing up trains, and a thirty-year- old El Pasoan named Tom Mix, who survived the Revolu- tion and went on to make his reputation as a Hollywood cowboy.

Gradually the revolutionary armies began to close in on Ciudad Juárez, the largest and most important of the border towns, where the garrison was commanded by eighty- year-old General Juan J. Navarro, a connoisseur of cognac and a soldier of the old school. Navarro had infuriated the *insurrectos* when, after one Federal victory, he had ordered that not only rebel prisoners but suspected revolutionary sympathisers should be shot.

As the rebel forces congregated along the Rio Grande to the west of Ciudad Juárez, a rumour spread in El Paso that Orozco would attack the Federals. By eight next morning thousands of people had made their way to the tops of tall buildings and to the nearby Franklin and Krazy Kat moun- tains. When no battle took place, the *El Paso Times* reported: 'The disappointment of the public was something tremendous.'

On 19 April Madero demanded the surrender of Ciudad Juárez but Navarro refused. Madero, still a man of peace, accepted the refusal meekly, believing he could get what he wanted by negotiation. In addition, he was afraid of creating an international crisis if, during the fighting for the town, there should be a repetition of the Douglas incidents and more American deaths.

So more talks were started between the Maderistas and a group of commissioners appointed by the Díaz government. The conference site was a grove of cottonwood trees on the banks of the Rio Grande about halfway between Ciudad Juárez and the main rebel camp. Though most of his officers were in favour of attacking the besieged town, Madero instead agreed to a ten-day truce, beginning on 22 April, by the terms of which the rebels were allowed to import food and clothing *through the Federal customs house* in Ciudad Juárez, but no arms or ammunition. For the first time in months the rebels were well fed and clothed, while the arms ban was no problem: all the guns and bullets they needed were smuggled across the Rio Grande to their camp. American sympathisers even threw silver dollars across the narrowest stretches of the river, until they were stopped by the U.S. authorities.

When the truce expired with the peace commissioners still arguing, Madero extended it by a further five days, while the impatient rebel armies fumed at the inaction and Madero vacillated unhappily in the midst of the rumpus which his oratorical eloquence had stirred up. Timothy Turner wrote of Madero's indecision: 'Madero, I think, was too kind-hearted ... to order a clash of these armed forces, too thorough-going a sentimentalist. His hesitation however, was not from fear.... One of his misgivings about the attack was that fire would kill Americans on the El Paso side and that this might lead to intervention by United States troops.'

On Sunday 7 May, unhappy over the lack of progress in the talks and worried about the possibility of American intervention, Madero announced that he intended to abandon the siege of Ciudad Juárez and move his army south into Chihuahua. His officers were astounded. Their troops, massed in the hills to the west of the town and supplemented by the stolen brass cannon and a home-made long gun, now heavily outnumbered the defenders. The town *must* fall to a determined attack.

Their disappointment turned to rage when copies of the next day's *El Paso Times* were delivered to the rebel camp. Added to the news of Madero's withdrawal announcement was a quote from Colonel Manuel Tamborell, second-in-command at Ciudad Juárez, accusing the rebels of cowardice.

The itchiest trigger fingers in the camp belonged to Villa and Orozco. Villa felt it was 'shameful to retire without an effort', so the two of them ordered small groups of their men into provocative action. Just to the east of the rebel-held territory an irrigation canal ran parallel to the river, then went on through the town. The Federals had, incredibly, left the space between canal and river unguarded and, in addition, the spring cleaning of the canal had resulted in a high bank of dirt being left as convenient cover. 'A prettier opening into the city could not have been desired,' according to Dr Bush. This was the route the rebels took.

Turner was interviewing Madero, who had just reaffirmed to the American newspaperman that there would be no attack, when firing broke out. 'Madero lost all self-control,' reported Turner.

A mounted subaltern was sent with a white flag and orders to stop the fighting but as he approached the battle scene his horse was shot from under him. Madero gave up all hopes of restraining his eager army and ordered a full-scale attack. But, a gentleman to the end, first he sent General Navarro a note informing him, albeit a little belatedly, that the truce was at an end.

Afterwards Villa was unrepentant. He explained: 'We contrived to launch our attack by military logic, circumventing Sr. Madero, who was no military man.... Sometimes a civilian chief is unable to see what is plain to the eyes of his military subordinate. If the success of a campaign or a revolution is at stake, that subordinate must be guided by his own judgment.'

Ironically, as the assault on Ciudad Juárez began, President Díaz was on his way to the Chamber of Deputies in the capital to make another conciliatory announcement. Edward Bell, an American who edited two Mexico City newspapers, *La Prensa* and *The Daily American*, was standing at the corner of Avenida San Francisco as Díaz passed in his state carriage:

'He was attended by twelve outriders of his presidential guard. As usual, their blue uniforms were spick and span, their silver helmets polished to glistening brightness.

'The top of the coach was lowered and, contrary to his custom, Díaz sat alone. He wore a black civilian suit and tall hat. The few people who halted at the street intersection waiting for a passage through, were all that had gathered. Not a cheer was uttered.... Straight ahead, with his stern features set in grim determination, the aged dictator stared as he rode along what proved to be his last visit to the Chamber.... The man who but a few weeks before would have been greeted with outbursts of applause wherever he moved had ceased to interest them.'

Díaz told the Deputies he would agree to resign 'when, according to the dictates of my conscience, I am assured that my resignation will not be followed by anarchy'. When the insurgents promised to lay down their arms, he would guide his people into smoother waters. Then he would go.

But it was too late. The only major battle of the Madero revolution was already under way and, with its success, the vaunted Porfirian régime was overthrown.

Though the defenders of Ciudad Juárez were well armed with machine-guns and mortars of French manufacture, they numbered only about 500, augmented by some 300 civilian auxiliaries, against Madero's 3000. But, apart from the vital flaw along the canal, their defences had been carefully worked out by Tamborell, who had arranged an outer defence of rifle pits, an inner defence consisting of buildings converted into strong points and barricades blocking the streets. It was such an impressive arrangement that the Boer, Viljoen, had pronounced the town impregnable unless the attackers had sufficient artillery, but the *insurrectos* soon proved their Foreign Legionnaire wrong.

The newspaperman Turner, seated on a hill just outside the town, watched the rebels go into action. Since no one wore a uniform, officers were distinguished by hat bands in the Mexican national colours of red, white and green. There were no regimental divisions and the rank and file were known merely as *gente* (people)—the *gente* of Orozco or the *gente* of Villa. 'They moved in no formation whatsoever,' wrote Turner, 'just an irregular stream of them, silhouettes of men and rifles. Thus they were to move in and move out ... throughout the battle. They would fight awhile and then come back to rest, sleep and eat, returning refreshed to the front.

'The European-trained soldiers raved at this, tried to turn them back, to make everybody fight at one time. But that was not the way of these chaps from Chihuahua. They knew their business and they knew it well. That casual way of fighting, I think, more than any other one thing, took Juárez. For by it the *insurrectos* were always fresh, with high spirits, while the little brown Federals, with no sleep and little food or water, with their officers behind them ready with their pistols to kill quitters, soon lost their morale.'

Turner was also a spectator of the two-gun bombardment of the town. The Frenchman Carpentier 'a dainty little chap who wore a pair of new kid gloves' was in charge of the cannon.

The first shot missed Ciudad Juárez altogether. Carpentier and his Mexican helpers lowered the muzzle of the long gun. The second shot struck the Federals' water tank in their barracks, a lucky hit which destroyed most of the defenders' water supply and which had much to do with the fall of the town.

'Then Carpentier tried another shot with his big gun. But the sound of it was not the same. Even with my untrained ear I knew that something was amiss. Carpentier started running back up the slope and, leaning over, he started to pull something out of the earth. He returned, lugging what proved to be the breech-block of the cannon. Examining it, he shook his head dolorously and, sitting down on a large rock, wept bitter tears of grief and exasperation.'

Despite this loss of half the rebel artillery force, Tamborell's elaborately contrived defences within the town proved no answer to an undisciplined army which failed utterly to abide by the accepted rules of war. Once they had overrun the outer defences, the Maderistas avoided the street barricades and strong points by entering houses at the top of a street and dynamiting their way through the walls until they reached the other end. Thus they were exposed only as they advanced into the next block.

Soon the town's water and electricity supplies were cut off and by nightfall the plight of the defenders was serious. But General Navarro curtly rejected a surrender demand.

'The scene at sunset was a picture,' reported the *El Paso Times*, 'Shrapnel shells were bursting in the setting sun; rifle fire was almost continuous.... A big American named Crum came staggering down the river to get a drink of muddy water just before dusk. He was with Garibaldi and they had reached the main street of the town. "We're lickin' hell out of 'em," he said. Which was the first official report of the battle to date.

'As darkness settled over the scene ... the firing ceased, since Mexicans make it a rule not to work at the battle business after dark. ...'

Next morning furious fighting broke out in every section of Ciudad Juárez, and soon the small rebel hospital operated by Dr Bush in a converted boarding house in El Paso was filled, and tents had to be erected in the front garden to accommodate the overflow. 'All the second day of the battle I stood over the operating table caring for the wounded until by night time I was worn out...' said Dr Bush.

One of his patients was a rebel who had been wounded at Galeana, 200 miles south of the border, before the Ciudad Juárez fighting broke out. His arm had been shattered by a bullet and, since there were no trains running north, he had walked all the way to El Paso. Dr Bush noted laconically: 'He made a speedy recovery but, by the irony of fate, attended a dance one rainy night, took pneumonia and died.'

Once again, as in the battles around Douglas, Mexicans weren't the only casualties. Mayor Henry Kelly of El Paso issued a warning to all Americans to keep off the streets and away from the border. But he was wasting his breath. Spectators lined rooftops, hilltops and the river bank, and even jostled for position on top of railway carriages, though the centre of El Paso was well within rifle range of the centre of Ciudad Juárez.

One American woman was killed on the banks of the Rio Grande, another stray bullet claimed a schoolboy, and a man sitting in the main square of El Paso reading a newspaper was struck in the ear. Five Americans died on their own soil and about two dozen were wounded during the battle. Bullets shattered windows and punctured wooden hoardings and, according to the *El Paso Times*, 'made the lee side of an adobe wall a most convenient and comfortable place to be'.

Despite further rumblings from Washington, however, the intervention that Madero so much feared never materialised.

By nightfall on the second day all of Ciudad Juárez except the bullring, the main church and the army barracks was in rebel hands. Next day Navarro and the survivors of his garrison made their last stand in the barracks where, thanks to Carpentier's lucky cannon shot, they were without water.

The rebels captured a mortar and began systematically to reduce the barracks; and when the attackers got close enough to start lobbing home-made grenades over the wall, the Federals had had enough. Just after noon on 10 May a white flag was run up and the Italian Garibaldi, the only rebel officer present at the time, received General Navarro's sword in surrender.

Of the town's defenders, 180 had been killed, including Tamborel, and 250 wounded. The rebel casualties were even higher but no figures were given.

The dead and wounded lay everywhere. Dr Bush found sanitary conditions 'indescribable' since Navarro's soldiers, mainly recruited in southern Mexico, had brought typhus with them to Juárez. Many typhus victims were lying alongside the wounded in the Federal military hospital where, during the three days' fighting, they had been left to shift for themselves. Apart from wounds and illness, many of them were nearly dead of thirst and starvation by the time help arrived.

Captured Federals were put to work cleaning up the town

and burying the dead, and two hotels—one of which had
changed its name overnight from the Porfirio Díaz to the
Francisco I. Madero—were commandeered as emergency
hospitals. Mexican and American doctors who had
answered the call for assistance treated the sick and
wounded.

No sooner had the firing stopped than the looting started.
All the shop windows had been smashed in, merchandise
was strewn around the streets and the rebels, their pockets
stuffed, were rummaging about for valuables.

When Turner passed a department store called 'Las Tres
B' he saw that some rebels had found a box of coloured silk
shirts 'and were in ecstasies'. Others were pawing over hundreds of shoes strewn about the floor and cursing because
they could not find two that would match.

Some of the rebels did their looting even as they fought.
Turner saw one man holding a sewing machine under his
left arm and carrying his rifle under his right. Before every
shot he carefully put down his prize in a safe corner.

One rebel wore five stolen sombreros, stacked one on top
of the other, a couple of bright shirts and a pair of yellow
shoes. 'He fairly squeaked with his recently acquired new-
ness', reported the *El Paso Times*. This newspaper also
noted that Federal prisoners were burying the dead where
they had fallen, 'throwing the bodies into less than the six
feet of earth to which every man is supposed to be entitled
as his last due'. One woman, gunned down as she tried to
cross the Plaza of Peace, was given such a perfunctory
burial in the plaza that one arm protruded from the ground.

Madero's arrival in mid-afternoon started the church
bells clanging and halted the looting. 'The whole city is
filled with a shouting multitude acclaiming Madero,' reported the *Daily Mail*. 'Captured Federal soldiers stripped
off their uniforms shouting "Viva la constitución".' The *El
Paso Times* commented, on Madero's arrival: 'More of the
product of Mr Winchester's well-known factory was wasted
on the desert air.'

On the heels of Madero came the American souvenir
hunters and curiosity seekers, swarming across the border
bridges and carrying off everything portable that had not
already been looted. Pieces of Federal equipment were

taken back into El Paso, together with typhus. The first
death of an American from the disease brought a prompt
embargo on the souvenir excursions, but the A. D. Foster
Company in El Paso catered for the souvenir mania by
manufacturing 'revolutionary spoons' which sold for two
and a half dollars each.

After Madero's arrival, groups of rebels demonstrated in
the streets, demanding the execution of General Navarro in
reprisal for the deaths of captured rebels. But Madero
insisted on according Navarro his rights as a prisoner of
war. Realising that the general's life was in great danger,
Madero jeopardised his whole future on a foolish act of
gallantry to save an enemy who, had the circumstances
been reversed, would have executed Madero without a
second thought.

Madero borrowed a car from an American journalist and
drove Navarro to the river-side home of Max Weber, the
German Consul in Ciudad Juárez. There Navarro was
given a civilian suit, a horse and his freedom. Rare old
campaigner that he was, the eighty-year-old general removed his suit, strapped it onto his back with his braces and
swam his horse across the Rio Grande to safety.

When the news of Navarro's escape became known,
Orozco and Villa, backed by their soldiers, burst into a
meeting of the rebel 'cabinet' and attempted to arrest
Madero. But the little chieftain managed to convince the
rebel duo that they were suffering from an excess of revolutionary zeal. The incident ended in embraces all round, and
a weeping Villa told Madero: 'I have committed a black
infamy and my heart is between two stones.' From then on
Villa was totally loyal to Madero, but Orozco was soon to
display his treachery anew.

An official exchange of letters between Madero and
Orozco (Villa could not write) was published as a handbill
and distributed among the rebel army in order to crush
rumours. A dangerous incident was closed, but it showed
just how brittle were the alliances of the Revolution, and
how difficult Madero's task would be.

Indeed, Madero's father was under no illusions. On the
evening after the fall of Ciudad Juárez, he told Dr Bush

prophetically: 'I greatly fear that this is the beginning of
chaos for Mexico.'

But for the time being the triumph of Ciudad Juárez was
enough. The town was a great prize for Madero, enabling
him to import arms and supplies freely from El Paso and to
pay for them with Customs revenues. More important still
was the psychological effect: rebel morale zoomed and that
of the Federals drained away.

The northern towns of Agua Prieta and Casas Grandes,
scenes of previous battles, now fell without a fight as the
Federals retreated towards Mexico City. In the south Zapata's ragged peasants captured the town of Cuatula, and
state capitals began to fall into the hands of Madero sympathisers.

By 17 May Díaz had been persuaded to face up to the inevitable—unconditional resignation. Weary and stricken with a jaw infection, he agreed to go before the end of the month, providing that vice-president Corral would agree, from the safety of Paris, to resign too.

Next day the London *Times* reported, 'The Cabinet Council at which President Díaz's resignation was announced was most pathetic. The aged president lay in bed in an anteroom with a swollen face, suffering great pain ... Señor Limantour ... was the only member of the cabinet who entered the sick room.'

Don Porfirio's illness had begun with toothache, which was diagnosed as an abscessed tooth. The dentist made a poor job of the removal, taking away part of the president's jaw with the tooth, and infection set in. Soon the whole of one side of his face was in a terrible state of inflammation and he was in such pain that he was hardly able to speak. The illness left him stone deaf in one ear for the rest of his life.

On the night of 21 May, on the outskirts of Ciudad Juárez, the peace agreement was signed at a table illuminated by the headlights of cars, since the electricity supply had still not been restored to the battered town. Government representatives reiterated Díaz's statement that he would resign and the Madero family agreed, over the objections of some rebel factions, that Francisco de la Barra, the former Mexican Ambassador to the United States and now Minister of Foreign Relations, should take over as provisional president pending an election, at which Madero would presumably be chosen president.

News of the treaty reached Mexico City on 23 May, the same day that Corral's resignation arrived from Paris. Still the promised departure of Díaz was not forthcoming, and howling mobs congregated outside the presidential home in Calle Cadena. American Ambassador Wilson went to pay a call on Díaz but had great trouble forcing a way through the crowds surging round the house. Once inside, he was 'ushered' through lines of sad and weeping people to the drawing room' where he found Señora Díaz 'in a state of profound agitation'. Díaz was in bed, in great pain, and his wife told the ambassador 'The tortures of his body are infinitely increased by the street demonstrations.'

When Wilson left the house, without seeing the sick president, the mob was seven blocks deep but apart from 'a few acts of playful familiarity' Wilson made his way safely through the crowd.

On 24 May the demonstrations grew fiercer. Students and workers roamed the streets, beating empty petrol cans and screaming for Don Porfirio's resignation. Gradually the various demonstrations began to converge on the Zócalo and by early evening the great plaza, where eight months previously Díaz had been fêted, was jammed with a crowd estimated at 75,000, all calling for his head.

But Díazpotism was not quite dead yet. Edward Bell reported:

'On the roof of the National Palace a dozen machine guns stood ready for action. In the towers and on the roof of the cathedral, on the north, were several companies of riflemen. On the roofs on the south side of the great square a regiment crouched behind the parapets. . . .

'Between 9 and 10 p.m. mounted police, issuing from the main entrance of the National Palace, made three attempts to force a passage through the mob but each time they were beaten back. The jam was too dense; and at each retreat the police were followed by yells of derision.

'The real carnage began about 10 p.m. On their fourth advance the police began shooting over the heads of the mob, who charged them in earnest. The police were dragged from their horses and the real battle was on. Then into the centre of that surging mass the riflemen on the tower poured their fire. No need to aim; to miss was impossible. Then the machine-guns opened up.

'For five minutes the Maxims directed their devastating fire full into the mob. It killed and maimed and maddened but did not effect a stampede. Suddenly the heavens opened . . . and the deluge cleared the plaza.'

Mexicans are notoriously reluctant to get wet, and a crowd who were willing to face bullets ran from the rain. In a few minutes the square was deserted, except for the fallen. The downpour washed away the blood of the dead and dying. Next day official reports gave the number of dead as seven and the wounded as forty. But the real total of killed was around 200, and more than a thousand were wounded. At one police station alone, 146 bodies were piled for collection.

The Zócalo massacre was the final straw. After refusing to sign three resignations prepared by de la Barra and thrust at him on his sick bed, Díaz finally gave in on the afternoon of 25 May. Almost delirious with pain and aided by his wife, he tottered to his study where, in a shaky hand, he penned his own resignation. Señora Díaz, unable to watch her husband's humiliation, left the room as he wrote the end to an era of Mexican history.

The resignation was read out the same evening to Congress. It was received in silence but its formal acceptance brought cheers from the public gallery. Within hours a monster parade formed, snaking its jubilant way through the streets. Police and peons, students and soldiers took part, the military celebrating with men at whom they had been shooting twenty-four hours earlier. One enthusiastic Madero supporter sent a telegram to his idol: 'Today I believe in God. Blessed are you, our Liberators.'

Hurried plans were made to get Díaz safely out of the country, and shortly after midnight the presidential party were on their way. They walked out of the house in Calle Cadena, leaving behind all their furniture and almost all their possessions. The dictator's son Porfirito, his wife and five children, including a ten-day-old baby, were also roused from their beds in the early hours and told to dress for Europe.

Three trains conveyed the group to Veracruz. The first and third were troop trains with a Federal guard of 300 under the command of General Victoriano Huerta, of whom Mexico was soon to hear much more, while the centre train carried the refugees. Díaz's prophecy 'I came to Mexico City in a shower of bullets and perhaps I shall have to go out the same way' came true when rebels attacked the train, but they were driven off.

When Díaz reached Veracruz he was so ill that he had to be carried to the house of J. B. Body, the manager of Lord

Cowdray's businesses in Mexico. At the house, he spent five days under the protection of the British flag waiting for a ship to take him to Europe.

So well kept was the secret of his flight that, on the morning following his resignation, Limantour and five other ministers turned up at the presidential home for a conference.

On 31 May a weeping Díaz boarded the German steamer *Ypiranga*, following into exile all the other Mexicans who had put ambition above country.

But not everybody was pleased to see him go ... Edith O'Shaughnessy, wife of an American diplomat in the capital, wrote: 'All those venerable tears should have been caught in a golden cup by a whole people on their knees, those eyes wiped dry with the cloth of gratitude and repentance, to be kept, cup and cloth, as long as the nation lasts. . . .'

To Mrs Tweedie, his departure was 'the greatest calamity Mexico has ever known', and another author felt that in the thirty years while he was 'practically the king of Mexico', Díaz had 'transformed Mexico from a land of disorder and demoralisation into a veritable Garden of Eden by comparison. . . .'

Ambassador Wilson thought that though Díaz governed 'autocratically and sometimes ruthlessly', he had possessed 'undeviating personal honesty, loyalty to obligations, a real patriotism and a lofty conception of Mexico's needs and future'.

The most scathing epitaph on the Díaz régime came from that implacable enemy of Díazpotism, John Kenneth Turner:

'He built a machine, enriched his friends and disposed of his enemies, buying some and killing others. He flattered and gifted the foreigner, favoured the Church, kept temperance in his body, and learned a martial carriage; he set one friend against another, fostered prejudice between his people and other peoples, paid the printer, cried in the sight of the multitude when there was no sorrow in his soul—and wrecked his country.'

Díaz and his party arrived in Paris on a June evening, to be met by Madame Lefaivre, wife of the French Minister to

Mexico. Mme Lefaivre was so moved by the ex-president's serenity and dignity that she sent to his hotel a magnificent bouquet in the Mexican colours, 'my usual economy disappearing in the face of this drama and this injustice of history'.

Díaz lived a simple, inexpensive life in Paris. It was reported that he rose early, bathed in cold water, rode horseback and attended to his own affairs, rather than hire a secretary. Other exiles like Limantour, who had followed Díaz to Paris within a week, lived in luxury, but Díaz maintained his simple habits until his death on 2 July 1915.

Victory had increased, rather than lessened, Madero's problems and responsibilities. His time and strength were dissipated in thousands of minor details, rather than with the major worries facing the revolutionary government, so his first message to the country on 26 May was a request to back the de la Barra interim administration. At the same time Madero renounced the provisional presidency he had assumed the previous November.

On 3 June Madero set out by rail from his home in Parras, Coahuila, for the capital. His train took four days to cover the 700 miles. Thousands of people gathered along the route at stations, bridges, level crossings and water tanks to greet him, listen to him, look at him and to touch his clothes. Women held up sick babies for him to touch, believing they might be cured by the mere laying on of his hands. Madero had become more than a victor; he was a saviour, a redeemer.

Almost a quarter of a million people flocked to the capital to greet Madero. Many of them were sleeping in the streets and parks when, shortly before dawn on 7 June, Mexico City was rocked by the strongest earthquake in living memory. It lasted for 14 minutes, 45 seconds and the tremor was recorded in such widely-scattered places as Sydney, Bombay, the Azores and Shepherd's Bush.

Great fissures opened in the streets, people were hurled from their beds, walls tumbled, roofs fell, electricity and power cables snapped, gas mains were shattered. The ancient church of Santo Domingo was wrecked; the San Cosme barracks collapsed, killing thirty-three soldiers. The central railway station crashed to the ground and a great crack appeared in one of the walls of the National Palace, displacing the keystone of the arch under which Díaz had passed daily during his long years of power. To the superstitious this meant that God was wreaking his vengeance upon the Mexican people for turning out Díaz.

Mrs Moats was in the capital during the earthquake. She grabbed her daughter from her bedroom and ran outside her house, which was on the outskirts of the city. 'As we sat there, shivering with the cold, I saw the earth literally rising and opening up before me in great crevasses. I looked across to the Country Club. It seemed to be bowing and swaying backwards and forwards. . . .'

The panic which followed the tremor was increased by the fact that so many extra people were in the city to welcome Madero. The final death toll was 207.

But within hours the disaster had been swept aside by the enthusiasm of the welcome for Madero. It took four hours for his cavalcade to cover the two miles from the railway station to the National Palace. Among the first of the revolutionary leaders to greet him was Emiliano Zapata, making one of his rare trips from the hills of his native state to meet the man who was supposed to be instituting a new deal for Mexico.

Great roars of 'Who wins?' were answered by more roars of 'Madero', though not all of the welcomers were at all sure why they were cheering.

The American journalist John Reed asked a soldier why he was wearing a Madero favour on his uniform. 'I don't know, Señor,' he replied. 'My captain told me he is a great saint.'

After his tremendous reception, Madero was suffering from a headache and loss of voice after his five-day string of speeches. He went to a house owned by his parents in the capital and rested for twenty-four hours.

The dove had arrived in Mexico City. But the sky was full of hawks.

Part Two: Madero

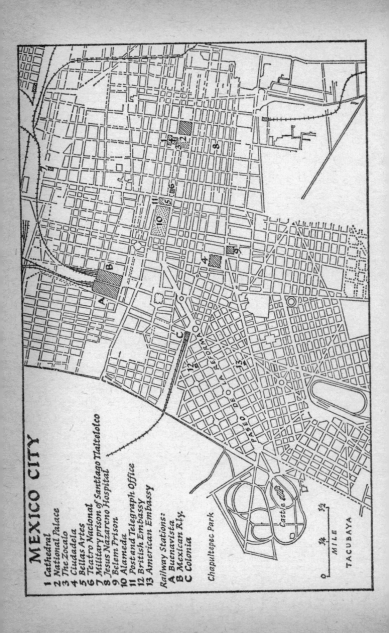

MEXICO CITY

1 Cathedral
2 National Palace
3 The Zócalo
4 Ciudadela
5 Bellas Artes
6 Teatro Nacional
7 Military prison of Santiago Tlatelolco
8 Jesus Nazareno Hospital
9 Belem Prison
10 Alameda
11 Post and Telegraph Office
12 British Embassy
13 American Embassy

Railway Stations:
A Buenavista
B Mexican Rly.
C Colonia

Chapultepec Park

TACUBAYA

Though the Díaz government had been toppled with incredible ease, few of the Díaz supporters had been destroyed, and they swiftly regrouped, awaiting a chance to
strike back. They did not have to wait long. Madero's
confirmation of Francisco de la Barra as provisional president was the first of a tragic succession of blunders made by
a well-meaning but inept politician. De la Barra was a Díaz
man and his appointment put an immediate check on the
progress of the Revolution.

Well educated, an expert in international law and a
professional diplomat, de la Barra had represented Mexico
in several countries, latterly the United States during the
Madero uprising. But he was hardly fitted for the monumental task of holding together the country's discordant
elements. He was described as 'a marshmallow made up to
look like a man ... at all times more concerned with his
personal appearance ... than with the grim business of
combating popular will'.

De la Barra made no secret of his anxiety to be rid of his
job. He told his first cabinet meeting that he had not wanted
the presidency and that the happiest day of his life would be
that on which he could relinquish it. But at least he possessed the prime virtue, for the moment at least, of being
acceptable to most elements of both new and old régimes
and, in the opinion of Mrs O'Shaughnessy, during the five
months he was interim president proved himself 'a very
good tightrope walker on a decidedly slack rope'.

Eagerly Díaz supporters and Madero men jostled for
position and promotion under the new president, while
Madero, standing in the wings, attempted to unite all
factions by his family policy of honesty and fair dealing.

Though Pancho Villa, content that with Madero's
triumph the struggle was won, went back to Chihuahua
City, married his sweetheart Luz Corral and opened a meat
business, other revolutionary generals wanted to transfer
their titles to the regular army, or even become members of
the government. The ambitions of Pascual Orozco, for
instance, suffered a severe setback when Madero 'rewarded'

him by appointing him military commander in the state of Chihuahua.

The revolutionary leaders were further alarmed, and understandably so, when the interim government began to disband and pay off the rebels, leaving the country in the hands of a regular army which had just conclusively proved its inability to defend it.

Zapata, in particular, was most reluctant to disband his troops until his cherished land reforms had been accomplished, so on 12 June Madero travelled to Cuernavaca, only forty-seven miles from Mexico City but in the heart of Zapata-dominated territory. Madero's sincerity impressed the rebel chieftain, who agreed to a partial demobilisation if his peasant soldiers were given land of their own. Madero agreed to this and further promised to pay each rebel £2 when he handed over his rifle. Seven hundred of them did so immediately.

Afterwards the Zapatistas staged a military parade through Cuernavaca in Madero's honour. It was attended by Mrs Rosa King, whose tea shop had been such a success during the Díaz days and who now also owned a hotel in the town.

'Surely all the strength of the Zapatistas was kept for action, for they wasted none on uniforms or martial drill,' she wrote. 'Poor fellows, in their huge straw hats and white cotton *calzones* with cotton socks in purple, pink or green pulled outside and over the trouser legs. They were equipped with rifles of all sorts and one poor little cannon....

'Among the troops were women soldiers, some of them officers. One, wearing a bright pink ribbon tied around her waist with a nice big bow tied in back, was especially conspicuous. She was riding a pony and looked very bright and pretty.

'Treacherous little ribbon! It gave the game away, for it was soon seen by that vivid bit of colour that the troops were merely marching around a few squares and reappearing before Madero....'

A delighted Madero returned to Mexico City and announced that the Zapata problem had been solved. For a time it appeared that his optimism was justified. By the end of July nearly 3000 Zapatistas had been paid off.

But de la Barra showed his true colours when he refused to negotiate with Zapata, announcing that he found it 'truly disagreeable that an individual with antecedents such as his should be permitted to maintain such an independent attitude'. He further antagonised the rebel chief by sending to Cuernavaca a Federal force under General Victoriano Huerta, the man who had escorted Díaz into exile and a bitter enemy of Zapata's, with orders to 'disarm the southerners if they were opposed to being discharged'. Zapata halted demobilisation and ordered his officers to be prepared to fight.

There was more trouble on 18 July, when a bunch of Madero generals issued a demand for de la Barra's compliance with the Plan of San Luis Potosí, the expulsion of *científicos* from his cabinet and their own confirmation as generals in the regular army. De la Barra stiffly refused even to consider their demands, so the rebel officers requested Madero to overrule the interim president. To their astonishment, he backed de la Barra, telling them they must not attempt to flout the authority of the government.

There were also frequent clashes between the Federal army and the suspicious rebel groups who feared, quite rightly as it turned out, that a successful revolution had somehow found itself in a minority in the new government. The Díaz clique still controlled the army and the state and national legislatures. In the executive departments of government nothing had changed except the heads.

There was a violent clash between government and Maderista troops in Puebla the day before Madero was due to speak there and the trouble was compounded when Madero, on arrival, publicly embraced the Federal commander, General Aureliano Blanquet, for his loyalty in suppressing the men who, less than two months previously, had been fighting for Madero. Just how loyal Blanquet was would soon be revealed.

Madero's attitude brought further disillusionment and bitterness among the rebel ranks. Just before he had boarded the *Ypiranga* and sailed into exile, Díaz is reported to have told a companion 'Madero has unleashed a tiger; let us see if he can control him.' The tiger was already proving difficult.

The main trouble spot continued to be the state of
Morelos. Madero returned there early in August and met
Zapata at Cuautla. Zapata promised to resume demobilisation as soon as Huerta and the Federals withdrew. Madero
agreed to this, but President de la Barra ignored Madero's
wishes, sent reinforcements to Huerta and ordered him to
push ahead with his campaign to disperse the Zapatistas. A
vigorous protest from Madero brought the bland comment
from the de la Barra administration that 'in view of the fact
that the disarming has been a farce, the government has
dictated the means conducive to guaranteeing the lives and
haciendas in that state, which has suffered so much'. On 30
August came the first battle between Zapata's men and
government troops at Chinameca: Morelos was again in
rebellion.

Fighting raged through September, with Zapata repeating
his willingness to negotiate. But the government demanded
his immediate surrender before any talks could take
place.

Madero, torn between his desire for conformity with legal
processes and sympathy for Zapata's point of view, was
bitterly disappointed over the failure of his mission, which,
he felt, reflected on his own sincerity. Instead of blaming de
la Barra, he considered General Huerta to be primarily
responsible for the renewed fighting and made repeated
efforts to have him replaced.

Huerta was bald, bullet-headed and suffered from poor
eyesight which he remedied by wearing dilapidated wire-
framed spectacles. He was a heavy brandy drinker and it
was said that his two closest friends were two Europeans,
Messrs Martell and Hennessy. Despite his drinking habits,
Huerta had proved himself an able soldier. Zapata hated
him, yet feared and respected his ability.

For the campaign against Zapata, Huerta made his headquarters in the Cuernavaca hotel owned by the British
widow, Mrs King. 'He allowed no laxness in his troops but
they adored him because he always led them to victory,' she
reported. 'He himself drank heavily and nearly every evening had to be led off to bed; but he was always up in the
morning, bright and early, looking as though he were not
even acquainted with the odour of drink.'

On one occasion, according to Mrs King, Huerta's forces
were lined up ready for an expedition against the Zapatistas. Huerta stopped off in the hotel bar to have 'one for
the road'. Then he had another, and another. Eventually his
troops stood all day in pouring rain waiting in vain for their
general to emerge from the bar. Next morning Huerta had
sobered up enough to mount his horse. As the troops moved
off, twenty-four hours late, Huerta assured Mrs King that
when he returned he would have Zapata with him as a
prisoner.

Huerta was pushing his campaign hard and successfully
when Madero's repeated complaints finally had their effect.
At the end of October Huerta was replaced as commander
of the Federal forces. He was furious at Madero's action
and at the public criticism which Madero had levelled
against him.

Mrs King commented: 'Huerta was very, very angry and
... swore revenge on Madero. He felt he had been made a
fool of. I marvelled at the incredible innocence of Madero,
who seemed to think he could play fast and loose with men
like ... the formidable Huerta.'

For the time being, however, Madero had plenty of other
worries which easily outranked Huerta's enmity. The presidential elections were due to be held on 1 October and there
was a dangerous split among the Maderistas over the choice
of a vice-presidential running mate for Madero. The leading candidate was Dr Francisco Vázquez Gómez, who had
been with Madero since the early days of exile in San
Antonio and had negotiated with Limantour in New York.
But Madero favoured José Pino Suárez, an obscure journalist from Yucatán who had taken no part in the Revolution.
There seemed little doubt that Dr Vázquez Gómez was
entitled to the nomination but Madero was insistent. Eventually he got his way and Pino Suárez was nominated. But
Madero incurred the resentment of another section of his
supporters.

That persistent fly, Bernardo Reyes, had also reappeared
in the ointment. Sent by Díaz on a military mission to
Europe, Reyes returned to Mexico a month after the
triumph of the Revolution. Madero, hoping to make capital

out of the general's undoubted popularity, tentatively offered him a cabinet post after the presidential election, but Reyes, arrogant, stubborn and ambitious, preferred to try again for the top post.

He simply could not believe that the people of Mexico would prefer Madero to a famous soldier like himself, and in August announced his candidacy at the forthcoming elections. Soon familiar accusations and recriminations filled the air and in September the bearded Reyes was badly beaten up by a mob of Madero supporters at an election meeting. Realising that they stood no chance of defeating Madero, the Reyistas petitioned Congress for a postponement of the elections. When this was refused, Reyes made a face-saving withdrawal from the race and left the country for Madero's old revolutionary stamping-ground, San Antonio.

The election, the most open ever held in Mexico, went ahead as scheduled, and the Mexicans indulged joyously in this new-found freedom. Some voted for Díaz, Limantour, Zapata, Orozco or even their favourite bullfighter, but Madero was still popular enough to claim more than ninety per cent of the total presidential vote.

The official swearing-in ceremony was not due to take place until 1 December, two months away. But with the country in such a critical condition, it was decided to bring it forward to 6 November.

When Madero went to the Chamber of Deputies to take the oath the confusion outside the building matched that of the country as a whole. Dignitaries and diplomats had to fight their way through an enthusiastic crowd and finally, suits crumpled and top hats battered, gained admittance by a small side door.

'There was indescribable confusion outside, since Madero had not called out the soldiery, wishing, as he said, to show his confidence in the people,' wrote Mrs O'Shaughnessy. 'Even the band of the presidential guard was scattered; the trombones sounded from one side and the bugles from another.'

After Madero's inauguration, Mrs O'Shaughnessy spoke to the German Minister, Admiral Paul von Hintze, who expressed pessimism about the outcome of 'so much legality in Mexico'. He told the American woman, 'You will intervene in the end.'

The period of interim government from May to November had proved an unmitigated disaster for Madero, and he had paid a bitter price for insisting on this measure to suppress any criticism that he had seized power through armed rebellion. Wrote Cumberland: 'Without official status and therefore powerless and unwilling to determine government policy, he was nevertheless held responsible for every ill-judged act of the government.'

Madero still enjoyed the support and goodwill of the masses, for the moment at least. But the more highly-organised and important sections of the community were building a daunting wall of antagonism.

First there was the Porfirian group, consisting of *cientificos*, Federal army officers, landowners and the Church. They had lost their leader but had survived almost intact and, in effect, were still running the country. Secondly, Madero faced the implacable opposition of the big business interests, whether owned by Mexicans, Americans or Europeans. Leadership of the businessmen settled on Henry Lane Wilson, whose energetic pursuit of private business interests and claims for damage conflicted seriously with his official rôle of American Ambassador and continually irritated the Madero administration.

Finally, Madero was up against growing disenchantment within the revolutionary movement. Zapata had already broken away, the Vázquez Gómez supporters were muttering ominously and others, like Orozco, who had hoped to gain from the Revolution's success and had been disappointed, were turning against him.

Madero decided to tackle the pressing problem of Zapata first. As soon as he was inaugurated he sent emissaries to the rebel, who was now styling himself the Attila of the South, promising Zapata freedom if he would surrender his forces unconditionally. But the wary Zapata would have none of this. Land for the masses was his aim, and so far Madero had given the masses no land. The rebellion went on, and Zapata set forth his own programme for the people, called the Plan of Ayala.

Standing on a table in a mountain hut on 28 November

1911, Zapata read out his Plan while the Mexican flag was raised and a band played the National Anthem. The Plan, which took its title from the name of Zapata's ancestral *hacienda*, advocated immediate seizure of all foreign-owned lands and of all properties which had been taken away from villages, the confiscation of one-third of the land held by *hacendados* friendly to the Revolution and full confiscation against owners who 'directly or indirectly' opposed the Plan. It also demanded the extradition, arrest and execution of Díaz, Corral and Limantour, the expulsion of all Spaniards from Mexico, the absorption of all revolutionary forces into one national army 'to prevent aggression by foreign powers'—and, surprisingly, support of Madero's Plan of San Luis Potosí.

All land held by the Zapatistas was immediately turned over to the people, and crude huts went up in the productive fields of fifty-three of the richest *haciendas* in the country, which were declared forfeit 'to the sovereign cause of liberty and equality'. Though the Indians were given buildings and machinery as well as the land, they preferred to live in their brush huts, haphazardly cultivating a small patch of ground.

The Plan of Ayala brought thousands flocking to the death's-head banner of Zapata and soon Cuernavaca fell before their advance. Mrs King described their entry into town:

'. . . A wild-looking body of men, undisciplined, half-clothed, mounted on half-starved, broken-down horses. Grotesque and obsolete weapons, long hidden away or recently seized in pawnshops, were clasped in their hands, thrust through their belts or slung across the queer old saddles. . . . But they rode in as heroes and conquerors, and the pretty Indian girls met them with armfuls of bougainvillaea and thrust the flaming flowers in their hats and belts. . . .

'All afternoon the wild-looking bands rode in. At six o'clock we heard shots and screams and feared that fighting had begun among them. Instead we found that the shots were fired in jubilation: the prison doors in the old palace had been opened and all the prisoners set free; political prisoners, murderers, all free! I shall never forget those men and women as they ran past my house seeking cover. In the old days they would have been shot as they ran, and they still believed they must be targets.'

Zapata had been hoping for the governorship of the state of Morelos as a true sign of trust on Madero's part. Commented Mrs King: 'I for one was quite content with this prospect. Rough and untaught as his followers were, they had treated us with true kindness and consideration during their occupation of the town. . . .'

Instead, Madero committed another incredible blunder by giving the governorship to General Ambrosio Figueroa, an owner of huge tracts of land and a man who could only succeed in driving the fanatical Zapatistas further away from the government. And so the rebellion dragged on through the Madero régime, a constant irritation, embarrassment and drain on the government's shaky finances.

Despite the nagging thorn of *Zapatismo*, Madero tried to turn his attention to the formation of a government which would be able to fulfil the extravagant promises he had poured out to his eager followers. But the Mexican people were prepared to settle for nothing less than an overnight miracle. And Madero was no miracle worker. He felt that Mexico's troubles were chiefly political and sincerely believed his own statement 'The people are not asking for bread, they are asking for liberty.'

Madero's most winning argument had been his assurance that he would cut up the great estates. When this didn't happen the masses tried to take land by the simple process of 'squatting'; and when they were prodded away at bayonet point they reacted with dismay and disenchantment. Delegations of barefoot, sombreroed peasants trudged from miles away to sit pitifully in government corridors, waiting in vain for a magic piece of paper which would give them their promised land.

Madero was by no means blind to the needs of the landless, but he did not appreciate the intensity of the hunger of the masses for their own land, and the need for prompt relief of this hunger.

Not wishing to see a further disruption of the fragile economy, Madero created a national agrarian commission to study the problem, and pleaded for patience. But the people had been patient for thirty years. Now they wanted action and the *hacendado*-dominated commission saw to it that they got precious little action—or land.

To make things worse, the first division of land proved a failure. Some Indians simply left the land lying fallow, others sold it to speculators or back to the *hacendados* from whom it had been purchased by the government.

But land had already become, and was to remain for many years, the Revolution's sacred cow and whether the land was being misused by some of the Indians or not, Madero needed to take massive steps to resettle the peasants, at least on the land stolen from them during the Porfirian régime. Instead he talked wistfully of creating a French-type class of small landowners.

Madero, still dreaming of leading his people to greatness by his own Christ-like example, did not readily appreciate things like disloyalty and duplicity. But he gradually realised that he was surrounded by men whose intentions were not always on the same high plane at his own. So he turned to his family, on whose honesty he felt he could rely.

He appointed his uncle Ernesto Minister of Finance, his cousin Rafael Hernández became Minister of Public Works and José González Salas, another cousin, took over as Minister of War. None of these men had had any previous connection with the revolutionary movement.

Madero's brother Gustavo became his political manager, and was immediately involved in a scandal over the repayment of the 375,000 dollars which he had 'loaned' to the Revolution. Agreement to pay back this money and quieten Gustavo's creditors had been included in the 21 May peace agreement signed in Ciudad Juárez, but the haste with which Gustavo presented his bill, the speed with which it was paid out of the emergency war fund and the stupid silence over the reasons for the payment of such a large sum to a member of the Madero family, instead of an honest explanation, all encouraged the rumours of massive corruption among the Maderos. The payment was the foundation upon which Gustavo's undeserved reputation as a grafter was built.

Resentment grew, unrest simmered, the government floundered. The next overt act of rebellion after Zapata's came from Bernardo Reyes. It was ill-timed and badly executed.

Reyes was blatantly fostering an uprising from San Antonio during November and when the Mexican government complained, the Americans reacted with much more celerity than they had done in Madero's own case the previous year. Reyes was arrested but released on bail pending his trial. On 4 December, however, he jumped bail and crossed into Mexico where he managed to gather a force of some 600.

But nobody else was interested in furthering Reyes' cause. 'The days passed and not even a single individual came to join me,' he complained. Gradually the original 600 melted away, and on Christmas Day 1911 Reyes surrendered to his old rival General Jacinto Treviño after watching a skirmish between government troops and his few remaining followers, who fled in panic.

'I called upon the army and called upon the people but no-one responded, so I resolved to discontinue the war,' said Reyes. He was sent to the military prison of Santiago Tlaltelolco in Mexico City to await trial.

The next uprisings were not to be so easily suppressed, however. Bands of rebels known as Vazquistas, supporters of the unsuccessful vice-presidential candidate Dr Francisco Vázquez Gómez and his brother Emilio, rebelled in Chihuahua, claiming that Madero was not fulfilling the promises of the Plan of San Luis Potosí.

As the government took steps to combat the rebellion, it received a staggering blow from across the border. President Taft, spurred on by alarmist reports from Henry Lane Wilson about the state of the Madero government and its inability to protect American-owned property, announced another of his amazing mobilisations on 4 February 1912; 34,000 troops were hurried to the Mexican border and the border states were asked to be ready to supply another 66,000 men. The mobilisation encouraged the Vázquez Gómez rebellion just as much as the previous year's massing of American forces had struck at the Díaz régime.

Taft backed up the troops with a strong warning that no more bullets must fall on American soil. Madero, again haunted by the fear of intervention, ordered the garrison of

Ciudad Juárez not to get involved in a shooting match at any cost, so on 27 February 400 Vazquistas under General Ynes Salazar entered Juárez without firing a shot.

But on this occasion, to the disappointment of the battle party hostesses, there were no border incidents and the only thing to be seen from American rooftops was the rather absurd spectacle of a huge American force again twiddling its thumbs by the Rio Grande.

At the beginning of March came an even more serious setback for Madero. Pascual Orozco turned traitor in Chihuahua. He defected with 6000 troops and vast quantities of military supplies, and sent an insulting message to Madero saying that he would soon be in Mexico City and proposed to hang the president from the biggest tree in the Zócalo.

Orozco had long been unhappy over his spoils from the Revolution. He had expected a rake-off of a quarter of a million pesos and a place in Madero's cabinet, instead of which he had been awarded 100,000 pesos (£10,000) campaign expenses and had been assigned to comparative obscurity as military commander in Chihuahua. To make things worse, when he ran for the state governorship he was overwhelmingly defeated by the popular Abraham González.

Orozco's dissatisfaction was soon noticed by the millionaire Luis Terrazas and other cattle barons, who cultivated his friendship. The U.S. Consul in Chihuahua, Marion Letcher, reported: 'The well-groomed gentlemen of the wealthy Chihuahua clubs, who would not have touched the hand of this person ... a year previously, began to flatter him with all kinds of social attentions, and it required a bare two months of this subtle work for Orozco to become their humble servant, body and soul.'

Orozco's ambition had provided Terrazas and the other landowners with the opportunity they were seeking to prevent agrarian reform by sparking off more unrest, to be followed, they hoped, by American intervention and the overthrow of Madero. Even the hesitant land reform steps so far taken by Madero were proving completely unacceptable to these owners of vast estates, on whose *haciendas* lived sixty per cent of Chihuahua's rural population.

Though the Revolution had swept across their lands, it had barely touched their wealth. The eighty-one-year-old Terrazas was the prime example. He travelled around in a gold-trimmed carriage pulled by white horses. He owned one and a half million head of cattle and was a millionaire six times over. When a Chicago meat company cabled Terrazas to ask whether he could supply them immediately with 15,000 cattle, he cabled back contemptuously 'What colour?'

The old man had been rewarded with huge land grants by President Juárez for his part in the defeat of Maximilian and the French. Later he became a firm friend of Díaz, which meant more land grants. When he became state governor, Terrazas confiscated cattle wherever he found them and transferred them to his own *haciendas*. At the time of Madero's victory Terrazas controlled merchant houses, mines, public monopolies and banks, and dominated the lives of 30,000 peasants.

He was reluctant to give up any of this, and Orozco's treachery seemed to present the perfect opportunity. He paid part of Orozco's campaign expenses, disguised as export taxes, and his son Félix served with the rebel forces.

Orozco's troops had gained control of most of the state of Chihuahua before the government could take steps against them; Madero's ability to raise an expeditionary force was hampered by the Zapata rebellion and other minor revolts which were occupying most of the Federal army. But at least there was token resistance to Orozco. It came from Pancho Villa, whose loyalty to Madero was exceeded only by his hatred of Orozco, the man he felt had fooled him into attempting to arrest Madero after the battle of Juárez.

When he heard of Orozco's latest treachery, Villa abandoned his meat business, slipped out of Chihuahua City and began to recruit an army to fight the rebels.

Villa quickly raised a force of 500 and moved against the mining town of Parral. Always fond of dramatic messages he ordered an ultimatum written to the town garrison saying, 'If you are loyal to the government come out and receive me, and if you are an enemy, come out to fight. I shall take the town in any case. Francisco Villa.' He occupied the town without resistance and next day fought off an attack by Orozco's men. But another, larger force was sent against him and after three days' occupation Villa had to evacuate the town, after extracting a forced 'loan' of £15,000 from the town's businessmen.

Some Villistas were cut off and captured during the retreat from Parral. One of the prisoners was an American soldier of fortune, Tom Fountain, a machine-gunner. The morning after his capture, Fountain was let out of the house where he had been imprisoned, given a silver peso and told to go to a Chinese restaurant down the street for his breakfast. As he started down the street a dozen of Orozco's officers, lined up on the pavement, drew their revolvers and gunned him down, preferring to give him the *ley fuga* rather than to execute him formally and risk American protests.

There *were* American protests, of course, but Orozco brushed them aside and in an extraordinary personal telegram to President Taft explained that Fountain had died 'because he was fighting us.... We mail you full explanation in the matter and feel confident you would approve it.'

Orozco's army, known to the Mexicans as *Colorados* and to the Americans as Red Flaggers, imposed a reign of terror on northern Mexico, burning, pillaging and robbing. Anyone resisting their advance suffered horribly. According to the American John Reed 'they cut the soles from the feet of one poor devil and drove him a mile across the desert before he died'. Pancho Villa never forgave them their cruelties and captured *Colorados* were always shot.

The Mormon colonies were early victims of Orozco's red flag. All the promises of neutrality were violated. Their homes were plundered, cattle and crops confiscated and most of their guns taken away. When the settlers complained and produced written promises of non-interference, they were told by the Orozco general, Ynes Salazar, 'Those are mere words, and the wind blows words away.' Mormon women and children were sent to the safety of El Paso and many of the men followed soon afterwards. In the American border town they were housed temporarily in an abandoned lumber shed until, with the defeat of Orozco in the autumn of 1912, they returned to what was left of their homes. Their settlement of Colonia Díaz had been burned to the ground but Colonia Juárez and Colonia Dublán were gradually re-occupied.

But not all Americans suffered so savagely. Eleanor Wilson, daughter of the Governor of New Jersey, Woodrow Wilson, who was to become president within a year, was seized by the rebels while on a car tour of northern Mexico. She reached the American border five days later covered in dust and wearing a Mexican shawl. She told anxious American officials that she had enjoyed herself immensely photographing the rebels. 'It was a splendid lark,' she said. 'I was sorry to leave the rebels, who were most polite.'

For three weeks Villa conducted a lone campaign against daunting odds, capturing small towns but never being strong enough to hold them for long. Eventually the government readied an army to take the field. The Minister of War, José González Salas, took personal command of the 8000-strong force, aided by Generals Trucy Aubert and Aureliano Blanquet, and they moved north to meet Orozco's army of 7000, which was marching towards the industrial town of Torreón. They met at Rellano, 800 miles north of Mexico City, on 24 March.

Salas travelled into battle by train with the bulk of the government troops, while General Aubert commanded a screening force to the left of the railway and General Blanquet covered the right flank.

A spectacular piece of warfare devised by the Orozco general, Emilio P. Campa, inflicted a crushing defeat on the Madero forces. An old railway engine was converted into a land torpedo by loading it with dynamite, and it was headed, its throttle jammed open and whistle screaming, towards the government trains. It rammed into the leading troop train, killing eighty soldiers and throwing the Federals into utter confusion. Salas panicked and ordered his headquarters train southwards with all speed, destroying the bridges behind him as he went. The demoralised army, bereft of its commander, was cut to pieces, and the humiliated Salas committed suicide in the train.

The Mexico City press, given its freedom by the new

régime, has reacted by becoming, in the main, violently anti-Madero and was proving an embarrassment and danger to the administration.

El Pais, which was particularly critical of Madero, greeted the Rellano news with the headline 'The Beginning of the End'. Had the rebels pushed rapidly southwards it might indeed have been the end for Madero, but they halted short of Torreón to celebrate. At an emergency meeting, the cabinet insisted on the recall of General Huerta, who had been sulking in semi-retirement since being relieved of his command against the Zapatistas. Madero objected on the grounds that Huerta was a heavy drinker but a cabinet member pointed out that this handicap had not prevented Abraham Lincoln from making use of General Ulysses S. Grant in the American Civil War. Madero gave way, Huerta was recalled and given the chance to re-establish his reputation. 'I will whip him. I guarantee it,' he told Madero.

Edward Bell, the American journalist, interviewed Madero just after the Rellano disaster and felt pity for 'the undersized frockcoated figure ... dwarfed by his huge responsibilities'. Bell wrote: 'He was greatly changed.... His cheeks, which used to curve smoothly from his broad forehead to his narrow chin, were now shrunken and lined; his brow was wrinkled; a dozen years had been added to his apparent age, a fair half of them in the last seven days. He showed loss of sleep and was extremely nervous, with the impatient manner of a man who is trying to do too many things at once....'

But with Huerta's assumption of command things soon began to brighten for the government. Huerta moved to Torreón and began to amass troops and supplies. He was joined by Villa, while Orozco dawdled in the north, giving Huerta the time he needed. When Orozco eventually decided it was time to move, Huerta was ready for him. They met at Bermejillo, near Torreón, on 10 May and Orozco's *Colorados* were routed. They fell back, destroying the railway as they went and slowing Huerta's advance. But on 22 May Huerta caught up with them at Rellano, scene of Orozco's great victory two months earlier. This time Orozco was the loser, leaving 600 dead and most of his equipment on the battlefield. Again Orozco ordered complete destruction of the railways as he fell back on Bachimba, only forty miles south of his headquarters, Chihuahua City. Doggedly the government troops rebuilt the wrecked track and pushed northwards.

But at the beginning of June Federal harmony suffered a setback with a clash between Huerta and Villa. From the beginning, their alliance had been an uneasy one. When Villa first reported to Huerta's headquarters he recalled 'Huerta and his staff officers did not get up from their chairs ... I was dusty and tired. All the men there were dressed in gala uniforms. But because I was not in the regular army I was wearing my usual old clothes. I never forgot the way those men looked me up and down as if I were a stray mongrel that smelled bad.'

But Villa admired Huerta's military ability. A teetotaller himself, he commented, 'If his judgment is sometimes at fault it is only because he begins to drink by seven in the morning and is hardly ever at his best. Not once in all the times I spoke to him was he altogether sober, for he drank morning, afternoon and night. His talents must have been very great.'

For his part, Huerta considered Villa was *tonto* (foolish) 'violent, undisciplined and refusing to take orders from anyone'. It was true that Villa was a difficult subordinate, and in Huerta he was working with a man who could tolerate nothing but strict obedience. Villa's rough manner and scruffy appearance were a joke among the regular army officers, who angered him by referring to him as 'honorary general'.

On 4 June Huerta ordered Villa's arrest on charges of persistent insubordination and refusal to return horses stolen from a rancher. An astonished Villa was turned out of bed in the middle of the night and, after a summary trial, sentenced to be shot at dawn.

Villa's description of the incident is worth recording, since he was one of the few men to stand in front of a Mexican firing squad and live to tell about it:

'As I stood in the square the first sergeant of the platoon went up to the wall and made a cross on it with a mattock. ... The sergeant ordered me to stand at the foot of the mark. ... I asked ... "Why are they going to shoot me? If I am to die, I must know why. I have served the government faithfully" ...

'I could not continue for the tears that choked me. At the time I hardly knew whether I was weeping from fear or mortification, but I see now it was because of the wrong they were doing me ...

'Again the sergeant ordered me to stand at the foot of the cross, and again, with tears in my eyes ... I demanded to be told why they were shooting me. As the sergeant tried to force me to the wall I threw myself to the ground, pretending to beg but only fighting for time.'

Emilio and Raul Madero, who were with Huerta's army, had been told of Villa's arrest and had telegraphed their brother in Mexico City requesting him to order a stay of execution until a full investigation could be made. They were still awaiting a reply when Villa went to the wall. Now Colonel Rubio Navarrete intervened. He managed to obtain from Huerta a temporary stay of execution and returned with it just as Villa was handing over his watch and money to the soldiers who were about to shoot him. Then came President Madero's confirmation of reprieve for Villa. When Villa was taken before Huerta he demanded to know why he had been ordered shot. Huerta merely told him, 'It was a matter of honour.'

Before being shipped off, under heavy guard, to the military prison in Mexico City, a grateful Villa had his horse saddled and he presented it, together with his sword, to Navarrete. He also offered Navarrete his house in Chihuahua City.

The incident closed, Huerta turned again to the pursuit of Orozco. Soldiers and gangs of levies slaved to repair the shattered railway, and a month after the Rellano victory the Huerta forces were within five miles of Bachimba, having advanced 228 miles in forty-six days since the Bermejillo battle on 10 May.

On 3 July Orozco's army, which had beeen reinforced and well supplied with arms smuggled across the American border, was smashed again at Bachimba. That night Orozco and his retinue fled by train to Ciudad Juárez and into the United States, leaving the Federal army to mop up resistance. Huerta entered Chihuahua City on 8 July, recaptured

Ciudad Juárez in mid-August and by October the uprising was completely crushed.

Huerta was the hero of the moment. When he returned to the capital he was unable to account for a £150,000 deficit in campaign funds, and commented tersely 'I am no book-keeper.' A frustrated Madero found himself promoting Huerta to major-general instead of charging him with embezzlement.

No sooner was the Orozco uprising put down than another rebellion broke out, this time in Veracruz. The general behind it was Félix Díaz, a nephew of the old dictator and a professional dissident. Díaz, who had been chief of police in Mexico City during his uncle's rule, was commander of the Federal garrison in Veracruz. Attempting to cash in on the mounting discontent with the Madero government, Díaz seized the port on 16 October, hoping to stimulate a nation-wide army revolt.

It was a measure of Díaz's ambitions that he presented no 'plan' for the people's approval. Instead, he contented himself with a letter to the *Mexican Herald* complaining that the army's honour had been 'trampled on' by Madero.

But there was still enough goodwill towards Madero among the army commanders to guarantee that the Díaz rebellion would be a failure. No other group outside Veracruz went over to him and soon the town was surrounded by government forces under General Joaquín Beltrán and blockaded by the Mexican navy, which had also remained loyal. The officers and men who had followed Díaz lost heart when they saw the overwhelming odds against them and Veracruz was easily recaptured on 23 October.

Two days later Díaz was convicted of treason and sentenced to be shot, along with twenty-six of his officers, at dawn on 26 October. But he had powerful friends in the Chamber of Deputies. They managed to obtain a stay of execution until the Supreme Court, which was also heavily loaded with Porfirio Díaz holdovers, handed down an extraordinary decision that since Díaz had left the regular army to start an insurrection he was technically a civilian at the time of his arrest and therefore not subject to military laws.

Still blindly faithful to the law, Madero went along with this fatuous ruling and Díaz was imprisoned in the island fortress of San Juan de Ulúa in Veracruz harbour. He was transferred to Mexico City in January 1913, a month after Pancho Villa had escaped from prison and got away to the United States.

Villa's confinement had not been onerous. Though he was given a cell which was, according to him, 'no more than a dustbin' he was allowed to spend his own money on cleaning and furnishing it. He passed the time by learning to read, write and use a typewriter, and soon his privileges were further extended ... 'A girl named Rosita Palacios was allowed to visit me. She was a great comfort in those lonely days and became the object of my most amiable attentions.' But he was still awaiting some form of trial or further review of his case. Appeals to the president brought no satisfaction, so Villa determined to get away.

He enlisted the aid of a prison clerk, Carlos Jáuregui, who agreed to open the necessary doors and to arrange a get-away car. Just before Villa broke out, he was visited in his cell by Antonio Tamayo, a lawyer friend of General Bernardo Reyes. Tamayo invited Villa to participate in a Reyes-led plot against Madero and told him, 'Give us your word and in six days you will be free again.' Tamayo said he would give Villa time to think it over and return in three days. But Pancho's dog-like devotion to Madero had not been dimmed by his misfortunes. News of the plot increased his determination to escape and warn the president.

Next morning, Christmas Day 1912, Villa walked boldly out of the prison, conspiratorially dressed in dark glasses and a black hat and accompanied by Jáuregui. Despite a scare when their car was stopped and searched by two soldiers, they drove safely to Toluca, forty miles from the capital, and from there made their way by rail and sea to the American border. On 2 January 1913 Villa, who was now calling himself Jesús José Martínez stepped across the International Line in the main street of Nogales. From there he travelled to El Paso, where he stayed at a small hotel in the Mexican district of the town known as 'Little Chihuahua'. He sent immediate word to the Chihuahua governor, Abraham González, about the latest plot against

Madero. González acknowledged the message and sent
Villa £150 but urged him not to return to Mexico 'as it will
compromise us'. So Villa fretted in exile, disturbed only
once when an *El Paso Times* reporter tracked him down at
his hotel hide-out on 12 January. The paper reported:
'Villa would not talk for publication. . . . At his room in the
hotel were four bodyguards. . . . When seen by the *Times*
representative, Villa was armed with two revolvers and a
large dirk.'

After a year of Madero democracy Mexico was in a mess. The country had been in a constant turmoil; three rebellions had been put down, but Zapata fought on in Morelos. The big business interests blocked every attempt at reform by the president, and when Madero imposed a tax on revenues of the foreign oil companies, who were reaping fantastic profits, there was an indignant outcry.

If he was proving unacceptable to the entrenched business interests, Madero was equally unsatisfactory as far as the masses were concerned. Their simple needs—land, water, food, schools—were not being met. Madero had promised; Madero was letting them down. And his amateurish attempts to promote harmony among these widely divergent groups only worsened matters.

One American writer commented: 'The concrete net results of Madero's half-hearted attempts to deal with the agrarian problem were exactly nothing.' While this judgment was perhaps over-harsh, it was nonetheless basically true.

The Madero government, in the opinion of Henry Lane Wilson, was 'apathetic, ineffective and either cynically indifferent or stupidly optimistic. Its councils were divided and moved in contrary direction from day to day.... Madero was one day a conservative ... a stern avenger of society against brigandage ... and the next day an apostle of peace, friend of the poor, apologist for bandits and criminals....'

The president's public image was not improved when he wept at a performance of the '1812' Overture, or by his increasing dependence on the forecasts of spiritualists. Yet somehow, in the crowded ominous months at the end of 1912, Madero regained his optimism, apparently by wilfully deluding himself that Mexico's problems were being solved. Wrote Bell: 'He had posted a deaf and blind sentry at the gateway of his life to cry "All's well" and there were times when he would hear no other voice.' He told foreign diplomats that prosperity was around the corner; worse, he discounted all talk of plots against his régime or his life. Villa's warning from Texas, passed on by Abraham González, was ignored like all the other information.

Ambassador Wilson was not far behind Zapata in the list of Madero's worries. Wilson's conduct in Mexico is one of the strangest episodes in American foreign diplomacy. Howard Cline has written that Wilson's attitude towards Madero was one of 'personal vendetta rather than a national policy'. Though his persistent hostility drove Madero to distraction, Wilson was never rebuked by the Taft administration.

In 1912 Wilson was fifty-five. A career diplomat, he had spent seven years as Minister to Chile and six as Minister to Belgium before replacing David E. Thompson as Ambassador to Mexico in 1910. Arriving amid the splendour of the centenary year, he had been much impressed by Díaz. He was quickly won over by American business interests in Mexico City and adopted their hostile attitude towards the new régime of Madero. This attitude was doubly unfortunate, since the United States was the only nation represented in Mexico by an ambassador. Wilson therefore ranked in diplomatic supremacy above the ministers from Great Britain, Germany, France, Spain and other nations.

Wilson had tried to bring about American intervention in February 1911 to crush the Madero insurrection and to protect American businessmen and property owners. He had travelled to Washington with a petition requesting intervention and signed by a group who called themselves The Committee of the American Colony. His attitude obviously had something to do with Taft's mobilisation order of 7 March which, contrary to Wilson's hopes, had merely served to strengthen Madero's hand and embarrass Díaz.

Wilson's darkest suspicions about the new president were confirmed when de la Barra expressed to him his 'serious apprehension' about the government's prospects and added that, in his opinion, Madero was unfit for executive work. And the Mexican's president's patent honesty only served to widen the gulf. Had he been more cunning and subtle, Madero might have been able to win over the American but his outraged reaction to Wilson's aggressive demands soon ensured that their relationship ceased to be that of adult men representing their countries. It became instead a campaign of annoyance which resulted in progressively worsening relations.

Bell considered Wilson's attitude in 1912 'unfortunate to the last degree. A superhuman tact on his part would have been required for the establishment of a merely tolerable status after the innumerable irritations of the past. But he took the contrary course. . . . He supplied advice to the government touching its negotiation of loans, tutored it in local policy and pursued an injudicious course in the matter of claims, taking up too many and pressing them inopportunely with detriment to his own dignity—and with no benefit to the claimants.'

Claims for damage to American property allegedly incurred during the Revolution gave Wilson the chance to make daily visits to the National Palace, where he soon became as familiar a figure as the president himself. He peppered Washington with pessimistic messages like 'Mexico is seething with discontent'. His endless alarmism was the principal cause of the second mobilisation of United States troops along the border in 1912 which helped to bring about the Orozco rebellion. Wilson had much to answer for.

In March 1912 he had telegraphed to Washington a request for 500 rifles for 'self-defence of the American colony', and a week later he demanded another 1000 rifles and a million cartridges. The American government refused to dispatch such a large consignment but did send a shipment of arms to the American Embassy.

By the end of 1912 Madero could stomach no more. He took advantage of the pending change of American presidents to instruct his Foreign Minister, Pedro Lascuráin, who was in New York negotiating compensation claims: 'Before returning here manage to obtain at all costs an interview with President-elect [Woodrow] Wilson for the purpose of earnestly insisting that Ambassador Henry Lane Wilson shall not further continue at this post. If it is necessary say to him that the Mexican government some time ago advised Washington that he was not *persona grata* but suspended action in order that the new president may dismiss him without rendering necessary representations by this government. Explain the Mexican situation to him. . . .'

But, to Madero's astonishment and annoyance, Washington did nothing. Taft was nearing the end of his term and chose not to mar his record by sacking Wilson and publicly admitting failure of his Mexican policy, while Woodrow Wilson, though anxious to act, was not able to do so until his inauguration in March 1913. By then it was too late.

As 1912 gave way to 1913 Madero continued his obstinate optimism while Mexico went steadily to the dogs. The newly-arrived Cuban Minister, Manuel Márquez Sterling, was told by the editor of a Mexico City daily paper:

'You have come at a bad time, Mr Minister; you will soon see the government collapse and Madero possibly sailing to Europe. He is an Apostle whom the upper class scorns and the lower classes suspect. He has deceived us all! He has not an atom of energy; he does not know how to use cold steel; and he has devoted himself to the mania of proclaiming himself a great democrat. He does not shoot, sir! Do you believe that a president who does not shoot, who does not punish, who does not make himself feared, who always invokes laws and principles, can preside? If within the Apostle there were a Don Porfirio, hidden and silent, Mexico would be happy. . . .

'Madero is good. But it is not a good man that is needed.'

Madero's reluctance to shoot was to prove his fatal flaw. In separate prisons in the capital were two generals guilty of rebellion—Bernardo Reyes and Félix Díaz. Both should have been executed. Instead, they were allowed regular visitors and began to plot the overthrow of Madero with dissident army officers on the outside.

News of the plot was given to Madero's brother, Gustavo, on 4 February by an army officer, who provided a list of twenty-two names. The nine most important on the list were Félix Díaz, Bernardo Reyes, his son Rodolfo, General Manuel Mondragón, the former Díaz army chief who had recently been allowed to return from exile in Cuba, General Aureliano Blanquet, who commanded 4000 troops at Toluca, General Joaquín Beltrán, commanding infantry forces in the Mexico City suburb of Tacubaya, General Rubio Navarrete, in command of the artillery at Tacubaya,

General Gregorio Ruíz, the cavalry commander, and General Huerta, against whose name a question mark had been written.

Gustavo hurried to the presidential residence in Chapultepec Castle to warn his brother. He came out an hour later and told a companion, 'Pancho won't believe it; he laughed at me.' Madero felt that Blanquet and Beltrán had already proved their loyalty beyond doubt, while the question mark alongside Huerta's name showed, in the president's opinion, that the list was false, since Huerta had more reason than anyone else to plot against the government.

Nevertheless the plot *was* real and had reached an advanced stage. The plan was that Bernardo Reyes should take over from Madero as provisional president until Félix Díaz could be elected 'constitutional' president for what remained of the six-year term begun by his uncle Porfirio in 1910. Mondragón was to be Minister of War, Rodolfo Reyes Minister of Justice and Huerta commander-in-chief of the army. Huerta, who did not consider either Reyes or Díaz of presidential calibre, had not finally agreed to the carving-up of posts, which accounted for the question mark against his name on the list of plotters.

The uprising had been tentatively scheduled for 16 March but when Gustavo Madero suddenly postponed a scheduled trip to Japan (he was due to give official thanks for the Japanese attendance at the 1910 centenary) and scurried into frantic action, the plotters realised they had been discovered, and brought forward the rebellion to that weekend.

By Saturday morning, 8 February, rumours of an uprising had become so strong that some army units whose loyalty to Madero was suspect were moved to barracks outside the capital. But the plotters went ahead, and the rebellion struggled into being late that night, though Mondragón could muster only 800 men, three batteries of artillery and the 600 cadets of the capital's military academy. The rebel troops moved out of their Tacubaya barracks, joined up with the cadets and marched into the city, where their first move was to release Díaz and Reyes.

Díaz was in the Ciudadela—the city barracks and arsenal. Here the commander, Colonel Mayol, refused to join the rebels and was imprisoned. At Santiago Tlaltelolco military prison the corrupt commander General Davila had been replaced at the last moment by a loyalist, General Villareal, but as he gave orders to oppose the liberation of Reyes an aide shot him in the back.

Shortly after 2 a.m. on Sunday the rumble of artillery moving into town along the Tacubaya road awakened an officer of the Chapultepec Palace guard, whose house stood near the road. He contacted Gustavo Madero, who decided to waste no more time pleading with his brother. His hat at a jaunty angle and a cigar clamped between his teeth, the bespectacled Gustavo set out by car to save the National Palace from the rebels. As his car rolled through the Palace gates his arrest was ordered by Colonel Morelos, who was waiting to admit Mondragón's troops. But Gustavo, using his car as a platform, addressed the Palace garrison and won them over with a brilliant impromptu speech. The bewildered Colonel Morelos was disarmed and imprisoned by his own men. Machine-guns were set up on the Palace roof and the defence of the headquarters of government was entrusted to General Lauro Villar, commandant of the Mexico City garrison, who hurried from a sick bed to take over the post.

On his release from prison, Reyes had assumed command of the rebel forces and at 7 a.m., with an escort of 200 cavalry, he rode into the Zócalo and made for the National Palace, expecting the gates to be swung open. Reyes was to occupy the presidential office and from there issue a manifesto to the nation proclaiming himself provisional president and announcing the bloodless overthrow of Madero. But a sharp challenge stopped the column in its tracks. General Villar emerged from the Palace to warn Reyes that he advanced at his peril. Refusing to believe that Villar, an old comrade-in-arms, would order his men to fire, Reyes pressed forward. A volley burst from the Palace roof and Reyes was killed instantly, only a few yards short of the presidential chair he had coveted for so many years.

The rebels fired back, wounding General Villar. Then the machine-guns opened up from the Palace roof, inflicting considerable casualties on the rebel cavalry and even more among the crowds of people who had paused on their way to early Mass at the near-by cathedral to watch the drama.

The Palace defenders charged into the Zócalo, routing the rebels and capturing the cavalry commander, General Gregorio Ruíz, who had lost his horse and was too fat to run away. As the firing broke out Díaz and Mondragón, at the head of the 600 cadets, were moving towards the Zócalo. They turned back and, joined by the remnants of Reyes' force, occupied the single-storey Ciudadela barracks about a mile and a half south west of the National Palace.

Gustavo Madero was delighted with the outcome of the battle. He contacted his brother, told him the rebellion had been crushed and cheerfully drove off to breakfast at the near-by home of a friend.

President Madero reached the centre of the city at 9 a.m., riding a grey horse and at the head of a thousand mounted police and cavalry. In the Alameda Park, about half a mile from the National Palace, he was warned by loyal troops to proceed with care, as dissidents were still roaming the narrow streets around the Zócalo. He ignored the advice, and as he rode past the unfinished Fine Arts Palace a sniper fired at him from the scaffolding, killing a spectator on the pavement.

Madero calmly rode on to the Zócalo, where he saw the bodies and realised at long last the seriousness of what had happened. And, for a change, he reacted with speed and ruthlessness. A specially-convened cabinet meeting passed sentence of death and immediate execution on Colonel Morelos and the fat General Ruíz.

It seemed at this stage that the rebels had been routed and that Madero had survived the fourth attempt in little more than a year to unseat him. But the key to the situation was, in reality, the bullet which had seriously wounded General Villar. Wrote the American journalist Edward Bell: 'My own opinion is that the whole clan Madero fell at that shot.'

Had Villar been able to retain command of Mexico City's loyal troops, who outnumbered the rebels by more than five to one, Madero would have been saved. But a new commander was needed to mop up the rebellion. The logical successor was General Felipe Angeles, the most able soldier in Mexico, intelligent, honourable and a loyal Maderista.

But he was in Morelos, fighting the Zapatistas and could not be summoned in time. The only ranking general available was Victoriano Huerta. So Madero reluctantly accepted the advice of his War Minister, General García Peña, and called on Huerta, whose name had appeared on the list of a plot which he now knew to be only too true, to take command of the government forces.

Huerta pledged his loyalty and the honest little president embraced his new commander. Madero had just signed his death warrant.

Huerta was born of a poor family in the state of Jalisco. In his early days his intelligence had attracted the attention of wealthy people in his home town and they had helped with his education and later sponsored his entry to military academy, from which he graduated with honours. He made rapid progress under Porfirio Díaz and by 1910 was a full general.

Henry Lane Wilson thought Huerta 'a man of iron mould and courage ... he possessed abundant vices but was not without great qualities of mind and heart. . . .' Wilson's incredible conclusion was that Huerta was 'in his own way a sincere patriot'.

Mrs Tweedie thought more realistically that Huerta possessed 'some of the best qualities but also the worst faults of his race'.

In the opinion of the historian Parkes, Huerta was 'a villain on an Elizabethan scale. An able general, with a masterful and magnetic personality, he was also a drunkard ... and a man for whom honour did not exist. From the time when he was appointed general of the government troops he resolved both to ensure the triumph of the rebellion and to manoeuvre himself to the head of it.'

It was incredible that Madero should have entrusted power to Huerta, since they had never got on. When Madero became president he told Henry Lane Wilson that Huerta was 'a very bad man'.

Yet within a few months he had promoted Huerta to commander of the Federal army against Orozco and, after Huerta's outstanding success, was obliged to promote him again. But Madero's open antagonism had convinced

Huerta that there was no future in backing the president and when the plotters sought his support he gave it, with that safeguard of a question mark.

The question mark was removed when fate gave into his hands the opportunity for which he had been waiting with Indian patience. He took it with consummate skill and infinite treachery, exposing Mexico City to a spell of bloody civil war and senseless killing which became known as the Tragic Ten Days.

Díaz and Mondragón, with their 800 men, could have been bombarded out of the Ciudadela in a couple of hours, with only a tenth of the bloodshed that actually occurred. Yet both Huerta and Díaz, who were in collusion from the start, began an aimless cannonade of the capital, during which the National Palace was struck only twice and the Ciudadela once, with the intention of causing widespread damage and, in the words of Bell, 'to destroy the appetite of the people for a voice in their government'.

Federal gun batteries were shifted from point to point in the residential and business sections, the only common factor in their siting being the fact that from none of them was the Ciudadela visible. Díaz positioned his artillery in the park in front of the Ciudadela and sprayed shells all over the capital. There were explosions, damage and death in all parts of the city except those supposed to be under bombardment.

Confusion was compounded on the first day of the battle when rebels threw open the doors of Belem prison, and thousands made their escape. But not all got away. One man who had been in jail for twenty years preferred to stay there rather than take his chances in the bullet-swept streets, and two more who had stayed behind to force the prison safe were re-arrested.

Entrusting Huerta with full command, Madero decided to go to Cuernavaca and bring back General Angeles and his forces to reinforce the loyal troops. The presidential party got out of the capital safely, arrived in Cuernavaca on 11 February and stayed the night in Mrs King's hotel, the Bella Vista, where a British flag was run up by Mrs King and a strong guard surrounded the hotel.

After consultation with the president, General Angeles

told Mrs King, 'We go to join Huerta, the new commander-in-chief.'

'The name was like a bell tolling,' wrote Mrs King. 'I had a remembrance of Huerta's face when he returned from his ill-fated campaign without his prisoner Zapata.

'Angeles' eyes met mine and he turned away.'

Next day Madero, Angeles and 2000 troops returned to the capital. But Huerta ordered Angeles' force back into the suburbs to guard against possible attack by Zapata; and after the overthrow of Madero, Angeles was court-martialled for 'exceeding authority' in returning to Mexico City at such an inopportune moment for the plotters.

As Angeles watched helplessly, the noisy farce dragged on to the confusion of the world and the despair of Mexico City's civilian population. The *Daily Mail* reported, 'Many people have been killed in the fighting and dead civilians are piled up in ghastly heaps in the streets. But the populace seems strangely indifferent. In many streets today the traffic went on as usual and the public gardens were crowded with loungers just as if nothing was happening.' But there was not destined to be much more lounging in the public gardens.

Trenches were dug in the streets, every home was soon in a state of siege, the capital was paralysed. Women ran in desperate search of food, carrying improvised white flags of sheets tied to broomsticks. Only two newspapers carried on publishing; they were eagerly sought, but paper sellers and buyers alike stood the risk of being gunned down on the street corners.

The seven-storey YMCA building became a battleground. Foreign students were thrown out of their rooms and replaced by rebel snipers and machine-gunners. On 12 February the *El Paso Times* splashed the headline 'TERRIBLE STREET ARTILLERY DUEL RAGED ALL DAY YESTERDAY IN MEX CAPITAL'.

Henry Lane Wilson, busy organising the accommodation of American refugees in the turreted, castle-like American Embassy, broke off long enough to wire Washington on 10 February 'Practically all the local state authorities, police and *rurales* have revolted to Díaz.' Next day he kept the pot boiling with this message to the State Department:

'Public opinion, both native and foreign, as far as I can estimate, seems to be overwhelmingly in favour of Díaz.'

The American Embassy was swamped by the flood of foreign refugees seeking protection. The overflow was accommodated, by agreement with the 'warring' factions, at the Hotel Génève, the immediate vicinity of which was established as a neutral zone. Civilians from the foreign colony formed a guard and patrolled this zone day and night to ensure that no soldiers from either side strayed into it. They kept out the troops, but not the bullets or shells, which regularly fell into the area.

The energetic Wilson was revelling in the situation. He organised a medical corps, a temporary bank and telegraph office and a rescue team to collect stranded foreigners.

Wilson's work was further complicated by the complaints of the British residents about the eccentricities of the British Minister, Sir Francis Stronge. Sir Francis was an Irishman who, surprisingly, deplored violence. He also had a consuming passion for parrots which according to the residents, exceeded his worries about the safety of British subjects.

He was described by Mrs Moats as 'a charming man with certain attractive oddities. He had, for instance, a parrot tamed to ride on his shoulder. . . .' Wilson suspected that the parrots participated in his councils: 'Whether in drawing room, at table, or in the chancellery, one of them was always perched on his shoulder, mingling affably in the conversation.'

The American Ambassador considered that Sir Francis would have been better suited to the 'quieter walks of diplomacy', though he felt the Briton was anxious to perform his duties 'so far as his natural antipathy to noise and violence would permit'.

Unfortunately for the peace-loving Sir Francis, machine-guns and cannon were set up in front of the British Legation. The Minister was forced to seek refuge in his cellar and from here sent out a message that he was in desperate need of fresh eggs daily. An English resident, Jack Cosgro, undertook to provide Sir Francis with the eggs and, by much bargaining and evasive action, managed to bring them each day. After the battle Sir Francis thanked Cosgro effusively for providing the food which had sustained his parrots through the fighting!

On 11 February battalions of troops known to be particularly loyal to Madero were sent by Huerta to attack the Ciudadela across exposed ground in a suicidal frontal attack. They were slaughtered.

Anxiously, a member of the Japanese Legation sought out Gustavo Madero. He assured the president's brother that within twenty-four hours he could muster 2000 Japanese, dressed as peons and armed only with knives, who could rush the Ciudadela by night and murder the entire defending force, ending the revolt at once. Gustavo loftily rejected this intriguing offer, saying that the Mexicans would fight their own battles.

On 12 February Wilson decided to take a direct hand in affairs. Together with the German Minister, Admiral von Hintze, and the Spanish Minister, Bernardo de Cologan, he set off by car from the Embassy for the National Palace. Despite being fired on by both sides the trio arrived safely and saw Madero. Wilson at once launched into a bitter protest about the continuation of 'indiscriminate hostilities' and the destruction of American property. Madero blamed Díaz for all the trouble but agreed to a cease fire so that the diplomats could go to the Ciudadela to talk to the rebels.

Sir Francis Stronge joined them for the visit to Díaz who, in turn, blamed the government forces for the destruction but promised to respect foreign property. As the diplomats' car left the Ciudadela it was struck by several bullets, causing Sir Francis to comment, 'This is very unpleasant.'

Huerta issued daily assurances that the rebels would soon be defeated but the bombardment worsened on 14 and 15 February. Dead and wounded civilians could be seen lying in the streets from the windows of the American Embassy. Cars flying British, American and German flags braved the bullets and shells to collect more members of the foreign colony and bring them to the comparative safety of the Embassy and the neutral zone, where more than 1800 people were now herded.

Water and light were cut off, 'producing intolerable sanitary conditions', according to Wilson. A shell struck the library of the American Club, injuring nobody but smashing a collection of portraits of American presidents. The only one to escape destruction was Theodore Roosevelt. 'Business is paralysed,' reported the *Daily Mail*. 'Dozens of buildings show great jagged holes. . . .'

Mrs Moats, who was in Puebla when fighting erupted in the capital, managed to get back by train to join her husband and daughter, arriving at Buenavista Station 'amid a perfectly audible bombardment'. She hired a coach, whose driver assured her he could get through to the neutral zone at the Hotel Génève.

'Everything went beautifully until we neared the Colonia Station,' she reported. 'Then came the most awful crashing of glass. Shells screamed and struck one after the other around us. We saw great branches of trees being cut down, and as we came up to the station realised we were directly in the line of battle.

'Bang, crash, bang, crash, went the windows of the station. Then I saw two men drop hardly ten or fifteen feet from us, caught by bullets. They fell like sacks dropped from a height and did not move.'

The coach driver hurriedly reversed and managed to get his passenger to the neutral zone by another route.

As the battle dragged on Wilson threw his considerable weight behind a demand that Madero should resign. He called a meeting of the diplomatic corps at the Embassy on 15 February, to which most of the ministers made their hazardous way. Sir Francis Stronge's car was repeatedly fired on as he drove to the meeting, and he was finally held up and robbed. Rather than hazard the return trip, he spent the night at the American Embassy, sleeping on a couch in the library.

Wilson managed to convince the meeting that they should urge the president to resign and place his powers in the hands of Congress. Since Wilson was hardly Madero's favourite diplomat, it was decided that the Spanish Minister, Cologan, should head the delegation which delivered the message. Madero received Cologan but denied the right of the foreign diplomats to interfere in a purely domestic problem. He rebuked the Spaniard and protested to Washington, charging Wilson with inciting the action of the diplomatic corps.

By the ninth day of the bombardment, however, the stricken city was ready to accept any steps that would guarantee a halt to the killing. Now Huerta made his move. The American Ambassador was told to expect Madero's overthrow, and he immediately wired Washington, 'Huerta notifies me to expect some action that will remove Madero from power at any moment; plans fully matured, the purpose of delay being to avoid any violence or bloodshed.'

But Madero hung on, rejecting all suggestions that he surrender or resign. On 16 February he had granted an interview to the *Daily Mail* correspondent L. C. Simonds who noted that 'though the strain on him during the last few days has been severe, he retains all his cheerfulness and his energy of manner and speech.

'I asked the president whether there had been any truth in the reiterated rumours of his resignation. "These rumours," he replied, "have no foundation. I have never for a moment entertained the idea. I was elected president by the free, untrammelled and *bona fide* vote of the Mexican people and I intend to be faithful to the trust committed to me by the people and the nation, though it should cost me my life.

' "My place is here—here" and the president struck with both fists the arms of the chair in which he sat.'

The interview appeared on 18 February, the day that Madero fell. The final treachery was perpetrated by General Blanquet, whose previous chief claim to fame had been that he was a member of the firing squad which had executed Emperor Maximilian forty-six years previously.

Madero, now suspecting Huerta, had ordered Blanquet and his 4000-strong 29th Infantry Regiment into the capital to take over defence of the National Palace. But Blanquet, too, had turned traitor.

Just after noon on 18 February Blanquet, tall and dignified in a black dress uniform, and accompanied by Lt-Col. Jimenez Riveroll and other officers, made an unannounced entry into the presidential office. Blanquet told Madero bluntly that the parlous state of the country necessitated his resignation and that he had come to insist that Madero step down at once.

When Madero refused, Blanquet drew his pistol, telling

the president, 'You are my prisoner.' Madero's bodyguards pulled their guns and fired at once, killing Colonel Riveroll and another officer. In the exchange of fire which followed, Madero's cousin Marcos Hernández was also killed. The president and his guard were overpowered and imprisoned, and by lunchtime all except two of the Madero cabinet were under arrest.

Promptly at noon, and *before* Madero had been arrested, the over-eager Wilson sent a message to Washington saying that he understood the army had 'taken control of the situation'. Shortly afterwards Huerta sent Wilson a message announcing Madero's overthrow and asking him to inform the rest of the diplomatic corps.

While the president was being arrested, Huerta and Gustavo Madero were lunching together at the Gambrinus Restaurant. A messenger arrived, telling Huerta he was urgently needed elsewhere. 'I have no revolver; will you lend me yours?' he asked Gustavo. Having thus obligingly disarmed himself, Gustavo was arrested a few minutes later.

By mid-afternoon the coup was complete. Madero's fifteen-month reign was at an end.

After the arrest of Gustavo Madero, Huerta returned to the National Palace. Messengers were sent to Félix Díaz in the Ciudadela telling him of Madero's overthrow. Next Huerta telegraphed all the stage governors 'By direction of the Senate, I have assumed charge of the government. President Madero and his cabinet are prisoners in my power.'

Later that afternoon Huerta and Blanquet, the arch-traitors in the affair, appeared on a balcony of the Palace and were cheered by a large crowd. Huerta told them: 'Mexicans, brothers; there will be no more cannonading. Peace has come.'

Henry Lane Wilson sent a hurried note to Huerta which, with unconscious humour, began, 'Without desiring in the least to intrude into Mexican domestic affairs, I beg to suggest...' and went on to suggest that Huerta put himself and his forces at the disposition of the Mexican Congress.

Next he invited Huerta and Díaz to the American Embassy for talks. It was here that they drew up a peace agreement known as the Compact of the Ciudadela, but contemptuously referred to among Mexicans ever since as the Compact of the Embassy. Wilson organised a champagne buffet, to which members of the diplomatic corps were invited, and provided escorts carrying American flags to bring the two generals to the Embassy.

Wilson told the astonished diplomats: 'Mexico has been saved. From now on we shall have peace, progress and prosperity.' When Díaz entered the room, Wilson led the applause and cried 'Long live General Díaz, saviour of Mexico.'

Despite some difficulty caused by the reluctance of the Reyes supporters to see Huerta take power, agreement was soon reached at the Embassy talks. Huerta was to become provisional president and Díaz was to be 'free to pursue his candidacy for the presidency'. As they left the Embassy the following statement was released:

'To the Mexican People:

'The unendurable and distressing situation through which the capital of the Republic has passed obliged the army, represented by the undersigned, to unite in a sentiment of fraternity to achieve the salvation of the country. In consequence the nation may be at rest ... within seventy-two hours the legal situation will have been duly organised.

'The army invites the people on whom it relies to continue in the noble attitude of respect and moderation ... it also invites all revolutionary factions to unite for the consolidation of national peace.'

Félix Díaz, V. Huerta.

Wilson informed the State Department of the 'happy outcome' of events and next day, still swept along on a flood tide of enthusiasm, cabled Washington 'A wicked despotism has fallen.' His happiness was shared by the American publisher of the *Mexican Herald*, whose headline on 19 February gushed 'Viva Díaz ... Viva Huerta ... after a year of anarchy a military dictator looks good to Mexico'.

After leaving the Embassy celebrations the Cuban and Spanish Ministers, Márquez Sterling and Cologan, obtained permission to see Madero, who was under heavy guard in the National Palace. At the request of Madero's uncle Ernesto, who feared for the president's safety, Márquez Sterling agreed to spend the night with the imprisoned Madero. Makeshift beds were prepared from chairs in the room and Márquez Sterling recalled that immediately after Madero lay down 'he fell into a quiet, childlike sleep'.

The names of Huerta's Cabinet were officially announced on 19 February, though Wilson had already read them out to the diplomatic corps at his reception the previous evening. Francisco de la Barra, recently the interim president, was made Minister of Foreign Affairs. De la Barra had been found sheltering in the cellar of the British Legation on 18 February and warned of his impending return to politics. General Manuel Mondragón became Minister of War and Rodolfo Reyes was appointed Minister of Justice. The Treasury post went to Toribio Esquivel Obregón, and Jorge Vera Estañol, after first refusing to serve, became Minister of Education. The Ministry of the Interior was taken over by the elderly Alberto Gracía Granados, who later paid for his Cabinet appointment with his life. Under the Carranza régime he was ordered to be shot, although he was on his deathbed at the time. He had to be tied to the execution post to prevent him falling over.

Once the Cabinet had been announced, the members of Madero's cabinet were released from prison and all of them resigned except Pedro Lascuráin, the forty-five-year-old Foreign Minister who ranked third in succession in the Madero government.

The next move was to obtain the resignation of Madero and Pino Suárez. The two men gave these when they had been assured that they and their families would be guaranteed safety.

A note, signed by the deposed president and his deputy, was sent to the Chamber of Deputies on the afternoon of 19 February: 'In view of the events which have occurred since yesterday in the nation and for its greater tranquillity, we formally resign our posts of President and Vice-President, respectively, to which we were elected. We concur in whatever may be necessary.'

The resignations were handed to Lascuráin, who took them to Huerta and begged the new dictator to spare the lives of the two men. 'Whatever you ask,' replied Huerta, and with a sudden gesture he pulled from beneath his shirt a medal of the Virgin of Guadalupe, the patron saint of Mexico, on a golden chain. 'I swear to you that I shall permit no one to make an attempt against the life of Señor Madero,' said Huerta, kissing the medallion. Lascuráin, a devout Catholic, was reassured and handed over the resignations.

They were placed before an emergency session of Congress the same evening and were accepted by a vote of 123 to four. So, in accordance with the Constitution, Lascuráin, the third in line, succeeded to the presidency and took the oath.

He was probably the shortest-lived president in history. His only act was to appoint Huerta Minister of the Interior and then, twenty-six minutes after taking office, he resigned.

Lascuráin's action placed Huerta next in line of succession and, this time without a dissenting vote, Huerta was elected provisional president pending a general election. On the surface at least, the constitution had been adhered to,

though Lascuráin's agreement to this flagrantly undemocratic act had only been secured when it was pointed out
that the alternative was more bloodshed.

And so, in ten days of deviousness unmatched in the
history of Mexico, Huerta had rocketed to power. He had
tricked the government, to which he had pledged support.
Now he was to prove false to his new allies; and the fist of
iron was quickly revealed when, after accepting the presidency, he telegraphed a message to the state government:
'Accept my authority or perish.'

Lascuráin's pious hope that his handing over of power
would prevent further bloodshed was shattered the same
evening with the murder of Gustavo Madero—the very
evening he had originally been due to depart on his goodwill mission to Japan. He was taken under armed escort
from the National Palace to the Ciudadela while Congress
was considering the resignation of President Madero. But
at the Ciudadela Félix Díaz wanted nothing to do with the
prisoner.

What happened next is the subject of controversy. Some
accounts have it that Gustavo was tortured inside the
Ciudadela by rebel officers, who rounded off the evening's
sport by emptying their revolvers into him. Other versions
of his death say that he was marched back outside the
Ciudadela, where—in the time-honoured version of *ley fuga*
—he made a break for freedom and was shot down by his
escort.

The evening of 19 February had been a busy one. While
the presidency of Mexico changed hands twice, arrangements were going ahead for the departure of Madero for
Veracruz. A special two-carriage train had been waiting at
Buenavista Station since 10 p.m. and by midnight Señora
Madero and Señora Pino Suárez, together with many members of their families, were on board. But they waited in
vain for the promised arrival of their husbands. At two in
the morning ex-president Lascuráin arrived, accompanied
by two Huerta officers, to explain that the departure order
had been countermanded. He said Huerta had been told that
the commander of the Veracruz garrison was a Madero
supporter and planned to free the deposed president as
soon as he arrived at the port.

Huerta was obviously undecided what to do about Madero. Should be send him into exile, and risk the possibility of facing a Madero-led invasion of the country, or should he allow the rebel hotheads to have their way and kill him?

Huerta asked Henry Lane Wilson whether he should send Madero into exile, have him impeached by Congress for 'violation of the constitution' or commit him to a lunatic asylum. Wilson, who had never before hesitated to thrust his nose into Mexican affairs, answered piously that Huerta should do 'what was best for the peace of the country', then told his government about the conversation.

Secretary of State Philander Knox wired back: 'General Huerta's consulting you as to the treatment of Madero tends to give you a certain responsibility in the matter. It moreover goes without saying that cruel treatment of the ex-president would injure ... the reputation of Mexican civilisation, and this government earnestly ... hopes to hear that he has been dealt with in a manner consistent with peace and humanity.'

Señora Madero went to the U.S. Embassy on the afternoon of 20 February to plead with Wilson to use his influence to save her husband's life, but the ambassador told her 'That is a responsibility I do not care to undertake, either for myself or my government.'

Then he told the shocked woman, 'I will be frank with you, madam. Your husband's downfall is due to the fact that he never wanted to consult with me.' And when Señora Madero also sought protection for Pino Suárez, Wilson became impatient, telling her 'Pino Suárez is a very bad man. I cannot give any assurances for his safety. He is to blame for most of your husband's troubles. ...'

Still Wilson poured out his telegrams, urging support of Huerta. He requested the State Department's immediate instructions 'as to the question of recognition of the Provisional Government, now installed and evidently in secure position', pointing out that it had taken office 'in accordance with the constitution and precedents'.

On 21 February Wilson telegraphed all American consular officials in Mexico, requesting them to advise loyalty to the new régime, which, he falsely informed them 'will be recognised by all foreign governments today'.

Madero, whose fortunes at the hands of the American government had undergone a drastic change and who had been harassed by a biased ambassador, met his death, ironically, on George Washington's birthday.

Earlier in the day Huerta and his new cabinet attended the annual ceremony at the Washington statue in the Plaza de Dinamarca. Afterwards Huerta appealed to his countrymen, in a manifesto to the nation, to co-operate in the re-establishment of peace. But he couldn't avoid ending on a threatening note: 'If, unfortunately, bad citizens, blinded by passion, insist on prolonging the strife ... I shall not hesitate an instant in adopting the measures of rigour that may be necessary for the rapid restoration of public peace....'

Late in the evening of 22 February Madero and Pino Suárez were told that they were being moved from the room in the National Palace, where they were imprisoned with General Felipe Angeles, to the city penitentiary where they would be safer.

As the two men were taken from the room Madero turned to Angeles and said, 'Adiós my general, I shall never see you again.' At 11.15 p.m. the Palace doors opened and two cars emerged. One contained Madero and the other Pino Suárez, both under heavy guard.

Journalists waiting outside the Palace tried to follow the vehicles on foot but were quickly outdistanced. One of them, the local correspondent for the *New York World*, was making his way towards the penitentiary when he heard about a dozen shots. When he reached the building he asked the guards if there had been any trouble and was told 'There has been some firing behind the prison.'

He went round the corner and halfway along the rear wall of the prison saw a group of men and the two cars.

'A gendarme came running towards me. I asked him what was the matter. He replied "Madero has been shot." An officer then came up and said "Madero is dead. There was a fight; they tried to rescue him and he was shot— Suárez too."

'He told me that I could proceed, as all was over. Before I could reach the group three men lifted each of the bodies. There was no blood to show where Suárez had been shot. I heard a soldier say he had been struck in the back of the head. I could scarcely recognise Madero, except for his beard. Blood flowing from his mouth nearly covered his face; his eyes were wide open. . . .

'I asked an officer how it happened. He replied "We had nearly reached the prison when we heard shots. Several men ran towards the cars. We thought it was an attempt at rescue, and Madero and Suárez jumped and started to run. Who shot them I don't know. The attackers finally fled and we found Madero and Suárez on the ground." '

Captain Francisco Cárdenas, in charge of the escort, told newspapermen afterwards that the two cars had been fired on by a group of a dozen men as they approached the prison. In the confusion, according to Cárdenas, both Madero and Pino Suárez had managed to get out of their cars and had run towards the group who were firing at the cars. 'They had come between the two fires and been killed,' he explained.

An even more fatuous version was put forward by Mrs Moats, who suggested in her book that the two men were shot inside the Palace and their bodies frogmarched into cars waiting in the patio. Outside the prison a sham battle had taken place and the cars had been riddled with bullets.

The autopsy, which no member of the Madero family was permitted to attend, proved the Cárdenas version to be false. Madero was killed by one bullet which entered at the base of the skull and lodged in the brain. Furthermore, no rescuing party would have been foolish enough to have fired upon the cars containing the men they wanted to liberate. A road block and a swift rush would have accomplished the purpose much more easily. And only men bent on suicide would have leapt from the cars and rushed into the line of fire.

Huerta's complicity in the murder of Madero was never proved. He denied all connection, and certainly no evidence was ever produced to implicate him. But Madero's supporters were in no doubt about whom to hold responsible and, even if Huerta was free of blame, he was certainly guilty of a serious political error in not protecting Madero's life.

An investigation was promised, but never took place, and Capt. Cárdenas was promoted to major for his part in failing to keep Madero alive. After the fall of Huerta, Cárdenas fled to Guatemala, disguised as a mule driver. He spent six years in exile but when, late in 1920, the Guatemalan government agreed to Mexican extradition requests Cárdenas committed suicide rather than return.

There were no queries in Henry Lane Wilson's mind, however. On 24 February he telegraphed Washington 'In spite of all the rumours which are afloat I am disposed to accept the government's version of the affair and consider it a closed incident. Certainly the violent deaths of these persons were without government approval.'

He went on to plead brazenly for recognition of the new government, saying that it was showing firmness and prudence and making the wild claim that 'adhesions to it, as far as I have been able to ascertain, are general throughout the Republic. . . .' Then came a final piece of what was, even for Wilson, tremendous gall: 'For the present, American public opinion should . . . accept with great reserve the lurid and highly-coloured stories which are being furnished by some few correspondents.'

But the Press wasn't so easily convinced. Said *The Times* on 24 February:

'This dark and sordid tragedy cries aloud for investigattion. . . . Civilised nations will place their own construction upon the lame and halting story which the successful conspirators who now rule Mexico have chosen to put out. To us it is by no means convincing. All who know the history of civil strife . . . in Mexico . . . still suspect that Francisco Madero and his companion have been murdered for the same reasons and in pretty much the same way as Gustavo Madero appears to have been murdered a couple of days earlier. . . .

'The trick of a sham rescue as a pretext for blowing out the brains of inconvenient prisoners is quite common. . . . Unless and until the new government can prove to the hilt the not very plausible story which they have published, foreign observers will remain of the opinion that the "re-

moval" of the two Maderos and Suárez is but a fresh proof
that the innate ferocity of Mexican politicians and military
adventurers remains untamed. . . .

'The most for which this unhappy country can hope is
the restoration of a rule not worse than that of President
Díaz.'

This produced a sharp complaint from Wilson to Washington. He felt that the published summaries of London
press opinion showed a vast ignorance about the true situation in Mexico. 'I would suggest that *The Times* correspondent in Washington have matters carefully explained
to him. . . .'

Henry Lane Wilson's later dismissal by President Wilson
and the heavy criticism of his actions made no difference to
his beliefs. In his autobiography the ambassador wrote that
he considered his actions during the Madero overthrow 'my
most valuable moment'.

The murdered men were buried on 24 February, Madero
in the French cemetery and Pino Suárez in the Spanish.
Only the nearest relatives were permitted to attend. Immediately afterwards, Madero's widow and other members of
the family left for Cuba, accompanied by the Cuban Minister, Márquez Sterling, who refused to represent his country
in Mexico any longer.

The same day the portraits and statues of Porfirio Díaz,
taken away during the Madero régime, were replaced in the
National Palace. The iron hand was back.

Madero was dead at thirty-nine, and with him were buried
the democratic ideals which had brought about his fall. He
had ruled for only fifteen months, hardly time for the most
brilliant of presidents to have made much impression on
Mexico's multiple maladies—and Madero was far from
being that.

'He was not a Strong Man with capital letters and Mexicans do like strong men,' commented one historian. 'He
might have survived if he had followed the Díaz dictum
"Better shed bad blood now than good blood later" and had
allowed Félix Díaz to be executed.'

Even some of his own family criticised his lack of force.
Gustavo Madero once commented bitterly that, of a family

of clever men, the only fool had been elected president.

The summary of one author that 'weak men have been the ruination of Mexico and Madero was simply a weak dreamer' is commonly seen in history references to Madero's rule. But these detractors mistook compassion, magnanimity and a love for legal processes for the actions of a weakling, rather than the idealist which Madero in fact was.

He showed no frailty in overthrowing a formidable dictator, and revealed lack of tact rather than weakness in dealing with the hysterical, hostile demands of Henry Lane Wilson. At least he had pointed the way, however hesitantly. Mexico would never be the same again.

The reasons for his fall were daunting. The first was the chaotic state of the country when he took over. Niggling rebellions and uprisings continued throughout his administration, dissipating the funds and energies of the government and preventing headway being made on education and public works. Then, too, Madero had fatally attempted a compromise with the Díaz element and, after the disastrous six months of provisional government, never managed to obtain full control or support among Congressmen.

Mexican and foreign landowners and business interests had fought him every inch of the way, and they were helped by a largely hostile press who revelled in their newly-granted freedom to attack the man who had given it to them. His refusal to pander alienated army generals and Henry Lane Wilson, and eventually it was the combination of these two forces which unseated him. The United States ambassador, rather than the American government, was heavily to blame, though the Taft administration was also at fault for permitting a man like Wilson to stay on in Mexico.

'Considering all the factors the wonder is not that so little was accomplished but that anything at all was done,' commented the historian Charles Cumberland. 'But the fall of the Madero government was a national disaster regardless of the merits of the government itself. Those who were responsible . . . had no substitutes which would be acceptable to the nation. Nothing was gained by his overthrow.'

Part Three: Huerta

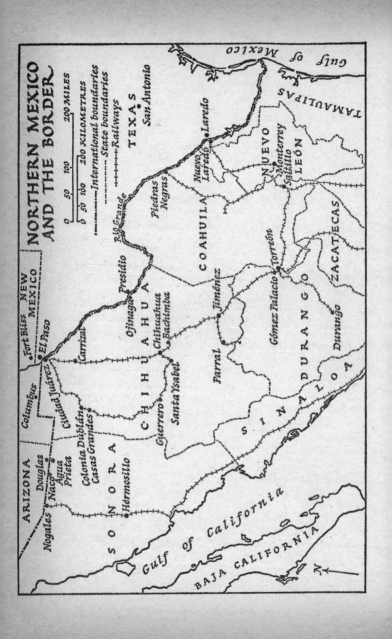

Huerta's assumption of power was hailed with relief by all those who had been deploring the lack of a 'strong man' since the fall of Díaz. The Porfirian element and the Army rallied to his support, landowners like Terrazas welcomed him, Orozco and the *Colorados* joined him, bankers offered loans; the Church lent him a million pesos, authorised sermons extolling the new leader and arranged a *Te Deum* in the capital's cathedral to celebrate the country's 'pacification'; a leading cigarette company produced a new brand with Huerta's face framed in laurels on the packet, and the Kaiser, impressed by Huerta's ruthless assumption of power, sent a message praising 'a brave soldier who would save his country with the sword of honour'. Huerta's supporters called him 'The Mexican Cromwell'.

Henry Lane Wilson was working unceasingly to obtain American recognition of the new dictator and assured Washington that Huerta was proving acceptable to all Mexicans. But this was far from the truth. On 26 February Venustiano Carranza, governor of the north-eastern state of Coahuila, protested to President Taft: 'The Mexican nation condemns the villainous *coup d'état* which deprived Mexico of her constitutional rulers by cowardly assassination ... I am certain that both the government of Your Excellency as well as that of your successor will not accept the spurious government which Huerta is attempting to establish. . . .'

On 1 March Louis Hotstetter the American Consul in Hermosillo, capital of the north-western state, Sonora, reported to Washington: 'The majority of people in the state are not at all in favour of Huerta . . .' and the next day Philip C. Hanna, U.S. consul general in Monterrey confirmed Carranza's rejection of Huerta with the terse announcement 'The state of Coahuila is in revolt.'

On 4 March Henry Lane Wilson's time ran out. Woodrow Wilson became President. It was Huerta's ill-luck that his assumption of power coincided with the change of presidents in the United States, and even worse luck that the Democrat Woodrow Wilson, much like Madero, regarded himself as an apostle, a man to sweep away the Republican Taft's mis-administration, restore integrity to U.S. politics and lead his people to greatness.

The death of Madero had shocked the new president and offended the sense of democratic processes which was so strong in this former President of Princeton University. From the very beginning his attitude towards Huerta was one of hostility.

A week after becoming president, Wilson made his attitude clear in his first statement of foreign policy. He typed it himself and released it to his Cabinet and the Press without even consulting his Secretary of State, William Jennings Bryan—an early indication that Wilson intended to be his own Secretary of State. With a man like Bryan, himself three times a Democratic presidential candidate and three times a disastrous loser, and perhaps the most improbable holder of the post in American political history, Wilson's attitude was readily understandable. Though he had been in politics for most of his adult life, Bryan's indiscretion and naïveté in political matters was matched only by the foolishness which he was to exhibit in later years in the famous Scopes 'monkey trial'.

Wilson's policy statement avoided direct reference to Mexico, but its wording left no doubt that it was aimed directly at Huerta. The co-operation (and therefore recognition) of the United States was only possible, said Wilson, 'when supported at every turn by the orderly processes of just government based upon law, not arbitrary or irregular force. . . . We can have no sympathy with those who seek to seize the power of government to advance their own personal interest or ambition. . . .'

Henry Lane Wilson still refused to give up. After receiving the president's policy statement, he cabled to Bryan the next day, 'Unless the same type of government as was implanted here by Porfirio Díaz is again established, new revolutionary movements will break forth and general unrest will be renewed.'

The Ambassador continually pleaded to be 'put in possession of the attitude of the administration on the question of recognition' but he knew well enough what the attitude was. Woodrow Wilson regarded Huerta as a usurper and a murderer and was determined to make an example of him in attempt to check the habit of revolution and bring democracy and order to the turbulent Latin American countries.

Wilson's antagonism ensured the eventual fall of Huerta, but the date of his overthrow depended purely on the volume of resistance to Huerta within Mexico itself.

It was quickly obvious that this resistance was going to be formidable. Zapata fought Huerta with even more determination than he had opposed Díaz and the Madero régime, but the main opposition was once more centred in the northern states. The rebels' first, and main, spokesman was Venustiano Carranza, who, like Madero, seemed an unlikely figure to inspire rebellion. His very appearance recalled a typical politician of the Díaz days.

Carranza was a tall, aloof landowner who had served as a senator in the Díaz government for twelve years but joined Madero's revolutionary government-in-exile in 1910. The personification of dignity and wisdom, he wore blue-tinted spectacles to protect his weak eyes and affected a large white beard, parted in the middle, which gave him a misleadingly benign and Biblical look.

Carranza was honest but implacably convinced of his own rightness, feeling that he was the only possible saviour of his country from the Huerta threat. Parkes felt it 'strangely ironical that this loquacious and self-complacent country squire' should have become spokesman for the resistance. In his opinion, Carranza 'had substantial virtues; he was financially honest and he had no love for bloodshed. Unfortunately, he was also domineering, egotistical, and remarkably ignorant of the history and needs of the people whom he proposed to govern.'

Carranza assumed the leadership of the anti-Huerta rebellion when, at the Hacienda de Guadalupe in Coahuila on 26 March 1913, he published the Plan of Guadalupe, a document which, by its very vagueness, proved acceptable to all factions of the rebellion. Its strongest article was the denial of recognition to Huerta and the appointment of the fifty-four-year-old Carranza as 'First Chief' of the Constitutionalists, the name adopted by those who were battling for restoration of a legal constitution.

The very word 'constitutionalist' convinced the democratically-minded President Wilson that in Carranza Mexico had found a new leader of the oppressed. Yet if the rebellion had depended solely on Carranza, victory would have been a long time coming. The self-designated First Chief was no soldier and the small force under his command in the north-east was badly led by Pablo González, who had gained a reputation as a general who never won a battle.

Fortunately, the anti-Huerta movement in the state of Sonora was better organised. It centred around Alvaro Obregón, a thirty-three-year-old rancher who claimed descent from Miguel Obregón (formerly known as Michael O'Brien), Irish bodyguard to the last of the Spanish Viceroys in Mexico. The author H. Hamilton Fyfe noted that Obregón, with his 'merry grey eyes, tip-tilted nose and healthy red round face with a jutting dented chin' had a face that was 'beyond doubt' that of an Irishman.

Obregón, though the youngest of eighteen children, managed to get an education at his village school before starting work at the age of thirteen as a *hacienda* mechanic. By the time the Madero Revolution broke out, Obregón had married, acquired a small plot of land on which he was raising chick-peas and had been appointed mayor of the Sonora hamlet of Huatabampo.

He took no active part in the Madero revolt, admitting frankly: 'The Maderista party was split into two sections; one composed of individuals responsive to the call of duty, who left their homes and severed every tie of family and interest to shoulder a rifle ... and the other of men who harkened to the promptings of fear, who found no arms, who had children liable to become orphans, and who were bound by a thousand other ties which even duty cannot suppress when the spectre of fear grips the hearts of men.

'It was to the second of these classes that I unfortunately belonged.'

But when Orozco rebelled against Madero, Obregón shed his reluctance to fight and organised a force of 300 men, nicknamed 'The Rich Battalion' since many of them were relatively well-off young farmers like himself. When Huerta demanded all states' allegiance, Obregón was one of the first men summoned into action by the anti-Huerta governor of Sonora, José María Maytorena.

Though he lacked the fiery dash of Villa and Zapata, or the solid military ability of Huerta, Obregón possessed tremendous organisational flair backed by infinite patience and a fantastic memory.

A socialist and an agnostic, he organised his military campaigns in a way unique among the rebels of those days, surrounding himself with competent, carefully chosen assistants whom he always consulted before making a move. His actions were a shrewd combination of the desirable and the practical. He was obviously destined to be one of Mexico's great men.

Obregón and his able lieutenants, Plutarco Elías Calles (like Obregón, destined to be President of Mexico), Benjamín Hill, Salvador Alvarado, Francisco Serrano and Adolfo de la Huerta, soon controlled most of their remote state and provided the Constitutionalists with an excellent revolutionary launching pad, far removed from Mexico City and handily placed for arms and supplies from the ever-willing merchants of the United States.

Huerta acted swiftly to prevent trouble in the trouble-prone state of Chihuahua. Abraham González, the pro-Madero governor, was arrested and superseded by a Huerta general, Antonio Rábago. On 7 March González was removed from prison in Chihuahua City and told he was being transferred by train to another town. When the train reached Bachimba Canyon González was thrown under the wheels and his remains were buried alongside the track.

News of the double murder of the men he most admired, Madero and González, followed by Orozco's return to Chihuahua, brought Pancho Villa back from exile in a hurry. On the night of 13 March, accompanied by eight followers mounted on horses stolen from an animal-hire firm in El Paso, Villa splashed through the shallows of the Rio Grande and back into Mexico.

The rebel element had got what it lacked in Chihuahua—a leader.

As Villa busied himself gathering an army out of the deserts, he sent a message to General Rábago: 'Knowing that the government you represent was preparing to extradite me I have saved them the trouble. I am now in Mexico, ready to make war upon you.'

Villa was exaggerating. He wasn't *quite* ready for war. But he soon would be.

Rábago countered with an offer of £10,000 and the post of divisional general if Villa would join Huerta. To this the leader of an army of eight replied, 'Tell Huerta that I do not need the rank as I am already supreme commander of free men ... and as for the money, let him swill it up in *aguardiente*.'

A week after crossing the border, Villa had penetrated to within sixty miles of Chihuahua City, but had enlisted only fourteen more men, among them his younger brothers Hipólito and Antonio. From that point, however, his force grew rapidly as the peons responded to the magic name of Villa. They came in from the villages, the *haciendas*, the mining camps, in their tens and fifties, sometimes on horse, mostly on foot; sometimes armed, mostly not, and invariably accompanied by their women and children.

These stolid women formed an essential part of Mexican armies, rebel and Federal, since neither provided medical services or a commissary while in the field. They accompanied their men everywhere. With children clinging to their skirts, and pots, pans and bedding strapped to their backs, they foraged through the fierce heat and chill night of the northern desert, stripping villages like an army of locusts if food was scarce.

Sometimes, too, the women fought alongside the men, earning the title *soldadera*. 'In exhibitions of strength, endurance and courage, the *soldadera* was her man's equal, if she did not surpass him,' said one author. If she lost her man in battle, a woman would spend the night in grief, then take another.

Villa's force soon looked less like an army in the accepted European sense than a disaster-stricken migration. But it was welding; and to get money to equip it Villa reverted to his old profession, rustling. Thousands of cattle belonging to Luis Terrazas and other *hacendados* were swept from the vast estates, driven to the American border and exchanged for guns and bullets.

Villa's force, now 700 strong, saw its first action in the

northern Chihuahua town of Casas Grandes, which was garrisoned by about 400 of Orozco's detested *Colorados*. Villa stormed the town after a two-hour battle and the *Colorados* fled, leaving behind forty dead and sixty prisoners. Next morning Villa had the prisoners lined up three deep and shot them that way 'to save ammunition by killing three with one shot'. The no-quarter mood had been set.

Carranza soon sent envoys to Villa requesting his allegiance to the Plan of Guadalupe. Villa willingly supported the Plan (he would have backed any anti-Huerta scheme) and recognised Carranza as First Chief.

Their alliance, however, was a union of necessity which never began to approach friendship. How could the landowning Carranza ever treat Villa, the epitome of a Mexican peon, with anything but suspicion? And how could Villa—earthy, passionate, barely literate—warm to an aloof, stubborn old man?

Villa's account of their first meeting was typically blunt: 'I embraced [Carranza] energetically, but with the first few words he spoke my blood turned to ice. I saw that I could not open my heart to him. As far as he was concerned I was a rival, not a friend. He never looked me in the eye and during our entire conversation emphasised our difference in origin ... he lectured me on things like decrees and laws, which I could not understand. There was nothing in common between that man and me.'

Perhaps that bear-hug from the barrel-chested, untidy peasant didn't help. The First Chief was not used to such rude contact with his followers.

Apart from isolated clashes, the spring and summer of 1913 were spent by the armies of Carranza, Obregón and Villa gathering recruits and supplies. Huerta was content to abandon the northern countryside to the rebels and concentrate on fortifying the towns, particularly the ones which straddled the main railway lines to the American border, while he manoeuvred desperately for United States recognition of his government. Without this he knew he would be lost.

But in the new American President, he was opposed by a

man every bit as unyielding as himself, and one who rarely sought the advice of others, unless their opinions happened to coincide with his. Wilson dug in his heels against the supplications of his ambassador in Mexico City and the cries for recognition from Americans with business interests in that country.

Wilson told his personal physician Dr Cary Grayson, 'I sometimes have to pause and remind myself that I am president of the whole United States and not merely of a few property holders in the Republic of Mexico.'

It was unfortunate that President Wilson was singularly unprepared for trouble in Mexico. Before taking office he commented that it would be the irony of fate if his administration had to deal with foreign affairs when his own preparation for the presidency had been so exclusively in domestic problems. However, he made a serious attempt to remedy his ignorance in the first crowded months of the presidency by reading as many books and reports about Mexico as he had time for.

Wilson was anxious that Britain should follow his lead in refusing Huerta recognition and early in March Irwin Laughlin, the American chargé d'affaires in London pending the arrival of the new Ambassador, Walter Page, was instructed to discover the attitude of the Foreign Office. According to Laughlin, he received an unequivocal answer that the British government would not recognise Huerta, either officially or tacitly. However, Washington's delight at the news quickly turned to anger.

While the British Foreign Secretary, Sir Edward Grey, sympathised with the moral purpose of Wilson's policy he did not believe that there was much to choose between Huerta and his opponents, and on 3 May Britain extended recognition to the Mexican provisional government on the understanding that free elections would soon follow and that Huerta would not run for the presidency. Germany, France, Spain and Japan followed Britain's lead, opening the way for Huerta to purchase badly-needed supplies and arms: Japan, for instance, immediately shipped ten million cartridges to the Federals.

Wilson, Bryan and others in the Democrat administration, ever suspicious of 'big business' as personified by the

Republicans, were convinced that Britain's change of heart resulted from pressure applied by Lord Cowdray in an attempt to preserve his interests in Mexico.

In July the British government further nettled Washington by appointing Sir Lionel Carden to succeed Sir Francis Stronge as Minister to Mexico. Carden, tall, suave and monocled, and a product of Eton, had gained a reputation for anti-Americanism during thirty years' service in various diplomatic posts in Central and South America. The Americans took such strong exception to Carden during his spell as British Minister to Cuba from 1911 to 1913 that the Secretary of State, Philander Knox, twice pressed for his removal. The British government's reply was to knight Carden.

Walter Page's biographer commented, 'If the British government had ransacked its diplomatic force to find the one man who would have been most objectionable to the United States, it could have made no better selection.' Page himself dismissed Carden as a 'slow-minded, unimaginative, commercial Briton, with as much nimbleness as an elephant'.

But, unlike the Americans who were objecting to his appointment, Sir Lionel was an expert on Mexico. He had spent seventeen years from 1882 as Minister in Mexico and was a good friend of Porfirio Díaz. Shortly before his appointment he had visited Díaz in Paris, seeking the ex-president's opinion of the Mexican situation in general and Huerta in particular. Díaz's answer that Huerta was 'the man of the hour' was passed on by Carden to the Foreign Office and undoubtedly had much to do with Britain's granting him recognition.

Carden's appointment coincided with the removal of Henry Lane Wilson by President Wilson. The American Ambassador had fought bitterly for recognition of Huerta and openly labelled his government's policy towards Mexico 'disastrous'. He was also indiscreet enough to invite Huerta to dinner at the Embassy. When President Wilson learned of this he wrote to Secretary of State Bryan, 'I think Wilson should be recalled.'

The Ambassador was brought back to Washington for 'consultations'. He met the president on 28 July, and a week later he was informed by Bryan that President Wilson had decided to accept his resignation because of a wide divergence in their views about Mexico.

As a further snub to Huerta, President Wilson refused to replace the sacked ambassador and the Embassy was taken over by the Second Secretary, Nelson O'Shaughnessy, who was promoted to chargé d'affaires. Unexpectedly, the change was to Huerta's liking. He was on friendly terms with the Catholic O'Shaughnessys. He referred to Nelson, who had been educated at Oxford, as 'son', and always took Mrs O'Shaughnessy's arm at receptions or dinners. This close friendship was to be of great value during the trying months ahead.

But Wilson was no more disposed to trust O'Shaughnessy than he had trusted the ambassador. The president was a great believer in using amateur diplomats and 'special agents', responsible only to Bryan or himself, to find out what he believed the professional diplomats were unwilling or unable to tell him.

To Charles W. Thompson, a veteran Washington reporter, these agents were 'a curious and unfit lot. They appeared, as a rule to be selected because they would give [Wilson] the side of the case he had already decided to be the right one, and the advice he had already given himself'.

The first agent to be sent to Mexico by Wilson was William Bayard Hale, a journalist who had been chosen to write Wilson's campaign biography the previous year. Although a brilliant journalist, Hale was temperamentally unfitted for the task. As one writer put it, 'His qualifications consisted of knowing nothing whatever about Mexico but a good deal about Wilson. A quick glance round was all he needed to report back what he knew Wilson wanted to hear; that Huerta was indeed the archfiend and his régime could not last.'

Hale, who went to Mexico in May, was particularly critical of Ambassador Wilson's conduct, and the ambassador, in turn, bitterly resented Hale's presence in the country as a slight on his own abilities. He even protested to Washington about Hale's interference.

The president took advantage of the removal of Ambassador Wilson to appoint another of his personal agents.

This time the choice fell on John Lind, the ex-governor of Minnesota, a tall, gaunt, sandy-haired man of Scandinavian descent who felt that prostitution and the Catholic Church were the main causes of Mexico's troubles.

On 4 August, the very day that Henry Lane Wilson's career was ending, Lind left Washington for Mexico, bearing with him this extraordinary letter of introduction from the president:

'To Whom It May Concern:

'This will introduce the Hon. John Lind who goes to Mexico at my request and as my personal representative to act as adviser to the American Embassy in the City of Mexico. I bespeak for him the same consideration that would in other circumstances be accorded a regularly accredited representative of the government of the United States.'

The letter, however, was no less extraordinary than the mission and the man chosen to carry it out. Lind carried with him proposals which the American president thought would put an end to Mexico's problems and, at the same time, remove Huerta. Wilson proposed an immediate cease-fire, to be followed by 'free elections' in which Huerta would agree not to be a candidate.

To carry out the delicate negotiations, Wilson had chosen a man without diplomatic experience, who knew next to nothing about Mexico and who did not even speak Spanish. Lind did, however, possess one qualification the recently-recalled ambassador had lacked: the ability to keep his mouth shut. When he reached Mexico Lind soon earned the nickname 'The Silent Man'.

He arrived at Veracruz aboard the American battleship USS *Louisiana* on 9 August and next day travelled up to Mexico City. He delayed delivering Wilson's proposals until 14 August, when he saw Federico Gamboa, the novelist who had taken over from de la Barra as Huerta's Foreign Minister. In the next two days Lind had several more meetings with Gamboa and at least one talk with Huerta, who spent most of the time trying to impress on Lind the size and efficiency of his army and his optimism about the speedy pacification of the country.

When Gamboa asked Huerta what sort of reply he

should make to Lind's proposals he snapped, 'Tell him to go to the Devil.' Then seeing the look of dismay on Gamboa's face he added, 'But put it in diplomatic language.'

Mexico's formal reply was made public on 16 August in a sarcastic note addressed to 'Mr Confidential Agent' which stated that Mexico could not 'for one moment' consider Wilson's interference in its politics. Gamboa further stated that, since Huerta's candidacy at the forthcoming presidential elections, scheduled for 26 October, would be constitutionally illegal, the Americans' main suggestion was not even valid.

Lind broke off negotiations and left for Veracruz; and on 27 August President Wilson went before Congress to announce the failure of the Lind mission. But he expressed confidence in his policy of 'watchful waiting', telling the Congressmen, 'We can afford to exercise the self-restraint of a really great nation which realises its own strength and scorns to misuse it.' How soon that statement was made to look foolish!

Wilson also told Congress that, in order to hasten a ceasefire, he proposed to impose a complete embargo on the sale of arms to Mexico. At this stage the president was so confident of a peaceful solution that on 29 August he wrote to General W. F. Sadler of New Jersey, who had offered his services in case of trouble with the Mexicans, 'There ain't goin' to be no war.'

John Lind, who had expected a recall to Washington, was instead requested to stay on in Veracruz, a silent, lonely representative of the president's 'watchful waiting' policy. He was to spend seven more months in the town before getting his longed-for recall. It was a farcical seven months.

Lind's biographer wrote, 'About five o'clock every afternoon, dressed in dark clothes and a pearl grey felt hat, he would take his walk, a very conspicuous figure in hot Veracruz. He was always followed by Huerta's spies at some distance. Lind never knew whether they were detailed to spy on him or protect him. Sometimes Lind would wave his handkerchief, at which signal they would come up to have a glass of beer or a cigar with him.'

In Mexico City, too, there was a touch of farce about the

political situation as Huerta began to concentrate power in his own hands. His high-handed ways soon brought the resignations of the Education Minister, Jorge Vera Estañol, and the Minister of the Interior, Alberto García Granados.

On 23 June General Mondragón, the Minister of War, was painlessly removed in a manner which typified Huerta's sense of humour. Mondragón and Huerta were guests of honour at a banquet organised by army officers. At the end of the meal Huerta told Mondragón that his presence was required immediately in the United States and that a train, with his luggage aboard, was waiting to take him to Veracruz. 'Accompanied' by half a dozen officers, the bewildered Mondragón was whisked to the station, where Huerta embraced his ex-Minister and assured him that his trip was 'for the good of Mexico'.

Félix Díaz, the man supposed to be in line for the presidency, was the next to go, sent away ostensibly to Japan on the mission of thanks which Gustavo Madero had failed to undertake. Before the end of July de la Barra, the Foreign Minister, was on his way to Paris as Mexico's new Minister to France, having been replaced by Federico Gamboa.

Rodolfo Reyes, the Minister of Justice, lasted until September. 'By then,' wrote Bell, 'Huerta's Cabinet was made up of men whose wills counted for little; he could look into a mirror and behold the sardonic visage of the whole Mexican government.' As one Mexican put it, 'Huerta no longer sought colleagues, but accomplices.'

Huerta was interested in power, not money. He scorned the use of the presidential palace at Chapultepec, and installed his wife and family in a quiet house in an unpretentious section of the city. He spent most of his free evenings at his 'retreat', a three-roomed bungalow surrounded by a high wall among the market gardens at Popotla, on the outskirts of the capital.

Usually dressed in a shabby suit and soft grey felt hat, Huerta dealt with the country's business in the oddest places and at the strangest times. He was rarely to be found at the National Palace. Instead, envoys had to scour Mexico City's saloons, cafés and parks in search of the dictator. His favourite haunt was El Globo, a fashionable tea room, where he would sit daintily sipping brandy from a teacup and matching coins with the girl cashier to see who should pay for his drinks. If the cashier lost, Huerta's bill was paid by the proprietor, who found him a great draw.

His favourite place for Cabinet meetings was the Bar Colón. According to Mrs Moats, one Cabinet member, awakened at 2 a.m. with the message that Huerta had called a meeting for 3 a.m. in the Colón, complained, 'That old Aztec will kill me yet.'

Rodolfo Reyes, soon to lose his cabinet job, grumbled that he always found Huerta 'in strange company, eating, singing . . . and acutely alcoholic'.

Most of Huerta's 'office' business was done in a car in Chapultepec Park. He would drive into the huge park, followed by another car containing a secretary and telegraph clerk; and there by the roadside the nation's business would be transacted.

Nelson O'Shaughnessy, who needed to see Huerta every day during the hectic months after Henry Lane Wilson's dismissal, became particularly skilful at tracking him down. Even so, Huerta sometimes refused to indulge in, or was incapable of, serious conversation. Once he cheerfully embraced O'Shaughnessy in an *abrazo*, the bear hug that passes for masculine greeting in Mexico, and told him playfully 'I arrest you.' On another occasion when O'Shaughnessy presented a diplomatic note Huerta waved it away with the statesman-like comment, 'How about the girls?'

A New York banker, F. F. Searing, was a member of an American business commission which was conducted to Huerta's bungalow to present a petition. After the business was concluded Huerta led his visitors to a bookcase and opened the doors to reveal shelves filled with bottles of liquor. 'These books make my heart merry,' he told Searing.

Huerta was genuinely fond of Americans and when the American residents of Mexico City, according to custom and in defiance of the Wilson administration, decided to invite the Mexican president to their Fourth of July celebrations, Huerta accepted, overriding Mexican objections with the comment 'I am not at war with the United States.'

Wearing his wrinkled grey suit and with his hat pulled well down over his eyes, Huerta managed to slip past the official welcoming committee waiting outside the Tivoli Hotel in morning coats and top hats, without being recognised.

A few minutes later an official ran outside to tell the reception committee that the president had arrived. They rushed into the hotel and found Huerta at the bar, drinking cognac. After polishing off half a bottle, he picked up the rest and put it in his pocket. 'This is very fine cognac. I will keep this,' he said. On leaving he thanked the committee: 'I have been greatly contented with my American friends.'

Through the summer of 1913 the Constitutionalist forces, united flimsily beneath the banner of Carranza and his Plan of Guadalupe, slowly built up their strength in the north.

Only in Carranza's home state of Coahuila were things going badly. There, the First Chief and his general Pablo González lost possession of the state capital, Saltillo, so in August Carranza turned over command of the north-east to González and removed his 'government' to the greater comfort, not to mention safety, of Sonora, where Huerta and the Federals had never been a threat.

In typically stubborn fashion, Carranza refused to cross into the United States to speed his journey to the Pacific coast. Instead, he made a laborious trip by horse and train to Sonora, where, protected by the armies of Obregón, he set up headquarters in Hermosillo.

One of the Carranza's first acts was to promote Obregón to brigadier general, but the army man was not over-impressed by the First Chief. He told an aide, 'He is a great man for little things and a small one for great ones. The individual trees would hinder him from seeing the forest as a whole. And he is persistent and dogmatic to boot.'

Newspapermen in search of a colourful story flocked to the dusty town to interview the First Chief, who had surrounded himself with sycophants and ceremonies in an attempt to disguise his squalid plight. Every evening Carranza and his 'government' walked from general headquarters to the dining area, accompanied by a military band.

The British writer Hamilton Fyfe visited Carranza and found him 'a man of striking personal dignity'. But he soon discovered that Carranza was a firm believer in his own statement that revolutions which compromised were revolutions lost.

Stressing the need for a return to democracy in Mexico, Carranza said that the Constitutionalists would refuse to recognise any president chosen in the October elections, and added, 'We shall execute anybody who does recognise him.'

Fyfe reported: ' "I beg your pardon," I said, "Would you kindly repeat your last statement?"

‘ "We shall", said the general calmly and as if he were making a perfectly natural remark, "execute anyone who recognises a president unconstitutionally elected and directly or indirectly guilty of participation in the murder of Madero." ’

When the American reporter, John Reed, went to interview Carranza he was shown into a darkened room.

‘As our eyes became accustomed to the light we saw the gigantic khaki-clad figure of Don Venustiano Carranza sitting in a big chair. There was something strange in the way he sat there with his hands on the arms of the chair as if he had been placed in it and told not to move. He did not seem to have been thinking nor to have been working.

‘He rose to meet us, a towering figure. I noticed with a kind of shock that in that dark room he wore smoked glasses and although ruddy and full-cheeked I felt he was not well. That tiny dark room where the First Chief of the Revolution slept and ate and worked and from which he hardly ever emerged seemed too small, like a cell. . . .’

While Carranza sat in Sonora, Villa was busy building an army out of the desert. As his migratory horde rolled south he was joined by many independent commanders and their forces; he was reunited, too, with bandit friends from his cattle rustling days.

One of these was Tomás Urbina, who brought 600 men and wagonloads of booty from the recently sacked town of Durango. A stocky, shifty-eyed man, Urbina was unable to read or write, and made his signature mark by drawing a heart. Urbina was known to his troops as the Lion of the Sierras, but he was a crippled lion these days. Years of hiding out in the harsh mountains had left him suffering badly from rheumatism.

Among Urbina's forces was a captain called Fausto Borunda, who was notorious for his cruelty even in a nation where cruelty was commonplace. Borunda was known as The Matador because he always killed his prisoners.

When Urbina sacked Durango there were few prisoners, so Borunda made a round of the town's saloons. In each one he picked out some unarmed citizen and asked if he was a Huerta sympathiser. When the terrified man said no, Borunda shouted that he was lying and deserved to die for not telling the truth. Then he shot the man in cold blood.

Among Urbina's group, too, was Rodolfo Fierro, who was to acquire the dubious distinction of being the most ruthless killer in all the Revolution. Tall, moustached and heavily-built, Fierro was said personally to have executed 300 *Colorado* prisoners in one marathon murder session, pausing only to massage a bruised trigger finger.

Fierro's background was different from that of most of Villa's lieutenants. A freight guard with the Mexican National Railways, he had thrown in his lot with Villa during the Madero Revolution. When he rejoined the Villistas with Urbina he was appointed chief of the force's railway transportation.

A story which typifies Fierro's cruelty is told by Edward O'Reilly, one of Madero's Foreign Legionnaires who stayed on to fight through the Revolution:

'When we entered Guadalajara Fierro discovered an old enemy living in the city. The man had quit the insurrection and was working as a carpenter. In an accident his leg had been broken and when discovered by Fierro he was lying helpless.

'The Butcher had the injured man brought to the [rail-way] depot and placed on his private car. Next day I chanced to be on Fierro's car when we left the city. He was playing cards with a group of officers as the train started on its journey. After about nine miles he told the conductor to stop the train. Grasping the injured man by the collar he dragged him down the car steps, dropped him like a sack of meal by the side of the track and shot him through the head, signalled the train to start and then, stepping aboard, picked up his cards and resumed the game.

'It was the most cold-blooded, dastardly act I have ever seen.'

Villa and Fierro often had violent quarrels. On one occasion in Ciudad Juárez, Villa was with Bill Greet, the El Paso county clerk, and as they approached the railway station they saw Fierro berating a soldier who was wearing a sombrero on top of the official cap which had recently been issued. Fierro snatched the sombrero, crushed it and struck the soldier hard across the face.

Villa raced towards Fierro, grabbed his hat, broke it

across his knee and then struck Fierro across the cheek. Greet dodged behind a handy telegraph pole expecting bullets to fly, but Fierro walked away without a word and Villa, as he saw the apprehensive Greet, burst into uproarious laughter.

Why did unscrupulous ruffians like Fierro, Urbina and Borunda make no attempt to do away with Villa when it would have taken only a split second to put a bullet in his back? Greet felt it was because 'Villa always had every faculty developed to the keenest degree. He seldom smoked, he never drank. He was one of the best shots I have ever known, a sure shot.... A man knew that if he shot at Villa and missed he could count his death number right there and then.'

While he was brave to the point of recklessness in battle, Villa had a deadly fear of the unexpected and the unseen, and harboured a suspicion of everything and everyone which sprang from his outlaw days.

One of his precautions against the possibility of assassination was a refusal to sleep in the place he had first chosen for the night. And, because of a fear of poisoning, Villa rarely ate with his officers. Instead, with rough camaraderie, he would wander among his troops, taking meat from one man's plate, beans from another, until he had eaten his fill.

Other commanders who joined Villa that summer included Maclovio Herrera, the Parral mine worker who brought 400 men with him, the sinister-looking Calixto Contreras, an out-and-out bandit, Toribio Ortega, a cattleman from Chihuahua who was known to his troops as 'The Honourable' because he never killed prisoners and refused to take a penny from the Revolution beyond his meagre salary, Agustín Castro, once a tram conductor, and the quiet, cross-eyed Eugenio Aguirre Benavides, a member of one of the cultivated Mexican families that had gathered round Madero in 1910.

The commanders of the now formidable, if loosely-knit, force decided to make their first big assault on the vital communications centre of Torreón towards the end of September. Torreón, according to Patrick O'Hea who operated a ranch nearby, was 'misbegotten on an arid site for no better reason than that of the intersection of the railway lines, north and south, east and west'.

He described it as 'unpiped, undrained, unasphalted, un-refrigerated ... life's utmost luxury was that of window-screening against the flies by day and mosquitoes by night. ...'

Unattractive it certainly was, even by Mexican standards, but it was without doubt a highly important centre, astride the main line from Mexico City to the American border, and a rich community too, since it sat in the centre of a heavily-populated cotton-growing area known as La Laguna. Control of the town could isolate the Federal garrisons in the north from their source of supplies and reinforcements, Mexico City.

On 29 September Villa convened a meeting of commanders at the Hacienda de la Loma, near Torreón, to elect formally a supreme chief. They quickly and unanimously chose Villa as leader of the newly-named Division of the North, though according to Villa 'it displeased Tomás Urbina for me to be commander instead of him'. Villa had no doubts about the wisdom of the choice, though ... 'Urbina was a man of courage and ability but he would not have made a better chief than I.'

So Villa, who six months earlier had entered Mexico with eight men, now commanded an army of more than 8000.

He ordered them straight into action against the Torreón area, which was garrisoned by 2000 Federals, stiffened by a force of *Colorados* who knew they were fighting for their lives, and a volunteer corps of ranchers, industrial workers and Spaniards—a total of about 3000, well-equipped, thoroughly prepared and deeply dug in.

Bitter and confused fighting raged in the foothills around Torreón for three days. Patrick O'Hea, far from his home in Wimbledon, was with the Division of the North at this time, at a point where the hills which shielded the Villistas from the fire of the Federals broke away in a narrow canyon, which the rebels called the *calzada de la muerte* (the highway of death).

'It was one of the diversions of the wilder spirits to run whooping across this deadly zone, that might be safe for

hours on end, then suddenly be swept by the fire from the
defenders of the town ... I was reclining lazily near the
calzada de la muerte reflecting uncomfortably upon the
necessity of my recrossing it within the next hour, a feat
difficult of achievement with that degree of leisurely dignity
which was to be observed with the eyes of the camp upon me
... Nearby, under the shelter of the hill, a band of some
score of pieces was playing remarkably good music, breaking at last into a selection of airs from *Carmen*.

'It must have been the impulse of that music of blood and
sand that did it, for suddenly I realised that there strutted
right up the middle of the death path a tattered figure with
a red cloak over one shoulder and held at the hip in true
torero fashion. The man paused only when he had reached
a rise in the path, then doffed his hat and gallantly bowed to
death. Apolonio, the butt of the camp, *monosabio** they
called him in derision of his oft-repeated desire to enter the
ring, the excitement of which was even now sending the
blood tingling through his veins. It was the music from
Carmen that had done it!

'The spectators ... were hushed as the man stood poised
there where none other had dared to pause, and we watched
him in silence as he swung off his hat at arm's length and,
with the grandiose gesture of the ring, addressed the audience, then flung the hat backward over his shoulder and
unfolded the faded cape from his body.

'As if in answer to his defiance as he fluttered his cape
toward the town, there whizzed past him, and exploded
somewhere beyond, a shell from the battery of French quick-
firers on an eminence outside the town, the pseudo-mata-
dor's body curving and his cape out-fluttering as he felt the
rush of wind go by. . . .

'Five shots more followed in rapid succession, the ragged
lunatic with his faded red banner apparently playing them
like charging bulls, pirouetting, stiffening, curving and
swerving with twirling cape in true *torero* style. There must
have been a genuine sportsman in command of the enemy
battery that day, for there was no musketry and, although
another salvo roared past the figure upon its deadly

* The name given to a horseboy at the service of a *picador*.

eminence that now claimed the gaze of both camps, the artillerymen evidently were timing their fuses to explode well beyond the man that stamped at them and taunted them.

'Meantime, under cover of the cliff the band continued to play, and shouts of applause greeted each graceful lunge or swing ... and whenever the breathless and grimacing hero swung back to the adversary after a successful play, seeking applause, the band would crash into the wildest of *dianas*, that riotous frenzy from *Carmen* that makes the bull-fighter's heart leap, as the climax of his emotion and reward in the game with death.

'And surely no Fuentes, Bombita, or Machaquito, the *matadores* of those days, ever rose to greater heights of emotion than did this poor scarecrow ... *Otro toro*, yet another bull, and again a great missile hurled past him with a rush of wind and a deadly crash beyond and again the crowd shrieked and waved, and flung hats at him in delight as he strutted; and again the band broke into the wildest of *dianas*.'

Eventually, the Federal battery commander received orders to end the game.... A charge of shrapnel, exploding some thirty feet ahead of him, laid low the gallant *torero* as he faced the next 'bull'.

By the evening of 1 October the rebels had penetrated to the outskirts of Torreón. That night, bareheaded at Villa's orders to avoid confusion in the hand-to-hand fighting, the Division of the North burst forward in a massive, enveloping attack from three sides.

After a sharp fight the heavily outnumbered Federals abandoned their positions and retreated eastward, protected from pursuit and further harassment by the flood-waters of the River Nazas. Between dark and dawn the most important centre in northern Mexico had fallen to Villa.

The booty totalled thirteen cannon, including the railway-mounted three-inch artillery piece called El Niño (The Infant) which became the pride of the revolutionary army. 600 grenades, 1000 rifles, half a million cartridges and six machine-guns—welcome addition to the Division's five home-made cannon and two machine-guns—and, more important, forty railway engines and a vast amount of rolling stock. Now Villa's newly-equipped army could really travel in style.

Appalled by the complete lack of facilities for his wounded, Villa ordered some of the captured carriages to be converted into a travelling hospital. Villa's hospital train, the only one of any effectiveness ever carried by a Mexican army, eventually came to be staffed by sixty American and Mexican doctors, headed by Dr Andres Villareal, a graduate of Johns Hopkins University, Baltimore, and a hundred nurses. Forty carriages, fitted with the most up-to-date medical equipment and appliances, enamelled inside and smartly painted outside, became operating theatres and wards, located only minutes from the fighting.

Villa set up his headquarters in the Hotel Salvador and, always a stickler for plundering in good order, levied a 'loan' of £300,000 from the Torreón banks and distributed money and food to the poor of the town.

In accordance with a decree issued by Carranza, all captured Federal officers who refused to join the Constitutionalist side were shot. Their execution caused the American magazine *Review of Reviews* to comment that the Constitutionalists had 'disgraced their cause'.

Villa's treatment of the Spanish residents of Torreón also brought a horrified reaction in the American and European Press. Convinced that all Spaniards were Huerta supporters —as indeed most of them were—Villa ordered them to 'get out of my Mexico' and told critics that he was treating the Spaniards no differently from the way they had for centuries treated his people. The luckless Spaniards had their property confiscated and were forced to leave Torreón under threat of death.

The fall of Torreón came at a bad time for Huerta. On 23 September a Senator, Dr Belisario Domínguez, denounced the dictator from the floor of the Chamber of Deputies and when the official Debates Diary discreetly omitted his speech, Dr Domínguez had it printed and circulated in the city. He was arrested at his home by secret police and his bullet-riddled body was found a few days later in a ditch.

When he was denounced in Congress for the murder

Huerta struck again; Congress was dissolved and 110 Congressmen were arrested in the Chamber during a sitting and carted off to prison in tramcars. The government newspaper *El Imparcial* failed to live up to its name by dismissing the incident in eleven lines.

Washington's indignation was increased when Sir Lionel Carden tactlessly chose to present his ministerial credentials to Huerta the day after the arrests occurred. Huerta, delighted with this boost from Britain, justified his actions by comparing Mexico to an ill man who needed an immediate operation.

Huerta issued public assurances that all would be well after the elections, scheduled for 26 October. As promised, Huerta did not put himself forward as a candidate, but as the date approached it became obvious that he intended to retain power, no matter what the election outcome.

There were four official candidates: Félix Díaz, Federico Gamboa, who had resigned as Foreign Minister to run for the presidency, Manuel Calero and David de la Fuente. Díaz returned from Japan a few days before the election in order to be constitutionally eligible, but was afraid to go to Mexico City, despite assurances of safe conduct. He stayed in Veracruz, at a hotel next to the American consulate, to await the outcome of the voting.

It was made plain that Huerta never intended to permit anyone to take over when he commented to O'Shaughnessy on Gamboa's candidature: 'I wished him well but if he had been elected president I should have had him shot.'

Not surprisingly, the election was a farce. On election day John Lind and the American consul in Veracruz, William Canada, went to watch the polling in the town. The only sign of activity was a lone official collecting ballots in a cigar box. He loyally put several slips in the box himself and, as far as the Americans were able to discover, they were the only votes cast in Veracruz.

Things were not much better in Mexico City. In many places the ballot boxes, consisting of anything from cardboard shoeboxes to chemists' jars, remained empty. Yet the government kept up the farce by reporting that returns were 'coming in slowly' and expressing doubt about the result.

In fact, there was never any doubt. Of the scattering of votes cast, Huerta, although not a candidate, received a majority.

Félix Díaz was in no doubt about the outcome, either. The day after the 'election' he fled from his judiciously-chosen hotel to the American consulate, where he sought political asylum, saying that his life was in danger. That night he was smuggled aboard the American gunboat USS *Wheeling* in Veracruz harbour, and then transferred to the battleship USS *Louisiana*, which took him to Cuba.

Taking its cue from Huerta, the submissive Congress, which now contained so many army officers that it was suggested a bugle should replace the chairman's bell, assembled in November, declared the elections void and called for new elections in July, 1914. Meantime, Huerta was 'authorised' to continue as interim president. Addressing Congress, Huerta excused his retention of power with the comment 'In saving the country one does not violate any law.'

The British writer Hamilton Fyfe watched Huerta address Congress and described the scene in a *Daily Mail* article headed 'A Barrack Room President':

'Through the crowded Chamber of Deputies ... there stepped lightly, with hand upraised to acknowledge the cheers which greeted him, a ... thickly built soldier whose briskness belied his fifty-nine years.

'He wore evening dress, as did all members of Parliament. The only distinction which set him apart from the rest was a broad sash of the Mexican national colours across his shirt front. His dome-like skull gleamed bald under the light. Closely cropped grey hair covered back and sides. His complexion was dark but it was only when you noticed the hand against his shirt cuff that you realised his pure Indian descent. Clearly his sight was very weak; he added another pair to the spectacles he already wore before he began to read his message to the new Congress.'

Fyfe went on to explain to British readers that Huerta 'is in private a jovial companion' and cited the example when, at a gathering of British residents, Huerta urged marriage upon an elderly spinster, offering her any rebel leader she might fancy.

But he pointed out, 'From a ruler two qualities are demanded in which Huerta is lacking—dignity and tact ...
Huerta brings the methods of the barrack room to the
Council Chamber: to that incongruity are attributable both
his weakness and his strength.'

Fyfe ended with a fascinating description of the Chamber: 'The Mexican Parliament, it is true, is not quite like
European Assemblies. The members smoke, for instance;
the liberal supply of spitoons on the floor of the House
would, I fear, shock Mr Asquith and Mr Bonar Law. It is
not the custom, either, of British M.P.s to keep firearms in
their lockers. When the desks of the arrested Congressmen
were searched most of them were found to contain loaded
revolvers.'

The farcical elections had hardened President Wilson's
determination into implacability: Huerta must go. On 1
November he requested the European nations who had recognised Huerta 'to impress upon him the wisdom of retirement...' But Huerta was not considering retirement. He
told an American newspaperman, 'I shall not retire until
I am six feet underground.' And to Luis d'Antin, a clerk
at the American Embassy, he said, 'Mexico is like a snake;
all its life is in its head.' Then he banged his head with
his fist and added, 'I am the head of Mexico, and until I
am crushed she will survive.'

Wilson's reaction was a message to all governments,
castigating Huerta's usurpation as a menace to the peace
and development of Latin America. The note sounded an
ominous warning: 'If General Huerta does not retire by
force of circumstances it will become the duty of the United
States to use less peaceful means to put him out. . . .'

But Wilson wrote to a friend, Mrs Mary Hulbert, confess-
ing 'a sneaking admiration' for Huerta's doggedness. 'It
makes the task of smoking him out so much more interesting.'

Wilson added that Huerta was 'always so perfectly in
character; so false, so sly, so full of bravado (the bravado of
ignorance, chiefly) and yet so courageous, too, and determined—such a mixture of weak and strong, of ridiculous
and respectable! ... He will not let go until he pulls the

whole house down with him ... he is seldom sober and always impossible and yet what an indomitable fighter for his own land!'

From Veracruz Lind bombarded Wilson with cables urging action against Huerta. He advocated the sale of equipment to the Constitutionalist armies and even planted in Wilson's mind the thought of military intervention which was soon to bear such terrible fruit.

Lind believed that in Pancho Villa the revolutionaries had 'an intrepid and resourceful leader, possessed of the highest moral, physical and mental efficiency', and on 15 November he informed Secretary of State Bryan, 'I should not worry if some of the verandahs and French windows [in Mexico City] were demolished. General Villa, for instance, would do the job satisfactorily.'

Lind was also scathingly critical of Britain, and particularly of Sir Lionel Carden. He felt that the timing of Carden's presentation of credentials had been a deliberate effort to strengthen Huerta, and even blamed Britain for the failure of his own mission. When he went to Mexico City, Lind turned down an invitation from Carden to have tea, and instead dined with the German Minister, von Hintze, who was delighted to hear of the American's hostility towards Britain.

On 14 December Lind cabled Bryan, 'England may talk fair in Washington but in Mexico I tell you she is manoeuvering every moment to ... place us in an embarrassing light before the world. ... The constant ridicule by Carden of the American government and American policies ... has its baneful influence.'

The next day O'Shaughnessy added his voice to the criticisms of Carden with this message to Bryan: 'I cannot too strongly appeal to you to bring the Machiavellian intrigues of the British Minister here to the attention of his government.'

At this time, with trouble looming in Europe, a row with the Americans was the last thing Britain wanted. So, in an attempt to clear up any misunderstandings over Mexico, the British government sent Sir William Tyrrell, the Private Secretary of Sir Edward Grey, to Washington.

His first taste of American officialdom was a ludicrous

interview with Bryan, who lectured him on the wickedness of the British Empire and said that the British oil barons in Mexico were the 'paymasters of the cabinet'.

Tyrrell who had a keen sense of humour, replied 'You are wrong. The cabinet have grown so greedy that Lord Cowdray hasn't the money to reach their price.'

'Ah,' said Bryan triumphantly, 'then you admit the charge.'

As he left, Tyrrell bowed to Bryan and said, 'You have stripped me naked, Mr Secretary, but I am unashamed.'

Tyrrell had a more satisfactory interview with President Wilson on 13 November and was delighted by the President's charm and intelligence. He assured Wilson that oil interests were not dictating British policy and stressed that his country was willing to accept any Mexican policy in which the United States would take the lead.

'When I return to England I shall be asked to explain your Mexican policy,' said Sir William. 'Can you tell me what it is?'

Wilson replied, 'I am going to teach the South American republics to elect good men.'

'Yes,' replied Tyrrell, 'but I shall have to explain this to Englishmen who cannot see the difference between Huerta, Carranza and Villa.'

The only answer Tyrrell obtained to this was that Carranza was the best of the three and that Villa was not so bad as he had been painted.

As a result of Tyrrell's talks, Britain fell into line with American wishes over Carden. Confidential word was passed to Ambassador Page in London that the British Minister's days in Mexico were numbered. Page, who had been campaigning tactfully for Sir Lionel's removal, happily informed his government, who committed the colossal blunder of releasing the information to the Washington press.

Carden was sacked in the finest British style by being promoted to the Embassy in Brazil, though he died in London the following year without ever taking up the appointment. Carden's brief stay in Mexico ended in farcical circumstances in February 1914. A large crowd turned up at the station when he left for Veracruz and the Briton was

Mobilisation – a Federal soldier bids farewell to his wife and child.

Pancho Villa (left) and a group of his supporters.

Emiliano Zapata

Revolutionary justice – execution of an unknown man, whose dog can be seen at his feet.

Pancho Villa was one of the few men to face a Mexican firing squad and live to tell the tale.

The Revolutionary song 'Adelita' celebrates this *soldadera*, the most famous of all the women revolutionaries.

The Revolution was perhaps the first war in which railways
played a vital part.

The historic meeting in the National Palace, December 1914.

Villistas hanged by General Murguia, who thought them
'not worth a bullet'.

The railway system was all too vulnerable; here a Villista force has successfully blown up a locomotive.

General Pershing's forces moving across border country in pursuit of Villa, 1916.

delighted with the cheers as his train pulled out. But the cheers were for a group of departing bullfighters who, according to Mrs O'Shaughnessy, 'were always first in the hearts of their countrymen'.

Huerta, who was finding international diplomacy rather too complicated, was steadily losing ground at home, too. The newspaper *Novedades* summed up his plight when it printed a cartoon showing two nurses beside an invalid Huerta. One nurse asked how he was progressing and the other replied 'No change. He can't move yet.'

Mexican waters were teeming with foreign warships hovering off the coasts to 'protect national interests'. The Americans led the field with sixteen, the Germans had three, Britain had the cruisers *Suffolk* and *Essex* and the French and Japanese were also represented.

By December 1913 Mexico's financial system, that solid structure of the Limantour days, had been reduced to utter chaos. In less than a year the peso had declined from its parity of forty-nine and a half American cents to twenty-nine. Currency was being circulated by the Constitutionalists and lavishly designed notes began to appear with pictures of smoking volcanoes, high-busted women and crossed guns and bandoliers, all covered with scrawled, and completely inadequate, signatures.

Shortly before Christmas Huerta had to rescue the banks, which were unable to meet the demand for gold and silver coin. He did it, in typical knot-cutting fashion, by decreeing a succession of holidays which enabled the banks to stay closed; first it was for three days, then ten days, then a month. The closure of the banks reduced the situation in the capital to absurdity. Rents and bills were impossible to collect, mortgages went unpaid and creditors found it useless to attempt legal action against debtors.

And in an effort to combat the growing Constitutionalist threat, Huerta authorised the stepping-up of conscription and press-gang methods, particularly in Mexico City. Seven hundred men were seized while watching a bullfight and marched off to barracks. When a big crowd turned out to a fire in the capital another thousand were roped in, including women, who were put to work in the ammunition factories. Mrs O'Shaughnessy wrote: 'A friend told me this morning that the father, mother, two brothers and sister of one of her servants were taken last week. They scarcely dare, any of them, go out after dark. Posting a letter may mean, literally, going to the cannon's mouth.'

A grocery store rang the American Embassy to apologise for failure to deliver an order: they explained that the delivery boy had been seized by the press-gang, together with the Embassy's groceries.

Another sixty-five conscripts were rounded up at a film show, which had been advertised as 'for men only'. When the audience discovered that the films were religious, they protested violently. The police were called in, the audience were arrested and enrolled in the army.

The conscripts understandably showed little enthusiasm for the régime that had dragged them from their homes and jobs, and they often had to be locked into the transportation which took them to the north.

Eduardo N. Iturbide, the governor of the Federal District in 1914 under Huerta, criticised the dictator's drafting methods. 'At the beginning of this practice ... the lower classes, the poor type of Indians, were the subject of the drafting. They were mere automatons, doing as they were bid to the letter but utterly lacking in initiative.... Eventually this class of recruit became exhausted and General Huerta then sent forth into all sections of the city and took each and everyone he could get ...

'In this abuse of a bad practice he gathered in the educated and the uneducated, schoolteachers, mechanics, chauffeurs etc. When they were confined in their barracks the men who had been drafted in this manner rebelled against the treatment they received and soon started making speeches to the others, so that in a short time instead of organisation in his army, General Huerta had insurrection bursting into flame in every quarter.'

Huerta remained content to defend the towns with the reluctant soldiers, and only Villa and his Division of the North were prepared to dispute Federal possession of the main centres in the closing months of 1913.

After his headline-making capture of Torreón, Villa was confident he could take Chihuahua City, and with it gain control of the state. He also realised that in Torreón his army was dangerously extended, out of touch with the

other Constitutionalist forces and a long way from its
source of guns and ammunition on the American border.
Villa risked a disastrous defeat if he chose to stand at
Torreón against the strong Federal relief force which would
undoubtedly be sent. So he decided to leave behind a garrison brigade, swing back north and attempt to take Chihuahua City, capital of the state which he regarded as his
base.

As the Division of the North rolled back into the desert
in a hooting procession of troop trains, their commander
rode, literally, in the van—a guard's van, painted red and
converted into his travelling home and headquarters. And
with him went his latest wife, a girl called Juanita Torres
whom he had met and wed after a whirlwind courtship in
Torreón.

Villa, honourable in his ardour, was a firm believer in
marriage. So much so that he had at least four 'legal'
wives—María Luz Corral, Soledad Seanez, Austreberta
Rentería and Juanita Torres—and after his assassination in
1923 five 'widows' claimed his estate.

María Luz Corral, his first wife, whom he had married
in 1911, is the one who has lasted the distance and won
wealth and reputation as Pancho Villa's widow. Seventy-
three years old, she is a small, stout woman with a ready
smile.

One feels she has had the last laugh on the unfaithful
Pancho and all his other women as she shows you round
the tiny museum in her house, Quinta Luz, on the outskirts
of Chihuahua City. She does a profitable business with the
procession of visitors who want to inspect Pancho's pictures, swords, guns and the bullet-riddled car in which he
met his end.

But during the Revolution Luz Corral suffered many
moments of degradation. Once, when she attempted to
cross from Ciudad Juárez into El Paso, she was stopped by
American Customs men and told that one Señora Villa had
already entered the United States. When she confronted
Villa with this, he shrugged, laughed and arranged to have
a letter written explaining that she was his first and legal
wife and that no other was to be recognised by American
officials.

At one time three Señora Villas were living in Chihuahua, and it was said that when Villa married Austreberta Rentería, who was Luz Corral's dressmaker, his first wife was forced to serve breakfast in bed to the honeymoon couple.

And, after the fall of Mexico City, Villa precipitated an international crisis when he abducted a pretty French receptionist from an hotel, taking her rejection of his offer of marriage as nothing more than shyness.

But, for the time being, Juanita Torres was the one in possession in Villa's travelling home which, apart from chintz curtains at the windows, had few homely touches. The interior was partitioned into two rooms—a kitchen and a bedroom. The bedroom, ten feet by twenty, was the heart of the Division of the North. In it were held the councils of war, when upwards of two dozen commanders crammed into the carriage.

On the walls were tacked pictures of the pin-up girls of those days, a large picture of Carranza, one of Villa himself and one of Fierro. Two double-width foldaway bunks were almost the only furniture.

But this was luxury indeed compared with the travelling conditions of the army and its followers. The carriages and goods wagons carried soldiers and their families three layers deep; the lucky ones inside, others on top and a few brave hearts, mostly boys and young men, in hammocks slung between the wheels. Soldiers, women and children camped out on top of the trains in all weathers, setting up ramshackle shelters of blankets and umbrellas. Every inch of space was taken. Some hardy women made their temporary homes on the front platforms of the engines themselves, building fires of twigs and baking their *tortillas* unconcernedly as the army crawled north to fresh battles, accompanied by the crackle of rifles loosed off by high-spirited troops at coyotes, cattle, donkeys—in fact, almost anything that moved within shooting distance of the railway.

As he approached Chihuahua City, Villa addressed a note 'in the politest of terms' to the fat little Federal commander, General Salvador Mercado, requesting him to surrender within twenty-four hours or move out of the city and fight at the spot of his own choice. When Mercado, whose garrison of Federals and *Colorados* totalled some 7000, ignored this courteous message, Villa threw his whole Division into violent assault on 5 November. By 10 p.m. two hills in the suburbs had been overrun and the fighting raged through the night. But next day the Federal artillery shelled the advance to a halt. The deadlock continued all that day, through the night and on through 7 November. That night Villa, running short of ammunition and reserves, broke off the action and withdrew south, heavily shelled by the jubilant Federals.

While supervising the withdrawal Villa had a miraculous escape. He had just walked away from his headquarters tent to receive a dispatch when a shell landed near it, killing Dr Samuel Navarro, chief of the Medical Corps, who had taken Villa's chair when he moved away.

Villa had been wrong. Chihuahua City had proved too strong. So instead, Villa devised a brilliant scheme for a surprise attack on Ciudad Juárez, the border town. Leaving behind his trains, his camp followers and most of his army south of Chihuahua City, Villa took 2000 men northward under cover of darkness on 13 November. They circled the city and next day ambushed a south-bound coal train and captured a railway telegrapher.

A pistol was put at the telegrapher's head and he was told to wire the following message to Ciudad Juárez in the official code: 'Line to Chihuahua burned by Revolutionaries. Send repair engine and orders.'

Back came the message that there were no repair engines to spare. Villa sent another message that a big cloud of dust was visible, perhaps rebels. The train was promptly ordered back to Ciudad Juárez. Promptly, Villa obliged.

The 200 miles to the border were swiftly covered and the Mexican Revolution's coal-black version of the Trojan Horse rolled through the town's defences and into the goods yard at midnight, unchallenged and utterly unsuspected.

As Villa's picked force surged through the sleeping town the only resistance came from the jail garrison, who were quickly surrounded. There was a shock for the border gamblers in the town casino when Villa's men burst into the gaming rooms. Employees and customers were lined up against the walls while the rebels cleaned out the gamblers, collecting about £30,000.

The Juárez garrison commanders were General Cesáreo Castro, one of the men who had persuaded Huerta not to execute Villa in 1912, and General Trucy Aubert, a French-descended Mexican. Three nights before the surprise attack the generals and their headquarters staff had paid a visit to the Crawford Theatre in El Paso, where, after the show, they were entertained by the cast, the Gilmore Brown Stock Company. On the night of Villa's attack the American actors were guests of the Federal officers at the Black Cat Café in Juárez, having been driven over the border after the show by the company chauffeur, Charles Seggerson. While the others went in to dine Seggerson stayed outside, saying he preferred to sleep in the car.

The Americans, entertaining the officers and café patrons, were halfway through the 'Miserere' from *Il Trovatore* when two dozen armed Villistas burst into the room. The Americans were led outside and, as they were being told they would be sent back to El Paso, they noticed the body of Seggerson slumped over the steering-wheel of their car. Stray shots, drowned by the singing, had killed him as he slept.

At dawn on 15 November the beleaguered jail garrison surrendered; Villa had captured Mexico's most important border town without losing a man. Huerta was so shaken by the fall of Juárez that he accused General Castro of having surrendered to Villa for 50,000 dollars.

The international bridges across the Rio Grande were reopened and captured Federal Army musicians were marched through the town, both to celebrate the victory and to assure American watchers that all was well. Villa met El Paso's mayor, E. C. Kelly, at noon at the Stanton Street Bridge and expressed regret about the death of Seggerson. Villa assured Kelly that all Americans within his zone of authority would receive full protection and promised he would meet the expected Federal counter-attack far enough south to avoid the danger of bullets flying across the border into El Paso, as had happened in 1911.

Villa did not forget that General Castro had helped to save his life a year before. The captured commander was allowed to cross into El Paso. But other officer prisoners were not so fortunate; seventy-four officials and army men were executed.

The morning after the capture of the town, many American curiosity seekers crossed into Juárez. One group of women approached the barracks and heard a volley, which they presumed was a rifle squad at practice. A man standing inside the barracks gates casually warned them not to come closer, since they would probably not care to see the Villista firing squads executing their prisoners. 'That was the twenty-first you heard just now,' he told them.

'Good gracious,' one of the women said to him, 'they're not going to shoot you, are they?' At that moment a guard touched the man on the shoulder. With a sweeping bow and a flourish of his hat he was gone. A moment later the horrified Americans heard the twenty-second volley.

On 16 November the American Sunday papers feasted on Villa's triumph. Overnight he became the best-known figure in the Revolution and *Collier's Magazine* even referred to the revolt against Huerta as 'Villa's uprising'.

The capture of Juárez was the turning point in the struggle against Huerta in the north. Now the revolutionaries could easily obtain the supposedly embargoed arms. Weapons flowed across the Rio Grande, hidden in piano cases, buried in wagons of coal, packed away in crates of tinned goods. The Constitutionalists were happy to pay the extortionate prices demanded.

The Federal reaction to the fall of Juárez was swift and predictable. As the Division of the North celebrated the third anniversary of Madero's Revolution on 20 November, news was flashed that a large enemy force was advancing north along the railway line from Chihuahua in eleven trains.

Villa ordered Rodolfo Fierro, his railways expert, to destroy the line and delay the Federals as long as possible. This Fierro did with habitual flair and coolness, wrecking the line about forty-five miles south of Juárez, within sight and cannon range of the advancing Federals.

Villa chose his battle site carefully, bearing in mind his

promise to Mayor Kelly. He decided to fight at Tierra Blanca, thirty-five miles south of Juárez, occupying high ground and forcing the Federals into a sandy plain where they would be unable to get water.

To prevent alarm on the frontier Villa ordered a review of his troops, fully armed and mounted, on the morning of 21 November, ostensibly as part of the anniversary celebrations. His forces, swollen by the arrival of most of the Division of the North, numbered over 6000. After the impressive parade, the troops moved off—but not back to their quarters. They wheeled out of town, climbed aboard waiting trains and headed south. They were just in time. That afternoon the Federals, about 5500 strong, reached Tierra Blanca.

Through the night and all next day the armies sullenly faced each other, the desert stillness broken occasionally as some nervous soldier let off his gun. On the night of 22 November Villa, growing impatient, ordered an attack but called it off when he received reports of Federal cavalry on the move, obviously preparing for action the next morning.

The Federals attacked at dawn, throwing their main weight against Villa's right flank in a bid to capture Bauche railway station and its precious water tanks. But they were beaten off. Next day the Federals, their water almost gone, tried again, this time on Villa's left, only to be forced back once more. The Constitutionalists, by contrast, were well supplied with food, water and ammunition from Juárez. Sympathetic Americans donated blankets, medicine and money. Private cars brought medical supplies and nurses from El Paso and the wounded were shuttled back by train to Juárez, where families converted their homes to accommodate them when the hospitals became full.

By 25 November fighting was raging along a front which extended almost to the Texas border. The Federals, now desperate for a breakthrough, began to force back Villa's army. Seeing that his left flank was in danger of collapse, Villa decided on his favourite tactic, *un golpe terrifico* (a terrific blow), a massed cavalry charge into the heart of the enemy. Two cannon shots signalled the charge, which swept through the white-uniformed Federals like a grass-fire. Their infantry were caught in the open, artillery was stranded in the sand. It became a rout, then a slaughter.

The survivors piled aboard their trains and hastily pulled back towards Chihuahua City. But not all made it. Fierro galloped alongside one train, leaped aboard, released the brake cylinder and halted it. All the occupants were massacred.

Villa reported triumphantly, 'I have completely routed the enemy. They are in full and shameless flight.'

In three days of bloody battle the Federals had lost almost a thousand men and three trains. They had also lost the state of Chihuahua.

Three days later General Mercado, commanding what was left of the Chihuahua garrison, abandoned a city he was no longer able to defend. Accompanied by a pathetic band of Huerta sympathisers and refugees, Mercado's force slogged painfully eastwards through the desert, harried all the way by small rebel bands. They finally reached the border town of Ojinaga on 7 December. At least a hundred had been killed during the march and an unknown number had died of exhaustion or deserted.

In Ojinaga, with the Rio Grande at their backs and the safety of the United States only yards away, the Federal force of 3500—which included forty-five majors, twenty-one colonels and eleven generals—dug in and waited for Villa to catch up with them. General Mercado, 'a pathetic, worried figure' according to John Reed, slumped in his headquarters blaming the defeat at Tierra Blanca on 'intervention of American soldiers'.

One of the Chihuahua 'refugees' was the multi-millionaire Luis Terrazas. Knowing that he would be the first target of Villa's execution squads, Terrazas collected his wealth, art treasures and heirlooms into twenty wagons, abandoned his estates and fled to Ojinaga. From there he moved to El Paso, where he rented the home of a Senator, Albert B. Fall. The family lived well, however, even in exile. One of the Terrazas children was late for school one morning in El Paso and when his teacher demanded an explanation he told her, 'My valet was not there this morning and I could not find which clothes to wear.'

But not all the Terrazas family escaped Villa's vengeance.

Luis junior, the fifty-two-year-old son of the hated *hacendado*, failed to get away from Chihuahua City in time, and took refuge in the British consulate, from which he was forcibly removed by Villa's men when they entered the town on 8 December.

Villa demanded a £50,000 ransom from old Terrazas in exchange for the life of his son, who was the father of thirteen children. Luis junior was held prisoner for three months in a marble house belonging to his family. Villa rejected appeals for his release with the comment, 'If some people had Pancho Villa a prisoner in the same circumstances do you think they would house him in a palace? No, they would parade Villa's head on a pike. The Terrazas family gained immense wealth by oppressing the people; now the people demand restitution.'

Eventually Villa announced that unless the ransom was paid, Terrazas would be sent as a common soldier to the battlefront 'where I cannot be responsible for his life'.

The dilemma was ended, however, when Luis managed to escape and make his way to safety in El Paso. But he had been so ill-treated that, according to Bill Greet, 'he could not look a man in the eyes'. Three months later Luis died as a result of the suffering he had undergone.

The Spaniards also suffered again when Chihuahua City fell to Villa. He summoned the British vice-consul, Mr Henry Scobell, who represented Spanish interests in the city, and ordered the expulsion of all Spaniards. 'Tell them to pack,' Villa said to Scobell. 'Any Spaniard caught within this state will be escorted to the nearest wall by a firing squad. . . .'

Scobell managed to obtain ten days' grace for the Spaniards but Villa refused them the use of the railways, and 400 men, women and children were forced to make their own way through 300 miles of desert and mountains, abandoning their possessions on the way, until they reached Torreón, which had been recaptured the previous month by Huerta's forces.

With the city swept clean of his enemies, Villa put his soldiers to work running the electricity plant, public transport, waterworks, telephone exchange, flour mills and slaughterhouses. He even tried to operate the brewery but failed because he could not find an expert maltster in his army. 'The only thing to do with soldiers in time of peace is to put them to work,' he reasoned. 'An idle soldier is always thinking of war.'

During the build-up for the drive south Villa set about re-equipping his army. Vast quantities of American khaki were purchased, together with the broad-brimmed Texas 'scout' hats favoured by the American forces at that time. Tinned meat and food was bought by the trainload. Clothing, shoes and war material rolled into Juárez. These purchases were often accompanied by job-lot accessories. One brigade was issued with—and proudly sported—magenta socks; another got silk bandanas and orchid shirts. Some of the cavalry took to wearing car goggles.

But many of Villa's soldiers remained in a picturesque state of raggedness. Some were clad in overalls, some in peasant white. Some had shoes, some sandals, some were barefooted. But none was without a rifle, a big flapping sombrero and a *sarape*, the all-purpose blanket which also served as overcoat, sunshade and makeshift tent. Some wore faded pictures of Christ and the Virgin pinned to the front of their sombreros. One extrovert in Urbina's brigade was weighed down by a floppy sombrero which carried five pounds of tarnished gold braid, once probably the pride of some wealthy *hacendado*.

The lessons of surprise and speed in his attacks, particularly in the brilliant capture of Ciudad Juárez, had not been lost on Villa. He chose this period of reorganisation to form an élite force, known as the *Dorados* (The Golden Ones) because of the gold insignia they wore on their olive uniforms and Stetsons. There were three squadrons, each of 100 horsemen. They were the pick of his cavalry, superbly mounted and armed. Each man owned two horses, a rifle and two pistols. Most important of all, the *Dorados* were unencumbered by camp followers, enabling them to strike swiftly. The *Dorados* were proud of their distinction, and their skill and daring paved the way for many Villa victories in the next eighteen months.

The year, which had begun on such a high note for Huerta, ended badly for him. In the north-west of the Republic Obregón had easily taken control of the lightly-defended state of Sonora, in the north-east Pablo González was preparing to move against the Federal-garrisoned towns of Monterrey and Saltillo and in Chihuahua the only remaining pocket of Federal resistance was in Ojinaga; and in the mountains around Mexico City the Zapatistas were still tying down a large government force.

Huerta remained pathetically eager for U.S. recognition and his public references to President Wilson were invariably couched in terms of respect and courtesy. He even sent Wilson a New Year's greeting: 'The Mexican Republic, through me, has the honour of wishing a happy year to the glorious people of the United States, so worthily represented by Your Excellency.'

But at a New Year's Eve reception in Chapultepec Palace he told assembled diplomats that, while he realised Mexico was an adolescent compared with the great powers like Britain, France, Germany and Spain (the United States was not mentioned) his country was entitled to be allowed to develop 'along her own lines'.

One author has compared Mexico's political development at this stage to that of pre-Bastille France. But Wilson was still persisting in expecting Mexico to behave like a modern democracy. His attitude was supported by most American public opinion, but there were occasional exceptions. The *North American Review* of December 1913 asked, 'What legal or moral right has a President of the United States to say who shall or shall not be President of Mexico?'

Huerta worried about his public image in the United States. He told Nelson O'Shaughnessy at a reception, 'After the country is pacified I am going to Washington in my best clothes just to show them I am not a blood-smeared savage clad in a breech-clout with a bottle of *aguardiente* in one hand and a *machete* in the other.'

The final pocket of Federal resistance in Chihuahua disappeared on 10 January 1914 with Villa's capture of Ojinaga. While the citizens of the Texas border town of Presidio watched from their rooftops in bitterly cold weather, Villa launched one of his *golpes terrificos*, ordering his men to take the town in an hour and a half. In fact, Ojinaga fell in less than an hour as the dispirited Federals, swollen to 5000 by women, children and camp followers, splashed frantically across the Rio Grande to internment in the United States. Among those who got away were Pascual Orozco, the man Villa would most have liked to lay his hands on, and General Mercado.

The Mexicans were herded into a vast corral by American soldiers and afterwards transported to the army camp at Fort Bliss, near El Paso, where a site of sixty acres was prepared for them and where most of them settled down happily, in conditions far better than those they had known in their homeland.

A few of the Ojinaga defenders managed to escape both Villa and the Americans. One of these was General Ynes Salazar, who got away into Texas only to suffer a tragi-comic fate. He was arrested on a train just short of the Mexican border for playing cards. 'I never suspected that in a free country you could not do such a thing,' he grumbled as he rejoined his companions in internment at Fort Bliss.

There was a lot of grumbling in the United States, too, about the hospitality being afforded the defeated Federals. *Collier's Magazine* published a full-page cartoon of Fort Bliss with the caption 'If You're Tired of Revoluting, Try Our Rest Cure. Uncle Sam Foots the Bills.'

When he heard of the loss of Ojinaga, Huerta declared his intention of having General Mercado shot if he ever returned from internment.

On 3 February another prop was knocked from beneath Huerta when Wilson changed his policy of 'watchful waiting' to one of active support for the Constitutionalists by lifting the embargo on arms to the rebels. Huerta was not over-disturbed by the news, commenting that Wilson's move would merely legalise the arms smuggling that had been going on. But the government newspapers of Mexico City were outraged. *El Imparcial* commented that Wilson was at last unmasked as the friend of bandits and assassins and called him, 'The Wicked Puritan with sorry horse teeth.'

When O'Shaughnessy lodged an official protest about the article, its author, Díaz Miron, announced his intention of shooting the American chargé d'affaires but never carried out the threat.

Von Hintze, the German Minister in Mexico, labelled Wilson's move as another step towards American occupation of all the land between Texas and Panama, and he offered to replace England's waning support of the Huerta régime with help from Germany if Huerta would guarantee to cut off oil supplies to Britain in case of war in Europe. Germany immediately backed up the offer by dispatching three arms ships, *Ypiranga, Bavaria* and *Kronprinzessin Cecilie*, from Hamburg. It was on this voyage that the *Ypiranga*, which had taken Porfirio Díaz into exile three years earlier, was to sail to fame as the ship which provoked the American invasion of Veracruz in April.

It was particularly unfortunate for the rebel cause that on the very day President Wilson lifted the arms embargo, an act of banditry caused the death of fifty-one people, including six Americans, in northern Mexico. A rebel leader named Maximo Castillo, who claimed allegiance to Villa, captured and burned a coal train in the Cumbre Tunnel, near Pearson in north-west Chihuahua. He then allowed a passenger train to plough into the wreckage in the tunnel in an attempt to obtain gold and valuables from the train.

At the time of the disaster Villa was in Ciudad Juárez. He ordered immediate pursuit and seven of Castillo's band were captured and shot near the Mormon settlement of Colonia Dublán. Castillo fled into the United States and was arrested near Hachita, New Mexico, and taken to Fort Bliss. Villa pleaded with American border officials, 'Give him to me; he shall have a fair trial and then I shall have him publicly shot.' But Castillo, who was suffering from advanced tuberculosis, died in imprisonment in the United States on 4 May.

President Wilson's blind faith in the Constitutionalists took another severe knock later in February. Again Villa was involved. This time, however, he sparked an international crisis. He was in Juárez on February 17, arranging for the purchase of a shipment of arms from the United States, when William S. Benton, a fifty-three-year-old

Scotsman, came to Villa's headquarters seeking an interview.

Benton, a native of Aberdeen, had lived in Mexico for thirty years and had carved a fortune out of the country. He owned a 150,000 acre ranch called Los Remedios, near Santa Ysabel in Chihuahua, for which he had paid £25,000 and on which he had made so many improvements that by 1914 it had become a showplace and was worth almost ten times as much. He also owned several mines.

Benton was hard-working, proud and strong-willed. His soldierly bearing and discipline bore testimony to the military background of his family. His maternal grandfather, a Colonel Hay, had taken part in the Charge of the Light Brigade.

Benton's property had suffered increasingly from predatory bands and by 1914 he had had enough. Benton, known to his workers as *el inglés turbulento*, the stormy Englishman, was not the type of man to take this treatment quietly. He decided to see Villa. Before he left for Juárez a friend, Charles Qualey, warned him, 'Be careful of Villa; if he gives you a lecture do not resent it. If you do you may get into trouble.'

Benton replied, 'If he lectures me I'll lecture back. I have never made a political move in Mexico and if he accuses me I'll have some accusations of my own to make.'

Two tempestuous men were on collision course. When Benton arrived at Villa's headquarters a violent quarrel broke out. What happened afterwards is the subject of many conflicting stories, but Villa maintained that Benton, in a rage, attempted to pull a gun on him and was disarmed by guards.

The unfortunate Benton had touched off Villa's explosive temperament and he paid the penalty. Villa ordered Fierro to shoot Benton that night. The execution was carried out at the village of Samalayuca, just outside Juárez. But after a grave had been dug, specially deep at Benton's request 'to keep the coyotes away', Fierro chose to kill Benton with a blow on the head instead of shooting him. He was buried still handcuffed.

As soon as the news of Benton's death got over the border a tremendous storm burst around the bewildered

Villa. An AP dispatch from El Paso, where Benton was
well known, reported that extra editions carrying the news
were 'frantically seized and read ... Mr Benton's ways were
blunt but his friends admired him for them and there were
moist eyes and muttered imprecations when they heard the
news'.

Though Benton was not an American citizen, an indignant meeting in El Paso passed a resolution demanding instant action by the State Department to prevent further out-
rages to foreigners in Mexico .. the *Montreal Star* pronounced loftily, 'If murder is proved against General Villa,
reparation must be exacted by somebody for whatever
measure of wrong has been done to a citizen of the British
Empire' ... *Le Temps* of Paris pointed out that Britain 'is
not in the habit of shutting her eyes in such a case' and
reflected that the American government, which was encouraging Villa, 'is much embarrassed'.

Benton's death had indeed highlighted American responsibility for Mexico. There was widespread acceptance of the
belief that since the United States, under the Monroe Doctrine, would not permit European intervention on the
American continent, she was morally responsible for the
conduct of the nations of that hemisphere.

But Sir Edward Grey was under no such illusions.
Answering questions in Parliament, he admitted that Britain had no means of communicating with Villa, except
through the United States, but that Britain did not hold the
American government responsible in any way for Benton's
death.

In France, however, the future Premier Georges Clemen-
ceau commented in *L'homme libre* that the United States
was responsible for Benton's murder and indeed for any
anarchy in Mexico because she would not allow England or
any other power to intervene. This attitude found popular
support in Parliament and throughout Britain generally.
There was much talk of 'sending the navy'.

From London, Ambassador Page wrote to President Wilson: 'Kill an Englishman at home and there is no undue
excitement. But kill one abroad and gunboats and armies
and reparations are at once thought about....'

The international rumpus worried Villa but failed to stifle

his sense of humour. George Carothers, former American
consul in Torreón who had been appointed one of Wilson's
'special agents' and attached to the Division of the North,
explained to Villa that he could not kill a British citizen
without bringing the British nation into the affair. But when
Carothers went on to point out that Britain possessed the
finest navy in the world, Villa laughed and said, 'What can
a navy do to me, here in Chihuahua?'

Villa would not permit Benton's body to be sent to the
United States, and made all sorts of excuses. He told
Marion Letcher, the U.S. Consul in Chihuahua, that the
body could not be removed because in Mexico it was not
permitted to disturb the dead after formal burial. But Villa
said he was prepared to admit a team of American and
British investigators into Mexico.

Asked to supply details of Benton's 'trial' and execution,
Villa instructed his legal advisers to prepare fictitious documents for release. These were quickly forthcoming, and in
grand detail. Full statements of 'witnesses' were even provided; newspapers on both sides of the Atlantic carried
columns of reports on a trial that never took place.

As demands for the delivery of Benton's body grew
stronger, a worried Fierro finally confessed to Villa how he
had killed Benton. Villa's solution was simple. He ordered
that the body be disinterred and shot, believing that this
would satisfy any commission of inquiry. But when one of
his doctors pointed out that an autopsy would reveal Benton had been shot after he was dead, Villa ordered a fake
autopsy issued, finding that Benton had been shot and given
a blow on the head as an act of mercy. On 1 March the
Americans published this 'official report' while an investigation team waited in vain at the border.

Two days later Sir Edward Grey told Parliament:

'All the efforts that have been made have failed to secure
an investigation of the facts. The persistent difficulties put
in the way of investigation create the strongest presumption
of a desire and an intention to conceal the truth on the part
of those in Mexico who are responsible for what has happened.

'It has been urged on me that we take immediate action. . . . There is nothing we can do effectively under the

present conditions. The government in Mexico City have no
control over the territory where the death of Mr Benton
took place, nor over those who were responsible for his
death. . . .

'We have no intention of engaging in what would be on
our part a fantastic attempt such as the sending of a
force. . . . In ordinary circumstances we might have taken
action at a port or by way of a blockade. Under present
conditions if we took such action and it had any effect, it
could only result in giving assistance to the contending
party in the north of Mexico.'

There were loud cheers from Members as he concluded,
'But I do not intend to let the matter rest, and as soon as by
any change of circumstances it is within our power to carry
the matter further we shall take whatever steps may be
practicable.'

Then Carranza clamped down. The First Chief insisted
that all further representations be made direct to him and
fired off a message to Villa saying that the entry of an
investigation team would 'violate Mexico's sovereignty'. He
ordered Villa to make no more statements to newspapers
without first consulting him.

This was one order from Carranza with which Villa was
only too glad to comply. One American writer who talked
to Villa afterwards noted that 'he was evidently worried by
the excitement the affair had caused and [was] anxious to
hush it up as quickly as possible'.

And there the affair dragged to its sordid end. By mid-
summer Benton's ranch had been taken over by hordes of
squatters, and in Europe the clouds of war obliterated British interest in Benton.

Despite the embarrassment of Benton's murder, Washington still lent enthusiastic support to the Constitutionalist
cause. But in an attempt to curb the excesses of Villa and
his followers, President Wilson asked the veteran American
general, Hugh L. Scott, to meet Villa and put the United
States' point of view.

In Scott, Wilson made a good choice. A former Indian
fighter wise in the ways of border life, Scott was also a highly
efficient military man, and fluent in Spanish. Villa was

impressed, and warmed to Scott at once. They remained friends, despite the troubles which Villa was to cause the American government, until Villa's death.

Scott thought that though Villa was 'as unmoral as a wolf ... nevertheless he had some fine qualities if you could reach them, and with all his faults I considered him to have a far better character than Carranza. He never violated his compacts with me.'

Their meeting, which took place shortly after the murder of Benton, was a clandestine affair. 'We met in the middle of the international bridge [between Juárez and El Paso] one dark night and sat on the back seat of his car for two hours,' reported Scott. He told Villa 'Civilised people look on you as a tiger or a wolf,' and when the Mexican expressed surprise, Scott told him of the horror aroused among Americans by the killing of prisoners and of civilians like Benton, and advised Villa that he was harming his own cause by persisting in these actions.

Scott gave Villa a pamphlet issued by the General Staff of the British Army on how to treat prisoners and conquered populations. Villa was fascinated. He had it translated into Spanish and distributed among his officers.

According to Scott, Villa was influenced by the pamphlet to the extent of refraining from shooting the next 4000 prisoners who fell into his hands, indicating, in Scott's opinion, that he was 'susceptible to good influences, even if it was only temporary'. But Villa still executed the *Colorados* whenever he captured them, explaining that they were *peons*, just like the revolutionaries, and that no *peon* would volunteer to fight against the cause of liberty unless he were a wicked man. He also continued to shoot captured Federal officers who declined to join the rebels 'because they are educated men and ought to know better'.

Even Villa's own troops suffered from his erratic temper. On one occasion, annoyed by the yells of a drunken soldier while he was being interviewed by an American journalist, Villa casually pulled his pistol and killed the man from the window, without interrupting his conversation.

Villa's temper was also demonstrated violently when Patrick O'Hea went to the rebel chief with a complaint that his house, near the railway just outside Torreón, was being shot up by trigger-happy soldiers as their trains went past. Villa refused to believe the story but was persuaded to go with O'Hea to a first floor balcony of the Hotel Francia, overlooking the railway yard, as a troop train began to move out. 'Just then some presumably drunken warrior on the train, out of habit, started shooting into the air,' wrote O'Hea. 'Villa threw me aside ... jerked a weapon from a blanching guard and emptied its chambers into the humanity atop of the moving caravan. I saw at least one man fall, crumbling, from the roof-top to the ground.'

Both Villa and Obregón were invited into the United States by General John J. Pershing, the commander of the border area, who attempted by diplomacy and displays of military force to impress on the Mexicans the U.S. Army's ability to protect American people and property south of the border. Pershing felt that Obregón was 'a sincere and able patriot' but Villa 'was of a different type. He was taciturn and restless, his eyes were shifty, his attitude one of suspicion. . . .'

On one occasion Pershing staged a military parade at Fort Bliss, attended by Villa and Fierro. 'When he saw the American cavalry and light artillery do their stunts Villa did not suppress his admiration and astonishment,' wrote the American journalist Timothy Turner. 'He sat there rather bashfully and was still more uncomfortable when, after the review, he was taken to the post commander's quarters, where tea was served. Fierro was so overcome that he forgot to remove his hat as he entered the house and Villa said to him, in a stage whisper, "Take off your hat, you brute, you animal."'

Turner, too, thought Obregón more promising than Villa, but it was Villa who was capturing the imagination and the headlines. The seventy-one-year-old Ambrose Bierce, one of America's best-known journalists, was so captivated by Villa that he crossed the border to follow his campaign in Chihuahua and disappeared for ever during the battle for Ojinaga in January 1914, leaving behind this note to a relative as an appropriate epitaph: 'If you should hear of my being stood up against a Mexican stone wall and shot to rags please know that I think it is a pretty good way to depart this life. It beats old age, disease or falling down the

cellar stairs. To be a *gringo* in Mexico—ah, that is euthan-
asia.'

At the beginning of March Villa was back in Chihuahua
City, readying the Division of the North for the spring
drive through the centre of Mexico towards Mexico City.
Obregón's forces prepared to push down the less heavily-
defended but vastly more difficult terrain of the Pacific
coast, while in the north-east Pablo González's army began
to threaten the oil-rich Gulf coast.

Equipping and paying three armies was rapidly depleting
Carranza's funds, and when Villa requested five million
pesos to finance his offensive, the First Chief replied that he
was unable to send so much money. So Villa printed his
own. Presses were set up in the basement of the Governor's
Palace in Chihuahua City and two million pesos paper
money was run off. 'I had all I needed from then on,' was
Villa's blunt comment.

The bills were printed on good quality paper, with Villa's
name splashed across them. They also bore the signatures
of revolutionary officials and carried portraits of Villa's two
martyred idols, Madero and Abraham González, earning
them the nickname *dos caras* (two faces).

Carranza dispatched three elderly emissaries, dubbed The
Magi by Villa, to complain that printing his own money
would cause endless complications to the Constitutionalist
cause. Villa sent them back to Sonora with the message that
if Carranza was unable to supply him with campaign funds
he would continue to print his own. Next Carranza sent one
of his top aides, the lawyer Luis Cabrera, who promised to
support Villa's request for more funds and managed to ex-
tract in return a promise from Villa that he would print no
more paper money than was absolutely necessary.

Soon afterwards Villa asked Carranza to free General
Felipe Angeles from his cabinet (where he was serving as
Secretary of War) to take charge of the artillery of the
Division of the North. Carranza agreed and Angeles travelled to Chihuahua to forge one of the most improbable, yet
highly-successful, partnerships of the Revolution—a Paris-
educated man serving as loyal subordinate to a primitive,
tempestuous peasant.

Angeles, who had been freed by Huerta after President Madero's death and sent on a study mission to Europe, abandoned the trip in France and made his way back to Mexico to join the rebels. Angeles had long admired Villa's fierce devotion to the Revolution and shortly after his arrival in Chihuahua City, he arranged a ceremony at the Governor's Palace at which Villa was to be presented with a medal by Angeles's new Artillery Corps.

Villa, who abhorred public functions, was not told until the last moment. He was dressed in an old khaki uniform with several buttons missing. He hadn't recently shaved, wore no hat and his hair matched the untidiness of his dress. According to John Reed, who witnessed the ceremony, Villa faced a scene of splendour rare in the ranks of the ragged Revolution.

'The officers of the Artillery Corps, in smart blue uniforms, were solidly banked across one end of the audience hall. . . . From the door of the chamber, around the gallery, down the state staircase, and across the grandiose inner court of the palace and out through the imposing gate into the street stood a double line of soldiers, their rifles at present arms. . . . Villa entered the aisle between the rigid lines of soldiers, walking a little pigeon-toed, in the fashion of a horseman, hands in his trouser pockets. He seemed slightly embarrassed and grinned and nodded to a *compadre* here and there in the ranks. . . .

'Finally, pulling his moustache and looking very uncomfortable, he moved towards a gilded throne, with lions-paw arms, raised on a dais under a canopy of crimson velvet. He shook the arms violently to test the throne's dependability, then sat down. There followed six speeches extolling Villa's bravery on the field.

'Through it all [Reed reported] Villa slouched on the throne, his mouth hanging open, his little shrewd eyes playing around the room. Once or twice he yawned but for the most part seemed to be speculating with some intense interior amusement, like a small boy in church, what it was all about. . . . Finally, with an impressive gesture, an Artillery officer stepped forward with a small cardboard box. The officers applauded . . . the crowds cheered, the bands burst into a triumphant march.

'Villa put out both hands eagerly.... He could hardly wait to open the box and see what was inside.... He held up the medal, scratched his head and, in a reverent silence, said clearly, "This is a hell of a little thing to give a man for all that heroism you are talking about."

'They waited for him to make a conventional address of acceptance.... Puckering up his face, as he always did when he concentrated intensely, Villa leaned across the table in front of him and poured out in a voice so low that the people could hardly hear, "There is no word to speak. All I can say is my heart is all to you." Then he sat down, spitting violently on the floor.'

Carranza was in danger of being left high and dry when the push towards Mexico City began. While Villa was arming the most powerful force in the history of Mexican warfare, Carranza was involved in the sort of ludicrous scene which saw him enrolling the support of Sonora Indians, whose bows and arrows had to be exchanged for rifles before they could be incorporated into the revolutionary army.

Many of his subordinates had already followed General Angeles from the dine-and-dance atmosphere of the Carranza headquarters to the business-like bustle of Chihuahua City. The First Chief decided to move too, and early in March he announced that Constitutionalist headquarters would now be established in Chihuahua City. Villa, preoccupied with plans for the push on Mexico City, received Carranza respectfully enough, but was openly scornful of the 'pantywaists and chocolate drinkers' who formed Carranza's court.

As Villa's campaign preparations neared completion, newspapermen swarmed in from the United States to report the fighting. To accommodate them, Villa provided a goods carriage, which was converted into a Press wagon. Rough bunks were built, a toilet was installed, a stove was provided, and with it came a Chinese cook called Fong. Timothy Turner wrote, 'There was a long built-in table of planks on which we ate and on which the pride of the car, an old, battered but faithful Remington typewriter sat....'

Villa was emphatic in denying reports from the United States that he was interested in the presidency. 'I am a soldier and an uneducated man,' he told reporters in Chihuahua, 'and I have not the qualifications for a president.' That said, Villa prepared to launch his second assault on Torreón in six months. Typically, Villa was preparing to head the Division of the North straight through the most heavily-defended part of Mexico—the string of towns which straddled Mexico's great central highway and railways from the United States to Mexico. Torreón was the most important, and the most heavily-guarded, of these. Since its recapture from the Constitutionalists, Huerta had poured in a garrison of 10,000 Federals and *Colorados* under the command of General José Refugio Valasco, who boasted that Torreón was now impregnable.

On 16 March, in the greatest secrecy, Villa made his move. Telephone and telegraphic communications were suspended, and trains and cars were forbidden to leave Chihuahua in case they should give warning to the Federals. Then the army on wheels steamed south through the undefended desert towards Torreón.

Heading the huge serpent of railway rolling stock were two construction trains, to repair any track damage; then came two artillery trains, loaded with twenty-eight cannons, the hospital train, Villa's headquarters train and Press carriage and finally the gypsy procession of troop carriers. They made rapid, unopposed progress and by the evening of 17 March the army had spilled into a huge encampment at Yermo, only seventy miles north of Torreón, where they dismounted to prepare for the attack.

Only one person was missing ... General Francisco Villa. The Division of the North camped uncomfortably at Yermo for three days waiting for Villa to turn up and give the order to attack. He had left the trains at Camargo, 100 miles south of Chihuahua City, to be best man at the wedding of one of his old friends, and when he finally arrived at Yermo early on 20 March, he was bedraggled and red-eyed from lack of sleep—hardly the condition in which to prepare for the most important battle of his military career.

With the arrival of their chief, the Division of the North moved on again towards the still-unsuspecting Federals. General Benjamin Argumedo, commander of the *Colorado* garrison at the outpost of Bermejillo, twenty-seven miles

north of Torreón had spotted huge clouds of smoke and
dust on the horizon but had done little except report the
matter to Torreón. While he waited for official reaction, the
storm burst upon him. Villa's cavalry broke into a gallop
five miles outside Bermejillo and poured into the town,
driving the garrison back towards Torreón in a running
fight that lasted for a further five miles and killed 106
Colorados.

The unprepared defenders had left intact the railway and
communications at Bermejillo, so Villa asked General Angeles to put through a phone call to General Velasco,
demanding the surrender of Torreón. Angeles managed to
get through to Velasco, who asked where the call was coming from. From Bermejillo, he was told, at which the courteous Federal commander congratulated the rebels on the
speed of their advance. But when Angeles requested the
surrender of his army, Velasco's good humour evaporated.
He hung up.

A little later the telephone rang in the railway office
which had been converted into a temporary headquarters.
Villa himself answered it. The call was from a Federal
officer in Gómez Palacio, about four miles north of
Torreón. He asked how many men Villa had. 'Oh, not
many,' replied Villa good-naturedly. 'Just a couple of regiments of artillery and ten thousand men.' But when the
officer expressed pleasure at the prospect of a fight Villa
suddenly lost his patience, bellowed that the man must be a
fool and jammed down the receiver.

Next morning at dawn the advance continued, but now
against an alerted enemy. At first the artillery, hospital and
supply trains were able to keep pace with the advance. But
nearer Torreón all railway bridges had been destroyed and
eight miles outside Gómez Palacio every yard of the track
into the town had been torn up.

While the repair gangs slaved away, Villa's men advanced to within two miles of Gómez Palacio, where the
Federals were deeply dug in. The first attack was disastrous.
The eager Villistas, without waiting for artillery support,
charged forward recklessly and were mown down in heaps.
The survivors fled in panic, abandoning their rifles and
equipment. Had the Federals followed up they could have

scored a crushing and perhaps decisive victory but they stayed in their trenches, afraid of a Villa trap. But it was no trap; Villa himself had to ride among the fleeing troops, rally them and persuade them to go back and pick up their belongings.

The wounded, roughly bundled in bloody *sarapes*, were passed back to the hospital train, delayed behind the toiling railway repair gangs. The Federals added to the casualties and the confusion by poisoning the water in the irrigation ditches in the cottonfields.

Soon however, the railway was repaired and General Angeles was able to get his artillery within effective range of Gómez Palacio. Clouds of thick smoke and the gagging smell of scorching flesh rolled over the rebel lines each evening as the town's defenders burned their dead, indication that the bombardment was having its effect.

The key to the defence of Gómez Palacio was a rocky, barren hill, the Cerro de la Pila, which dominated the town. The hill was bombarded by day, while at night waves of troops were thrown in against the Federals who, though outnumbered, put up a gallant defence from their well-prepared entrenchments. On the night of 25 March Villa launched a massive attack on the hill. Six waves were beaten off with fearful losses but the seventh time the rebels literally overran the defenders, reaching through loopholes to disarm riflemen and machine-gunners.

General Velasco threw in a desperate counter attack, and after a hand-to-hand struggle lasting more than two hours the rebels were dislodged from the summit. At dawn they were back where they had started. That night Villa grimly went ahead with plans for another *golpe terrifico*, but as the attack got under way it drew no answering fire from the hill. The Federals had used the recapture of La Pila to cover their withdrawal from Gómez Palacio to Torreón. The town, which had cost Villa nearly a thousand dead and three times as many wounded in three days of furious assault, eventually fell without a fight.

Patrick O'Hea, who at that time was managing a soap factory in Gómez Palacio, had been trapped in the town during the battle. He described the entry of the rebels:

'They were not viciously aggressive, save in isolated

cases, but they pressed into our poor remaining shops and cleaned them out, for payment with *villista* currency; into our offices, into our very homes, not as a matter of vindicative looting, but in quest of something, anything, to alleviate the hardship of the desert. . . .'

Before moving against Torreón, Villa made one further attempt to avoid bloodshed. He summoned the British vice-consul in Gómez Palacio, Mr Herbert Cunard Cummins, and asked him to take a message to General Velasco, calling on him to surrender and promising to spare the lives of his officers and men. Cummins refused. He maintained that, as a neutral, he should not be asked to mix in a political affair.

Villa became angry and abusive. Foreigners were demanding that he protect them, he stormed, yet they refused to help when they could. But the outburst quickly abated. Villa's personal physician, Dr Rauschbaum, had recently advised him to give up eating meat in an attempt to stabilise his emotions and perhaps this had something to do with Villa's reasonableness. Or perhaps it was the memory of the Benton affair. Whatever the reason, Villa calmed down, apologised and shook hands. Cummins, no doubt startled, thawed too and promised to deliver the message.

He told Villa's following of journalists, 'General Villa has asked me to go to Torreón and to carry with me a demand on General Velasco to surrender the town. I said that my status as a neutral might make it embarrassing but he rather insisted. Anyway, I have decided to do it. I wanted you to know about it so in case anything should happen to me you can explain it all.'

Then, carrying a clothes pole on which had been tacked a white pillowcase, Cummins set out. He wore a light summer suit and a straw hat and, according to the reporters, looked as if he were off on an outing. Nor did he seem excited or nervous. He bowed, said 'Good afternoon, gentlemen' and walked away.

'The last we saw of him he was walking down the railway tracks towards Torreón, the clothes pole over his shoulder and the pillowcase flying in the breeze,' wrote Turner. 'They began to fire at him very soon but, without stopping, he waved his flag and presently the fire stopped.'

But Cummins' gallantry was wasted. Velasco flatly rejected Villa's demands. The battle for Torreón itself began. Villa threw in his entire Division in an effort to smash the resistance. They battered forward, street by street, yard by painful yard. Federal defences were dynamited by rebels who crawled literally under the muzzles of machine-guns, holding sticks of dynamite sewn in cowhide, lighted cigars clamped between their teeth. Angeles' artillery pounded away at point-blank range, and the defenders' position daily grew more hopeless.

On 30 March Cummins came through the lines again, this time with a message from Velasco requesting a forty-eight hour truce so that he could bury his dead and attend to the wounded. Suspecting that the Federal commander might use the truce to bring up reinforcements, Villa refused. Instead, he sent Cummins back with another ultimatum, repeating his offer to spare the lives of prisoners if Velasco surrendered.

Cummins arranged to have a Union Jack waved from a Federal outpost if Villa's ultimatum was rejected. Shortly after Cummins went back the British flag was hoisted and fighting broke out again. But the Federals were unable to hold out for much longer. On 2 April Velasco abandoned the town, skilfully extricating most of his forces and escaping to the east under cover of a dust storm.

Had he been able to wipe out or neutralise Velasco, Villa could have pushed ahead swiftly to Mexico City. But with a large Federal force to the east of Torreón threatening his communications Villa was forced to turn aside and hunt them down. This, coupled with Carranza's mounting distrust and jealousy, was to cost Villa the honour of being first into Mexico City.

For the time being, however, Villa's capture of Torreón was triumph enough. Now he controlled a territory twice as large as the British Isles. On the evening of 2 April he cabled Carranza, informing him of the fall of Torreón and adding bluntly, 'The cost has been great and painful.' Next morning the Division of the North made its formal entry into the town.

The population had suffered terribly during the protracted battle, and when Timothy Turner entered the town with the Villistas he noticed ragged old men sorting through the horse manure in the streets looking for partially digested grain with which to make *tortillas*.

Villa's victory was the most telling so far for the Constitutionalists. It was celebrated as far away as Ciudad Juárez where, according to the *Daily Mail*, 'In a series of Bacchanalian scenes women from across the American border danced the two-step with Mexican soldiers until the early hours of the morning.'

John Reed, too, was quite carried away by Villa's success, writing that he was 'the greatest leader Mexico has ever had. His method of fighting is astonishingly like Napoleon's.'

The temptation to rest in Torreón must have been great, but Villa ordered immediate pursuit of Velasco's forces, who had linked up with a Federal relief force under General Joaquín Maass at San Pedro de las Colonias, about forty miles north-east of Torreón. Furious assaults failed to dislodge the Federals from the town but Villa enjoyed a stroke of luck when Velasco and Maass fell out over the question of which one outranked the other. In a fit of temper Velasco abandoned San Pedro on 15 April and headed for Saltillo, which was still in Federal hands, leaving Maass to fight on alone. Maass decided the odds were too great and later that day followed Velasco, abandoning most of his equipment and many of his troops. Hundreds of Federal soldiers deserted, some to join the Constitutionalists, others to head hopefully for their homes from which they had been dragged to fight in a war of which they knew little and cared less.

Huerta had been smashed on his strongest front. The road to Mexico City lay invitingly open but the Division of the North, which had been in action continually for a month, was in urgent need of supplies, reinforcements and rest. 'Some of our horses had carried saddles so long that their blankets were stuck to their backs,' reported Villa.

'As soon as the firing began I went out to look over the positions of the two forces,' he write. 'If the Constitutional-City, were rounded up and imprisoned in the vaults of the Laguna Bank while Villa decided what to do with them.

After confiscating all their property and possessions, Villa assembled the Spaniards and, in a violent speech, accused them of aiding the Federal defenders of Torreón. He would have been justified in executing all of them, he maintained, but he had decided instead to expel them from Mexico. Some 700 unfortunates were driven at bayonet point into goods wagons and shipped 500 miles north to the American border with hardly any food or water.

An American protest to Carranza about Villa's treatment of the Spaniards met with no sympathy. The First Chief told the American envoy, George Carothers, that he too wished to expel all Spaniards from Mexico, and that if they did not leave the capital before he arrived there he intended to have many of them executed for assisting Huerta.

On the Pacific coast Obregón's Division of the North-West took advantage of Huerta's preoccupation with Villa to make swift progress. The only serious resistance came at the port of Mazatlán, which was left in a state of siege as Obregón pressed southward. The besieged port figured in two incidents, one historical and one comical. In April 1914, for the first time ever, an aircraft was used for warfare when a rebel plane, piloted by Captain Gustavo Salinas, bombed the Federal defenders of the port. Apart from that, the besieged garrison was hardly disturbed until American and Japanese warships in the harbour fired a salute to mark the funeral of the Dowager Empress of Japan on 25 May. The Constitutionalists, thinking the Federals were trying to break out, opened up on the town with artillery and machine-guns.

In the north-east, too, Pablo González was stirring. After testing the defences of Monterrey and Saltillo and finding them too strong for his liking, González pushed south towards the oil port of Tampico. The British journalist, Hamilton Fyfe, was in Monterrey when a Constitutionalist force of some 4500 under Jesús Carranza, brother of the First Chief, attacked the town.

'As soon as the firing began I went out to look over the positions of the two forces,' he wrote. 'If the Constitutionalists had known how small the garrison was, and if Mexican troops ever fought in any but their own way, the defences could have been rushed. The losses would have been heavy but the city must have fallen.

'Mexicans, however, are not in the habit of rushing. Their only method is to get behind something and fire their rifles, seldom with any particular aim. Many I saw did not raise them to their shoulders. Of those who did this, few looked along the barrel. As I passed the hospital during the fight a dozen men or so were letting off their rifles on the roof, a strange place to choose, but typically Mexican. I could not see one of them aiming. They shot into the air ... I am speaking now of the Federals; the *insurrectos*' fire was rather more careful.

'I saw twenty or thirty shots fired from a distance of eighty yards or so at an old *Carrancista* who had somehow got into the city and was riding, gloriously drunk, down the main thoroughfare. Not one of them hit him. He turned into a side street, where two officers rode up and killed him with their revolvers.

'During two days rifle fire was kept up with few intervals. An enormous amount of ammunition must have been used. Yet only a few hundred men in all were hit. That also is typical of Mexican battles. If either side could induce its soldiers to use the bayonet or was enterprising enough to train a few regiments of Lancers, and if further, they could break themselves of the habit of sitting down after victories instead of following them up, the civil war could soon be decided. ...'

But while he was highly critical of Mexican tactics and marksmanship, Fyfe admired their bravery. 'At Monterrey I saw soldiers walk calmly across a fire-swept square. They knew, no doubt, what bad shots the men on the other side were, but still, when bullets are zipping through the air, it is not easy to be unconcerned.'

After the capture of Torreón, vast quantities of cotton fell into the hands of the Constitutionalists. Some of it was sold in the United States to finance the purchase of war materials, and attempts were made to dispose of the rest in Europe. But to ship the cotton, the rebels needed a port. For this reason, and for the value of the revenue from the foreign oil companies based there, González was urged to take Tampico, which his forces had been threatening for some time.

The area around Tampico was the richest in the country. The discovery of oil had made a boom town of Tampico, and its population mushroomed from about 5000 to 30,000. It had a bigger foreign colony than any other centre except Mexico City.

As early as the previous November, Lord Cowdray's Mexican Eagle Company wells to the south of Tampico had fallen within the sphere of domination of rebels under General Aguilar, who demanded huge tolls. Despite the alternating control of rebels and Federals, Eagle carried on producing oil under the most difficult circumstances, including one occasion when all the company employees were lined up and threatened with execution because the management refused to pay the extortionate tolls demanded. Lord Cowdray, persuaded to remain in England because of the danger of being kidnapped and held to ransom if he returned to Mexico, praised his workers: 'I am as proud of my army as any general could be. . . .'

By the end of March a Constitutionalist force was poised within ten miles of Tampico, and on 5 April the long-expected attack began. It was to bring far heavier consequences than either side could ever have believed.

5: Salute the Flag

It had been a long and boring winter in Veracruz for John Lind, the almost-forgotten Wilson emissary. With little else to do but cable suggestions and complaints to Washington, Lind had, by March, concocted a ludicrous plan for the capture of Mexico City and the bloodless overthrow of Huerta.

Lind felt that his plan would not entail the loss of a single life. On his instructions, an American marine officer, posing as a railways official in search of a missing employee, had travelled to the capital and drawn up a detailed map of its defences. Lind had even got together a small raiding party prepared to carry out his plan. The idea was to arrive in Mexico City before daylight and, rather vaguely, 'possess the city before noon'.

Huerta was to be held until he could be turned over to the 'proper domestic authorities to be dealt with according to the law'. Lind had even prepared suitable proclamations. The only thing lacking was President Wilson's authority. When Lind requested this, the only reply he received was a telegram from Bryan saying that the president 'did not contemplate any immediate action'. Disillusioned by the rejection of his cherished plan, Lind cabled Bryan on 29 March asking to return to the United States for a few weeks. Permission was given and he sailed from Veracruz on 6 April, missing by a mere two weeks the action he had been advocating for so long.

Though O'Shaughnessy wrote to Lind expressing regret at his departure, the two men had not hit it off too well, mainly because of age and religious differences, and Mrs O'Shaughnessy was a good deal less formal about the envoy. She noted: 'Lind leaves tonight for Washington, so exit from the tragic scene Don Juan Lindo (I sometimes feel like calling him Don Juan Blindo) who commenced life in a Scandinavian town as Jon Lind and who has ended up by dreaming northern dreams in Veracruz in the hours of Mexico's agony.'

The Americans, with huge oil interests at stake along the Gulf coast, had for years maintained an intimidating number of warships in the area. Philander Knox, President Taft's Secretary of State, once said that the purpose of the ships was to keep Mexicans 'in a salutary equilibrium, between a dangerous and exaggerated apprehension and a proper degree of wholesome fear'. In 1914 the Fourth Division of the Atlantic Fleet, under Rear Admiral Frank F. Fletcher, was at Veracruz, and the Fifth Division, commanded by Rear Admiral Henry T. Mayo, was off Tampico. Also at Tampico were the British cruiser HMS *Hermione* and the German cruiser *Dresden*, watching over the interests of their nationals in the area.

Mayo, a veteran with more than forty years' service, had two battleships, USS *Connecticut* and USS *Minnesota*, in his division, but since the 'port' of Tampico was situated ten miles inland up the shallow Pánuco river which neither ship could negotiate, he chose the gunboat USS *Dolphin* as his headquarters vessel inside the river. *Dolphin* had had a distinguished career. It had served as the Presidential yacht during Grover Cleveland's two terms and since then had been a dispatch boat used by Secretaries of the Navy.

After the rebel attack on Tampico had begun, Rear Admiral Mayo and Clarence Miller, the American consul in Tampico, were kept busy organising the evacuation of American oil workers and their families and attempting to dissuade both sides from damaging the extensive oil installations along the Pánuco river.

By 7 April the rebels had reached the Iturbide Bridge spanning a canal which marked the northern boundary of Tampico. For the next two days the bridge and the canal constituted an uneasy front line.

Incredibly, since they were in the middle of one of the world's richest oilfields, the Americans ran short of fuel for *Dolphin* and the smaller naval boats being used as messenger and supply launches to the bigger warships anchored off the coast. Since the American-owned refineries had been closed because of the fighting, *Dolphin*'s captain, Lt Cdr Ralph K. Earle, went ashore in Tampico to try to arrange the purchase of fuel. He was put in touch with a German, Max Tyron, who offered to sell the Americans some petrol stored in his warehouse on the canal which had become the first line of Federal defence.

The Americans sent a whaleboat, under the command of an inexperienced ensign, Charles Copp, to collect the petrol. With blind disregard for the war going on around them, the Americans sailed up the canal and up to the warehouse, their boat flying the Stars and Stripes fore and aft. As the crew were loading the petrol cans into the boat they were arrested by a squad of Federal soldiers, whose officer had orders to keep everyone except combatants away from the area.

The unarmed Americans were marched through Tampico's streets to the headquarters of Colonel Ramón Hinojosa, who commanded the Federals in that part of the town. After pointing out to the Americans the folly of being in the front line, Hinojosa released the crew and had them escorted back to their whaleboat, where the loading of petrol was completed before the boat returned to *Dolphin*. When news of the Americans' brief detention was passed on to General Ignacio Morelos Zaragoza, commander of the Tampico garrison, he made a profuse apology to Lt Cdr Earle and the American consul Miller, explaining that the soldiers who had made the arrest were members of the state guard and 'evidently ignorant of the first laws of war'.

In view of the crew's quick release and Morelos Zaragoza's equally quick apology, both Miller and Earle considered the incident closed. Their view was not shared, however, by Admiral Mayo, who was aboard *Dolphin*. Brushing aside Morelos Zaragoza's oral apology, Mayo sent an officer in full dress with a note demanding from the garrison commander a formal expression of regret, an assurance that the officer responsible for the arrest of the sailors would be punished and Morelos Zaragoza's promise that the Mexicans would hoist the American flag 'in a prominent position on shore' and give it a 21-gun salute, 'which salute will be duly returned by this ship'.

Mayo made his demands without reference to Washington. He did not even consult Fletcher, his fellow rear-admiral in Veracruz. Morelos Zaragoza, alarmed by the severity of Mayo's note, said he would have to refer the matter to Mexico City. The sailors' arrest was on the way to becoming an international incident.

Later that day Mayo informed Fletcher briefly of what

had happened and what steps he had taken. Fletcher backed him up and forwarded the news to Washington. President Wilson was at the Virginia resort, White Sulphur Springs, with his wife Ellen, who was ill, when the brief account which Fletcher had received of Mayo's actions was forwarded to him by Bryan. On 10 April he cabled Bryan, 'Mayo could not have done otherwise. O'Shaughnessy should be instructed to handle this matter with the utmost earnestness, firmness and frankness, representing to [the Mexicans] its extreme seriousness. . . .' Then he went back to his golf and his ailing wife, declining to talk to the Press about the matter.

On receiving Bryan's instructions, O'Shaughnessy's first act was to contact Roberto Esteva Ruiz, the Under Secretary for Foreign Relations. Together they set off to track down the elusive Huerta. When the two men found him, O'Shaughnessy was obliged to introduce the Mexican president to his own minister, since Huerta had never heard of Esteva Ruiz before!

Huerta's first formal reply to the United States demands came on 12 April when he announced that he considered Morelos Zaragoza's apology sufficient and, since Col Hinojosa had been arrested, that was ample punishment. Huerta refused to order the salute to the American flag, adding with ironic humour that in any case the United States was demanding a salute from a government it did not even recognise.

President Wilson's return to Washington on 13 April coincided with the arrival in the capital of John Lind. They met immediately to discuss the Tampico incident, and Lind obliged by giving Wilson the advice he wanted to hear: be firm with Huerta. It was becoming increasingly clear that this was in fact the opportunity Wilson had been seeking to force out Huerta.

A Cabinet meeting on 14 April gave unanimous backing to Wilson's demands that the American flag must be saluted, and that afternoon the president ordered the rest of the Atlantic Fleet to Tampico. When he learned of Wilson's instructions to the fleet Huerta commented, 'Is it a calamity. No, it is the best thing that could happen to us.' Huerta obviously expected Mexican opinion to unite in the face of this threat to the Republic, thus preserving his tottering dictatorship. After O'Shaughnessy had had another interview with Huerta on 14 April he reported to Bryan, 'The old Indian was more eloquent than I have ever seen him ... I believe that he will probably not yield.'

The situation was inflamed further by two more incidents which, like the Tampico affair, were exaggerated out of all proportion by the American president. An American naval mail orderly was arrested in the Veracruz post office on 11 April by a Mexican soldier who had seen a Navy poster advertising a reward for an A.W.O.L. sailor and who hoped optimistically that he had apprehended the missing American. The matter was quickly sorted out: the sailor was released, and the chastened Mexican was turned over to the military authorities for punishment. Rear Admiral Fletcher reported to Washington, 'The attitude of the Mexican authorities was correct; there is no cause for complaint against them and the incident is without significance.'

The same day, a diplomatic message from Washington was delayed in the Mexico City censor's office for fifty-five minutes, due, according to O'Shaughnessy, 'to a misunderstanding of duty by the censor'. Like Admiral Fletcher, O'Shaughnessy thought the matter of little significance.

But Wilson thought otherwise. On 15 April he summoned members of the Congressional foreign relations committees to the White House to inform them of the steps he proposed to take. He said the United States had suffered 'intolerable insults' and added, 'For some time past the Mexican government has seemed to think mere apologies sufficient when the rights of American citizens or the dignity of the United States government is involved.' The politicians gave Wilson enthusiastic assurances of support when he outlined tentative plans to seize Veracruz and Tampico, and Senator Chilton of West Virginia told Wilson, 'I'd make them salute the flag if we had to blow up the whole place.'

What Wilson was demanding was precisely what Huerta was seeking so desperately to avoid—public apology and humiliation. Even so, on 15 April Huerta gave way a little and told O'Shaughnessy he might be willing to apologise. O'Shaughnessy suggested that Huerta 'might arrange the matter quietly', perhaps giving the salute at sunrise. Huerta proposed instead a 'gun for gun' salute by batteries of both sides. O'Shaughnessy thought this a fair solution and forwarded Huerta's proposal to Washington, where it was joyfully received by the eternal optimist, Bryan. But Wilson immediately rejected the idea. Now Huerta too refused to budge and on Saturday 18 April the State Department received a message from O'Shaughnessy saying, 'I regret most profoundly my failure to bring [Huerta] to reason.'

President Wilson was having his customary Saturday morning round of golf at the Washington Country Club when O'Shaughnessy's dismal news was received. A messenger found Wilson on the fourteenth hole and the president was on his way back to the capital when he met his secretary, Joseph Tumulty and Bryan on the Potomac Bridge, carrying the cable from Mexico. While dozens of newspapermen camped in the corridors of the State Department waiting for a release, Wilson returned to the White House and on his own typewriter composed an ultimatum to Huerta.

Wilson announced that unless the Mexicans agreed to comply with Admiral Mayo's original demand within twenty-four hours he intended to place the matter before Congress on the following day 'with a view of taking such action as may be necessary to enforce the respect due to the nation's flag'.

Wilson spent the next day at White Sulphur Springs with his ailing wife. Though the ultimatum expired without further news of Huerta, Wilson did nothing that night. But he was back in Washington early on Monday, 20 April. His first move was to call a cabinet meeting, at which he mapped out the speech he intended to make to Congress that afternoon. He also passed on to the cabinet the news received the previous day from William Canada, the U.S. consul in Veracruz, that the German merchant ship *Ypiranga* was due to dock there on 21 April with 200 machine-guns and fifteen million cartridges for Huerta. At the end of the meeting Wilson told his cabinet, 'If there are any of you who still believe in prayer, I wish you would think seriously over this matter between now and our next meeting.'

The fact that this arms shipment might prolong Huerta's resistance caused the American government, with the lack of logic which had dogged the whole crisis, to shift the scene of activity from Tampico, where the insult to the flag had occurred, to Veracruz. Admiral Mayo, who had perfected plans for the seizure of Tampico, was abruptly instructed to move his fleet to Veracruz to join Fletcher. The rest of the Atlantic Fleet, which had been steaming at its leisure towards Tampico, was now ordered to make for Veracruz at full speed. The might of the American Navy was being summoned to halt one merchant ship.

After the cabinet meeting Wilson told a Press conference, 'In no conceivable circumstances would we fight the people of Mexico. It is only an issue between this government and a person calling himself the provisional president of Mexico, whose right to call himself such we never have recognised in any way.' In other words, the United States was proposing to wage war on an individual. Wilson concluded, 'I have no enthusiasm for war; but I have an enthusiasm for the dignity of the United States.'

It was a busy day for the President. That afternoon he addressed a joint session of Congress, stressing, in an eloquent speech, that American honour must be restored through armed action against Huerta, and requesting the approval of Congress—though he did not need it—for his actions. His speech received a standing ovation from the two Houses and was promptly approved by the House of Representatives by a margin of 337–37.

But in the Senate a group of Republicans, spearheaded by the former Secretary of State Elihu Root and the principal Republican spokesman Henry Cabot Lodge, wanted to intervene, not only against Huerta, but also in the areas controlled by the Constitutionalists, to 'protect American lives and property'. The Senate debated Wilson's request until the early hours of 21 April, and another day had passed before the Democratic majority forced it through on a straight party vote.

But by then it was irrelevant. Wilson had already acted.

Wilson had gone to bed without waiting for the decision of the Senate. Just after 2 a.m. a message from Consul Canada in Veracruz confirmed that the *Ypiranga* would be docking that morning. He added that three trains were waiting at dockside to speed the ship's cargo to Mexico City. The news brought a three-way telephone conversation, which became known as The Pyjama Conference, between President Wilson, Secretary of State Bryan and the Navy Secretary, Josephus Daniels.

When Wilson asked his opinion, Daniels, whose pacifist convictions must have been badly strained, replied 'I do not think the munitions should be permitted to reach Huerta.' Wilson told Daniels to issue orders for the immediate seizure of the Veracruz Customs house to prevent the arms being unloaded, then went back to bed in the blithe belief that there would be no bloodshed.

After all, as Wilson's confidant, Colonel Edward House, had told him only a few days previously, 'If a man's house was on fire he should be glad to have his neighbours come in and help him put it out. . . .' But the Mexicans could not understand this simple logic. They wanted to shoot the firemen.

At 8 a.m. on 21 April Admiral Fletcher received his instructions from Daniels: 'Seize Customs house. Do not permit war supplies to be delivered to Huerta government or any other party.' Though neither Mayo's ships nor the rest of the Atlantic Fleet had arrived, Fletcher moved into action immediately. Consul Canada was informed that American forces would start landing at 11 a.m. When the landing commenced he was requested to telephone the Federal commander in Veracruz, General Gustavo Maass, and tell him of the Americans' decision. Although he had sent most of his ships to Tampico to bolster Mayo's force, Fletcher managed to muster a landing party of nearly 800 sailors and marines. Meanwhile the battleship USS *Utah* steamed out to intercept *Ypiranga*, which was ordered to anchor outside the harbour.

Just after 11 a.m. the first boat-load of marines approached the Veracruz dockside. Consul Canada, watching the scene through field-glasses from the consulate, telephoned General Maass as ordered. 'No, it cannot be,' exclaimed the shocked Mexican. Canada promised that the landing force would not proceed beyond the waterfront and requested co-operation of the Federal troops in maintaining order in the town, but Maass instead issued orders to 'repel the invasion'. It was no more than token resistance, however. Maass had sent off most of his forces to help defend Tampico, and to fill the gaps had been taking convicts from the fortress prison of San Juan de Ulúa and converting them into makeshift soldiers.

By 11.30 a.m. the Americans were pouring ashore, watched by a large crowd whose enthusiasm and curiosity turned to hostility when they realised what was happening. The Customs house was soon occupied. So too, in excess of orders, were the railway station, cable office and post office.

Maass had sent an urgent message to Mexico City requesting instructions. He was told not to oppose the landing, but to move his forces to the small town of Tejería, about ten miles inland, and await further orders. But Maass was too late to stop the fighting. Small groups of Federal soldiers, acting independently, had already opened fire on the invaders. Thanks to the Mexicans' poor marksmanship, American casualties were light that day. Canada wired Washington, 'Four of our men killed, twenty wounded, firing all round the consulate.'

During the night the Americans ashore were reinforced by the arrival of the Atlantic Fleet and the ships from Tampico and, by daybreak on 22 April, 3000 marines and sailors were ready to complete the occupation of the port. According to the *Daily Mail*, the crews of the British cruisers HMS *Essex* and HMS *Berwick* in Veracruz harbour 'lined the decks and cheered to the echo' as the American reinforcements went in.

On the first day of the landing there had been much confusion among the white-jacketed American sailors, who had several times found themselves shooting at each other in mistake for white-uniformed Federals. In order to overcome this, many of the new landing parties stained their whites with iron rust and coffee grounds, effecting rudimentary identification and camouflage.

Since the Federal garrison had withdrawn from Veracruz to Tejería, the advance through the town met little organised resistance. But the Americans were harassed by civilian snipers and the armed convicts-turned-soldiers. It was the snipers who inflicted the majority of American casualties—and it was the reaction of the American marines as they hunted down snipers, both real and imagined, which sent the Mexican casualty rate soaring.

Typical of the hopelessness of the Mexicans' resistance was that put up by the cadets of the naval academy in Veracruz. As the Americans approached the academy across open ground and in close formation they suffered heavy casualties from cadets shooting from the dormitory windows and sheltering behind mattresses. Covering fire was requested and the warships USS *Prairie*, USS *Chester* and USS *San Francisco*, lying in the harbour close to the naval school, opened up over the heads of their advancing comrades. Mattresses proved no match for shells and soon the firing ceased.

By mid-morning Veracruz was in American hands. The landing force had lost nineteen dead and seventy wounded. Mexican casualties ran into the hundreds: a few soldiers, many snipers, even more civilians suspected of being snipers, and men, women and children who simply happened to get in the way of American bullets and shells. The house-to-house search for snipers went on all day but by evening the American force ashore, which had now grown to about 6000 was engaged mainly in cleaning up the town and getting essential services running again.

Now came the storm of reaction. On 22 April Huerta told the nation, rather misleadingly, 'In the port of Veracruz we are sustaining with arms the national honour.' And to newspapermen he commented, 'The Republic of Mexico has been, is and always will be in the right. The government serenely awaits events.'

But the Mexican Press was by no means serene. *El Imparcial* urged 'We may die, but let us kill,' and *La Patria* called for 'Vengeance, Vengeance, Vengeance!' A Mexican cartoon, captioned 'The true forces of the opponents', showed Wilson seated on a heap of money bags, faced by Huerta holding a basket of eggs. *El Independiente* revealed the real danger in the situation when it trumpeted 'Federal bullets will no longer spill brothers' blood but will perforate blond heads and white breasts swollen with vanity and cowardice.'

There was indeed a real fear that Mexico would unite behind Huerta to repel the hated *gringos*. Carranza, for instance, had loftily declined to discuss the Tampico argument, dismissing it as another example of Huerta's bungling. But when the Americans occupied Veracruz Carranza's nationalism came to the surface. He warned Washington, 'The invasion of our territory ... may indeed drag us into an unequal war' and requested the American government to 'suspend the hostile acts already initiated, ordering your forces to evacuate'.

Obregón, too, was reported to be in favour of all Mexicans uniting to repel the Americans, and announced that his troops were prepared to fight 'until they have exhausted every effort to resist'. But not Villa. With typical bluntness he commented 'It is Huerta's bull that is being gored.' After a talk with Villa, George Carothers, the American consular agent attached to the Division of the North, reported to Washington that, as far as Villa was concerned, 'we could keep Veracruz and hold it so tight that not even water could get in to Huerta. . . . He said no drunkard ... was going to draw him into a war with his friends.'

Despite the attitude of Carranza and Obregón the Constitutionalists stood to gain heavily by the Americans' action. Veracruz was Mexico's principal port and the cutting off of supplies and revenues was certain to throttle Huerta in a short time. Villa foresaw this and was satisfied with the American assurances that they intended to advance no further inland. And there seems no doubt that Carranza, though he never ceased to complain about it, fully realised the advantages of having the Americans in Veracruz.

The landings brought wild outbursts of anti-American feeling in Mexico City, however. The statue of George Washington, unveiled two years previously, was torn down, dragged through the streets and dumped at the foot of the statue of Mexico's great president, Benito Juárez. On the empty pedestal was placed a small bust of Hidalgo, their own hero of independence. American flags, about which so much fuss had been made by Mayo and Wilson, were torn down, trampled on and burned, and one Stars and Stripes was tied to the tail of a donkey and used to sweep the streets. The American Club was set on fire three times. Mobs chanting 'Death to the *gringos*' roamed the streets,

smashing and looting American-owned shops and businesses, invading hotels and hurling insults at Americans
and stoning the offices of the American-owned *Mexican
Herald*, which prudently removed its headquarters to Veracruz. After threats of an attack on the U.S. Embassy, 100
mounted police were sent to guard the building. The Embassy was also protected at night by squads of armed
American residents, who circled the area in cars.

There was anger in the American border states, too.
Texans queued up to buy guns after three Americans were
killed by shots fired into Laredo from across the border, an
incident far more serious than the Tampico affair, but
which brought no threat of punitive action. In El Paso
hysterical rumours circulated of a conspiracy among Mexican servants to poison their American employers.

As the situation worsened, President Wilson, badly
shaken by the news of the deaths in Veracruz and the
Mexican outbursts, again suspended the shipment of arms
to the Constitutionalists. So the Mexicans went back to
smuggling in what they needed. After American Customs
men had caught girls carrying cartridges concealed under
their blouses across the international bridges into Ciudad
Juárez, orders were issued to search every Mexican crossing the border.

The tenuous thread between the United States and the
Huerta régime was severed on 22 April when Huerta, in-
formally dressed in a sweater and soft felt hat, visited the
American Embassy to tell the O'Shaughnessys that they
were to be handed their passports and would be expected to
leave the next day. Then he put his arm round Nelson
O'Shaughnessy's shoulders and told him, 'I hold no rancour
towards the American people, nor towards President Wilson. He has not understood.' On the evening of 23 April a
train specially provided by Huerta for the O'Shaughnessys
and other Embassy personnel left the capital for Veracruz.
However, other Americans who tried to board the train in
Mexico City and *en route* were turned away. When the
train neared Veracruz the track had been torn up, so the
Embassy staff had to walk the last two miles into the port
under a naval escort.

After a tour of the battered town, Mrs O'Shaughnessy

noted in a letter to her mother, 'I think we have done a
great wrong to these people; instead of cutting out the sores
with a clean, strong knife of war and occupation, we have
only put our fingers in each festering wound and inflamed it
further.... What we are doing is war accompanied by all
the iniquitous results of half-measures.'

The O'Shaughnessys, in Wilson's black books because of
their friendship with Huerta, were sailing into political
oblivion, but they left in grand style. They were taken back
to the United States on board Admiral Badger's special
yacht *Yankton*, which had formerly belonged to the actress
Sarah Bernhardt and which had a huge golden figure of
Cleopatra on the prow. When they landed, O'Shaughnessy
was congratulated by one newspaper on being relieved of
'the daily task of delivering ultimatums to, and being hug-
ged by, Huerta'.

On 26 April the American flag was raised over the British-
built railway station in Veracruz. It received a 21-gun salute
from the battleship USS *Minnesota*. But the flag was never
saluted by Mexicans. Nor was the other cause of American
intervention, the *Ypiranga*, halted from her purpose. Later
in the month she sailed southwards to Puerto Mexico (now
Coatzacoalcos) and, joined by another German ship, the
Bavaria, which was carrying two million rounds of ammunition and 8000 rolls of barbed wire, completed delivery
of her munitions to the Federals. It was difficult to avoid the
conclusion that nineteen Americans and many more Mexicans had died to no purpose.

As fears grew for the safety of American residents in
Mexico, on 24 April Wilson authorised the mobilisation
of the Regular Army of 54,000 and the 150,000-strong
National Guard. With the two countries poised on the brink
of war, it became imperative to get American residents out
of Mexico as quickly as possible. The Royal Navy was of
great assistance in two cases.

At Tampico, Captain H. M. Doughty of HMS *Hermione*,
assisted by officers of the German cruiser *Dresden*, managed
to evacuate all Americans from the area by taking them in
small boats flying conspicuous British and German flags,
and transferring them to American ships outside the
Pánuco river. On 25 April a train flying the British flag

arrived in Veracruz from Mexico City carrying 100 British refugees and 150 Americans, who had got away by posing as Britons. But there were still some 700 Americans trapped in the capital. Huerta, while sympathetic towards their plight, would give no undertaking of safe conduct. Angry Mexican government officials hampered arrangements for their evacuation, and one Huerta colonel even talked of shooting them all. Since American forces were being fired on if they ventured further inland than Veracruz, Commander Hugh Tweedie of the British cruiser HMS *Essex* volunteered to rescue the Americans. He set off at 3 a.m. on 16 April with an interpreter and two unarmed Mexicans carrying a Union Jack and a white flag 'for the information and enlightenment of all whom they might concern'. They walked along the torn-up railway track as far as Tejería, passed safely through the Federal lines and, after an interview with General Maass, were given an engine and a wagon to take them to Mexico City.

In the capital Tweedie failed to see Huerta but the vice-president, General Blanquet, agreed to co-operate in the evacuation and provided three trains. Though Blanquet was unable to supply crews, Tweedie managed to persuade English engineers still in the city to operate the trains. At ten that night the refugee column pulled out of Mexico City, guarded by a squad of fifty soldiers. On the way Tweedie also managed to obtain the release of 113 American members of a farming colony, who had been imprisoned for five days. These Americans were in a pitiful state, having lost everything. When they asked for food and drink, a guard had told them 'You will all be shot at sunset; why worry about food?'

Commander Tweedie also managed to talk himself and his flock of 800 past a truculent Federal officer at Tejería, then escorted them along the torn-up railway to safety in Veracruz. After handing over the refugees to American marines. Tweedie reported that he 'cut across country and caught a tram back to the docks to dodge reporters'. The *New York Tribune*, in a dispatch from Veracruz dated 29 April told how the refugees 'wrung Cdr Tweedie by the hand, thanking him as their deliverer'. And the newspaper quoted the interpreter who had accompanied Tweedie to

Mexico City as saying 'It was good to see him lashing the British lion's tail in Huerta's face.'

The threat of war was dispersed somewhat when a mediation offer was made on 25 April by Argentina, Brazil and Chile, the three most powerful Latin American countries known as the ABC Powers, and was accepted by both the Americans and the Huerta government. Carranza and the Constitutionalists were also invited to take part in the talks, which opened in the Canadian town of Niagara Falls on 20 May. The mediation talks have been summed up neatly by Robert Quirk as resembling 'an elaborate quadrille from *Alice in Wonderland* in which nothing anyone did or said made sense to anyone else'.

Huerta seized on the talks as a means of dignified escape from a position which was rapidly becoming untenable, while Carranza, within sight of victory in Mexico's civil war, limited his interest to a settlement of the differences between Huerta's régime and the United States. He would tolerate no outsiders meddling in the affairs of his country—or threatening to cramp his presidential ambitions.

For his part, President Wilson was not prepared to stop at mediation. He sent a confidential memorandum to the conference delegates saying that 'no settlement could have any prospect of permanence ... that did not provide for the entire elimination of General Huerta and the immediate setting up in Mexico of a single provisional government acceptable to all parties. ...'

That Wilson still saw his rôle as that of a knight in democratic armour aiding a downtrodden people against oppressors and ruling classes was apparent from the interview he gave to the *Saturday Evening Post* the same month. He said, 'My passion is for the submerged eighty-five per cent of that Republic who are now struggling towards liberty.' That liberty could never be won, Wilson added, while Huerta remained in power, and he promised that American forces would stay in Mexico until Huerta either resigned or was eliminated.

On 28 May the ABC mediators proposed pacification of Mexico by the transfer of executive power from Huerta to a provisional president and four cabinet ministers who would be acceptable to all factions; the arranging of new elections by these five men; and a prompt recognition of the new government by the United States.

Huerta agreed on the condition that at the time of his withdrawal 'Mexico shall be pacified', but he refused to accept a revolutionary as provisional president. Carranza would not even consider any proposal for a provisional government in which Huerta or his followers would take part, and he warned the mediators that 'under no circumstances' would he accept their findings, no matter how much they might be in his favour.

The ABC conference finally reached agreement on 24 June, calling for the establishment of a provisional government made up of all parties involved in the civil war. Nothing was said about Wilson's cherished elimination of Huerta, and nothing was said about the salute to the American flag. The agreement was promptly invalidated, however, when Carranza, whose Constitutionalists were by then on the brink of victory, refused to sign it, as he had threatened.

Wilson's part in the conference was hailed enthusiastically in the United States, despite Carranza's attitude. On 26 June the *New York Times* said 'The result of the Niagara Falls conference ... is such a triumph for President Wilson's much misunderstood policy as to astonish even the staunchest supporters of the President....' But the Republicans were not impressed. Their backing for Wilson had evaporated when it became clear that he was not going to order his forces to advance beyond Veracruz, and they criticised his sit-tight intervention as a 'hesitation waltz—one step forward, two steps backward, and then side-step'.

By the beginning of May the U.S. Army's Fifth Brigade had joined the marines in Veracruz. Many of them expected—and indeed hoped—to continue their march until they reached Mexico City. Their expectations were shared by their peppery little commander, General Frederick Funston. 'Merely give the order and leave the rest to me,' he assured the Secretary of War, Lindley Garrison. Garrison, too, was willing enough but was shackled by Wilson's policy of 'Veracruz and no further'.

So the 7000-strong force of soldiers and marines was destined to sweat through a disagreeable summer, impotent observers of the fall of Huerta and the outbreak of another bitter civil war.

By the end of April the tide was running irrevocably against Huerta. On 24 April, Monterrey, the biggest city in the north, fell to the army of Pablo González. On 10 May a heavy attack was launched against Tampico. A big oil storage tank was set on fire and the rebels used its light to press home night attacks. The town fell on 14 May after both sides had sustained heavy losses. General Morelos Zaragoza lost more than half his 5000 garrison killed or captured, and the Constitutionalists suffered 1500 casualties.

A Dutch warship landed a guard to protect oil installations belonging to the Shell company, but none of the other foreign warships hovering off the port put ashore an armed party. Representatives of the five biggest American oil companies at Tampico appealed to President Wilson to land troops, but the Americans had their hands full in Veracruz.

Of the northern towns only Saltillo, which had been bolstered by the remnants of the garrisons of Torreón and Monterrey, still remained in Federal hands. It was the question of who should capture Saltillo which forced into the open the ill-concealed rift between Carranza and Villa.

Villa was preparing in Torreón for an advance southwards against the mining town of Zacatecas, the final obstacle between the Division of the North and Mexico City, when Carranza arrived without warning and ordered Villa to turn his forces aside and capture Saltillo, which he claimed was a danger to the Constitutionalists' flank. Saltillo did indeed constitute a problem but it was ludicrous that Villa should have been asked to eliminate the Federals there, since a strong section of Pablo González's Division of the North-East was at Monterrey, only fifty miles from Saltillo, while Villa's forces would be compelled to trek 180 miles east from Torreón.

Villa and General Angeles proposed that they should take Zacatecas first, and then return to subdue Saltillo, but Carranza knew that if the Division of the North went any further south it would not stop until it rolled into Mexico City—and the First Chief was willing to go to any lengths to prevent that happening.

If Villa occupied the capital, Carranza feared that his dreams of the presidency would quickly evaporate. So he insisted, bringing to bear all the stubbornness which was to exasperate politicians and military men for the next six years, and eventually Villa gave way. 'Well, we'll do it to please the Chief,' he said impetuously to Angeles.

The Division of the North began to move against Saltillo on 11 May. The inhabitants, who had long been awaiting a rebel attack, had been filling their bathtubs each night in case the attackers should suddenly cut or poison the water supply. By 17 May the Division of the North was approaching the perimeter town of Paredón, garrisoned by 5000 Federals. The disheartened government troops were no match for the 8000 cavalry Villa flung into action and within an hour the battle was over. The Federals lost 500 dead, 2500 wounded and prisoners and all their equipment. 'Some of my men had the pleasure of bringing in fifteen or twenty prisoners each,' reported Villa.

After the capture of Paredón Villa was lunching outside the town when some of his soldiers brought in two captured Federal officers and asked what should be done with them. Without looking up from his meal, Villa ordered that they should be shot. When Jesús Acuña, a member of Carranza's retinue who was with the Division of the North as an observer, tried to intervene on the prisoners' behalf, Villa rounded on him and shouted 'Why are you afraid to see the laws of the Revolution carried out? You chocolate-drinking politicians want to triumph without remembering the blood-drenched battlefields.' Then he had the two officers shot in front of the luncheon table to teach Acuña a lesson. The bodies lay there throughout the meal.

On 20 May Saltillo fell without a fight; the Federal troops deserted *en masse* or made their way southwards in small groups, and Villa remained there until the end of May, when he handed over the town to Pablo González. According to Villa, he had a cordial talk with González at which the two agreed that, with Obregón's forces, they should make a triple, triumphant entry into Mexico City. But Carranza intended to let nothing of the kind happen.

While Villa was preoccupied with the Saltillo campaign, the First Chief travelled to Durango where he met Pánfilo

Natera, the Constitutionalist chief in the state of Zacatecas. Natera's forces were entrusted with the capture of the town of Zacatecas, but proved incapable of doing so. After a costly and fruitless three-day assault Natera sent a request for reinforcements.

On 11 June Carranza passed on the request to Villa, who was by now back in Torreón, ordering him to detach 5000 men from his forces to help Natera. Villa, preparing to move all his men south, demurred, saying he preferred to keep the Division intact. When Carranza repeated the order, Villa requested a telegraphic confrontation on 13 June. Surrounded by their officers and advisers, the two men sat—Villa in Torreón and Carranza in Saltillo—in the railway station offices dictating a conversation to the operators. The wires were soon humming with angry words. Carranza was adamant that Villa should detach part of his forces to help Natera. Villa, equally dogmatic, was eventually goaded into signalling Carranza, 'Señor, I resign command of this Division. Tell me to whom to deliver it.' This was an unexpected stroke of luck for Carranza. His most dangerous rival had offered to eliminate himself.

Villa's officers were wandering around, angry and depressed, when General Angeles, who had missed the dramatic resignation, entered the Torreón railway office. General Maclovio Herrera had just ordered the terrified operator to send the message 'Señor Carranza, I am informed of your treatment of my General Francisco Villa. You are a son of a bitch,' and was standing over him with a loaded revolver to make sure the message was transmitted, while another general, José Trinidad Rodríguez (soon to be killed at Zacatecas), said sadly, 'I am going up and eat roots in the mountains.' Angeles quickly restored unity of purpose to Villa's officers, and next day they signalled a rejection of Carranza's demand that they should get together and nominate a successor as commander of the Division.

Villa was by now regretting his impulsive action and was anxious to retain command. But Carranza flatly refused to reconsider his acceptance of Villa's resignation, and reiterated that the other generals should pick a new leader.

Forced to choose between disloyalty to their chief and

rebellion against Carranza, Villa's officers took the second
course and Angeles telegraphed the First Chief: '... We do
not accept your decision.... We know well that you were
looking for the opportunity to stop General Villa ... because
of your purpose to remove from the Revolutionary scene
the men who can think without your orders, who do not
flatter and praise you....'

The break had come. But it did not immediately affect the
rebel cause or prove of any relief to Huerta. On 17 June,
without consulting Carranza, Villa moved the Division of
the North towards Zacatecas. By 20 June a force of 23,000
was assembled on all sides of the town. Two days were
spent preparing the troops and siting Angeles' artillery.
Villa sent in his Division against a Federal garrison outnumbered two to one at 10 a.m. on 23 June, ordering them
to take Zacatecas that day.

The most bitter fighting centred around the three
northern heights which dominated the town. One by one
they were shelled, climbed and captured. While Villa and
Angeles were with a forward battery watching the progress
of the battle they had a narrow escape. Villa described it:
'... An enormous explosion enveloped us. My only feeling,
as I remember, was one of admiration for the enemy who
were bombarding us with such accuracy. But when the
smoke and dust cleared away we saw that no enemy shell
had fallen ... the men at the nearest gun all lay on the
ground, either dead or wounded. We ran to the spot and
learned that a shell had exploded in the hands of the gunner
as he was getting ready to fire it.'

As the final height in front of Zacatecas was captured,
Federal resistance crumbled. The rebels poured fire down
into the town and the terrified conscripts of the garrison fled
in any direction to escape the bullets. By early evening all
resistance had been crushed and Zacatecas was in Villa's
hands. 'Later reports confirmed my estimate that out of
12,000 defenders of Zacatecas no more than 200 escaped,'
wrote Villa afterwards. 'They left us their cannon, their
machine-guns, and almost all their rifles. They left us their
supplies and their munitions....

'The next day at nine in the morning I entered Zacatecas;
and as I contemplated the battlefield and the streets, the

magnitude of the holocaust was visible. Those who came out to meet me, men, women and children, had to leap over the corpses to greet me. Beside the enemy dead many of my soldiers lay resting, sleeping in pools of blood.'

Villa was in such good humour after his overwhelming triumph that he unexpectedly spared the lives of captured officers. But there was almost a repetition of the Benton incident when Villa's men arrested Donald St Clair Douglas, the British vice-consul in Zacatecas, and accused him of assisting the Federals during the battle. Douglas faced a summary trial and execution until Villa ordered that no hasty action be taken. Theodore C. Hamm, the American vice-consul in Durango, hurried to Zacatecas to observe at the trial, which resulted in the acquittal of Douglas. But he was ordered to leave the country immediately.

Still in benevolent mood, Villa sent Carranza a report of his successes at Zacatecas as if no dispute had ever taken place. Though Villa was willing to forgive, Carranza was not. The one thing Villa had *not* captured at Zacatecas was a supply of coal for his trains, and when Carranza cut off his supplies of fuel from the north, Villa's division lay immobilised at Zacatecas. Reinforcements and supplies were diverted instead to Obregón, now nearing Mexico's second largest city, Guadalajara, and to Pablo González. The severing of coal supplies for Villa's trains proved one of the most decisive steps of the Revolution.

The split between the Revolution's two top men was distressing President Wilson, who ordered that George Carothers, the Wilson agent with Villa's forces, and Leon J. Canova, who had a similar post at Carranza's headquarters, should attempt to talk the two leaders towards a reconciliation. On 1 July the two Americans had a long interview with Carranza in Saltillo. The First Chief launched into a tirade against Villa, complaining that all the Constitutionalists' troubles, such as the Benton affair, emanated from Villa-held territory.

He further charged that when he had supplied Villa with five million pesos to redeem the currency issued in Chihuahua, Villa had simply spent it, instead of calling in what Carranza considered counterfeit money. Such lack of discipline could not be tolerated, said Carranza.

Villa, on his way north to negotiate for coal and supplies, saw Carothers in Torreón on 3 July. He expressed willingness for a reconciliation with Carranza, but made it clear that he regarded this as purely a temporary expedient. He told Carothers the Constitutionalist armies were realising that Carranza was not the man they wanted as president and he predicted that, after the fall of Mexico City, the generals would choose another leader.

Pablo González, too, attempted to heal the breach by holding a conference of generals from his own army and the Division of the North at Torreón. They presented a pact for Carranza's approval but, still fearful that attempts were being made to sidetrack him, he rejected it.

Carranza was hanging on, hoping for someone other than Villa to take Mexico City. Obregón was daily becoming the best bet. On 6 July his Division of the North-West, at last over the Pacific coast mountains, burst upon Guadalajara, routing the Federal garrison. Now nothing stood between Obregón and the capital.

A day before the fall of Guadalajara, Huerta's régime had gone through the formality of the 'elections' promised for July after the abysmal flop of the previous October. This time, however, there was not even a list of candidates for the public to choose from. No official result was ever given; nor did it much matter. The rebels were rapidly closing Huerta's remaining escape routes and the dictator, facing certain death, would be forced to flee within days.

On 9 July Huerta took the first step by appointing Francisco S. Carvajal, Chief Justice of the Supreme Court, as his Secretary of Foreign Relations, thus placing Carvajal next in line for the presidency after himself and General Blanquet. Carvajal had been Díaz's peace commissioner during the border talks with Madero in 1911, Mexican Minister in London and latterly a staunch Huerta supporter.

On 15 July Huerta submitted his resignation to the Chamber of Deputies. Afterwards he made his way to his favourite drinking place, the Colón, followed, according to the *Daily Mail*, 'by an immense crowd shouting *vivas*. Many shook him by the hand, others embraced and kissed him. The stern veteran, overcome by the demonstrations, raised his glass and said, "This will be my last glass here. I drink to the new President of Mexico." '

Huerta's resignation was hailed by the *New York Times* as 'Another Wilson Triumph', and the paper declared 'The wisdom of the President's course has ... been clearly proved.'

Like Díaz before him, Huerta sailed into exile on a German ship. He boarded the cruiser *Dresden* at Puerto Mexico on 17 July. The *Dresden*'s captain and his entire officer complement stood at attention on the railway platform in Puerto Mexico to welcome the departing dictator and to escort him to their ship.

Huerta landed in Spain on 1 August 1914 ... three days before Europe exploded into war.

Part Four: Carranza

Hostilities between the Constitutionalists and the government forces ended on 18 July with the capture by Jesús Carranza of San Luis Potosí, 250 miles north of Mexico City. The stand-in president, Carvajal, tried to initiate negotiations for the peaceful takeover of the capital, but Venustiano Carranza thrust aside all suggestions of talks. He was interested only in the unconditional surrender of the Huertistas, and his assurance that no excesses would be permitted against the conquered element was tempered by a threat that all those who had supported Huerta, whether civilians or military, would be punished as 'enemies of democracy'.

By the end of July Obregón had moved his forces as far as the railway junction of Irapuato, 200 miles north-west of Mexico City. And, with Pablo González's Division of the North-East established at Querétaro, seventy miles to the east of Obregón, there was now no way for Villa's Division of the North to get to the capital, except by risking the possibility of a clash with other Constitutionalist troops barring their way. Villa, however, was already preoccupied with the approaching confrontation with Carranza, and spent most of July in the northern part of the Republic, recruiting for his Division and organising supplies and ammunition. On 25 July Marion Letcher, the U.S. Consul in Chihuahua City, told Washington, 'Nobody here doubts the purpose of his activity.'

The problem of the peaceful hand-over of Mexico City was further complicated when, in the face of Carranza's insistence on unconditional surrender, Carvajal decided not to run the risk of facing a firing squad and followed Huerta into exile. This left Eduardo N. Iturbide, governor of the Federal District (which is comparable with the District of Columbia in the United States), in charge of maintaining law and order. His task was a monumental one, since Zapata's forces were harassing the suburbs of the capital, and if the Federal garrison were withdrawn—as Carranza insisted—before the take-over, the Zapatistas would be in a much better position than the Constitutionalist armies to move in on the undefended city.

Eventually Carranza saw the necessity of maintaining armed defenders in the capital until his forces could move in. The First Chief's acceptance of the Federals' offer to man their positions until the Constitutionalist take-over immediately alienated Zapata, who recognised it for the act of hostility it undoubtedly was. As he had opposed Díaz, Madero and Huerta, Zapata would now oppose Carranza for five more bitter and bloody years. The fact that Zapata and Carranza had both fought Huerta was, as Robert Quirk has put it, 'a historical accident': during the whole of the anti-Huerta uprising there had been no communication between the First Chief and the self-styled Attila of the South.

By 9 August Obregón had reached the tiny railway station of Teoloyucan, twenty miles north of Mexico City. Two days later a delegation from the capital, headed by Iturbide, who had taken the precaution of making his will and resigning his military rank of brigadier which went with his gubernatorial position, travelled to Teoloyucan to arrange for the hand-over of the city. In view of the Constitutionalists' habit of shooting all Federal officers, the negotiating group, which included ministers representing the foreign element in Mexico City, travelled unescorted.

According to Iturbide, 'Obregón began by telling me he could not understand why I had come ... when no Federal officer or subordinate had ever come out alive from a Constitutionalist camp. I replied that I had something to discuss with him of much more importance than my life ... we must talk of Mexico City, which was in an awful condition. ...'

Over lunch another Constitutionalist general, Francisco Coss, did little for Iturbide's peace of mind by telling the Federal District governor that he would be shot the next day; and another officer added that if Carranza tried to defend Iturbide they would shoot him, too.

Carranza arrived by train in Teoloyucan at nine that night, but refused to see the Mexico City delegation until the following morning. When Iturbide eventually faced Carranza he was again threatened with death as the First Chief vowed that all Huerta supporters in the capital 'would soon pay for their crimes'.

Iturbide found Carranza 'very stubborn and hard to convince' but eventually the First Chief agreed to Iturbide's suggestion that the Federal troops defending Mexico City should move out south-eastwards towards Puebla and that the capital's police force should attempt to maintain order until the take-over was complete. Obregón, however, insisted that the Federals should leave behind their arms and ammunition before evacuating, and Iturbide returned to the city to negotiate this point, promising to return the next day.

It says much for Iturbide's nerve that he refused to take this last chance of escaping to Veracruz and exile. On 13 August he stuck his head into the lion's mouth once more by going back to Teoloyucan to sign agreements calling for the withdrawal and disbanding of the Federal forces and, on Obregón's part, a promise that the city's inhabitants would not be molested. Carranza would promise nothing.

Next day the Federals pulled out—all, that is, except the units of Orozco's *Colorados* who had retreated south as their cause withered. Knowing they could expect no mercy from the Constitutionalists, they went over to Zapata who, badly in need of reinforcements for the looming clash with Carranza, welcomed them.

Obregón entered Mexico City on 15 August 1914. He immediately imposed martial law and banned the sale of alcohol. Iturbide, having safely negotiated the peaceful occupation of the capital, offered himself as a prisoner of war but Obregón, impressed by his bravery and honesty, sent him home after exacting a promise that he would not try to leave. Three days later Carranza made his triumphal entry, which was only slightly marred by the fact that Pablo González refused to take part because he resented the First Chief's request that he ride on the left of Carranza while Obregón occupied the position of honour on his right.

Carranza immediately announced a cabinet for his provisional régime and vainly set about trying to make friends with Zapata, who warily refused to leave his mountain headquarters, commenting brusquely that Carranza's Plan of Guadalupe was 'more worthless' than Madero's Plan of

San Luis Potosí had been and demanding, as his price of co-operation with the new régime, complete allegiance to his own Plan of Ayala. Agreement to this, implying as it did subordination to Zapata as leader of the Revolution, was, of course, completely unacceptable to Carranza and was rejected out of hand.

Carranza's threatened retribution against the capital's Huerta supporters was not long in coming. Within twenty-four hours of arriving in Mexico City he had halted the railway service to Veracruz, thus cutting the last escape route, closed the courts and suspended the legal guarantees of the country's constitution. After a clash between the police and the rebel troops, Carranza ordered that the police should be disarmed. Now there was no one to prevent the widespread looting and killing. The example was set by the generals. Lucio Blanco, the first leader into Mexico City at the head of Obregón's forces, moved into the home of the wealthy Casasús family on the Paseo de la Reforma, the capital's main thoroughfare, and Obregón occupied a mansion on the same boulevard. The ordinary soldiers contented themselves with looting homes, confiscating horses and cars and settling private scores—or, as one rebel officer smilingly told an American official, 'finishing with their enemies'. On the night of 26 August alone, forty-two civilians were killed and thirty-seven wounded by revolutionary troops, according to a Red Cross report.

While the troops of Zapata and Carranza faced each other uneasily on the outskirts of Mexico City, trouble broke out unexpectedly in the north, where a pro-Carranza garrison under General Plutarco Elías Calles, one of Obregón's top men, was besieged in Naco, which straddled the Mexico-United States border, by forces under the Sonora state governor, José María Maytorena, who was a Villa supporter.

Hoping to prevent more border trouble, Obregón received permission to confer with Villa about the Naco problem. The two chieftains met in Chihuahua City on 24 August, and Villa extended a friendly welcome to the apprehensive Obregón. They travelled to the American border where, on 29 August, they talked to the contending factions. An 'agreement' was quickly worked out which, however, was a shelving, rather than a solution, of the dispute. Calles' force was left in control of Naco and Governor Maytoren's besieging force withdrew to the south.

Back in Chihuahua City, Villa and Obregón had further long talks about the need for preserving revolutionary unity and on 3 September they produced a nine-point plan designed to guide the Revolution into smoother waters. The main requirements, pressed home fiercely by Villa and agreed to by Obregón, who at this stage was willing to sacrifice Carranza for the sake of a settlement, required Carranza to become interim president, to appoint judges and mayors and then to arrange presidential elections which would exclude the First Chief himself.

When Obregón got back to Mexico City with the plan on 9 September he found that Carranza had already taken steps to silence criticism that he was well on the way to becoming Mexico's next dictator. He had called an assembly of Constitutionalist leaders for 1 October and told Obregón that only a meeting of this stature could discuss the future of the Revolution. The matters which Obregón and Villa had agreed upon 'should be laid before the entire nation', Carranza maintained.

The uneasy peace in the north was soon shattered by a resumption of fighting between the Villista and Carrancista factions in Sonora, and Obregón left Mexico City by train on 13 September for more talks with Villa in Chihuahua. He also carried an invitation for Villa and his advisers to attend the October conference in the capital.

Obregón arrived in Chihuahua City early on 16 September, Mexico's Independence Day. Villa had prepared an impressive military parade, which the two generals reviewed from the balcony of the Governor's Palace. Villa recalled that the parade lasted 'three to four hours, as there were so many brigades and they marched slowly, to display their good appearance'. When Obregón asked if his arms stockpile was equally impressive, Villa showed his visitor buildings stacked with crates of rifles and seven million cartridges.

Hopes that their latest round of talks would be fruitful

were ruined the next day when Villa received news from
Governor Maytorena that the Obregón generals, Benjamín
Hill and Plutarco Elías Calles, were violating the truce
agreement in Sonora. Villa, convinced that Obregón was
deceiving him, launched into a furious tirade which was at
its height when Leon Canova, the American presidential
agent, arrived at Villa's headquarters for an appointment.

Suddenly Villa turned to his secretary, Luis Aguirre
Benavides, and ordered 'Bring a platoon of twenty men to
shoot this traitor.' Soon the building was surrounded.
Canova, who told his superiors in Washington that he did
not wish to appear to be 'eavesdropping', moved away to a
more discreet distance, thus robbing the scene of an im-
partial observer.

Villa threatened to shoot Obregón on the spot unless he
sent a telegram to his generals in Sonora ordering them to
abide by the ceasefire agreement of the previous month.
When Obregón had agreed to this (though later he managed
to send off a secret message countermanding his instructions), Villa stormed out of the room 'in search of repose'.
A little while later Villa calmed down, sent away the
execution squad and rejoined Obregón.

'He sat down and invited me to be seated beside him'
(wrote Obregón in his autobiography). 'Never before was I
so ready to accept an invitation.... With signs of deep
emotion ... Villa addressed me thus: "Francisco Villa is
not a traitor. He is not the man to kill unarmed people, and
least of all to kill you, comrade, who are my guest. If you
had come to this place with troops a good deal of powder
and ball would have passed between us. But as you have
come alone you have no ground for misgivings. The des-
tinies of the Republic are in your hands and mine. United,
you and I dominate the country ... and as I am a grey,
obscure, uneducated man, it is you who will be the president."

'My situation had become delicate' (Obregón continued).
'All I said to him was "The contest is over now. We need
not give our thoughts to war any more. At the next election
that man will rise to the top who has acquired the sympathies of the majority".... Thereupon a dead silence
ensued.... It was at length broken by the arrival of a lad,

who suddenly stalked into the room and cried "Supper is ready". Villa rose, dried his tears, turned to me and said "Come and have supper, dear comrade, now that everything is over and done with." '

Obregón and Villa worked together amicably for the next three days. Villa agreed to be represented at the 1 October conference, though he refused to attend in person. He also sent a telegram (addressed, significantly, to 'Señor General' Carranza, not 'First Chief') demanding that the Zapatistas be invited too.

On 21 September Obregón left for Mexico City, accompanied by Villa's generals José Isabel Robles, Eugenio Aguirre Benavides—the brother of Villa's secretary—and Roque González Garza, who were to represent their commander at the conference. In the meantime, however, reports had filtered back to the capital of the row between Villa and Obregón. Carranza was told that Obregón was a prisoner, and fearing an attack by the Division of the North, he suspended communications with the north and ordered railway tracks to be torn up. When, in turn, Villa heard of Carranza's actions, he was furious.

He formally withdrew recognition of Carranza as First Chief, rescinded his decision to be represented at the October conference and, ominously, ordered that Obregón's train should be halted and brought back to Chihuahua City. The train was stopped at Ceballos, a small station just north of Torreón, and Villa's orders were passed on to the mystified occupants. When the train pulled into Chihuahua City Obregón was confronted by Villa, waving the bunch of telegrams he had exchanged with Carranza and so angry that he could hardly speak. Obregón was the innocent target on whom Villa vented his fury against Carranza. Obregón's life again hung by the undependable thread of Villa's common sense and, though he repeatedly told Obregón he intended to have him shot—and was supported in his threats by cut-throat aides like Tomás Urbina and Rodolfo Fierro—Villa eventually calmed down and was swayed by the advice of Angeles, González Garza, the Aguirre Benavides brothers and Robles to allow Obregón to return to Mexico City.

That evening, over an anxious dinner, Villa told

Obregón he was being allowed to return to Mexico City, but when Obregón heard that the travel arrangements were being handled by Fierro he realised that he was escaping formal execution only to be assassinated *en route*.

Now the situation acquired overtones of Mack Sennett. Just before Obregón's train was due to depart on the evening of 23 September, another train under the command of General Mateo Almanza left Chihuahua City with orders to waylay Obregón *en route* to Torreón and kill him. But during the night, while Almanza's train had pulled into a siding for repairs, Obregón's train passed it without exciting comment, for Almanza had told no one else of his orders.

When Villa learned that Obregón had eluded Almanza, he telegraphed ahead of the train, ordering it to be stopped once more. There are widely differing accounts among the participants about the end of this bizarre incident. Villa maintained he was persuaded once again by the three generals accompanying Obregón to allow him to live 'but I consider that I did wrong'. Obregón wrote in his memoirs that he and his aides leapt from the train, prepared to die fighting rather than face certain execution in Chihuahua City and made their escape. In fact, he had come so close to death that some newspapers in the capital carried reports of his being shot. Whatever the truth of the matter, Obregón *did* make his way to safety and his extremely lucky escape from Villa's vengeance changed the course of Mexico's history. Villa had spared the one man who was to prove capable of overcoming the formidable Division of the North.

The prospect of a showdown with Carranza was one which pleased Villa. When he told Leon Canova of the break the American reported that 'his eyes were dancing, apparently in delight over the decision'. On 30 September, as his army began to move south again, Villa issued a 'Manifesto to the Mexican People' repudiating Carranza and inviting all Mexicans to join him in replacing the First Chief with a civilian government.

Now that Villa was taking steps to crush Carranza, some generals had to decide on which side of the fence they belonged. Most of Villa's officers were solidly behind him, but he was shocked to lose the support of one of his dearest allies, Maclovio Herrera 'whom I had protected and carried to his greatest triumphs'. The Arrieta brothers, Domingo and Mariano, based in Durango, also refused to back Villa.

As elements of the Division of the North, based in Torreón, began to menace as far south as Zacatecas, there were frantic moves from peace-minded Constitutionalists to effect a reconciliation between the stubborn Carranza and the violent Villa.

Villa wanted only to rid Mexico of Carranza's influence and was willing to go to any lengths to achieve this, even suggesting that he and the First Chief take part in a joint suicide pact—'I am ready to propose not only that he and I leave our country but that we depart this world altogether.'

The peace-minded elements, still led—despite his perilous time in Chihuahua—by Obregón on one side and Generals Robles and Eugenio Aguirre Benavides on the other, conferred in Zacatecas and decided that a full convention representing all elements of the Revolution should meet in the town of Aguascalientes, 330 miles north-west of Mexico City on 10 October to attempt to restore unity and to plan for Mexico's future.

This decision effectively neutered the conference called in Mexico City by Carranza, although it still took place. Seventy-nine delegates, all Carranza supporters or personally invited by the First Chief, gathered in the Chamber of Deputies. No representatives of Villa or Zapata were present.

The delegates' first act was to vote to adjourn the conference on 5 October and to reconvene in Aguascalientes five days after that. Although the conference was now of little importance, one vital step was taken. It occurred on 3 October when Carranza, wearing a blue suit and a blue peaked cap which made him look, according to one of the delegates, like a ship's steward, came to the Chamber to address the conference and ended by offering his resignation. Not surprisingly, since the vast majority of the voters were hard-core Carrancistas, the First Chief's offer was rejected, but Obregón probably spoke for many when he suggested that the offer be turned down only on the grounds that it was 'inopportune' in view of the forthcoming, and far more important, convention at Aguascalientes.

The only other decision taken by the conference, on the final day, 5 October, was that only military men should be permitted to attend the convention—a decision which brought bitter protests from Carranza's legal brain, Luis Cabrera. And so the speech-making scene moved to the fateful Convention of Aguascalientes.

Aguascalientes (Hot Waters) proved to be aptly named. Situated roughly on the boundary of the areas controlled by Villa and Carranza, it housed the strangest gathering even in Mexico's turbulent and colourful history. The quiet spa town was crowded with military men. In the Morelos Theatre, which housed the Convention, the delegates sat clutching their rifles and revolvers, signifying applause by crashing rifle butts on the floor. Speeches were punctuated by pistol shots. In this circus atmosphere was decided Mexico's tottering course for the next few years.

'I had only to take one look at that military assembly to be convinced that nothing would come of its deliberations,' wrote Martín Luis Guzmán, whose political imprisonment at the hands of Carranza was terminated just in time for him to attend the Convention as an observer. '. . . It lacked the civic consciousness and the far-seeing patriotism that was needed at that moment.

'But . . . as a show it was a brilliant success. . . . At times the show provoked laughter; at times it left one perplexed and bewildered; at other times it produced its catharsis, for it was a tragedy in fact if not in form, with its fatal struggle between two irreconcilable forces. Two profound aspects of the same nationality were locked here in a death struggle. . . .'

In the beginning, at least, there was a solidarity. After appointing Antonio I. Villareal, a Carrancista but a radical, President of the Convention, the 152 delegates came forward one by one to sign the Mexican flag hanging on the stage. Then Villistas and Carrancistas exchanged embraces. The first five days of the Convention were spent in speculation about the Zapatista delegation which had failed to arrive. On 16 October the Convention decided to send General Felipe Angeles to Zapata's headquarters with a verbal invitation to attend the talks as quickly as possible.

The next day Villa, who had set up headquarters at Guadalupe, 100 miles north of Aguascalientes, travelled south to take his oath of allegiance to the Convention. Villa's incoherent speech to the delegates was rendered even more difficult to follow when he broke down and wept in the middle of it. Afterwards, in an unexpected gesture of forgiveness on both sides, Villa and Obregón exchanged bear-like *abrazos* outside the theatre. Though some delegates complained that they had been approached by drunken soldiers and forced at gunpoint to shout 'Viva Villa', it seemed that Villa was making a determined effort to maintain a neutral attitude, and to stay at a neutral distance, from the Convention.

Carranza, however, refused to attend the Convention or to send a personal representative. It was a carefully calculated move. Had he attended, he would have been reduced to the level of 150 other delegates. Even to have sent a spokesman would have amounted to admission of the legality of the Convention. This Carranza was extremely careful never to do.

That this attitude aroused deep feeling among some delegates was made clear when a documentary film of the Revolution was shown at the Morelos Theatre one evening. The event proved a popular one and Martín Luis Guzmán and the Obregón general, Lucio Blanco, were unable to find seats. So they went backstage, appropriated a couple of chairs and watched the film from behind the screen.

As the various heroes of the Revolution appeared, there were cheers and *vivas* from the packed audience. But when Carranza's face shone on the screen, a cry from the hall of 'Long Live the First Chief' was answered by a storm of boos and hisses. The next scene, showing Carranza making a triumphal horseback entry into Mexico City, brought an uproar of boos and cheers, culminating in two revolver shots. Both of them perforating the screen at the height of the First Chief's chest and struck the wall inches above the heads of Guzmán and Blanco.

'If the First Chief had entered Mexico City on foot instead of on horseback, the bullets would have found their mark in us,' wrote Guzmán. 'Ah, but if he had entered on foot he would not have been Carranza, and if he had not been Carranza there would not have been any shots, for there would have been no Convention!'

From Morelos, Angeles sent word that he would return to the Convention with twenty-six Zapata delegates (including five generals and sixteen colonels) on 25 October, but when a welcoming delegation went to meet the train it roared straight through Aguascalientes station and carried on to Guadalupe, since the Zapatistas had asked to meet Villa first, in order to 'exchange impressions'. Next day the wary Zapatistas entered the Morelos Theatre, looking, according to the Convention's recording secretary, Vito Alessio Robles, like a troop of soldiers crossing a dangerous defile.

They were a picturesque group, wearing huge sombreros, skin-tight trousers and peasant blouses. Even their leader, the lawyer Antonio Díaz Soto y Gama, was dressed this way. 'Anybody who did not know him would have taken him for the driver of a *pulque* wagon,' Guzmán commented.

With their arrival the Convention burst into life. According to Guzmán it also underwent a serious moral and cultural decline. The Zapatistas quickly threw off their wariness and began to bombard the Convention with demands for the unconditional recognition of Zapata's Plan of Ayala —the first time Zapata had secured a public hearing for his programme of land and liberty.

The spirit of friendliness towards the Zapata delegation underwent a violent change on 27 October when Antonio Díaz Soto y Gama rose to speak. He was a brilliant orator and a rabid Socialist. Robert Quirk has written of him, 'At the age of thirty, Díaz Soto was already an accomplished revolutionary.... He knew nothing of the battlefields; his forte was the quintain of parliamentary oratory. Díaz Soto had a propensity for inciting dislike. He talked too much, heaping abuse and scorn upon his listeners as unfeelingly as though he were unloading garbage.... His subsequent rationalisation was that he was an "anarchist", though this is scarcely an explanation for his bizarre behaviour.... Perhaps all that can be said is that he was the complete revolutionary, in the intellectual, if not the physical, sense of the word....'

Díaz Soto began his speech on a balanced enough note, urging the Convention to speak what was in their hearts, in defiance of Carranza and Villa. He went on to list the great leaders of humanity: Buddha, Jesus Christ, St Francis, Karl Marx and Zapata. Then suddenly he seized the Mexican flag, the sacred flag bearing the signatures of the delegates, crumpled it and shook it at his audience.

'What is the good of this dyed rag, bedaubed with the image of a bird of prey?', he asked. 'How is it possible, gentlemen of the Revolution, that for a hundred years we have been venerating this silly mummery, this lie?'

As cries of 'No, no' rose from the astonished delegates, Díaz Soto plunged on: 'I, gentlemen, will never sign this banner. We are making a great revolution today to destroy the lies of history, and we are going to expose the lie of history that is in this flag....'

The rest of his words were lost in uproar. Leon Canova, who witnessed the scene, wrote to William Jennings Bryan that:

'The members [of the Convention] rose to their feet, faces livid with indignation, trembling and shaking their fists at the speaker, who stood calmly in the tribune above them, awaiting the passing of the storm. The beautiful flag, which was affixed to the left side of the tribune, was snatched away and borne to the centre of the stage while on the floor pandemonium was rampant. Delegates screamed at one another, with left hands pounding their chests, and right hands on their pistols.... The chairman was pounding the bell for order, but no sound of the bell could be heard.... From the crowded boxes and galleries of the theatre, humanity was tumbling over itself in a mad effort to escape imminent danger....'

Through it all the foolhardy Díaz Soto stood calmly, facing a forest of pistols. When the uproar abated he said quietly, 'When you have finished, I'll go on.' Díaz Soto, realising he had overstepped the mark, *did* go on—to explain that he had been misunderstood and that he had meant no disrespect for the flag. The damage had been done, however. The Zapatistas came to be recognised as erratic extremists and when they allied themselves with the Villistas later in the Convention, the more moderate ele-

ments among the Constitutionalists chose what they considered the lesser of two evils and stuck by Carranza.

The obdurate Carranza was still the stumbling block. On
29 October Obregón dramatically opened a sealed envelope
from the First Chief and read out his message to the
Convention. Carranza said that if the Convention decided he
was an obstacle to unity he was 'disposed to retire'. But in
return he demanded the retirement of Villa and Zapata.
The Zapatistas were outraged that their leader should be
lumped with Carranza and Villa as a threat to revolutionary unity, and heckling and fighting broke out in the theatre
among the delegations. When order was restored the Convention continued in secret session, and quickly voted overwhelmingly in favour of the retirement of Villa and Carranza. Only twenty delegates wanted to keep Carranza.
However, no decision was taken on the First Chief's demand for the retirement of Zapata.

When General Angeles telegraphed Villa asking for his
support of the Convention's decision, he received this
answer: 'I propose not only that the Convention retire
Carranza from his post in exchange for retiring me from
mine, but that the Convention order both of us shot.' It
seemed that Villa was still willing to go to any lengths to rid
Mexico of Carranza.

As the Convention moved into its second month the
delegates took steps to complete the replacement of Carranza by naming their own provisional president. Once
again the Morelos Theatre was the scene of squabbling, dissension and deadlock over the rival claims of the favourite,
Antonio I. Villareal, and his opponent José Isabel Robles.
The Zapata and Villa delegations refused to support Villareal because he was a Carrancista, albeit a radical one,
and the bulk of the Carranza Constitutionalists rejected
Robles because he was a Villa man. Eventually, on 2
November, the Convention settled on a compromise candidate, Eulalio Gutiérrez, nicknamed mockingly by the
Zapata delegation *el presidente accidental*. Gutiérrez had
the acceptable background—a fighter for Madero and an
opponent of Huerta. A former fisherman, stevedore, small
shopkeeper and petty lawyer, he first made his mark in the
Revolution as a dynamiter of 'bold and inventive capaci-

ties'. He was an honourable man, but his political experience was strictly limited. The Convention had chosen a small man to fill a dauntingly large seat.

On 3 November it was decided to send a commission, headed by Obregón, to Mexico City to deliver to Carranza the news that he had been superseded by Guitérrez. But Carranza was not around to meet them. On 1 November he had left the capital for Tlaxcala, seventy-five miles to the east. Carranza had no intention of seeing the prize for which he had worked and schemed so hard snatched from under his nose. When he wrote to the Convention he had been careful to say that he was 'disposed' to retire, providing certain conditions were met. Now he could equivocate endlessly about those conditions in the certain knowledge that the Convention, already irrevocably split, would soon destroy itself.

As Obregón vainly tried to pin him down, Carranza, first moving to Puebla and then to Córdoba, wrote to the Convention that the conditions for his retirement had not been complied with and that, further, he was receiving assurances of continued support from many state governors and military men who did not want him to retire.

This was too much for the Convention. On 5 November they gave Carranza five days to deliver the executive power to Gutiérrez. Villa, despite his suggestions of suicide, was no more disposed to give up his command than Carranza—at least until there was some proof that the First Chief had stepped down. And he further complicated an already delicate situation by moving sections of the Division of the North nearer Aguascalientes.

On 8 November Carranza published a scathing reply to the Convention's ultimatum. He dismissed the Convention as a 'junta' whose sovereignty 'I have never for a moment recognised.' He refused to accept orders from military men sitting in Aguascalientes and ordered all members of the Convention under his command to withdraw before the expiration of the ultimatum.

Obregón and his commission finally caught up with Carranza in Córdoba on 9 November, when the First Chief put forward more objections—that Gutiérrez had been appointed before he himself had resigned, that Gutiérrez did not possess the qualifications for president and, most bitterly of all, that Villa had not kept his promise to retire.

This ludicrous 'after you' situation was the crux of the tragedy. Carranza refused to quit until there was proof that Villa had stepped down; Villa would not retire until Carranza had formally resigned. And, in a welter of accusations and counter-accusations, Mexico drifted back into war.

As the ultimatum expired Gutiérrez declared Carranza in rebellion, and appointed Villa to command the Army of the Convention. This at once brought General Francisco Coss out on Carranza's side, and by the time the final session of the Convention was held on 13 November, most of the Carranza delegates had complied with the First Chief's order and left Aguascalientes to follow their leader into rebellion. The remaining members voted to adjourn until Villa's forces had captured Mexico City—an admission that civil war had broken out again and that the Convention had been a failure.

The biggest question mark hung over the head of Obregón. Whose side would he take? He had worked energetically for a peaceful solution and, further, had pressed at Aguascalientes for Carranza's resignation. But his personal experiences of the erratic behaviour of Villa, the actions of the Zapatistas at the Convention and Gutiérrez's selection of Villa as commander-in-chief of the Convention forces drove him, however reluctantly, into the welcoming arms of Carranza. His decision was the critical one. Without Obregón's organising genius and loyal soldiers Carranza would have fallen quickly.

On 19 November in Mexico City, Obregón formally declared war on Villa, at the same time preparing to evacuate the capital. Trains, cars and horses were commandeered to expedite the exodus of Carrancista officials to join their First Chief in Córdoba and on 22 November Obregón left Mexico City, turning over its command to his young general, Lucio Blanco.

Carranza was now in charge of a government without a home. But he was soon to be provided with one by the timely withdrawal of the Americans from Veracruz.

During the occupation of Veracruz throughout the summer of 1914 the biggest problem for the commanders of the American force had been keeping the troops busy. Business quickly returned to normal after the capture of the town, many Mexicans prudently choosing to ignore the clause in the Republic's constitution which made it high treason for any Mexican to hold employment under a foreign flag during enemy occupation.

By the end of May Veracruz had become virtually a new town. As the rainy season got under way at the end of May, bringing with it mosquitoes and the threat of disease, American troops and a large Mexican labour force were put to work cleaning up a town which they treated as if it had hardly seen a broom in its 400-year history. Strict sanitation rules were enforced in the public markets, which were, to American eyes, indescribably filthy. Fines, and even imprisonment, were the punishment for people contravening the new regulations.

The vast flock of vultures, tolerated by Veracruzanos for centuries as 'nature's garbage men' could find nothing to scavenge and moved inland to better pickings. A vigorous programme of drainage or oil-covering of pools and canals virtually wiped out the malaria menace in what would normally have been the high season for mosquitoes. The battle damage was made good, with interest. The town's lighting system was repaired, streets were paved, new bridges were built and the water supply was vastly improved.

Schools were re-opened, postal services were re-established and, where possible, taxes collected: in fact, the military eventually took over virtually every function of the former civil régime. Robert Quirk wrote, 'In effect, the American government was a despotism ... Yet it was by all accounts a benevolent despotism, the best government the people of Veracruz had ever had. ...'

It was also, as far as Carranza was concerned, a great bone of contention. Possession of the port, and of its Customs revenues, was of vital importance to the First Chief after the fall of Huerta, and he badgered the Americans ceaselessly about its return to Mexican rule, pointing out that the government against which the invasion had been directed no longer existed. It was quite true that, with the overthrow of Huerta, the Americans had lost even their slender excuse for occupying Mexican territory, and they were more than willing to negotiate a withdrawal which would not involve too much loss of face.

With a neat sense of timing, the Americans informed Carranza on 16 September, Mexico's Independence Day, that the troops would be withdrawn. But the handing over of Veracruz proved much more difficult than its capture. The town was clogged with refugees, and the Constitutionalists threatened harsh measures against these unfortunate people and also against those who had co-operated with the Americans during the occupation.

When President Wilson sought guarantees of safety for all Mexicans in Veracruz, Carranza stubbornly refused, though his need for the port was becoming daily more pressing as Villa prepared to make war on him. October passed with still no settlement—and by then, as a result of the discord at the Convention of Aguascalientes, the Americans found themselves confronted with yet another delicate problem: to which faction should they surrender the port?

Since Carranza found himself forced to flee from Mexico City at the beginning of November, it was he who eventually backed down and gave the assurances required by the Americans about the treatment of civilians. The Convention had already given similar assurances, so on 13 November Washington ordered the evacuation to get under way, omitting, however, to tell the occupation forces to whom they should deliver their prize. But the Carrancistas were the only ones in a position to reoccupy the port quickly.

Early on 23 November the evacuation began. Led by a military band, the American troops marched through the streets to the dockside. By mid-afternoon the withdrawal was complete. The homeless Carranza, his supporters—and the vultures—were soon in firm occupation again. Despite his promises, Carranza punished those who had co-operated with the Americans and refused to employ them, even the schoolteachers.

Carranza's luck was holding. Now he had a base of operations, with a convenient bolt-hole at his back and an assured source of revenue. This good fortune in being closer to Veracruz than anyone else when the Americans withdrew was to prove a major factor in his eventual victory over Villa.

As the hordes of Zapata moved in to occupy Mexico City after Obregón's November evacuation, the civilian population, who for years had been hearing stories about their cruelties, awaited the invasion with understandable trepidation.

But the Zapatistas, described as 'little brown fellows, with heavy cartridge belts buckled around their gaunt bellies and over their shoulders, and antiquated arms in their holsters', filtered into the capital, to all appearances more afraid of their strange surroundings than the inhabitants were scared of them.

They gazed at Mexico City's fine buildings in wide-eyed, rustic astonishment, and peered innocently into the windows of the shops which had been hastily barred by their trembling owners. But the Army of the South made no attempt to loot stores or homes, even though their meagre rations were soon exhausted. Instead they knocked on doors, asking humbly for a little food, or approached a passer-by to beg a peso. If he was offered three or four pesos, the *peon* soldier would refuse the money, saying he was permitted to ask for one peso, no more. When he was hungry again, he would beg another peso.

When it came to horses, however, the Zapatistas shed their restraint. Here was loot of a different calibre. The animals were appropriated wherever and whenever they were found. Mrs Leone Moats, who lived through the shifting occupations of that winter of 1914–15, was driving through the city when she saw 'a most disconsolate-looking bride and groom sitting in their carriage minus the horse, which had been led away by Zapatistas. They presented a thoroughly pathetic spectacle, poor things, marooned there in the middle of the main thoroughfare. . . .'

One well-known Mexican polo player saved his entire string of ponies by secreting them in the empty house next door to his own home; an American woman, Hattie Welton, who owned a riding stable in the city, had to wage a ceaseless battle against the rebels who wanted to steal her animals. Since her horses were her livelihood, she managed to obtain from General Lucio Blanco, who had by now deserted Obregón and joined up with Villa and Zapata, a signed authority that her horses must not be molested. When this proved insufficient she also managed to obtain a written order from Zapata's brother, Eufemio, which was signed by someone in his name, as he could not write. Eufemio also gave the startled Miss Welton a hearty *abrazo* and a peso note with 'Viva Zapata' written on it.

Zapata himself arrived in Mexico City by train on 26 November. But in his reticent, suspicious manner he refused to go to the National Palace, preferring instead to spend the night at a small hotel near the suburban railway station at San Lázaro. He stayed in the capital only three days, scurrying back to his mountain stronghold like a wild animal when he heard of the approach of Villista troops under General Angeles.

His soldiers, too, were inordinately suspicious of anything unusual, and when a fire engine hurried through the city with its bell clanging it was charged by a group of mounted Zapatistas, who picked off several firemen before the shooting could be halted.

Villa was determined not to repeat the mistake made by Carranza in occupying Mexico City in the face of Zapata. He waited at Tacuba, just outside the city, until negotiations had been completed for a first meeting between the two great rebel chieftains on 4 December. Zapata was still reluctant to move completely out of the territory under his domination, even to meet Villa, and would come no nearer than Xochimilco, twelve miles south of Mexico City. So Villa, with a small escort of *Dorados*, rode out for the historic meeting, which was held in the municipal school building of the market town. The Villistas got a great reception. 'So many were the bouquets and wreaths', wrote Villa, 'that our men could not carry them and our horses were walking on them while we rejoiced in our hearts.'

The conference was witnessed by the American presidential agents, Carothers and Canova. According to Canova's account, Villa, tall and florid, was wearing a tropical pith helmet, a large, loose woollen sweater, khaki military trousers, gaiters and riding boots: Zapata, shorter and slighter, was far more neatly turned out in black coat, blue silk neckerchief, lavender shirt, tight *charro* trousers decorated with silver buttons down the seams and a massive sombrero.

After the obligatory *abrazo*, the two men and their aides opened a hesitant conversation. It was not until the name of Carranza was mentioned that their talk struck fire. Then their mutual hatred of the First Chief poured out in torrents. After they had agreed to make a joint triumphal entry into Mexico City on Sunday, 6 December, Zapata called for a bottle of cognac to seal their friendship and, despite Villa's protests, poured two large tumblers full of brandy. '*Compañero*, I accept this drink solely for the pleasure of joining you, for the truth is that I never drink liquor,' Villa told Zapata. Then he swigged the glass of fiery spirit straight down and, with livid face and tears running down his cheeks, huskily Villa called for a glass of water.

The formal occupation of Mexico City began on the morning of 6 December and the parade lasted until five that afternoon. Villa wrote 'The people of the city welcomed us all with the greatest enthusiasm and affection.... How the young ladies showered us with their flowers! They made a little basket of Zapata's hat until the bouquets bent the brim with their weight and overflowed....'

Allene Tupper Wilkes described in *Harper's Weekly* the parade of 'Soldiers afoot in khaki and felt or straw sombreros, mounted soldiers in the most original of *charro* suits, wearing hats that were large to the point of being caricatures. Wonderful hats, some gold or silver trimmed.... A few hours earlier General Villa had passed us, riding side by side with Zapata. A stern, heavy-bodied man, dressed in an elaborate suit of dark blue and gold, hardly recognisable as the Villa I had seen on the border.'

Villa was again outshone by the dapper Zapata, who was sporting a silver-braided *charro* suit with elaborate silver buttons and a twenty-gallon white sombrero and riding a superb white horse.

Later that day Eulalio Gutiérrez, the provisional president, held a banquet at the National Palace for the generals, ministers in his newly-formed Convention government and those diplomats who had hung on in Mexico City through the troubles. Next day Villa and Zapata saw Gutiérrez

again to inform him of the plans they had laid at Xochimilco for the crushing of Obregón and Carranza. It was
obvious, from the way the two war chiefs chose to *inform*
Gutiérrez of their plans rather than consult him about
them, that they intended to pay little attention to his office.

Villa was to drive north-east from Mexico City, then
swing south-east towards Veracruz, while Zapata pushed to
the south-east on the direct route towards the coast through
Puebla. After the conference Villa and Zapata parted, with
lavish expressions of comradeship. They were never to meet
again.

The military situation in the last month of 1914 was one
of utter chaos. Generals, colonels and self-styled leaders of
armed groups wavered in an agony of indecision about
which side to support. The countryside from Mexico City
to the northern border (the south of the Republic, apart from
Zapata's immediate area of operations near the capital, saw
comparatively little fighting during the Revolution) was a
patchwork of various factions, supporting either the forces
of the Convention (Villa and Zapata) or Carranza's Constitutionalists.

A historian of the Revolution has written: 'The supreme
gamble of the Mexican officer was whether to join a revolt
against the government or participate in its suppression. In
the roulette wheels of rebellion, the officer stakes a dis-
honourable death against a promotion, and the men who
reach divisional generalship are those who always place
their swords on the winning number.'

The confusion, and the war, could have been brought to a
quick end if Villa and Zapata, with their combined army of
60,000, had gone through with their plans for a quick thrust
against Carranza in Veracruz. The campaign started well
enough. Puebla fell to the Zapatistas just before Christmas.
But there, 200 miles short of his target, Zapata halted.

Neither he nor his soldiers really cared about conquering
fresh, and to them unknown, territory. Morelos was their
state, their *patria chica*, and further than that they were not
interested. For them the Revolution was over. After the
capture of Puebla, Zapata sat tight and was virtually useless
as an ally to Villa.

Villa, too, hesitated—and was lost. Instead of thrusting

straight for the sea, he worried about his supply lines from the United States and the fidelity of his followers in the north. And Villa, like Zapata, also thought primarily of his own part of the country. Faced with the possibility of being cut off from his northern supply bases of Chihuahua City and Torreón, Villa elected to clear his lines of communication before falling on Veracruz.

And, while he should have been mopping up the Constitutionalist threat, Villa chose to spend most of December living it up in Mexico City. His example was followed by many Convention officers and, after their misleadingly orderly occupation, the new conquerors embarked on a saturnalia of debauchery, looting and revenge.

There were arbitrary arrests and executions, and prominent men had to exhibit nimble tongues and legs to avoid death. Eduardo Iturbide, who had handed over the capital to Obregón and Carranza the previous August, was forced to go into hiding in the British Legation to escape a squad of vengeful Zapatistas. Gutiérrez, however, issued a safe-conduct order for Iturbide, and the Zapatistas respected it. Iturbide left Mexico City quietly with the American agent, Canova, but when Villa heard of Iturbide's departure he ordered his arrest. Iturbide and Canova abandoned their north-bound train and made their hazardous way through the desert on foot to Ojinaga, then across the Rio Grande into Texas. Canova's help in saving Iturbide's life meant the end of his valuable mission in Mexico. Villa publicly denounced him and Canova wisely chose to remain in the United States after that.

But not all were as lucky as Iturbide. 'What days those were,' Martín Luis Guzmán wrote, 'when murders and robberies were like the striking of a clock, marking the hours that passed.'

Even two members of the Convention, David Berlanga and a leading Zapatista, Paulino Martínez, were murdered by Villa's henchman, Rodolfo Fierro, after publicly criticising the northern chief.

Berlanga's fate was typical of the treatment accorded to any critic of the new conquerors or anyone to whom they took a dislike. A group of Villa's officers dining in Sylvain's, a restaurant owned by a Frenchman who had been a chef to the Czar, refused to pay for their meal and when the waiter complained bitterly that he would have to make good the bill out of his own wages, Berlanga, at a near-by table told the waiter 'I will pay.' When the Villistas asked who he was, Berlanga told them 'I am a revolutionary who does not want to see the uniform you wear dishonoured.' The officers reported the matter to Villa, who ordered Berlanga's arrest and execution.

When Gutiérrez demanded to know why Berlanga, a distinguished member of the Convention, had been assassinated, Villa told him, 'I ordered Berlanga killed because he was a lapdog who was always yapping at me. I got tired of so much noise and finally took care of him.'

It was typical of Gutiérrez's predicament that he dared not order the police to arrest Fierro for his blatant double murder. Nor could he attempt to control the excesses of the capital's garrison. He was trapped in Mexico City, virtually a prisoner himself.

In the first week after the Convention's occupation of the capital the American State Department was informed that 150 people had been shot 'for alleged political crimes'. Despite strong American protests the executions continued, even on Christmas Day. Minor, and assumed, crimes were heavily punished, too. The Zapatistas hung three bodies outside a police station, with notices above them giving the reason for their execution. One sign read 'This man was killed for being a thief', and another said 'This man was killed for printing counterfeit money'. The third said simply 'This man was killed by mistake'.

By Christmas Gutiérrez had had enough. He planned to assemble a new coalition of forces, eliminating the three danger men, Villa, Zapata and Carranza, and began to woo Obregón and other generals whom he thought might be interested in his aims.

When Villa, who was in Guadalajara, heard of Gutiérrez's scheming, he hurried back to Mexico City, ordered communications to the north cut to prevent Gutiérrez escaping and then summoned members of the Convention's Permanent Commission to a meeting at which he denounced Gutiérrez, unjustly accusing him of planning to desert to Carranza and Obregón. After Villa's harangue, several terrified members of the Commission, convinced they were all about to be shot, fled from the capital.

Next Villa, still in a towering rage and ominously accompanied by Fierro, went to Gutiérrez's home, which had been surrounded by Villista troops. Gutiérrez may have lacked tact but he was not short of courage. He faced up to Villa's fury, denying that he intended to join Carranza but admitting that he planned to leave Mexico City since no one respected or obeyed his orders as president of the Convention government. 'I want to free my conscience of the crimes that the Villistas and Zapatistas are committing under my government,' he said. When Villa told him that communications to the north had been cut, Gutiérrez retorted that he would, in that case, ride out on a donkey. 'You try it and I'll lay you out cold,' Villa threatened the supposed president of his country. Though the meeting ended on a more cordial note with *abrazos* there was now no doubt that Gutiérrez was clinging to his office only on Villa's sufferance.

Despite his danger, Gutiérrez continued to correspond with Obregón, hoping that he and other reasonable revolutionaries would agree to form a new coalition. Early in January 1915, while Villa was in the north for talks with the Americans about a further outbreak of trouble in Naco, General Angeles captured documents and correspondence after a victory over Antonio I. Villareal and Maclovio Herrera at Ramos Arizpe. The documents included letters from Gutiérrez to Villareal, formerly the President of the Aguascalientes Convention, outlining proposals for the elimination of Villa and Carranza.

Villa was informed of the discovery by Angeles, and immediately sent a message to José Isabel Robles, the Convention's Minister of War and an old campaign comrade, ordering Gutiérrez's execution. But Robles chose to throw in his lot with the provisional president and showed the telegram to Gutiérrez.

In the early hours of 16 January, Gutiérrez, accompanied by several members of his cabinet, three brigades of Villista soldiers and part of the division belonging to the vacillating Lucio Blanco, who had now changed sides three times in two months, fled from the capital heading north-east by horse and car. Gutiérrez took with him thirteen million pesos from the Treasury, leaving behind only ten million pesos and fewer than 5000 troops to garrison the capital. He had been president, in name only, for sixty-six days.

Gutiérrez and his escort, which was gradually whittled away by desertions and casualties in skirmishes with pursuing troops, made their hazardous way towards Gutiérrez's home town of San Luis Potosí only to learn that the town was held by Villa's general, Tomás Urbina. Eventually Gutiérrez and his decimated band settled in a tiny desert town called Doctor Arroyo, which was so insignificant that no faction had bothered to claim it. Here he clung to his title, still dreaming grand dreams of uniting all Mexico, until June, when he renounced the presidency, which had in any case long been taken away from him, and returned quietly to civilian life.

His military supporters were not so lucky. Lucio Blanco fled to the United States, where he remained in internment until the Revolution was over; the former Villista generals Eugenio Aguirre Benavides and Mateo Almanza, the man who had failed to catch Obregón in the epic train dash of the previous year, died in front of firing squads but José Isabel Robles, literally taking his life in his hands, surrendered himself, his forces and his equipment to Villa early in April, apologising for his misguided actions and promising to remain faithful to Villa in future. Surprisingly, Villa forgave him.

The Convention of Aguascalientes, which had reassembled officially in Mexico City on New Year's Day, 1915, met on 16 January and named the 29-year-old Villista, Roque González Garza, who was President of the Convention, Provisional President of Mexico in Gutiérrez's stead. He formed another government, most of them Villa supporters, enforced martial law in Mexico City and the Federal District and set about tackling the chaotic currency problem, which had been rendered even more acute when Gutiérrez made off with more than half the Treasury. Currency issued by Villa, Carranza and other revolutionary leaders had been circulating freely but on 23 January González Garza invalidated all Carranza currency. During the next few months, as Mexico City changed hands several times, paper notes of one side or the other—known derisively as 'milk tickets'—became worthless so fast and so often that merchants refused to take anything but gold and silver coins, except at the point of a gun.

While the presidency was changing hands, Villa was involved with the continuing troubles in the border town of Naco, where the forces of the Sonora governor, Maytorena, once more had the Carrancistas, Calles and Hill, penned in the Mexican half of the town. Fighting had flared on and off since October, and although Colonel W. C. Brown, the commanding officer of the garrison in the American part of Naco, had marked out the border 'very clearly' with a row of flags, American territory was regularly violated and shots fell into the United States.

On the American side of the line, wooden houses were riddled and their occupants had to move into the greater safety of adobe brick dwellings. Every window facing Mexico was blocked up by steel plates, bales of hay or blocks of wood, and hotelkeepers in Naco and other American border towns announced the availability of 'bullet-proof rooms' as proudly as they did hot and cold running water.

By the end of 1914 one American civilian had been killed and eighteen wounded in Naco. The 10th U.S. Cavalry had suffered eight casualties and the regimental commander's tent had been pierced four times by bullets. Eventually the American troops suffered the galling experience of having to withdraw a mile north of their own border to avoid further casualties. The fact that they managed to refrain from returning the fire earned from President Wilson the commendation 'This is the hardest kind of service and only the troops in the highest state of discipline would stand such a test.'

By January, as the fighting continued, the Americans found the situation intolerable. General Hugh Scott, who had now become Army Chief of Staff, was asked to negotiate with both sides.

Calles and Hill, who were being hard pressed, agreed at once to evacuate Naco under a guarantee of safety but Maytorena, who felt he was on the verge of victory, refused to sign an agreement, saying that he had lost 800 men during the siege and did not intend their sacrifice to be in vain.

So Scott asked for a border meeting with Villa. This took place in the middle of the international bridge between Ciudad Juárez and El Paso on 7 January. The next day Villa crossed the border for further talks with Scott and, according to the American, they were 'locked for two hours like bulls with their horns crossed'. Eventually, however, agreement was reached, and once again it was Villa who gave in to American wishes. He had promised that, given eight hours, he could clean out the Carrancistas but when Scott said he did not intend to permit even eight minutes of further conflict, Villa signed a promise that Maytorena's forces would be pulled back from the border. When the paper was taken to Maytorena on 9 January for his signature, the Sonora governor seized a pen, signed the paper, threw the pen onto the floor and burst into tears of rage and frustration.

In accordance with the agreement both sides evacuated the area of Naco. Calles and Hill moved east to the frontier town of Agua Prieta and Maytorena took over the border point of Nogales, further west.

With Villa occupied in the north, Carranza and Obregón made good use of the reprieve granted them. For the first time in his life Carranza was willing to take advice; and his circumstances compelled him to issue far-ranging proposals and a social programme in an attempt to attract support for his cause. The Revolution's hobby horse—land for all—was given a fresh gallop, and Carranza also announced his intention of promulgating electoral reforms, improvements in the living conditions of workers and peasants, the abolition of peonage and the introduction of minimum wage and maximum hour levels.

Carranza also gave his blessing and assurances of government aid for organised labour when Obregón signed a pact with the *Casa Del Obrero Mundial* (House of the World Worker), the most powerful of Mexico's nascent trade unions. The *Casa* recruited six Red Battalions for Carranza and these worker-soldiers played a large part in Obregón's decisive victories over Villa during the summer.

The Constitutionalist forces were regrouped in Veracruz

under Obregón's command and were renamed the Army of Operations. By 5 January they had driven far enough inland to retake Puebla from the Zapatistas after a bloody, day-long battle. A second task force pushed to within sixty miles of Mexico City. With the defection of Gutiérrez from the Convention soon afterwards, Carranza ordered Obregón to move on the under-garrisoned capital at once. By 25 January Obregón had reached the archaeological site of San Juan Teotihuacán, thirty miles from Mexico City.

The news caused the Zapatista element in the capital's garrison to bolt back to their mountains, and on 26 January the Convention decided to follow them, voting to adjourn and to reconvene in Cuernavaca, which was in Zapata-dominated territory. They were just in time. Obregón's ten thousand-strong Army of Operations entered an unde-fended city on 28 January. They were destined to remain until 11 March, a spell of occupation which was to bring fresh agony to the hapless capital and was to prove one of the unhappier interludes in Obregón's otherwise highly suc-cessful military career.

That Obregón had no intention of staying in Mexico City was soon made plain. He made no serious attempt to clear away the Zapatistas from their positions, on the outskirts of the city, and Carranza was quite content for the time being to remain in the greater safety of Veracruz. Indeed, in an effort to force the diplomatic corps away from Mexico City and to his side, thereby implying recognition for his régime, he decreed that Veracruz was to be the new capital of the Republic, but nothing came of his order. The diplomats stayed put and Carranza quietly dropped the scheme.

Obregón busied himself with stripping Mexico City of anything worth removing. Factory equipment was dis-mantled and transported to Veracruz, and hospital beds and equipment went the same way. Cars and horses were 'con-fiscated', even schools were shut down and the teachers forcibly removed to Veracruz to replace those teachers who had stained their characters in Carranza's eyes by working during the American occupation. According to Mrs Moats 'It was unsafe to venture forth in your own motor car. Cars were too likely to be commandeered by some officer and that was the last you would see of them. . . .'

On 3 February Obregón decreed all Villa currency worthless, substituting it with Carranza money, despite the fact that government employees and public transport workers had been paid in the now-valueless Villa currency earlier that day. Obregón's action, though not unexpected, merely served to hasten the economic collapse in Mexico City. On the day the currency change was announced, the Brazilian Minister Cardoso de Oliveira, representing American interests in Mexico, reported to Washington, 'The situation grows worse every day. The indescribable uncertainty of the paper money which one day is given forcible circulation and next day is declared of no value creates in general a condition very near to despair.' When banks and businesses shut down in protest against the chaotic financial situation, they were forced to open again at gunpoint, and any Villista currency found was confiscated.

The food and water situation was even more serious. The Zapatistas blew up the water pumping station at Xochimilco and the pressure in the capital became so low that water was available only between five and six each morning. The water pressure was insufficient to flush drainage from houses or to clear the city's sewers and the stench was soon overpowering.

Because of the Zapatista blockade, food could only be brought into Mexico City from the east, and precious little was forthcoming. Many grocers hoarded what food they had in the certain knowledge that the Carranza currency would be declared worthless as soon as Obregón left the capital. In an attempt to halt this tendency, Obregón rounded up a number of grocers who had hidden their stocks and forced them to sweep the streets.

By the end of February the food situation was critical. What few *tortillas* there were commanded ridiculously exorbitant prices. There was no bread or meat. Prices had trebled since Obregón's arrival, and dressed alley cats were on sale in the markets for £3. 'It was a time of filth and pestilence,' wrote Mrs Moats. 'The city was full of lice, and there was a terrific epidemic of typhus fever ... the poor people were absolutely starving. In her entire history Mexico has perhaps never experienced such widespread privation.... Even foreign colonies suffered....'

With Obregón's return to the capital, the Church finally began to reap the consequences of a hundred years of consistently backing the wrong political horse. In the early days of the Independence struggle, the Church had excommunicated the revered patriot priests, Hidalgo and Morelos, it had supported Maximilian against Benito Juárez, it had condoned the brutalities and excesses of the Díaz régime and had provided financial stiffening for Huerta.

As a child, Obregón had been influenced by a teacher who was a rank agnostic, and his anti-Church feeling had increased during his revolutionary campaigning. In an interview with the *Mexican Herald* on 21 February Obregón referred to the Church as a 'cancerous tumour', and while he conceded that there might be 'some well-intentioned members of the clergy', he felt they were so few that 'the wickedness of the rest neutralises their actions'.

Taking their cue from Obregón, Carrancista soldiers sacked many of the city's finest churches. Santa Brigida, the smartest church in the capital, came in for the most severe treatment. Officers rode their horses up the aisles and on to the altar, smashing statues of the saints with swords and rifles. Drunken troops staggered through the streets with their heads thrust through religious paintings, the gold frames hanging round their necks; others carried valuable crucifixes or the battered statues of saints. The attack on the capital's churches was one of the first of the anti-religious demonstrations which were soon to become so common in Mexico. One of Obregón's generals, Salvador Alvarado, explained: 'It was for the deliberate purpose of showing the Indians that lightning would not strike that generals rode their horses into church and publicly smashed the statues of venerated saints.'

The attacks, however, were made upon the institution rather than the system of faith. One historian has written of this strange paradox: 'In the last 100 years the Catholic Church in Mexico has been reduced to a hierarchical skeleton. It has lost its lands and its power; it has largely been destroyed as an organisation. But this change has had little effect upon the essential faith of the common people. They are no less Catholic today than they were a hundred years ago.'

On 12 February Obregón demanded a payment of £50,000 from the Mexico City archdiocese 'to alleviate the present distressing situation of the working classes' and gave the Church five days to find the money. By 19 February no payment had been forthcoming, so Obregón summoned all the clergy to the National Palace. Only 168 of the city's 400 priests turned up. The ones who stayed away proved to have been wise. Obregón told the assembled priests that they would be held prisoners until the money was paid, and if the Church continued to be uncooperative they would be recruited into his army.

The foreign priests among the group were soon set free after diplomatic protests, but they were sent under military guard to Veracruz to be deported. By the time Obregón abandoned Mexico City on 11 March the money had still not been paid, though most of the remaining priests had managed to bribe their way to freedom by then. But twenty-six still remained in custody, refusing to pay their captors even a nominal sum for freedom. Obregón sent this recalcitrant group to Veracruz, but they were quickly freed by an embarrassed Carranza and in most cases made their way back to the capital.

Mexico City's businessmen were also victims of Obregón's wrath. He imposed a crippling capital tax on all businesses, including foreign-owned ones, and when 150 of the leading professional men met at the Hidalgo Theatre to protest, Obregón turned up in person to address them. He told them not to be too alarmed about the tax 'for others will soon be published which will alarm you more', and he added ominously 'I am determined my orders shall be obeyed.' When the businessmen tried to leave the theatre they found the doors locked and the building surrounded by troops armed with machine-guns. All were arrested and those who failed to produce receipts showing they had paid the new tax were jailed.

Obregón's treatment of the priests and businessmen, among whom there were several Americans, stretched relations between Washington and the Carrancistas to the breaking point. Though President Wilson was the son of a Presbyterian clergyman, he was only too aware of the heavy Catholic voting potential among the Democratic Party.

Strong protests about Obregón's actions were sent to Carranza and Wilson wrote to Bryan 'Ask Daniels [the Navy Secretary] if he has any ships with long range guns ... which he could order to Veracruz at once.' And Bryan wrote to Carranza, 'When a factional leader preys on a starving city to compel obedience to his decrees by inciting outlawry ... a situation is created which it is impossible for the United States to contemplate longer with patience.' Intervention was in the air again.

But the situation was temporarily resolved by a further change of régime in the capital. On 9 March the imprisoned businessmen were released and late the next night Obregón's army, which had no further use for Mexico City, prepared to entrain for Pachuca, to the north-east of the capital, for a showdown with Villa. As they pulled out they were followed into the city by a cautious advance guard of Zapatistas. The populace were so relieved at Obregón's departure that church bells were rung to welcome the new occupiers.

Obregón explained his tough attitude in Mexico City in his autobiography:

'From the moment when I first occupied the City of Mexico I became aware of the prevalence of a marked hostility on the part of the clergy, the big houses of commerce, bankers, wealthy industrialists and the bulk of foreigners. ... I sincerely believe that the opposition was less the outcome of conviction than of expediency, for the elements in question could not get it into their heads that our army ... would be able to withstand the hosts of Villa and Zapata. ... It was, therefore, natural to assume that our army would shortly be wiped out; that Villa and Angeles would treat the citizens who had given in to us with more or less rigour. Consequently their main object was to further their own interests.

'I had to choose between two alternatives—to withstand all the enemies of the Revolution or, yielding to the pressure of those perverse influences, to confess myself beaten. The former a thousand times sooner than the latter was my decision. And in the depths of my conscience I swore by my honour as a man to fling down the glove and deal with those enemies as their attitude merited.'

It was quite obvious from the way that Obregón had left

Mexico City that he regarded occupation of the capital as a problem rather than an advantage. Villa, too, showed no interest in returning, concentrating instead on clearing north-east Mexico of Carrancistas before turning to meet Obregón. When the Convention announced its intention of following the Zapatistas back from Cuernavaca Villa warned, 'I think ... you will find yourselves obliged to flee again,' and offered to accommodate the Convention in Torreón or Chihuahua City. Nevertheless, the Convention, now increasingly dominated by Zapata's delegates, preferred Mexico City and reconvened there on 21 March under the provisional president, Roque González Garza.

With the return of the Zapatistas, living conditions in Mexico City immediately improved. The water supply was restored to normal and there was more food available, though it continued in short supply. The foresight of the merchants who had dragged their heels over accepting Carranza currency was borne out when Villa's *dos caras* were again made legal.

By now, however, the Convention government was almost bankrupt and there was little money to pay Zapata's troops until more could be printed. On their return to Mexico City the Zapatistas were not so particular about appropriating property, inflicting damage and casualties or picking up ready cash wherever they could get it. This was illustrated in a letter written to Mrs O'Shaughnessy by Madame Simon, the French wife of the Inspector of Finances of the National Bank in Mexico City.

She was alone at home one afternoon when she was told that four of Zapata's officers wished to speak to her husband urgently. 'A glance from the window revealed a carriage full of *hats*—you see the picture,' she wrote. 'Nothing daunted, I said to the alarmed servant "Tell the ranking one to come in."

'A moment later a tall, handsome brigand with a very large and decorative hat in his hand, his torso almost concealed by cartridge belts and armed with rifle and knife appeared at the door. He bowed with excellent manners and asked if I preferred to speak Spanish or English. My English being the better of the two we carried on the politest of conversations in that language. I offered him a cup of tea. Between dainty sips he told me he had been educated in the United States and had studied law there. His history between his American studies and brigandage in Morelos he did not reveal.

'The gentle object of his visit was to obtain 30,000 pesos which he needed to pay his men. My husband appeared at this moment and he repeated his demand with the additional remark that if he didn't get the money he would proceed to the sacking of Mexico City. There being no choice but to comply, my husband went to the telephone, saying he had no such amount in his home. There was no one at the bank and it was impossible to get hold of anyone else at that hour.

'The general began to get very impatient, suspecting of course that some trick was being tried on him, and said finally in a loud tone "If the money isn't in my hands by ten o'clock I will give orders for the sacking of the city. The responsibility will be on your hands. I must have money to pay my men."

'My husband prevailed upon him to wait until nine o'clock the next morning, telling him to present himself at the bank at that hour. This he did, received the money and departed. We thought the affair forever closed. A little later, however, the whole sum was repaid to my husband.'

Some others were not so lucky. An American, John B. McManus who owned a dairy farm just outside the capital, had shot several Zapatistas when they tried to take his cattle with them on their previous retreat from Mexico City.

When the Zapatistas returned, a group approached his farm and asked for food and water. McManus pointed to the American flag waving over his home and told them he would give them nothing, whereupon he was shot dead in front of his wife. Zapata promised a full investigation and punishment of those responsible for the murder, and provided a large sum of money for Mrs McManus and her five children when they returned to the United States.

Private property was increasingly subject to ill-treatment. The Country Club was converted into a barracks and the ballroom became a stable. The ground floors of many magnificent homes on the Paseo de la Reforma were turned over to the horses and the upper rooms taken over by peasant soldiers and their women. The residence of José Yves Limantour, Treasury Minister under Díaz, was sacked. The floor of the ballroom, covered in expensive Chinese tiles, was dug up so that the barefooted women could dance without slipping. The library, which contained more than 11,000 volumes on the New World alone, was used as fuel for camp fires set up on the floors of the various rooms. In another beautiful home, the Zapatistas chopped huge chunks out of the hardwood floors; they had slipped, they explained, in trying to walk on such a surface.

Churches, too, fell victim to the new spate of sacking and even some of the chapels in the main cathedral were looted, and their contents disposed of in the National Pawnshop, which was compelled to buy or face being looted in its turn.

While Zapata cooled his heels in Morelos and his men cavorted in the capital, satisfying themselves with occasional forays of little significance towards Carranza-held territory, the military situation around Mexico City rapidly worsened for the Conventionists. Obregón, now ready to meet Villa, began to move his Army of Operations from Pachuca north-west towards Querétaro and Celaya at the end of March, and the Convention again faced the unpalatable fact that they were about to be cut off from Villa.

The delegates bickered and wavered for several days about taking belated advantage of Villa's offer to accommodate them in the north. By the time they decided to move north, however, it was too late. Obregón had severed rail communications between Mexico City and the north.

During the early months of 1915 Villa's main concerns were to keep his supply lines clear and to dominate the fertile central plateau of Mexico, running north from Mexico City to San Luis Potosí and west to Guadalajara. The biggest threat to his control of this area came around Guadalajara, where two Carrancista generals, Francisco Murguía and Manuel M. Diéguez, drove the Villa commanders, Rodolfo Fierro and Calixto Contreras, out of Guadalajara in a fierce fight on 17 and 18 January.

Villa gathered all available reinforcements for the recapture of Mexico's second largest city, and even took away the 5000 remaining Villista troops garrisoning Mexico City, despite an appeal from Roque González Garza that they should stay in the capital to protect the Convention.

Villa maintained (and one can hardly blame him for his attitude) that since the Zapatistas were contributing little else towards the overthrow of Carranza, they should be able to look after the defence of Mexico City. When the two men held a telegraphic conference about the matter, Villa told González Garza that if the Zapatistas could not defend the capital alone, they should abandon it. González Garza maintained, 'It is important to our prestige to keep the capital from falling into the hands of the enemy,' to which Villa replied, 'It is important to win battles in war and then let the battles provide the prestige and deliver the cities.'

When González Garza insisted, 'The Convention needs forces to protect it,' Villa ended the conference with the dismissive comment, 'The Convention was not created to fight. If you want to be safe, go to any of my cities in the north.'

Fierro received a roasting from Villa for his loss of Guadalajara but in the end Pancho forgave his bosom companion with the words 'Very well, the defeats also are battles.' Early in February, Villa launched a three-pronged drive westwards from Irapuato to recapture Guadalajara and by 12 February the city was once more in the hands of Convention forces.

Next Villa received an urgent message from Angeles, in charge of operations in the north-east, requesting assistance to repel the threat posed by three Carrancista armies under Pablo González, Maclovio Herrera and Antonio Villareal. Villa paused only long enough to stop the vengeful Fierro shooting all prisoners, officers and troops, who had helped to defeat him the previous month ('Discontinue this shooting, since every man killed is one less to work on repairing the railroads') before leaving Fierro in charge of operations in the west and hurrying north with the main body of his troops to assist Angeles.

Villa found Angeles on the defensive in Monterrey and was appalled to learn that some of his prized cavalry were being used as front line infantrymen. Villa urged Angeles to move onto the offensive, and the reinforced Villistas defeated the forces of Villareal the very next day. Villa cockily told Angeles, 'You see, Señor General, these Carrancistas flee at the jingle of my spurs.' Villa's jubilation at further victories in the north-east over Herrera and Pablo González was dampened when he heard that Fierro had again been defeated in the state of Jalisco, with the loss of 2000 men, 800 horses—and the city of Guadalajara.

He immediately moved south again, just in time to run into Obregón, who had dug in at Celaya, a small town about 150 miles north-west of Mexico City and famous for its candied fruits. Typically, Obregón had chosen his site with infinite care. The area around Celaya, laced with canals and irrigation ditches, was ideal defensive country and it was soon made even more so when a German officer on Obregón's staff, Colonel Maximilian Kloss, put into effect the barbed wire and trench tactics which were already proving so deadly in Europe.

After overrunning Obregón's outposts with ease, Villa's cavalry threw themselves against the Celaya entrenchments on 6 April. Tangled in the barbed wire, they were decimated by machine-guns. It was here that the pride of Villa's army, the *Dorados*, were virtually wiped out. By sunset the Division of the North had left more than a thousand dead in front of the Celaya trenches and the hospital trains were crammed with wounded.

Next morning, however, Villa ordered another mass assault. This time a spearhead burst through the defences and into the centre of Celaya. Jubilant Villistas rang church bells to celebrate the town's capture, but they were premature; they were soon driven out again. By now Villa's situation was becoming serious. He was desperately short of ammunition and his cannon were reduced to firing homemade shells. Wherever Obregón's troops were forced back they flooded the fields to delay Villa's advance. By midday the Division of the North had been fought to a standstill. It was then that Obregón threw in his cavalry reserve under General Cesareo Castro against Villa's flanks.

The dispirited foot soldiers of the Division of the North wavered then broke, and Villa, whose own cavalry had been slaughtered the previous day, was forced to acknowledge defeat. He managed to extricate most of his artillery but the two-day battle had cost him 2000 dead. Villa pulled back to his base at Irapuato, thirty-eight miles to the west, and Obregón chose not to follow up his victory. Instead he reinforced the Celaya defences, in the certain knowledge that Villa's impetuosity and damaged pride would mean another attack on the town.

In the week's reprieve that he was granted, Obregón received reinforcements of men and a million cartridges. For his part, Villa collected all available troops and supplies from the centre of the Republic but was in too much of a hurry to gain revenge to wait for the arrival of Angeles and his force from the north. Villa's swiftness, audacity and courage had swept him to an unbroken series of victories. Now those very qualities were to drive him to irretrievable defeat. Villa explained his second gamble at Celaya with these words 'I knew ... Obregón would never fight unless he was fortified and entrenched and I would have to conquer him like that or let myself be conquered.'

First, however, Villa tried his favourite gambit of sending neutral consular officers to Obregón under a flag of truce, inviting him to come into the open and fight to avoid unnecessary bloodshed among the people of Celaya. Obregón and his forces, secure behind their wire and trenches, were not interested in committing suicide. So on 13 April began the biggest and bloodiest battle on the continent since the American Civil War: 25,000 Villista troops against the

15,000 defenders of Celaya. Villa's advantage in manpower and artillery was offset, however, by Obregón's superiority in machine-guns.

Villa had sworn that this time he would teach his 'perfumed opponent' a lesson and he sought desperately for two days to smash Obregón into submission. Time and again his brave soldiers rushed the trenches, only to be shredded on the wire and massacred by machine-guns. As Villa's badly-mauled army moved forward doggedly once more on the morning of 15 April, Obregón repeated his successful move of the previous battle by launching a flanking cavalry attack against them.

Despite the pessimism of some of his officers, who sought to persuade him to break off the battle and withdraw eastwards to Querétaro, Obregón had managed to hold Villa at bay without committing General Castro's 6000 cavalry to the defence of Celaya. It was this force, falling upon Villa from the north, which sent the attackers reeling in hysterical flight. The rout was so complete and so swift that Villa lost twenty-eight of the thirty-four cannon he had committed to the attack, and his shattered soldiers, throwing away their rifles, were rounded up in huge, dispirited batches.

Estimates of Villa's losses varied, according to the source. Villa himself admitted losing 3500 dead, wounded, prisoners and 'dispersed' in the second battle of Celaya, while Obregón claimed 8000 prisoners and a similar number of casualties inflicted. An American, J. R. Ambrosins, who passed through Celaya just after the battle, said he had seen 5000 Villista prisoners entering the town and he estimated that Villa's dead must have numbered 4000. 'Bodies were strewn on both sides of the [railway] track as far as the eye could reach,' he reported.

Villa, retreating northwards with the shattered remnants of his once-proud Division, admitted he had suffered 'a very serious defeat' and is said to have added bitterly, 'I would rather have been beaten by a Chinese than by Obregón.' Reporting his triumph to Carranza, Obregón explained wryly, 'Fortunately the enemy was directed by Villa.'

Celaya was a massive reverse from which Villa, despite his desperate efforts that summer, never recovered.

Villa halted at Aguascalientes to reorganise. He withdrew his forces from the western and north-eastern battlefronts, relieving the pressure on the Carrancistas in the Tampico area and in Guadalajara. Obregón's victory also meant that Mexico City could be reoccupied whenever the Carranza forces chose to do so. The Convention delegates, protected by nothing more reliable than the Zapata garrison, were now living on borrowed time and by the end of May the Convention had virtually ceased to function.

Villa was in grim mood as he regrouped at Aguascalientes, still convinced that he could smash Obregón. He wrote in his memoirs, 'I wanted everyone to understand that the main thing was not glory but perseverance in the struggle for justice. To make them understand me better, I sent wives of chiefs and officers away to Chihuahua, as I was sure this would make them more apt to fulfil their duty. Every morning and afternoon, after ... disposing of business I would leave my train, accompanied by my chiefs, and with an axe split wood, saying "The people will benefit, and we will return to what we were." '

The splitter of wood was now in even more suspicious mood than usual, and convinced that he was surrounded by treachery. One of his generals, Dionisio Triana, was unfortunate enough to have an uncle, Martín Triana, who was a commander in Obregón's army. When some of his officers urged him to relieve Dionisio Triana of his command, Villa sent for the man. According to Villa 'I saw in his glance that he was a traitor.' This was enough. He ordered Triana shot 'as an example'.

Obregón, now possessing an advantage in numbers, advanced slowly north along the railway line down which Villa had travelled in triumph a year before. By the end of May he had reached León, about halfway between his base in Celaya and Villa's headquarters at Aguascalientes. Villa, who, it seemed, had not learned a bloody enough lesson at Celaya, prepared to attack Obregón again at León. General Angeles advised Villa to let Obregón take the offensive and to meet the attack in Aguascalientes, where Obregón's supply lines would be much more extended. But Villa brushed aside all thoughts of caution, telling Angeles, 'I am a man who came into the world to attack, and if I am defeated by attacking today, I will win by attacking tomorrow.'

What was left of the Division of the North was flung recklessly into action at León on 3 June. The battle was almost Obregón's last. He was conferring with a group of officers near the front when a shell landed in their midst. Obregón's right arm was blown off at the elbow. Covered in blood and convinced that he was dying, Obregón decided to speed the end. With his remaining hand he drew a small pistol which he always carried, put it to his temple and pulled the trigger. But one of his aides had cleaned the pistol the previous day and had forgotten to reload it—a piece of carelessness which was to affect Mexico's future course profoundly.

The pistol was snatched away and Obregón was rushed to hospital. Even the loss of the Army of Operations' leader could not turn the tide in Villa's favour, however. Obregón's able generals combined to inflict yet another defeat on the Division of the North.

After its three quick successes the Army of Operations was a revitalised force. According to one writer 'It was the best and most capable Mexican army I ever saw ... the majority of the men were in uniform and virtually everyone wore shoes.'

Despite the severity of his wound Obregón was soon back at the head of his troops, driving steadily north against a dispirited opposition which daily lost its strength as hordes of Villistas, tired of the war, melted away into the deserts.

An indication of Obregón's cheerfulness at this highly successful point in his career came when he was visited by his brother José, who expressed dismay at his condition. Obregón quipped to his brother, who had recently shaved off his moustache, that he looked worse without it than he himself did without his arm.

Among those who deserted Villa after his triple setback was his oldest companion, General Tomás Urbina, who took with him the Division of the North's war chest containing thousands of pounds' worth of gold, and fled to his *hacienda* in the state of Durango. Villa and Fierro, accompanied by a small group of *Dorados* were soon on his trail. They hurried west across Mexico by train, surrounded

Urbina's *hacienda* at night and moved in at dawn.

Urbina, coming sleepily out of the house to see what the noise was about, was felled by a shot, whereupon Villa, suddenly full of compassion, halted the shooting and promised to get his old friend to a doctor in the nearest town. But when Villa managed to find only a small part of the war chest (the rest of it has never been recovered and is believed to have been buried by Urbina) he agreed to Fierro's argument that 'there is no end but death for a traitor'. Villa rode away and left the killing to Fierro.

Obregón's successes tightened the Carrancistas' grip on most of the area around Mexico City and by early May the food situation in the city had again become desperate. This time all classes were affected; notices were hung in the windows of fine homes offering to exchange pets, pianos and even cars for food. Many poor people, in desperation, ate the prickly fruit and leaves of cactus plants.

On 20 May, while the Convention was debating the problem, a huge crowd of hungry women gathered outside the Parliament building and eventually burst in on the Convention, thrusting empty baskets and crying babies under the noses of the startled delegates. Many of the members handed over all their money to the starving women and children, merely ensuring that a bigger crowd than ever would be there for a hand-out the next day.

The Convention voted an appropriation of £500,000 to purchase food which would be sold at fixed prices to the public, but there were two drawbacks to this fine plan: there was no food to be had, and the Convention was bankrupt. Roque González Garza blamed the lack of funds on Zapatista wastage of campaign funds when no campaigning had been done, and—a sign of the inflationary times—requested permission to issue more paper money including, for the first time in Mexico's history, 100-peso notes.

Next day, 21 May, the Zapata and Villa elements in the Convention almost came to blows over the food problems, each blaming the shortage on the other. At one stage the leading Zapata orator, Díaz Soto y Gama, launched into such a vitriolic speech that the Villista delegates tabled a formal motion asking that he be examined as to his sanity

by two doctors. Further acrimony was thrust aside when
another horde of starving people, predictably larger than
the mob of the previous day, burst into the debating chamber pleading for food. According to the *Mexican Herald*
they cried 'We want corn! In the name of the Virgin Mary,
do not deceive us! We want to eat! We want to live!'

Reports of the terrible conditions in Mexico City and the
rest of the Republic, and exaggerated accounts in the American Press about people in the capital eating rats and a starving mob tearing a dead mule to pieces, finally forced President Wilson into another policy statement. At the beginning
of the year he had told an audience in Indianapolis 'It is
none of my business and it is none of yours how long [the
Mexican people] take in determining what their government should be.... The country is theirs.... Have not the
European nations taken as long as they wanted and spilt as
much blood as they pleased in settling their affairs? And
shall we deny this to Mexico because she is weak? No, I
say.'

But by 2 June his attitude had changed. In a speech
which was half-appeal and half-threat, he detailed the har-
rowing conditions in Mexico and the misery brought about
by the revolutionary struggles.

'Mexico is apparently no nearer a solution of her tragical
troubles than she was when the Revolution was first
kindled,' said Wilson. 'In these circumstances the people
and the government of the United States cannot stand in-
differently by.... They want nothing for themselves in
Mexico. Least of all do they desire to settle her affairs for
her, or claim any right to do so. But neither do they wish to
see utter ruin come upon her.' Wilson went on to say that
his government 'must soon lend its active moral support to
some man or group of men ... who can rally the suffering
people'. He called upon the warring factions to resolve their
differences quickly and ended with this warning: 'If they
cannot accommodate their differences ... within a very
short time, this government will be constrained to decide
what means should be employed by the United States
in order to help Mexico save herself and serve her people.'

The reaction of Carranza was, not surprisingly, a disappointment to Wilson. The reply from Constitutionalist

headquarters stated simply 'Foreign Ministry today expresses General Carranza's thanks and states there is no reply.' After all, Carranza was winning the civil war and had no intention of halting to parley with the defeated enemy. Zapata took no notice of the Wilson speech and the attitude of most Mexicans was summed up by one Carrancista officer in the port of Mazatlán, who told the local American consular officer 'What a witty man Mr Wilson is.'

Villa, on the other hand, was losing the war and was anxious for a settlement while he still retained a little bargaining power. He sent messages to Carranza, Zapata and González Garza, the provisional president, asking them to discuss unification, as Wilson had requested, and holding up the bogey of American intervention and the possible restoration of *científico* rule in Mexico by the United States.

Early in June, William Jennings Bryan, whose pacifist convictions clashed with President Wilson's stern attitude towards Germany's submarine warfare in the Atlantic and the sinking of the *Lusitania*, with the loss of American lives, resigned and was replaced as Secretary of State by Robert Lansing.

One of the first communications Lansing received in his new post was from the presidential agent, George Carothers, who had spoken to Villa in Torreón about Wilson's proposals. Carothers reported that Villa would accept 'any reasonable proposition' since his treasury was empty, his commanders were deserting and there was great suffering among the people of northern Mexico.

Carranza's answer to Villa's peace feelers was a manifesto to the nation, in which he claimed over-optimistically that he controlled seven-eighths of Mexico and nine-tenths of its population. He called on the warring factions to submit to him, stressed the claims of his own régime to legitimate power and expressed the hope that he would soon earn the recognition he deserved from other countries. It was becoming daily more obvious that, whether they liked it or not, Carranza was the man to whom the United States would soon have to extend recognition.

In Mexico City confusion was increased by the Convention's election on 9 June of yet another new man, Francisco

Lagos Cházaro, to the now meaningless office of Provisional President. Lagos Cházaro, a former governor of Veracruz, was an insignificant personality, which was why the Zapatistas preferred him to Roque González Garza, whose relations with them had grown increasingly strained since the Convention had reoccupied the capital.

Three days after the change of president, while the Convention was debating a suitable, if belated, reply to President Wilson's proposals, news was passed to the delegates that Carranza's forces were again converging on the city. Carranza wanted to be sitting in Mexico City when the Americans recognised his régime; and for the new push towards the capital the First Chief had formed an Army Corps of the East under the command of Pablo González. On 13 June González sent an ultimatum to the Convention demanding the surrender of the city within forty-eight hours and the Convention's acceptance of Carranza's Plan of Guadalupe. The Convention proposed instead a thirty-day armistice to allow time for the contending factions to agree on peace. They rejected the Plan of Guadalupe, since it referred mainly to political matters relating to the overthrow of Huerta, which was now a dead issue. González, in turn, found the Convention's proposals 'completely unacceptable' and the Convention, in no position to argue, prepared to defend the capital.

Some delegates left for the front line, others fled the city while there was still time. Zapata did not move from his mountain headquarters to help organise the defence, but on 18 June he ordered 'all generals, chiefs and officers ... who are passing their time in Mexico City in theatres, *cantinas* and houses of ill fame, to report at the front for duty'. His duty done, Zapata lapsed into silence and indifference again.

The certainty that Mexico City was once more about to change hands caused another currency crisis. Some merchants flatly refused to accept Convention and Villa money, while others doubled and tripled their prices to discourage customers. As González tightened his grip on the Valley of Mexico, food became virtually unobtainable, and two women were killed when police fired on starving people looting a market.

The Convention continued to meet sporadically during the attack on Mexico City and on 7 July held what proved to be its final full meeting, when its only, and rather tardy, act was to raise the pay of the Zapatista soldiers. Finally, thanks to the intervention of foreign diplomats, the defending commanders agreed to allow González's army unopposed entry into the capital in order to avoid useless bloodshed and damage. González entered Mexico City on 11 July, but to the utter consternation of the civilian population (and in keeping with his timorous nature) he evacuated again six days later when he heard that Fierro and a force of Villista cavalry were operating to the north of the capital and attempting to join up with the Zapatistas to cut his lines of communication.

By now all semblance of law and order had disappeared in Mexico City. The Brazilian Minister, Cardoso de Oliveira, wrote in despair to Lansing on 18 July, 'The money question is worse than ever because no money is accepted by anybody ... I really consider the position hopeless in the true sense of the word.' Zapata's soldiers nervously reoccupied the capital after González's unexpected departure but every rumour or gunshot was enough to send them galloping off madly into the southern suburbs, shooting at anything that moved. Mrs Moats wrote, 'There were days on end when one could not leave the house. It required only a rumour to cause the evacuation of Mexico City....'

Many non-combatants were killed or wounded during the Zapatistas' panicky retreats and cautious reoccupations in the dark days at the end of July. A British author, Charlotte Cameron, who was in the capital then, wrote 'You may go out fifty times and nothing happens, yet the fifty-first time your life may be forfeit.'

Fierro's cavalry force passed through Mexico City at the end of July before moving west and north to try to rejoin Villa. Many Villista delegates in the Convention took this final chance of escaping to the north, while the rest fled into Zapata's mountains. The Convention government, which since Celaya had been existing on dreams, was finally scattered. González reoccupied Mexico City on 2 August. The capital had changed hands for the last time.

During the troubled summer of 1915 the exiled dictator Victoriano Huerta made an unexpected reappearance in the wings. After fleeing Mexico Huerta had settled in Barcelona, where, in February 1915, he was visited by a German naval officer, Captain Franz von Rintelen, who offered German backing for a military coup which would restore Huerta to power and, far more important to the Germans, further divert American attention and resources from the European war.

Von Rintelen arrived in New York bearing a forged Swiss passport on 3 April and began to organise the financial side of Huerta's restoration to power. Eight million rounds of ammunition were bought in St Louis and another three million ordered in New York. An account of more than £200,000 was opened in Huerta's name in the Deutsche Bank in Havana and arrangements were even made with the perennial dissident Félix Díaz, to lead a rising in southern Mexico when Huerta crossed the northern border.

Huerta arrived quite openly in New York on 13 April. His group was dogged from the first day by American Secret Service men and Carranza agents who, according to Barbara Tuchman's account, were 'tripping over one another as they sniffed in and out of New York hotels on the scent of the conspirators'.

Huerta's presence in the United States brought requests for his extradition both from Carranza and the Convention government. Though the Americans were uneasy hosts, they refused in the knowledge that the minute Huerta was handed over he would be as good as dead. Though they knew of his plans to re-enter Mexico, the American authorities might not have been so reluctant to see him extradited had they been aware of the German involvement and of Huerta's assurances to von Rintelen that as soon as he regained power in Mexico he would take up arms against the Americans. Despite these promises, it is extremely doubtful that the wily old Huerta would ever have considered such a wild scheme seriously.

As the war between the Carranza and Villa factions raged through the early summer of 1915, Huerta finalised his plans for an invasion of northern Mexico. One of the allies he managed to recruit was Pascual Orozco, the leader of the *Colorados*, who had been preserving his skin in Texas exile since the collapse of the Huerta régime. On 25 June Huerta made his move. He boarded a west-bound train in New York, telling newspapermen he was going to see the San Francisco Exposition. But he switched trains at Kansas City and headed south.

The move was discovered by Zach Cobb, the Collector of Customs in El Paso, who was also a zealous sniffer-out of Mexican plots. Cobb contacted Lansing, told him of Huerta's sudden switch of direction and asked for instructions. The Secretary of State ordered Cobb to 'co-operate' with Department of Justice agents in the area. To Cobb, this amounted to licence to take the affair into his own hands. He discovered that Huerta planned to leave his train at Newman, a small halt twenty miles north of El Paso, where he was to meet Orozco and complete the journey to the Mexican border by car. Rounding up a support force consisting of an army colonel, twenty-five soldiers and two deputy marshals, Cobb hurried to Newman, arriving at dawn on 27 June, just ahead of the train. As Huerta stepped down from his Pullman compartment to greet Orozco, Cobb emerged from behind a baggage crate and arrested both of them. For the first time in his life Huerta was a prisoner.

The two men were taken to El Paso, where they were released on bail. Huerta put up his own 15,000-dollar bond and also guaranteed the 10,000-dollar bail for Orozco. The plotters were kept under the strictest watch in El Paso while Cobb urged their re-arrest or removal from the border area, claiming that their presence was causing unrest.

On 2 July Washington ordered that Huerta and Orozco be taken into custody again. Rather than face re-arrest, however, Orozco jumped bail, stole some horses and fled with five companions eastwards into Texas. They were next heard of at the ranch of a man named R. C. Love, where they forced a Mexican servant to cook them dinner and shoe their horses. They were just riding away as Love returned. Shots were exchanged and the Mexicans fled. Thinking they were bandits on a border foray, Love telephoned the sheriff at the nearest town, Van Horn. A posse was sent out and found Orozco and his companions camped in a dead-end canyon. All six Mexicans were killed in the gun battle which followed, but it was not until wagons brought the bodies into Van Horn that Orozco was recognised. Orozco was buried in El Paso's Concordia Cemetery and Huerta, now in detention at Fort Bliss military camp, seven miles from El Paso, sent a large wreath of lilies of the valley tied with mourning tulle.

At Fort Bliss, Huerta was quartered in a derelict hospital building with little furniture—and no brandy to console him. He was watched continually, day and night, by a squad of six Secret Service agents—a civilian prisoner in a military camp under the guard of government agents. Wistfully he told a *New York Times* reporter who visited him, 'I have not had a drink these one-two-three-four days' and complained that the water brought to him by his captors was 'a little thin'. He took to studying English from a child's primer to while away the long hours of confinement.

Huerta's wife moved to El Paso soon after his arrest, rented a house on Stanton Street, near the border bridges and visited her husband every day. The unaccustomed confinement and the sparseness of his quarters soon affected Huerta's spirit and health. He took little exercise and when Bill Greet, the El Paso County Clerk, visited him with a case of brandy Huerta refused it.

Tom Lea, a former mayor of El Paso, became his legal representative, and when Huerta fell ill with yellow jaundice Lea managed to secure his removal from the hospital building to a comfortably furnished officer's quarters in another part of the camp. But Huerta's health showed no improvement. Day after day he lay on his bed, his face turned to the southern wall, towards Mexico. Eventually in November Lea obtained permission for Huerta to live at his wife's home in El Paso, though he still suffered the indignity of a bedside guard which was not removed until he fell into a coma. Huerta died in the Stanton Street house on 14 January 1916, and next day was buried alongside Orozco.

Even by August 1915 the United States had not given up all hope of finding an alternative to Carranza as the next ruler of Mexico. William Jennings Bryan had come to the remarkable conclusion earlier in the year that Villa was 'perhaps the safest man to tie to', influenced no doubt by the fact that Villa was a fellow-teetotaller. Even after Villa's summer of disasters Bryan's successor, Robert Lansing, had not abandoned hope that another candidate might replace Carranza.

Villa, desperately short of money for arms, was imposing all sorts of taxes and levies on companies and businesses—many of them American-owned—in the north of Mexico, so on 6 August Lansing, in all seriousness, asked the Department of Agriculture to establish a meat inspection point on the border to facilitate the entry into the United States of the cattle which Villa had stolen to help pay for guns and bullets. Lansing sent Wilson a copy of this request, explaining that it would give Villa a 'legal' means of disposing of his cattle and 'relieve his strained financial situation'. Understandably, the President confessed himself 'a little puzzled' by the proposal, though he did not countermand it.

On 5 August a conference on the Mexican problem was convened in Washington. It was attended by ministers from Argentina, Brazil, Chile, Bolivia, Uruguay and Guatemala and they readily accepted a proposal by Lansing that all the 'secondary chiefs' in Mexico should be called upon to choose a government which would exclude the factional leaders.

But by now Carranza was in possession of Mexico City and on the verge of realising his dreams. He brushed aside the Washington proposals as 'meddling' and kept the mediators waiting a month for his formal rejection. When the Washington conference began, Colonel House, Wilson's adviser, discussed the situation with the President. 'We agreed that if Carranza was to be recognised he must guarantee religious freedom, give amnesty for political offences, institute the land reforms which had been promised, give protection to foreigners and recognise their just claims,' wrote House.

Carranza would guarantee nothing. On 11 October the conference faced up to realities and announced that Carranza's régime was 'the only party possessing the essentials for recognition as the *de facto* government of Mexico'. Eight days later the United States extended *de facto* recognition and though *de jure* recognition did not follow until 3

March 1917, Wilson immediately embargoed the supply of arms to all Mexican factions other than Carranza's. United States recognition was quickly followed by that of Britain, France, Italy, Russia, Japan, Germany, Spain and most Latin American countries.

The reaction of the American public was, on the whole, dubious. The *New York Globe* thought the move 'a doubtful solution to a perplexing problem', though the *Kansas City Journal* felt that Carranza would be acceptable 'provided due arrangements are made to watch him every minute and see that he carries out his promises instead of his vengeances and greed'. Reaction among the Catholic Press was more predictable. The *Catholic Review* regretted the recognition of 'a man wholly unfit for the task of reestablishing justice, freedom and stability in Mexico', while the *New Orleans Morning Star* called on the American people to defeat Wilson at the polls in 1917 'as an answer to this insult against Catholics and religious freedom'.

The *Louisville Times* probably came closest to Wilson's thinking when it pointed out that while the European war lasted, it was better to let Carranza bear the blame for conditions in Mexico than for the United States to shoulder the responsibility.

Wilson had reluctantly but realistically recognised Carranza because, after Villa's eclipse, there was no other leader of sufficient stature opposing the First Chief and his Constitutionalists.

Wilson could have delayed the recognition but, like the *Louisville Times*, the American president felt that, with the increasing involvement of his country in the World War, his administration needed to devote most of its attention to European affairs. His recognition of Carranza was, in effect, a relegation of Mexico to the back seat of American politics.

There was much sympathy for Villa. General Scott, his chief ally in the United States, felt that his government's step 'had the effect of solidifying the power of the man who had rewarded us with kicks on every occasion and of making an outlaw of the man who had helped us'.

During September Villa had been pushed steadily northwards by the Carrancista armies. He had lost Torreón, and with it the source of revenue from cotton lands sur-

rounding the town, and the news of the Washington conference's announcement that Carranza possessed the only
régime qualified for recognition reached him in Chihuahua
City, where he was reorganising his depleted forces.
According to an American, Frank Rhoades, who spoke to
him at this time, Villa took the news quietly, merely commenting that the war had just begun and that a dozen
nations could not keep Carranza from failure.

By the time the formal American recognition announcement came, Villa and his army of 6500 had disappeared
into the mountains of the north-west. Villa, who had lost all
his ports of entry except Juárez, was on his way to subdue
the state of Sonora and the long-troublesome border town
of Agua Prieta, thereby freeing himself from a Carrancista
threat to his rear and giving himself another entry point to
the United States where he could smuggle arms.

The first news of American *de facto* recognition of Carranza reached Villa as he approached Agua Prieta after a
hazardous and arduous slog through the mountains. This
time, according to the presidential agent George Carothers,
who was still with the Villa forces, Villa became very angry
and declared his intention of having no further dealings
with the United States. He maintained that he would still
take Agua Prieta and that he was willing to fight both Carranza *and* the United States, if necessary.

Although he was desperately short of pack animals, Villa
had managed to transport two batteries of field artillery and
thirty machine-guns across the Sierra. Men and animals
died attempting to cross mountain streams swollen by
autumn rains, and food was so short that precious horses
and mules had to be slaughtered. Villa's troops arrived, exhausted and hungry, in front of a town which had been
turned into an impregnable fortress by its shrewd commander, General Calles.

The lessons of Celaya had been well learned by Calles,
who had surrounded the town on three sides with deep
trenches, protected by masses of electrified barbed wire and
machine-gun emplacements; and he had the comforting
presence of a friendly United States at his back. The two
things that Calles had lacked, reinforcements and ammunition, became freely available after U.S. recognition of Car-

ranza. President Wilson, not wishing to see Villa establish himself along the American border, with the consequent risk to American lives and property, agreed to allow Agua Prieta to be reinforced by the only possible route—through the United States. As Villa's forces toiled through the bleak Sierra, trainloads of troops and ammunition poured into Agua Prieta from other Carranza-held border points via American territory. The First Chief was reaping quick fruits of recognition.

Word had spread along the American border that there would soon be another battle to watch. Local railways ran special excursions into Douglas, Agua Prieta's twin border town, and by the time Villa appeared on the south-east horizon there were some 4000 American spectators gathered round the touchlines, rather like supporters at a football match. American forces under General Frederick Funston, who had commanded the occupation troops in Veracruz the previous year, took the precaution of manning trenches around Douglas in case the Villistas overran the border during the fighting.

Villa opened the assault on the morning of 1 November, taking care to bombard Agua Prieta from the east and west, so that no shells would fall over the American border, inviting retaliation. The artillery barrage was followed by a massed advance over open ground and a full-blooded cavalry charge in typical, but now outmoded, Villa fashion.

The result was a repetition of the Celaya massacre. Men and horses tangled in the wire and were slaughtered by concealed machine-guns. The attackers fell back but tried again after dark, only to run into another unpleasant product of the war in Europe—searchlights. The advancing Villistas, caught in the open and blinded by the powerful beams, were smashed to pieces like fairground targets, and the survivors fled in panic.

Much has been made by some Mexican historians of the rumour that the searchlights were operated from the American side of the border by U.S. troops. This was not true, but there is little doubt that the electric power for the searchlights was supplied from the United States.

By the afternoon of 3 November, Villa and some 3000 survivors of the Agua Prieta débâcle were retreating along the international line to the next border point, Naco, which was in Villista hands. Villa had many desperately wounded men, and when George Kingdon, the manager of an American copper company at Cananea, heard of their sufferings he sent two of the company's physicians, Dr Miller and Dr Thigpen, to their assistance. They were warmly received by Villa but when he learned that reinforcements for Agua Prieta had been allowed to pass through the United States and as the rumour about American-operated searchlights spread through his army, Villa summoned the doctors and accused them of being spies. Though they hotly denied this, the two Americans were imprisoned and told they would be shot. Each morning for several consecutive days they were brought out to be executed, then returned to their cells when Villa changed his mind.

When the copper company learned of the doctors' plight they opened negotiations for their release and eventually agreed to pay Villa 25,000 dollars 'taxes'. When the money was received the unfortunate doctors were turned loose near the American border and left to find their own way to safety in Arizona. When they were picked up they were suffering from exposure and exhaustion, and Dr Miller later died as a result of his experiences.

The Mormon settlement at Colonia Dublán in Chihuahua also suffered as Villista stragglers and deserters, angry and hungry, began to filter south from the border battle. They blamed the United States for their disastrous defeat and for several days squads of them terrorised the town, robbing and looting.

Now in desperate need of an operations centre remote from the Carranza armies, Villa moved southwards from Naco intending to make Hermosillo, capital of Sonora, his new headquarters. He expected to be joined in the town by the forces of the state governor, Maytorena, and had sent funds to his ally for the purchase of arms. But, like Urbina, Maytorena proved nothing more than a fair-weather friend. He fled to the United States with Villa's money and, instead of a friendly reception, Villa found Hermosillo fortified by the timely arrival of a force of Carrancistas under General Manuel M. Diéguez.

The dejected Villistas besieged Hermosillo but, despite an overwhelming superiority in numbers, could manage nothing more than half-hearted probing attacks. The outnumbered defenders repulsed these by transferring soldiers from one side of the town to the other by car. Eventually Villa gave up and drifted back towards the American border with a force which could now be numbered in hundreds rather than thousands. Villa's career had come full circle. By the end of 1915 he was once more reduced to the status of outlaw chief.

It was at this time that Villa lost his closest friend, Rodolfo Fierro. Fierro was in charge of a battalion moving west from Ciudad Juárez into Sonora and wanted the troops to ford Lake Guzmán in order to save time on the march. When they hesitated Fierro plunged forward crying 'Here I'll show you. You are cowards, watch me.' When he had ridden some fifty yards out his horse stumbled, throwing Fierro into the water. In addition to the fact that he could not swim, Fierro was suffering from the further handicap of wearing a money belt containing a large amount of gold. Villa hurried to the scene and offered a large reward for the recovery of Fierro's body. It was found on the lake shore some days later by a gardener, the money belt untouched. Villa paid the reward from the money he took from Fierro's belt.

Villa's bitterness against Americans was shared by his hard-core followers and when the survivors of the wretched Sonora campaign reached the border their hatred flared into violence. An argument between two Villista officers and American Customs men ended with a band of about thirty Villistas riding over the international boundary and threatening the Americans. There was trouble, too, at Juárez where, just before they abandoned the town without a fight to a force under Obregón on 21 December, Villistas opened fire across the Rio Grande into El Paso, killing an American railway inspector. American troops were rushed to the border but trouble was averted when Obregón's soldiers took over the border points later that day.

By the end of the year, with most of Villa's old territory in the hands of Carranza's forces, much of the danger which had caused a mass exodus of Americans from the northern part of Mexico seemed to have passed, though as the Revolution moved into its sixth year Mexico itself was in a wretched state. Epidemics were sweeping the country, people were starving to death, mine buildings and *haciendas* lay in ruins. The new régime assured all foreign companies that Villa no longer constituted a threat and urged them to restart production to help get Mexico's economy moving again. Though the American State Department warned all its subjects to stay out of Mexico until conditions became more settled, this advice was ignored as Americans flocked back over the border to resume operations.

One of the organisations which believed the Carrancistas' assurances was the Cusi Mining Company, which wanted to reopen its mine at Cusihuiriáchic in Chihuahua. Charles Watson, the general manager of the company's Mexican operations, arrived in El Paso from Chicago on 5 January 1916, carrying with him more than £5000 in gold. At the border he joined up with the rest of his American staff. After receiving promises of safe conduct the party of eighteen Americans and their Mexican assistants travelled to Chihuahua City, where on 19 January they changed trains to complete the journey to the mine.

A few hours later, near Santa Ysabel, the ranch which had belonged to the ill-fated Scot, Benton, the train was stopped by a band of some seventy Villistas, led by Colonel Pablo López. What happened next was told to an El Paso newspaperman by a Mexican employee of the Cusi Mining Company, José María Sánchez, who was travelling on the train.

'We were in two coaches, one occupied by Americans and the other by twenty of us Mexican employees. No sooner had the train been brought to a standstill by the wreck the bandits had caused ahead than they began to board the coaches. They swarmed into our car, poked Mausers into our sides and told us to throw up our hands or they would kill us. They rifled our pockets, took our blankets and baggage and even our lunches.

'Then Col. Pablo López ... said "If you want to see some fun, watch us kill these *gringos*. Come on boys," he shouted to his followers. They ran from our coach crying "*Viva* Villa" and "Death to the *gringos*." I heard a volley of rifle-shots and looked out of the window. Manager Watson was running towards the Santa Ysabel river, a short distance away. Four other Americans were running in other directions, the Villistas shooting at them. Some of the soldiers dropt [sic] to their knees for better aim. Watson fell after running about a hundred yards. He got up, limping, but went on a short distance further, when he threw up his arms and fell forward, his body rolling down the bank into the river....

'While this was going on, other Villistas crowded into the Americans' coach. I could not see what happened in there, as a frightful panic broke out in our car. Later I learned that the Americans were unarmed. Pearce was shot as he sat in the coach. I saw Wallace's body on the ground at the car-step. He had been shot through the back. Another body was on top of Wallace's. The other Americans were herded to the side of the coach and lined up.

'Colonel López selected two of his soldiers as executioners, and this nearly precipitated a fight among the bandits over who should have the privilege of shooting the Americans. The two executioners used Mauser rifles. One would shoot his victim and then the other soldier would take the next in line.

'Within a few moments the executioners had gone completely down the line. The Americans lay on the ground, some gasping and writhing in the cinders.... Col López ordered the "mercy-shot" given to those who were still alive, and the soldiers placed the ends of their rifles at their victims' heads and fired, putting the wounded out of misery.

'All bodies were completely stript [sic] of clothing and shoes.'

Seventeen Americans were murdered. Only one of the party, Thomas B. Holmes, managed to escape. He made a break at the same time as Watson and, as the Mexicans opened fire, fell into some bushes. The bandits left him for dead and Holmes crept into some thicker undergrowth, where he hid until the Villistas had departed.

Villa strongly denied involvement in the killings, explaining that Pablo López, the man he had authorised to plunder the mining train, had grossly exceeded his orders. Twelve days after the massacre Teodoro Prieto, a Villista major, arrived in El Paso and told the authorities that Villa had had nothing to do with the murders. 'Villa did not know of the tragedy until days afterwards. He instructed me to say he will execute the men responsible.'

Whether Villa ordered the murders or not, there was no doubt that the Americans were killed by Villistas and that Pancho was therefore responsible. It seems highly unlikely, as some writers had suggested, that Villa perpetrated the massacre to bring about American intervention in Mexico. The presence of United States troops in the country would have been of no benefit to him, as was soon to be proved. The Carranza government, on the other hand, had a real fear that Santa Ysabel would bring soldiers swarming over the northern border. Carranza himself expressed profound regret at the incident and promised that no effort would be spared to hunt down the killers. This was easier said than done, for Carranza's forces were spread very thinly, coping with Zapata and other smaller rebellions. Within a week two of Villa's officers had been captured and executed, though their involvement in the massacre was doubtful. The body of one, José Rodriguez, was displayed in its coffin at Ciudad Juárez shortly afterwards for American citizens to inspect if they wished. The Carrancistas claimed that eleven members of the gang had been captured and executed within two days of the massacre.

The murders threw the border area of the United States into uproar. There were angry editorials, protest meetings, petitions. A volunteer posse of 1000 miners and cattlemen threatened to invade Mexico and hunt down the Villistas unless the Army was sent in. On 14 January, the night that Huerta died in the town, the bodies of the murdered mining men were brought to El Paso. Their arrival sparked off a huge demonstration. A mob which was heading for the Mexican quarter of El Paso was turned back at gunpoint by police and troops, and martial law was proclaimed.

Away from the area of involvement, however, American reaction was surprisingly mild, though President Wilson's political opponents made the most of the incident. Former Republican President Theodore Roosevelt complained that 'this dreadful outrage' was an inevitable result of Wilson's watchful waiting policy and warned, 'If we don't do our

duty in Mexico, one or all of (the European powers) will
surely seize Mexico themselves.'

In the House of Representatives James L. Slayden, a
Democrat, voiced the feelings of his fellow-Texans: 'The
rising anger of Americans on the border is dangerous and
cannot be trifled with.' Two resolutions were introduced in
the House calling for armed intervention but were heavily
defeated after bitter debates.

The American Press, too, was largely against intervention, though the *Cincinnati Enquirer*, in an editorial entitled 'Clear The Decks For Action!' thundered, 'If it takes
the bayonets of our infantry, the cannon of our artillery,
the guns of our Navy, to make our citizens safe in Mexico,
it must be done,' and the *Washington Post* demanded, 'Let
us proceed to it, by a punitive expedition, by intervention,
by invasion, no matter what it is called.'

But the *St Louis Post Dispatch*, commenting on 'the folly
of intervention', said, 'This is no time to tie up the American
Army and Navy,' a feeling which was undoubtedly shared
by President Wilson in view of the steadily worsening relations with Germany. The *San Francisco Star* felt sure that
Carranza would make every effort to punish those responsible and went on, 'At any rate, that is Carranza's job, and
no American has any right to go into Mexico for that
purpose without the consent of the Carranza government....

'In times past the Chinese have been robbed, assaulted
and even ruthlessly murdered here in California by Americans, but there was never a demand by the Chinese that
their government should invade this country.'

But there was little doubt in the minds of Americans living in Mexico City that intervention was at hand. One visitor entered the American Club there to find the place
crowded with 'my drinking, hilarious countrymen' who
urged drinks upon him. When he asked the reason they told
him that seventeen Americans had just been murdered in
northern Mexico.

'But why do you celebrate the killing of Americans?' he
asked them.

'Don't you see?' he was told. 'It means intervention. You
don't suppose that those blankety-blank pacificists in the

Wilson administration can refuse to send an army now, do
you?'

However, the Santa Ysabel massacre brought about nothing more serious than an abrupt termination of the American nation's honeymoon with that romantic bad man,
Pancho Villa....

Though Villa and his gang dropped completely from
sight after the massacre, Americans along the border remained tense and worried. The British journalist Hamilton
Fyfe wrote, after visiting the area, 'I begin to understand
how much loss and suffering have been caused to subjects of
the United States. The fact that some 60,000 Mexicans have
been killed [in the Revolution] concerns Mexico alone....
If they lived on a barren island all by themselves they might
go on fighting until they were all exterminated and no one
would greatly care. But when one learns that 200 Americans have been killed, not to mention the enormous losses
suffered, one is driven to ask with Mr [Theodore] Roosevelt whether it is not the duty of a government to protect its
subjects?'

The other side of the picture was just as grim, however.
George Marvin wrote in the American magazine, *World's
Work*, 'The killing of Mexicans through the borderland in
these last four years is almost incredible. Some Rangers
have degenerated into common man-killers. There is no
penalty for killing, for no jury along the border would ever
convict a white man for shooting a Mexican.

'Their ranks are swelled by so-called deputy sheriffs.
Some of these men are responsible citizens, but others are
unstrung gunmen.... You feel almost as though there
were an open game season on Mexicans along the border.'

On 17 February, at the request of a New Mexico Senator,
Albert B. Fall, President Wilson sent to the Senate a re-
port, prepared by Lansing, which listed the number of
Americans killed as a result of the Mexican Revolution as
159. Of these, forty-seven were killed in Mexico during the
first three years of the Revolution and a further seventy-six
met their deaths in Mexico in 1913, 1914 and 1915. Twenty
American citizens and sixteen soldiers were killed on
United States soil. The report officially listed ninety-two
Mexicans killed in the United States during the Revolu-

tion, though Marvin's figure of 400 would seem nearer the mark.

The number of American dead did not include the victims of Santa Ysabel, and the grim total was soon to be boosted even higher when Pancho Villa struck across the border at the unsuspecting town of Columbus, New Mexico.

Columbus was (and still is) a straggling, dreary place in the New Mexico desert, seventy-five miles west of El Paso and two miles north of the wire fence which marked the border with Mexico. Seared by the sun and threatened with burial by drifting sand it was, according to one writer, 'as Western a town as you might have seen in the movies'. Other descriptions, particularly by soldiers unlucky enough to be stationed there, were a good deal less Hollywood-like.

Pershing's biographer, Richard O'Connor, wrote that it was 'afflicted with windstorms and rattlesnakes; neither electricity nor telephone service had reached it ... and its only communications with the outside world were the telegraph and the El Paso and South Western Railroad, from whose westbound "Drunkards' Special" every midnight tumbled men who had been celebrating brief furloughs in El Paso'.

Columbus was the headquarters of the U.S. 13th Cavalry Regiment, under the command of Colonel Herbert J. Slocum. The regiment consisted of seven rifle troops, a machine gun troop commanded by Lt John P. Lucas (later, as Lt Gen. Lucas, to command the Allied landing at Anzio in the Second World War), and a headquarters troop—a total of twenty-one officers and 532 men. The 13th Cavalry was assigned sixty-five miles of border, to be patrolled at Slocum's discretion. The 13th Cavalry had been on routine border patrol on an unusually quiet stretch of the international line for five years, though it had been alerted many times by false alarms. Too many times, as it turned out. . . .

On 27 February, 1916, Villa and a group of 450 followers left their hide-out at San Geronimo, Chihuahua, and began to move towards the American border, amid rumours that Villa himself was on his way to Washington to deny personally any involvement with the Santa Ysabel massacre.

According to one of Villa's *Dorados*, 'We rode stealthily over mountain trails and dirt roads during the nights and made camp in daytime with strict orders for no fires.' Despite their precautions, on 7 March the raiders ran into a group of Mexican cowpunchers and their American foreman, Arthur McKinney, from the American-owned Palomas Land and Cattle Company. One of the Mexicans, Antonio Muñoz, managed to get away but the others were made prisoner. Muñoz carried warning of the Villistas' presence to another American cowboy, Bill Corbett, who decided to ride into Villa's camp in an attempt to obtain McKinney's freedom. Muñoz sensibly kept going in the other direction.

On Villa's orders McKinney and Corbett, together with another American, James O'Neill, the Palomas company's camp cook, who had also fallen into Villista hands, were hanged, to save ammunition. The Villistas had also been spotted that day by Juan Favela, another employee of the Palomas Company. He reported the news to Col. Slocum in Columbus next morning, but the garrison commander chose to disregard Favela's information, relying instead on other intelligence he received the same day that Villa had started south again, away from the border. The Columbus garrison bedded down for the night on 8 March without taking any extra safety precautions.

The raiding force moved off after dark on 8 March, and shortly after midnight they broke through the border wire about two and a half miles south-west of Columbus without being detected. Things were so quiet in camp at Columbus that night that Lt James P. Castleman, Officer of the Day at regimental headquarters, strolled over to the railway station to meet the midnight 'Drunkards' Special' which was bringing back the 13th Cavalry's polo team, among them Lt Lucas, who had been playing in a competition at El Paso. After inspecting the guard, Castleman returned to the Officer of the Day's hut about 1 a.m. on 9 March. He was unable to sleep, and lay reading until four o'clock, when he prepared to make his final inspection.

At precisely that moment the main force of Villistas, moving in to Columbus from the west in pitch darkness, blundered into a sentry, Private Fred Griffin. He challenged a Mexican who replied by shooting and mortally wounding him.

As Griffin cried out 'My God, I'm shot,' Castleman raced from his hut, pistol in hand. Right outside the door he ran into a Mexican who fired at him from point-blank range and missed, though the bullet knocked off Castleman's hat and the blast seared his face. Castleman shot the bandit dead in his tracks and sprinted across the parade ground under heavy fire to the guard house, where he organised the first resistance.

In the early stages there was utter confusion among the defenders, the inevitable result of such a surprise attack. Guns were locked up and, since the keys were in the possession of officers who were not on hand, the American soldiers had to smash the weapons free. Panic-stricken members of the regiment's medical detachment locked themselves in their bullet-proof adobe hospital building in the middle of the battle area and refused to open up, even when members of the Machine-Gun Troop, badly in need of illumination in a safe place to change a broken firing pin, demanded admittance.

As the Mexicans spread through the camp, non-combatants among the garrison attempted to repel the attack with a variety of improvised weapons. One soldier in the stable crew killed a Villista with a baseball bat, and when the bandits broke into the kitchens, the cooks drove them off with boiling water, axes and butcher's knives.

In Columbus itself, the main targets of the Villistas were the bank, and two buildings, the Mercantile Store and the Commercial Hotel, owned by Sam Ravel, a Jewish businessman. The Villistas seemed particularly anxious to find Ravel (it was rumoured that he had taken money from Villa for clothing and guns and had failed to deliver the promised goods) and the fact that he was in El Paso having treatment for sinus trouble undoubtedly saved his life. When raiders broke into the store Sam's brother Louis hid under a pile of hides, leaving a third brother, fifteen-year-old Arthur, to face them in his underwear. The Villistas demanded the combination of the safe and when Arthur told them he did not know it they fired several shots into it in a vain attempt to blow it open.

Then they ransacked the store, looking for the other Ravel brothers. Most of the hides under which Louis was sheltering were thrown aside but he escaped detection. Convinced that Sam Ravel was hiding at the Commercial Hotel, a bunch of Mexicans marched Arthur to the building.

As they arrived there, stray bullets struck two drums of petrol, stored across the street from the hotel. Blazing petrol flew in all directions, setting fire to it and other near-by buildings. Several writers have claimed that Villa deliberately put the torch to Columbus. This is not so. The fire was accidental and, in fact, was the major cause of the heavy casualties among the bandits.

A group of about twenty-five riflemen under Lt Castleman, who had advanced into the town itself, and Lucas' machine-gunners, on the south side of the railway line, now had plenty of background illumination and were able to make their fire power tell. Castleman reported, 'As soon as the light was bright enough we made every shot count and soon thoroughly discouraged the invaders.'

The Commercial Hotel blaze probably saved Arthur Ravel's life. Two Villistas were marching him back from the hotel towards his brothers' store when both were picked off by some particularly sharp shooter among the American cavalrymen. Ravel needed no further urging. Still dressed in his underclothes, he started to run and did not stop until he got to the Columbus school building, about a mile away.

The plight in which Major Frank Tompkins found himself was typical of that of most married officers. He was awakened by shots and shouts of 'Viva Villa' and 'Viva Mexico' immediately outside the bedroom window of his married quarters on the north-western edge of Columbus. He tried to get outside the house but found it surrounded and decided to stay to protect his wife and two other officers' wives who were in the building.

Wives who were alone had even more terrifying experiences. Mrs Ryan, whose husband Capt. Thomas Ryan, was on border duty, decided to make for her adobe garage, which was bullet-proof, when firing broke out. As she ran from the house a Villista grabbed her and asked 'Adonde va?' ('Where are you going?'). 'Nowhere,' Mrs Ryan replied, at which, incredibly, the Mexican released her.

In the absence of her husband, Mrs Castleman grabbed her two children and crawled under her bed, while their coloured servant Carson Jackson contributed probably the most athletic achievement of the night by squeezing under the family bath—a position which, under ordinary conditions, no one could have managed—and remaining there throughout the battle. The Castlemans' house was riddled by bullets and their car, parked outside, had nineteen bullet holes in it.

The battle raged until dawn, when Mexican bugles sounded the retreat. Major Tompkins managed to get out of his house and into the camp, where he located Colonel Slocum and requested permission to pursue the Villistas. Slocum authorised Tompkins to take Troop H.

After crossing the border 'for the loss of one horse killed', Tompkins' tiny pursuit force found a rearguard screen of Villistas holding a small hill about 300 yards south of the boundary. The Americans charged the hill with pistols drawn, and the Mexicans broke and ran, taking up a new defensive position about a mile further south. After requesting, and receiving, permission from Slocum to proceed deeper into Mexico, Tompkins was joined by a further twenty-seven soldiers of Troop F under the indefatigable Lt Castleman, and again charged Villa's rearguard, driving them back with losses. The Americans penetrated fifteen miles into Mexico in pursuit until the Villistas, realising how few men were chasing them, turned round and attacked Tompkins' gallant band. Heavily outnumbered, horses exhausted and ammunition almost gone, they fell back to the border. They had not lost a single man, though Tompkins reported laconically, 'I received a slight wound in the knee, a bullet through the rim of my hat and my horse was wounded slightly in the head.' His bravery won him the Distinguished Service Cross.

Tompkins' tiny force enthusiastically claimed between 75 and 100 Villistas killed on Mexican soil alone, but this figure seems altogether too high. In fact, the total number of Mexicans killed and captured in the whole Columbus affair probably did not exceed this number, though no official figure has ever been given, since the bodies were dumped in the desert and burned within a few hours of the battle.

American casualties were incredibly light: eight soldiers and ten civilians killed, six soldiers and two civilians wounded. That the death rate was not higher was attributable to two factors—the Mexicans' terrible marksmanship, and the fact that they were generally more concerned with booty than killing unarmed civilians. In addition to eighty horses, Villa's men got away with thirty mules and a heavy haul of military equipment, including 300 Mauser rifles, though some of this was abandoned during the headlong flight back across the border, and the number of stolen horses did little more than make up for the ones they lost during the battle.

As the Columbus news broke across a stunned United States, the most elaborate theories began to circulate—and in fact are still being propounded—about the reasons for Villa's raid. James Gerard, the American ambassador in Berlin, telegraphed to Lansing on 20 March, 'Am sure Villa's attacks are made in Germany,' and on 15 April *Collier's Magazine* followed up by blaming 'a certain European nation now at war whose interest is to keep the United States very busy'.

Though Villa never explained his reasons for attacking Columbus, there seems little doubt that the prime object was to pick up guns, horses, money and as much incidental booty as possible. Since the reimposition of the Americans' arms embargo, Villa had been in desperate need of supplies. This, allied to his newly-acquired anti-Americanism, meant that an American town near the border, and preferably an isolated one, was the obvious target. Columbus filled the bill in all respects but one: the garrison turned out to be much bigger, and reacted much more efficiently, than Villa had expected, causing grievous losses among the bandits.

The Columbus Raid brought an uncharacteristically prompt apology from Carranza, who promised Washington that he would use 'the most vigorous means' to hunt down Villa 'and avenge his horrible acts'. But according to presidential agent John W. Belt, who presented the American protest to Carranza, the First Chief's immediate reaction to the news was to boast that Villa had entered the United States because of his fear of Carrancista troops.

This time, whatever Carranza's promises, President Wilson had to act. . . .

In the early evening of 10 March the State Department issued a Press statement that 'an adequate force will be sent at once in pursuit of Villa ...' and General Frederick Funston, C.-in-C. of the Southern Department, received orders at the same time to prepare an expedition 'with the sole object of capturing Villa and preventing any further raids by his band, and with scrupulous regard to the sovereignty of Mexico'.

These arrangements were made before the United States received Carranza's reply to their note of protest, in the happy belief that the Mexicans would be only too glad to receive Big Brother's help in hunting down their most notorious bandit.

Indeed Carranza's note seemed to back up the Americans. He was unusually apologetic and polite. He even suggested that there should be reciprocal pursuit agreements enabling Mexican forces to cross freely into United States territory and giving American troops the same privilege '*if the raid at Columbus should unfortunately be repeated*'. To save time, Carranza's reply had been forwarded to Washington in its original Spanish, the consular officer responsible feeling sure that someone in the State Department would be able to translate it. Apparently, the note was either hastily or not fully translated, since Carranza's final comment, authorising American forces to enter Mexico in case of *future* incidents, was overlooked and plans went ahead to mount an expedition.

Its command was entrusted to the fifty-five-year-old General John J. Pershing, who as a lieutenant fresh from West Point had campaigned in northern Mexico in pursuit of the Apache chief Geronimo. Pershing was at that time commandant of Fort Bliss, outside El Paso.

General Funston, his immediate superior, perpetrated one of the understatements of military history when, commenting on Pershing's appointment, he told a newspaperman in San Antonio, 'John's up against a lot.'

Pershing faced, first of all, the monumental task of conjuring up an expedition from an army which was unbelievably ill-prepared. Then, too, he was being asked to find an unusually elusive needle in an extremely large and hostile haystack, and to operate in a country where the supposedly friendly government troops in fact caused most of the Punitive Expedition's casualties and whose president, in a fit of pique after learning that American troops had crossed his border, refused them permission to use Mexican railways for supply purposes.

Organising the expedition proved a daunting task. Despite her vast financial resources, America did not possess a single military unit ready or equipped for operations in Mexico. In fact, the *Detroit Free Press* felt that the country was indebted to Villa for revealing that its army 'was not prepared even for a fourth-class skirmish'.

Troops, equipment and supplies flooded into Columbus, the staging area for the expedition, but the Army was so short of transport that it had to advertise for lorries, and eventually spent almost half a million dollars buying fifty-four vehicles, fitting them out for the campaign and, in many cases, hiring civilian drivers and mechanics until soldiers could be trained to operate them.

If it had shown itself painfully unprepared for Villa's raid and the aftermath, the Army exhibited some typical American hustle in getting Pershing's command ready for the road. On 15 March, six days after the Columbus battle, the Punitive Expedition moved off. It was divided into two columns, the object being to trap Villa between them. The largest of the columns, comprising about 4000 men and led by the 13th Cavalry, still smarting from Villa's surprise attack, headed straight south from Columbus ignoring a warning from the commander of the Carrancista garrison at the border town of Palomas that he would resist their 'invasion' of Mexico. Discretion overcame the Mexican officer's valour, however, and the American force, known as the Eastern Column, crossed the border without incident shortly after noon on 15 March.

Departure point for the Western Column, led by Pershing himself, was Culberson's Ranch, about fifty miles west of Columbus. In this 2000-strong force, unhindered by transport wagons, were the 7th Cavalry Regiment, once the command of Custer, the 10th Cavalry (a Negro regiment with which Pershing had once served, earning him the nickname 'Black Jack') and a battery of field artillery. This column set off half an hour after midnight on 16 March. Both columns converged on the Mormon settlement of Colonia Dublán, some 125 miles south of the

border. The faster Western Column covered fifty-five miles
on 16 March and sixty-eight the next day, reaching the
Mormon colony on the evening of 17 March. Relief was
almost certainly mutual ... the troops and their mounts
were desperately tired and the Mormons had been living in
daily fear of massacre since the Columbus Raid.

The larger and slower Eastern Column did not arrive at
Colonia Dublán until 20 March. Its journey had been dusty,
tiring and devoid of incident except for the discovery, on the
second day's march, of the body of an unidentified American, blindfolded, hands tied behind his back and shot
through the head. He had been dead about a week.

In view of Carranza's refusal to allow the Americans to
make use of Mexican railways, arrangements had to be
made to feed and supply the huge field force by motor
transport, since the contents of mule-drawn wagons consisted almost entirely of fodder to sustain the animals during the journey. Another 200 lorries were purchased to
make the increasingly difficult journey from the source of
plentiful supply at Columbus to the expedition. In the early
stages of the operation the southward trail was indicated by
nothing more than wheel ruts or Signal Corps telegraph
lines across the broken, empty countryside. But soon the
trails became badly cut up and almost impassable. The road
was so bad that the supply lorries often travelled up to sixty
miles without getting out of first gear. By the closing stages
of the Punitive Expedition, however, army engineers had
vastly improved the main supply route and proudly named
it the Lincoln Junior Highway. It had also picked up other
refinements such as mobile brothels, and stalls set up in the
middle of nowhere by enterprising Chinese to cater to the
troops' various needs.

If conditions were bad for the lorries, they were appalling
for the troops who made up the pursuit columns. Dirty,
dusty, thirsty and fleabitten, the cavalrymen crawled their
weary way south, gradually shedding the antiquated and
inadequate equipment with which they had been burdened.
The troopers' regulation sabres quickly became an embarrassment and were thrown away. Two lorries made the return journey to Columbus laden with discarded sabres. One

officer reported that fifty-nine of the seventy-nine saddles in his troop were defective; the rifle scabbards were not the right shape or size to fit the saddles, and stirrup leathers were too clumsy and too heavy. Horses and soldiers were permitted ten minutes rest every hour, though the men were ordered to remain standing 'otherwise they would drop off to sleep and there was much difficulty and delay in rousing them', while the hungry horses, unable to find forage in the barren countryside, chewed their halter shanks.

'The weather was one of the real hardships of the campaign,' Major Tompkins reported. 'Hot days were followed by freezing nights. Many times we experienced a difference of ninety degrees between noon and midnight. Sometimes it was so cold no one could sleep, man or beast....' Icicles formed on the soldiers' beards and the water in their canteens often froze solid.

When Pershing's more mobile Western Column reached Colonia Dublán he was told that Villa had retreated southeastwards to a village called San Miguel. Despite the punishing march they had just completed, and without waiting for the Eastern Column to arrive, three flying columns immediately prepared to pursue Villa. The first to leave, only a few hours after reaching Colonia Dublán, was the 7th Cavalry (29 officers and 647 men) under the command of Colonel George Dodd, who was only a few months away from the compulsory retiring age of sixty-four. Dodd was ordered across the Sierra Madre mountains, a little to the east of where Villa was supposed to be.

But Villa had not halted at San Miguel, as had been reported. Instead he pressed on south with about 300 men towards the town of Guerrero, one of his favourite hideouts.

Villa fell on the town's unprepared Carrancista garrison in the early morning of 28 March, routing them with ease. But during the storming of Guerrero he was struck by a stray bullet, which entered the back of his right leg and came out four inches below the knee, shattering the shinbone. The wound was extremely painful and, much more important, totally disabling.

Within a few days—and for the only time—the Americans came very close to trapping Villa. It was the veteran Dodd and his 7th Cavalry who chanced to be closest on the bandits' trail. Dodd pushed his command mercilessly. Buffeted by snowstorms as they hurried along mountain trails, they outstripped their supply wagons, and men and animals were forced to exist on *frijoles* (Mexican beans) and parched corn. On this sparse diet, the 7th Cavalry covered 225 miles in a week over the most appalling country, at an altitude of about 7000 feet.

On 28 March Dodd was only thirty-six miles from Guerrero and when he learned that morning that Villa had just taken the town, exhausted horses and weary men were pressed into another forced march. They pushed on through the night, hoping to reach Guerrero before dawn, but they took the wrong trail in the dark and at daylight on 29 March were still two miles from the town. The Villistas were still taken by surprise, however, since they had spent the night celebrating their victory over the Carrancista garrison. Thirty Mexicans were killed and an unknown number wounded in a running fight which cost the Americans five wounded. When the Villistas fled they could not be pursued because of the pitiful condition of the 7th Cavalry's horses.

Dodd's command captured two machine-guns, forty-four rifles, thirteen horses and twenty-three mules. But no prisoners were taken and Dodd was particularly disappointed to find that the wounded Villa had left Guerrero in a carriage the previous evening. Still, it was a morale-boosting success. Though Villa had not been captured his band was utterly dispersed and it was not until the end of the summer, when Pershing was tied down by political restrictions, that Villa was able to regroup.

By 1 April Pershing's mobile headquarters had reached Bachíniva, about thirty miles north-east of Guerrero. Here he caught up with Major Frank Tompkins, the man who had chased Villa back across the border after Columbus, and two troops of the 13th Cavalry. When Pershing asked where he thought Villa had gone, Tompkins replied that whenever Villa was hard pressed he headed for the vicinity of Parral, another 150 miles to the south-east. Pershing told

Tompkins, 'Go find Villa wherever you think he is,' and the next day the small force (12 officers and 160 men) moved out.

Tompkins' men set off with only two days' rations and no supply wagons or pack mules. They did not even possess a map of the country through which they were to ride. 'But each man had a belt full of ammunition with an extra bandolier over his shoulder, so I rejoiced, for we were after Villa and I had real soldiers at my back,' wrote Tompkins.

The column entered Parral (about 400 miles from Columbus and the most southerly point the expedition was to reach) shortly before noon on 12 April. Tompkins' high spirits were quickly dissipated. The garrison commander, General Ismael Lozano told Tompkins Villa was to the north and expressed surprise that the Americans had entered Parral in view of the strong pro-Villa feelings among the population. Tompkins agreed to withdraw as soon as he had picked up provisions and could be guided to a suitable camp-site near by.

As General Lozano escorted the Americans northwards out of Parral, they were followed by a crowd crying 'Viva Mexico' and 'Viva Villa'. As the Americans reached the selected camp-site some of the mob began to fire on them. General Lozano hastened back to stop the shooting, but when some of his soldiers disobeyed him and began to take up threatening positions on the Americans' flanks Lozano sent word to Tompkins advising his immediate withdrawal, as he could no longer control the situation. As Tompkins stood up to yell at the Mexican soldiers, telling them to go back, they fired at him, miraculously missing him but killing a sergeant, Jay Richley, who was peering over the top of the railway embankment on which Tompkins was standing.

In three hours the Americans covered sixteen miles from Parral and reached the village of Santa Cruz de Villegas. They were harried and fired upon by Carrancistas all the way, replying only when the Mexicans became too bold. During this time another soldier, Private Hobart Ledford, was killed and six wounded, including Tompkins himself, who was hit in the left shoulder. Seven horses were also killed. The men of the 13th Cavalry halted at Santa Cruz de Villegas and held off the Mexicans until they were relieved later in the day by a force of the 10th Cavalry.

The Americans remained in camp at Santa Cruz de Villegas for a further week, reinforced by two more cavalry columns until the force numbered nearly 650. There were no more clashes with Mexican troops and on 21 April they pulled back north towards the new expedition headquarters at San Antonio, midway between Guerrero and Chihuahua City, where Pershing intended to concentrate all his forces in an attempt to avoid any more trouble with the Carrancistas.

Meanwhile, relations between the two governments remained strained. Carranza was uncooperative and sulky, though understandably reluctant to see the situation escalate into open war. In an attempt to clear up the problems raised by the Punitive Expedition's entry into Mexico it was agreed to hold border talks in Juárez. General Obregón, newly-appointed Secretary of War in Carranza's government, was the Mexican spokesman, while Generals Scott and Funston represented Washington. The first meeting was held in the Juárez Customs house on 30 April. It was a dismal flop. Obregón insisted on immediate withdrawal of Pershing's force and would discuss nothing else until the Americans agreed to this point. This was too much for the fiery General Funston. According to General Scott, Funston 'lost his temper and didn't return to any more of the meetings'.

Two days later Obregón contacted Scott, requesting a secret meeting in an El Paso hotel. Scott was spotted making his way there and dozens of newspapermen camped outside their room while the two generals thrashed out an agreement. It took twelve hours and involved a struggle of wills which the old Indian fighter Scott told Washington 'was not equalled by any similar struggle with the wildest and most exasperating Indian hitherto encountered'.

Scott wrote in his memoirs, 'How I kept Obregón from leaving I have never known. He was the secretary of war of a friendly power and he could not be struck on the head with a sandbag and kept locked in a closet until he signed. . . .' But Obregón *did* sign the agreement, which called for a gradual (and undated) withdrawal of the Punitive Expedition and, on the Mexicans' part, a promise to intensify their efforts to wipe out Villa and his followers. The American government readily approved the agreement but again Carranza proved a stumbling block, refusing to sign until a date was set for Pershing's withdrawal. So the hard work of Scott and Obregón proved to have been wasted and Count von Bernstorff, the German ambassador in Washington, reported cheerfully to Berlin, 'It seems to be increasingly probable that the Punitive Expedition against Villa will lead to a full-dress intervention.'

The Americans, fully aware of the dangers, were imposing all sorts of restrictions on the unfortunate Pershing in order to reduce the possibility of further incidents between his cavalry and Mexican troops. Funston's instructions that Pershing should pull back to San Antonio (300 miles south of Columbus) and operate from there had already severely affected the striking ability of the expedition, though Pershing still managed to seek out and destroy occasional groups of Villistas operating in his area.

At dawn on 5 May, 330 men of the 11th Cavalry surprised a group of Villistas at a ranch called Ojos Azules (Blue Springs), near Cusihuiriáchic killing forty-four and capturing several more. The force's Apache scout, First Sgt. Chicken, described it as 'damn fine fight'.

The next blow against Villa was struck by the Carrancistas, when they captured the formidable Pablo López, who had led the Santa Ysabel massacre. López was badly wounded during his capture, and when he was executed in Chihuahua City in June he faced the firing squad standing on crutches.

A keen hunt was mounted by Pershing for the chief of Villa's *Dorados*, General Julio Cárdenas, who was reported to be operating near the expedition's camp. On 14 May the search paid off, in unexpected fashion. A brash young lieutenant named George Patton, who was to become famous in the Second World War, was ordered to take a party of six soldiers and a civilian interpreter in three Dodge cars to buy corn. Patton, eternally hopeful of some action, drove towards a ranch known to be owned by Cárdenas' uncle and, in his eagerness, approached it alone and on foot. As he did so three horsemen galloped from the yard, firing at him. Patton, a crack shot, returned the fire with his pistol, knocking one of them, who turned out to be Cárdenas, from his horse. While Patton was reloading the other two galloped past, shooting at him—and missing—from about ten feet. Next Patton killed one of the horses, which fell on its rider. With a risky sense of chivalry, he refused to fire again until the Mexican freed himself of the horse and rose to shoot at Patton. Then the American killed him with a single shot.

The third rider was killed by Patton's soldiers, who then approached the wounded Cárdenas. He held up his hands as if to surrender but suddenly opened fire. He managed to get off only one shot before he was brought down by a hail of bullets. Patton drove back to camp with the three dead Mexicans draped over his car bonnet like hunting trophies.

Sheer luck also played a part in the death on 25 May of Colonel Candelario Cervantes who, according to Pershing, was 'next to Villa himself, the most able and the most desperate of Villa's band'. A dozen American soldiers were hunting wild cattle in a canyon near Namiquipa when they were attacked by a group of about twenty Villistas, who killed one trooper and wounded three others. In reply, the Americans toppled two of the attackers, one of whom turned out to be Cervantes.

Next to the capture of Villa himself, this was the greatest coup the Punitive Expedition could have achieved and capped a highly successful month. Had they only known it, the end of May would have been a good time for the soldiers to have returned home, at the peak of success. But they stayed, and successful May gave way to disastrous June....

Early in June Pershing was ordered to pull back even nearer the border and set up headquarters near the Mormons at Colonia Dublán. Patrolling was reduced to little more than a formality, designed mainly to keep Pershing aware of the movement of Mexican government troops rather than of the now-scattered Villistas.

The first hint of impending trouble came on 16 June, when General Jacinto B. Treviño, the Carrancista commander in Chihuahua, sent a message to Pershing that he had been ordered to 'prevent by the use of arms new invasions of my country by American forces' and went on to warn Pershing that he would be allowed to move his troops in one direction only—north. 'Your forces will be attacked by Mexican forces if these indications are not heeded,' he ended.

Pershing's reply was brief and to the point. No such restrictions on the movement of his troops had been imposed by his own government, he told Treviño, and he would continue to use his own judgment about their disposition. However, only four days later, an American officer was to blame for the worst clash yet between the Punitive Expedition and Mexican soldiers. It came at a village called Carrizal, about sixty miles east of the main American camp.

Pershing had ordered a reconnaissance of that area after rumours that Carrancistas were massing for an attack on the expedition. But in sending Captain Charles T. Boyd in command of forty-one men of Troop C of the Negro 10th Cavalry, Pershing chose badly. Boyd was a brave but headstrong officer whose 'death or glory' attitude ended in death for himself and the most humiliating defeat suffered by the Punitive Expedition.

Captain Lewis S. Morey, commanding Troop K of the same regiment, was also operating in the area of Boyd's patrol and on 19 June the two columns met at an American-owned ranch called Santo Domingo near Carrizal. Boyd, the senior of the two troop commanders, took charge and, over Morey's objections, decided to ride through Carrizal the next day to discover at close quarters the strength of the Carrancistas there.

Early next morning the two Troops, totalling eighty-four men including two civilian guides, approached Carrizal. Boyd rode forward to request permission of the Mexican commander, General Félix U. Gómez, to ride through the village. When this was refused Boyd led his Negro cavalrymen forward on foot across open ground into what can only be called a miniature Balaclava; fewer than a hundred utterly exposed troops against 400 entrenched Mexicans armed with machine-guns. The Americans' foolhardy attack was repulsed with the loss of twelve dead and twenty-three prisoners. The Mexicans' admission that they had suffered thirty-three casualties was testimony to the accuracy of the Americans' marksmanship under the most adverse conditions. Both Capt. Boyd and General Gómez were among those killed.

Once more, Mexico and the United States stood on the cliff edge of war. Washington bombarded Carranza with protest notes demanding the return of the twenty-three captured cavalrymen, international bridges over the Rio Grande were seized in readiness for a full-scale attack on Mexico and units of the National Guard were ordered to border duty. Alarmed by the severity of American reaction, Carranza ordered their release on 28 June.

Despite the ravings of extremists on both sides of the border (one cartoon in the Mexico City newspaper *Acción Mundial* depicted a bold Mexican, rifle in one hand and knife in the other, towering over a cringing Uncle Sam) good sense prevailed. Both nations backed away from a confrontation and the Americans once more set about arranging to withdraw an armed force from Mexico without too much loss of prestige. Both nations agreed to the setting up of a six-man peace commission (three from the U.S. and three from Mexico) which sat for six months in New London, Atlantic City and later Washington without being able to reach agreement on the exact date or manner of withdrawal.

Long before then, however, Pershing's rôle in Mexico had been effectively neutralised. The disastrous Carrizal episode was the last action in which the Punitive Expedition participated.

By the end of June the expedition had settled into what was to prove its home for the next six months in the Casas Grandes–Colonia Dublán area, and it was forbidden to patrol further south than 150 miles from the American border. Pershing's greatest problem was to keep up the morale of his troops, who were living in tented camps seared by the fierce sun and occasionally lashed by sandstorms. Elaborate drills and training exercises were devised to keep the soldiers occupied, but their greatest unfulfilled needs were women and liquor. Eventually Pershing permitted the establishment of a red light area, well removed from the shocked eyes of the Mormon residents of Colonia Dublán.

By autumn the Punitive Expedition had become just as much an embarrassment as the Veracruz Expedition had been two years previously. The *New York Herald* summed up the feelings of most Americans—and probably the majority of the expedition's soldiers, too—when it commented, 'Through no fault of his own, Pershing's Punitive Expedition has become as much a farce from the American standpoint as it is an eyesore to the Mexican people.... Each day adds to the burden of its cost ... and to the ignominy of its position. General Pershing and his command should be recalled without further delay.'

The *Kansas City Journal* took sarcastic note of the expedition's failure to run down Villa: 'Since General Pershing was sent out to capture him, Villa has been mortally wounded in the leg and died in a lonely cave. He was assassinated by one of his own band and his grave was identified by a Carranza follower who hoped for a suitable reward from President Wilson. Villa was likewise killed in a brawl at a ranch house where he was engaged in the gentle diversion of burning men and women at the stake. He was also shot on a wild ride and his body cremated. Yet through all these experiences which, it must be confessed, would have impaired the health of any ordinary man, Villa has not only retained the vital spark of life but has renewed his youth and strength. He seems all the better for his vacation, strenuous though it must have been.'

Villa was indeed feeling much better. Free from the attentions of Pershing, he had soon recruited another force, a thousand strong, and on 16 September, in celebration of Mexico's Independence Day, he seized Chihuahua City from its Carrancista garrison, captured sixteen wagon loads of arms and ammunition, liberated those of his comrades who were held in prison, enrolled some government soldiers in his force and rode off again into the desert. To prove that his victory had been no fluke, Villa fell on Chihuahua once more on 23 November. This time he captured the city only after three days' bitter fighting, though he held on to it until the arrival of a large government relief force on 7 December.

Just before Christmas Villa switched his attentions to another of his favourite places—Torreón. He descended on the town on Christmas Eve, capturing it with ease from

government troops under the command of General Sever-
iano Talamantes who, according to Patrick O'Hea, was 'an
improvised but amiable soldier from Sonora'. The unfortunate Talamantes preferred suicide to facing Carranza's
wrath over the loss of Torreón.

The raid was so swift and unexpected that an English
resident of Torreón, Harry Purkis, alighted from a tramcar
right in the middle of a bunch of Villista cavalry. When the
horrified Purkis looked up and recognised Pancho Villa
himself among the horsemen, he made haste to explain that
he was no American *gringo* but a Briton. The terrified
Purkis was trembling so badly that Villa threw him a silver
peso and told him to buy a plate of soup with it, since he
was obviously suffering from a chill. After extracting a
forced 'loan' from Torreón's banks and businesses, Villa
disappeared northwards again.

That Christmas was a doubly frustrating one for Pershing.
He chafed at his politically-imposed confinement while
Villa plundered undisturbed to the south; and then, to add
to the expedition's miseries, the elaborate Christmas festivities which had been arranged to celebrate Pershing's
recent promotion to major-general were blighted by what
Pershing himself described as 'a combination between a
Montana blizzard and a Sahara dust storm' which tore tents
to shreds, wrecked the camp and spoiled the barbecued
steers which had been specially prepared. But next day the
weather relented and the party went ahead.

The Punitive Expedition's days in Mexico were now
almost over. By early January, 1917, agreement had been
reached between the two governments about the withdrawal,
which commenced on 30 January. Pershing's force re-
crossed the border, appropriately at Columbus, on 5 February, followed by a migratory horde of civilians who had
grown to depend on the American troops for protection.
The only visible signs of Pershing's success were twenty-one
Villista prisoners and a small quantity of captured arms,
which provoked one National Guardsman on border duty
to wonder why it was called the Punitive Expedition, 'since
nobody got punished'.

An American historian, Hudson Strode, has called Pershing's mission 'a failure in every respect'. The *Cleveland*

Leader dismissed it as 'a record of barren futility', and Major Tompkins complained that the expedition's inglorious end was 'consistent with Mr Wilson's Mexican policy, which was a hodge-podge of interference and non-intervention, of patience and petulance, of futile conferences and abortive armed invasion. . . .'

But the expedition had not been a failure in *every* respect. True, Villa was still at liberty and though in the early stages of the Pershing Expedition his forces had been harried and scattered, he had now re-assembled them at leisure and was once again strong enough to menace any town in northern Mexico. The benefits of the 130 million dollars spent on the expedition were to be felt within two months, however, when the United States declared war on Germany. The Villa chase proved a most useful dress rehearsal for France, not only awakening the American Army but also the American populace to the shortcomings of its forces.

Fate had great things in store for 'Black Jack' Pershing. Two weeks after the expedition returned to the United States, General Funston died of a heart attack and was replaced by Pershing as commander of the Army's Southern Department. When the American Expeditionary Force to France was formed later that year the command of it, which would almost certainly have gone to Funston, was given instead to Pershing.

With the removal of the Pershing thorn, relations between the United States and Mexico improved. Carranza emerged triumphant at elections held on 11 March (he polled 797,305 votes, against Pablo González's 11,615 and Alvaro Obregón's 4008). The Americans, who had just re-elected Woodrow Wilson for four more years, promptly extended *de jure* recognition and sent Henry P. Fletcher to Mexico City as their new ambassador, while Ignacio Bonillas was appointed Mexican ambassador in Washington. Despite this, Carranza's anti-American attitude persisted and it was the First Chief who was partly, if perhaps unwittingly, responsible for America's entry into the World War on 6 April 1917.

Carranza had shown himself to be such a Germanophile that von Eckhardt, who had replaced von Hintze as German Minister in Mexico, reported to Berlin that he was willing to permit German submarine bases—and perhaps even shore bases—in Mexico, and further prepared to halt the flow of oil from Tampico for the British Navy. Understandably, the Germans eagerly cultivated the First Chief's friendship. Their 4000-strong community in Mexico ran a Union of German Citizens which had twenty-nine branches, and an Iron Cross Society which reported seventy-five branches in the Republic. German residents also subsidised a propaganda picture newspaper which disseminated German-angled war news. There were, too, some fifty German officers serving as 'advisers' in Carranza's army. One of them, Maximilian Kloss, who had helped Obregón to defeat Villa at Celaya, had been promoted to general and was now director of Mexico's munitions manufacture. He wrote home proudly to his parents, 'I now have nine (Mexican) decorations and three high orders to pin on my tunic and the Cross of Honour to wear round my neck.'

In January 1917, Germany, desperate for a winning gambit to end the war's stalemate, decided to begin unrestricted submarine warfare on 1 February, despite the risk of American involvement should her ships be torpedoed. The United States, still pursuing President Wilson's 'watchful waiting' course, was anxious to stay out of the war and had even gone to the lengths of allowing the Germans to use the State Department's cable route to exchange messages between Berlin and Count von Bernstorff in Washington, supposedly about proposals to keep the peace between Germany and the United States.

Not knowing that British Intelligence had broken his country's top code, the German Foreign Secretary, Arthur Zimmermann, used the State Department's supposedly neutral cable route to put forward an outlandish proposal that Mexico should be invited to make war on the United States. The message, known as the Zimmermann Telegram, was sent on 16 January to von Bernstorff for forwarding to von Eckhardt in Mexico City. It read:

'We intend to begin unrestricted submarine warfare on the first of February. We shall endeavour in spite of this to keep the United States neutral. In the event of this not succeeding, we make Mexico a proposal of alliance on the following basis: make war together, make peace together, generous financial support and an understanding on our part that Mexico is to reconquer the lost territory in Kansas, New Mexico and Arizona. The settlement in detail is left to you.

'You will inform the president (of Mexico) of the above most secretly as soon as the outbreak of war with the United States is certain and add the suggestion that he should, on his own initiative, invite Japan to immediate adherence and at the same time mediate between Japan and ourselves.

'Please call the President's attention to the fact that the unrestricted employment of our submarines now offers the prospect of compelling England to make peace within a few months. Acknowledge receipt.'

The Germans were confident that the Americans would stay out of the war, even when the submarine packs were released into the Atlantic to prey upon all shipping. And in any case the threat of United States military involvement was dismissed as a negligible factor. At a Reichstag meeting on 31 January Admiral Capelle told the Kaiser 'From the military point of view America is as nothing. I am convinced that almost no American will volunteer for war

service. That is shown by the lack of volunteers for the
conflict with Mexico.'

The United States *did* stay out of the war after Germany
unleashed her submarines, though von Bernstorff was
handed his passport and diplomatic relations were broken
off.

On 5 February Zimmermann sent von Eckhardt a coded
message—again intercepted by the British—urging him to
pursue urgently the question of military alliance with
Mexico. However, Zimmermann's timing could hardly have
been worse. That same day the main reason for Carranza's
hostility towards the United States had been removed when
Pershing led his Punitive Expedition back across the border.

With the United States still neutral the British decided to
act. The sensational Zimmermann Telegram was leaked to
the Americans, with its designation carefully altered to
make it appear that it had been intercepted in Mexico. In
this way the Germans remained unaware that their top
secret code had been broken. Incredibly, Zimmermann
admitted that the telegram was true and the resulting diplomatic explosion blew the United States into the war. The
Mexicans and Japanese promptly denied all knowledge of
the Zimmermann proposals, though in fact Carranza's
Foreign Minister, Cándido Aguilar, had discussed the matter with the Japanese minister in Mexico on 20 February.

The Germans were stunned and furious. Arrogantly certain that the British were too stupid to have cracked their
complicated code, they vented their fury on the unfortunate
von Eckhardt, blaming him for the leak. British Intelligence
spent hilarious hours decoding the agonised messages flash-
ing back and forth. Desperately attempting to clear himself
of suspicion, von Eckhardt told Berlin that their messages
to him had been read out to him 'at night, in a low voice' by
his German manservant and that afterwards they had been
burned 'and the ashes scattered'.

Still Zimmermann persisted with his Mexican pipe
dreams. On 13 April, a week after the United States had
entered the war, he cabled von Eckhardt, 'Please state sums
necessary to carry out our policy.' But Carranza was not
now to be tempted. Next day the disconsolate German

Minister wired Berlin the bad news that Mexico had decided
to stay neutral: '[Carranza] say the alliance has been
wrecked by premature publication.'

However, the sympathies of many Mexicans still lay with
the Germans ... if only because of the fact that they were
now in active opposition to the detested Colossus of the
North. At Carranza's formal inauguration as President of
Mexico on 1 May 1917, von Eckhardt was greeted by cheers
while Fletcher, the new American ambassador, was hissed
and booed as he took his seat at the ceremony. But unpopularity could be endured. The important thing was that
Mexico had stayed out of the war, and American troops
would be free to strengthen the Western Front.

With his inauguration as president, Carranza considered the
Mexican Revolution over. Though six years of bloody civil
war had changed Mexico irrevocably, the Revolution was in
fact far from ended, as Carranza was to discover at the cost
of his life. But for the time being the First Chief went
serenely ahead, forming what was to be called, with some
truth, 'the most corrupt administration in the annals of
Mexico'. What Carranza in fact sought to re-establish was a
government on the Díaz lines—strong and authoritarian—
but with the vital difference that Mexico would no longer
dance attendance on the United States.

Carranza possessed several admirable qualities, some of
which—untiring industry, tenacity of purpose, a firm grasp
of detail and a sincere desire to make his country great—
were rare in Mexico. But they were outweighed by his lack
of political vision, his unfailing tendency to alienate people
and his unwillingness to mix with the masses. To sit in the
National Palace planning Mexico's greatness was not
enough. In his leisure time Carranza studied history. He
would have been better occupied creating it.

Obregón's biographer, Dr E. J. Dillon, has written of
Carranza, 'He was always a respectable, never a popular,
figure. He lacked not only the personal magnetism which
draws and captivates the multitudes but also the straightfor-
wardness, trust and affability ... which form the cement of
ordinary social relations. ... He resembled most Mexican
reformers in his set purpose so to better his country that he

himself should be its lord and master.'

In fact, Carranza was totally incapable of enforcing order in his chaotic and miserable country. The governors and *jefes políticos* of the Díaz days had been replaced by the army's 500 generals, and much of Mexico had been broken up into virtually autonomous little states under the leadership of bandits-turned-generals or generals-turned-bandits. Even in Mexico City, high military officers continued to loot and kill virtually as they pleased. Typical of the rampant graft was Pablo González's daily allowance of £100 'expenses' on top of his general's pay. Whenever Obregón, the Secretary of War, approved these payments, he always wrote carefully alongside them, 'By special order of the First Chief'.

On the day of Carranza's formal inauguration Obregón resigned in protest against the prevailing corruption and, after briefly contemplating exile in South America, went back to chick pea farming in his home state of Sonora. Before resigning from Carranza's government and following Obregón back to Sonora, General Plutarco Elías Calles criticised the corruption among the First Chief's entourage: 'They speculate with everything; they sell offices and concessions, they authorise thefts from the national treasury; they traffic ... even with the pensions of the widows and orphans of the Revolution....'

But graft was, and in many cases still is, a way of life in Mexico. The Mexican politician and author Francisco Bulnes had this to say about it: 'In Mexico to steal is to live; not to steal is to fall into the pit dug for cowards and honest men, and the hope of stealing is implanted as deeply in the soul of the revolutionist as the hope of heaven in the Christian's soul.'

Even Obregón recognised the inevitability of graft. 'All of us are thieves, more or less, down here,' he joked with the Spanish author Vicente Blasco Ibañez after becoming president in 1920. 'However, the point is that I have only one hand, while the others have two. That's why the people prefer me.'

Well-meaning Mexicans and foreigners attempted without success to point out to Carranza that many of his followers were living contradictions of the political principles

for which he had fought, though once he admitted to Dr
Dillon, 'I confess that I should be glad to be rid of some of
them. But I cannot dismiss them, at least not at once. They
stood by me in times of need and it would be a piece of
baseness on my part were I to turn my back upon them in
the hour of triumph. Besides, if I did I should be jeopardis-
ing the work accomplished.'

The government's corruption became so blatant that a
new verb, *carrancear*, meaning 'to steal', was coined and
gleefully taken up by the masses.

However, despite the hardships and disappointments of
Carranza's régime, his name ranks among the most highly-
regarded Mexican presidents for two reasons. The first was
his courageous foreign policy. One thing guaranteed to
unite Mexicans was an appeal to their chauvinism. This
Carranza did continually, resenting all intrusions into
Mexicans affairs and resisting what he considered en-
croachments on Mexican rights by the United States. Prime
examples of this were his immediate protest against American occupation of Veracruz, even though his own success
hung in the balance at that time, and his refusal to accept
American conditions for recognition of his régime—which
he proceeded to obtain without conditions. Though President Wilson regarded him, sometimes with justification, as
tiresome, bigoted and intransigent, Carranza's insistence on
Mexico's rights as a sovereign nation and his defiance of
the mighty northern neighbour helped the Mexicans to
tolerate the First Chief long after his government had become a sour joke.

Carranza's second, and infinitely greater, achievement
was the Constitution of 1917, upon which Mexican law is
based and which stands as the oldest operating Constitution
among major Latin-American nations. Its acceptance by
Carranza was, in the opinion of the historian Frank Tannenbaum, 'the most important event in the history of the
Revolution'. The constitution proposed a revolution more
sudden than any other in the history of labour (the Russian
Revolution had not then taken place). A stroke of the pen
gave Mexican workers and peasants rights, powers and prerogatives for which workers in other parts of the world had
been struggling for many years.

In September 1916 Carranza had ordered the setting up of a convention to decide what changes had been made necessary in Mexico's constitution by the years of revolution. The convention met in December in the same theatre in the town of Querétaro in which the Emperor Maximilian had been condemned to death. Carranza had prepared and presented to the convention a mild document which put the emphasis on political, rather than social, reform. But the delegates chose to throw their weight behind the proposals of a radical group led by a young general, Francisco Múgica, the son of a country schoolteacher from Michoacán. Poised ominously behind Múgica was Obregón, the one man who could overthrow Carranza whenever he chose to do so.

It was Múgica who secured the adoption by the convention of two historic articles which completely changed the format of the constitution. The first, Article 27, was designed to remove the two most disastrous acts of the Díaz days—the acquisition of property and oilfields in Mexico by foreigners, and the alienation of Indian-owned lands. It declared the State the original and sole owner of all lands, waters and subsoil wealth, and decreed that only Mexicans by birth or naturalisation and Mexican companies had the right of ownership or development. While Article 27 conceded the right of development to foreigners, it insisted that 'they agree to be considered Mexicans in respect of such property, and accordingly not to involve the protection of their government. . . .' Foreigners were prohibited from owning land within thirty miles of the Mexican coastline and sixty miles of the border, and the government was authorised to expropriate foreign-owned properties with appropriate compensation. This rule paved the way for the sensational nationalisation in 1938 of all foreign-owned oil companies in Mexico. In addition, all *ejido* lands taken from the Indians during and since the days of Díaz were to be returned, and any additional land needed by the villages was to be provided from private properties and *haciendas*.

The second, Article 123, is often called the Magna Carta of Mexican Labour. It proposed a revolution in the lives of industrial and agricultural workers: an eight-hour day, six-day week, minimum wage, and equal pay for equal work, regardless of sex or nationality. It also abolished peonage, child labour and the practice of collecting a man's debts from his children. The right to organise unions and to strike were legalised. Finally, Article 123 called for profit-sharing with employees, and compensation both for industrial injuries and dismissal without proper cause. It was probably the biggest gift package ever handed to the working class of any nation.

The Constitution of 1917 also re-enacted, in even more stringent form, the anti-clerical laws of Benito Juárez, while conceding the freedom of worship, in whatever form. Monastic orders, religious schools and religious processions were forbidden, and even church buildings were declared the property of the nation. Foreign priests were banned and Mexican priests were defined as persons exercising a profession and therefore subject to law. They were forbidden to organise political parties or criticise the government and were barred from voting.

The historic constitution was published on 5 February 1917, carefully timed by Carranza to coincide with the day Pershing and his expedition marched out of Mexico. On paper, at least, it represented a magnificent victory for the working classes; but it was a victory for which Mexico's masses, and its rulers, were woefully unprepared. It is to Carranza's everlasting credit that he accepted and signed the new constitution, though it bore little resemblance to the draft document he had presented to the Querétaro convention. The fact that he chose not to, or in some cases was unable to, implement it was another matter entirely. Like other Mexican constitutions before it, the Constitution of 1917 was a statement of aspiration rather than of intention. Its implementation was bitterly resisted by the Church, by landowners and by foreign owners of mines, ranches and oilfields—and in some cases by Carranza himself.

Ten years after its adoption, the provisions of Article 123 had not been enacted into a national labour law, though some states had adopted local codes based on its provisions. Labour's very lack of organisation, productivity and efficiency, too, for long proved a handicap. Parkes has written of the post-constitutional period: 'The history of Mexico for the next generation was to be the history of a long struggle to make the [constitution] a reality; and though the progress was to be painfully slow, at times imperceptible, it was to be genuine.'

The distribution of land was an example of the slowness in putting into effect the Constitution's provisions. Under Carranza, the promise of land for the landless remained a promise. Of Mexico's ten million land-hungry peasants, only 48,000 benefited from the agrarian reforms during the remaining three years of Carranza's presidency. Even these fortunate few usually possessed neither water, seeds nor tools and were often forced to return to work for the local *hacienda*. By 1920 less than half a million acres had been redistributed among the people—a total which was still, despite the Revolution, far less than the land holdings of some individuals.

The history of the *ejidos* and land distribution was subsequently happier. Though there was only a slight improvement in the rate of distribution during Obregón's presidency, his successor, Calles, stepped up the rate so that by 1927 half a million families had received land of their own. Mexican agrarian reform has been called 'a qualified success' by one economist; by 1964 about 133 million acres (an area about equal to the remaining privately-owned land in Mexico) had been granted to some two and a quarter million people. Many of Mexico's economists feel that the *ejido* system, though very much a political sacred cow, remains a straitjacket, hampering agricultural productivity, and the emphasis has been gradually shifting over the past few years from distribution of land to the improvement of farming techniques among those Mexicans who already own land.

Now that he no longer needed their support in his armies, Carranza's relations with industrial workers, and the unions, were markedly less cordial. He did nothing to implement the provisions of Article 123 and when electricians in Mexico City staged a strike Carranza labelled it treason and their leader, Luis Morones, was sentenced to death, though this was commuted to imprisonment. But other labour leaders *were* shot and, for the moment, the workers' new rights remained nothing more than paper promises.

Press opposition, too, was squashed by Carranza. When, after Germany's defeat in Europe, the Mexico City newspaper *A.B.C.* attacked the government for its pro-German attitude, saying, 'It is unfair that the Mexican nation and people should suffer the consequences and mistakes, whims and inefficiency of certain short-visioned authorities,' its publication was suspended and the editor physically attacked.

Mexico's peace under Carranza was an exhausted, fitful one, disturbed by a succession of small uprisings and rebellions, and the ever-present menace of Zapata and Villa. Life and property remained insecure and cheaply forfeited. Trains never ran at night, and even in daylight their military escorts could not prevent them from frequently being blown up or attacked. In Baja California a separatist government had been proclaimed by a man named Cantu; in the rich oilfields around Tampico General Manuel Peláez had rebelled against the government and was extracting a rich tribute for 'protecting' foreign properties there; and north of Veracruz even Félix Díaz was in arms once more.

Typical of the minor rebellions was the one started in 1918 by General Aureliano Blanquet, former vice-president under Huerta, who had been living in Cuba since the dictator's flight from Mexico. Blanquet landed on the Gulf Coast between Veracruz and Tuxpan in a small boat with half a dozen followers. After waiting in vain for several days for a promised rendezvous with Félix Díaz, the party moved inland where they ran into a force of government troops. Trying to escape, Blanquet plunged to his death in a ravine. By Carranza's orders his head was exhibited on a pole in Veracruz as a deterrent to further rebellion.

Carranza's most determined military efforts were directed to the extermination of Zapata and Villa. He found the presence of an uprising so close to Mexico City a political embarrassment and finally ordered General Pablo González into Morelos to smash for ever what he called 'the Zapata rabble'. Quickly realising that he was fighting a whole population, González systematically began to lay waste to a countryside which had already been ravaged by seven years of civil war. Whole villages were burned; crops were destroyed; women and children were herded into detention camps and every man González could lay his hands on was hanged. The entire sugar industry of the state was wrecked as González looted what factories and *haciendas* Zapata had left untouched. Even the huge copper vats in the distilleries were melted down and the metal sold.

Zapata struck back with equal ferocity. *Haciendas* and towns were put to the torch. Mrs King, the English widow who had lived in Cuernavaca and who finally fled with a refugee column at the height of the savagery said 'The Zapatistas treated all alike—masonry, dumb animals and human beings; there was only devastation, desolation. . . .'

Captured landowners and army officers faced agonising deaths at Zapata's hands. Some victims were crucified on telegraph poles or on giant cactus trees; others were staked out over ants' nests and smeared with honey, or sewn up inside wet hides and left to suffocate as the hides dried in the sun. One of Zapata's favourite execution methods was to stake out a man on a rough framework of branches over the top of a fast-growing maguey cactus. During the night the thorn-tipped blossom stalk of the plant would grow a foot or more, driving itself inch by inch through the staked-out victim.

Finally, in April 1919 Zapata was killed. His assassination was engineered by a half-breed Yaqui named Jesús Guajardo, a colonel in the army of González. Guajardo sent word to Zapata that he and his 800 troops wished to desert Carranza, bringing with them plenty of new rifles and ammunition. Though he was in sore need of men and munitions Zapata, ever suspicious, ordered Guajardo to prove his intentions by capturing the government-held town of Jonacatepec. Guajardo did so, throwing his troops against their unsuspecting Carrancista comrades. And, as further proof of his devotion to the Zapata cause, Guajardo had all the prisoners shot. Zapata was suitably impressed and accepted Guajardo's invitation to meet him at the *hacienda* of San Juan Chinameca.

Zapata arrived at the *hacienda* with ten followers and, as he passed through the gates, bugles blared out in his honour. Inside the *hacienda* courtyard a row of Guajardo's troops were drawn up facing the gate. At the command 'Present arms' they raised their rifles and fired, mowing down Zapata and his group. Guajardo's reward for his treachery was £5000 and promotion to brigadier-general.

But in attempting to hunt down his old enemy Villa, Carranza was no more successful—in fact a good deal less successful—than Pershing had been. Through 1917 Villa steadily built up his strength, though he was continually harassed by another 'Pancho', General Francisco Murguía, a photographer-turned-soldier who, though a devoted Carrancista, favoured the field uniform of the old Porfirian army, including a peaked kepi. Because of his fondness for hanging prisoners, Murguía was known as 'Pancho the Rope' to differentiate from Villa, 'Pancho the Pistols'. These two matched cruelty for cruelty, savagery for savagery, though not on the total scale of González's campaign in Morelos.

On 30 May 1917 Villa suddenly appeared out of the desert to attack Ojinaga and drove the government garrison across the Rio Grande into Presidio, Texas, producing a repetition of the panic-stricken flight when he had sacked the town with a much larger force in January 1914. Villa, in his first border appearance since the Columbus Raid, made no attempt to hold Ojinaga, but moved off into the desert after stripping the town of supplies and arms.

Next Villa tried another raid on Chihuahua City. But this time he found the grim-faced, efficient General Murguía waiting for him. The attack was beaten off and when Villa retreated he had to abandon a group of his men who had advanced into the heart of the city along one of the main roads, Columbus Avenue. Murguía lived up to his nickname by hanging all 256 of them in grotesque bunches on the trees along the avenue, with the comment that the lives of the Villistas were not worth the bullets that would otherwise have killed them. Columbus Avenue is still known by the people of Chihuahua City as the Avenue of Hanging Men.

On 15 November the wretched garrison of Ojinaga was again put to flight across the Rio Grande when Villa, at the head of a thousand men, pounced on the town for provisions. Again he was content with a brief stay. In 1918 Villa kept well away from the American border, contenting himself with a series of guerrilla raids against small towns and isolated garrisons, mainly in Chihuahua. He also took to kidnapping Americans in order to provide himself with campaign funds.

In October Villa abducted Frank Knotts, the owner of the Erupción Mining Company, near Villa Ahumada in northern Chihuahua, and held him to ransom for 20,000 dollars. The kidnapped man's brother, A. W. Knotts of El Paso, delivered the money to Villa in a huge wad of dollar bills, but Villa refused to accept them, saying he hated the faces of the *gringos* printed on them. He demanded instead that the ransom be paid in gold. When this had been arranged Knotts was released, unharmed, on 18 November.

Those Mormons who had not fled to the United States when Pershing left Mexico also suffered from Villa's depredations. The Mormon Elder, Anthony W. Ivins, wrote, 'Most people feel the pincers of the tax collector once a year but the Mormon colonists in Chihuahua not only pay the federal government the regular tax, but hand over any available surplus to Villa and his band of expert and lawless collectors now and then. When Villa needs more money he swoops down on the defenceless colonists and takes it. If the money is not forthcoming he kidnaps some wealthy and influential citizen and holds him for ransom. If the amount is not secured in time, he kills the citizen by way of warning for the future.'

Ivins cited the case of A. M. Tenney, a wealthy Mormon rancher, who was kidnapped along with two American min-

ing engineers. When no ransom money was received, Villa
sent Tenney back to collect the 20,000 dollars, threatening
that if he did not return with the money the mining men
would be shot. He returned with the money in time to save
them, but not, according to Ivins 'before they had been
tortured by the evident preparations for execution'.

On 12 December Villa raided the long-suffering mining
camp as Cusihuiriáchic, stealing 10,000 dollars from the
company's safe and burning the entire stockpile of wood,
with the explanation that the company would now have to
buy more wood and that this would provide employment
for the Mexican people.

By the spring of 1919 Villa had increased his strength to
about 1200 men and he received a further boost when
General Felipe Angeles, who had spent several years farming in the United States after the eclipse of Villa in 1915,
returned to join him and was appointed second-in-command.

Parral was the next town to suffer Villa's vengeance.
After capturing it on 25 April, he hanged the Carrancista
mayor and his two sons in the main square and also strung
up as many male relatives as he could find of Maclovio
Herrera, his former ally who had deserted to Carranza.
Villa systematically sacked the town, and though he respected foreign property and companies they were required
to contribute to Villa's fighting fund, which benefited by
more than £100,000. With enough money to purchase plenty
of arms, and confident that he was now strong enough to
capture a major border town, Villa headed north for
Ciudad Juárez.

He launched a surprise attack on the night of 14–15
June, bombarding the town from the east so that the danger
of damage to El Paso would be lessened. Within two hours
the Villistas had taken most of Juárez but at daylight a
counter-attack by government troops cleared them out of
some parts of the town. Late in the afternoon of 15 June
Villa attacked again, and this time bullets flew across the
border; by nightfall one American soldier had been killed,
another wounded and several civilians had been hurt. Brigadier General James B. Erwin, commanding the U.S.
forces at El Paso, decided to delay no longer.

Just before 11 p.m. two columns of the 7th Cavalry crossed the Rio Grande east of El Paso on pontoon bridges; and soon afterwards American Negro infantrymen marched across the international bridge into Juárez after Colonel Francis Glover, General Erwin's Chief of Staff, had warned the Carrancistas, 'Get out of the way if you don't want to be hurt.' The battle which followed was short, sharp and decisive. The Villistas' main camp at Juárez racecourse was bombarded with shrapnel and high explosive and at dawn the Americans moved in. The cavalry units, led by Colonel S. R. H. 'Tommy' Tompkins, brother of the Columbus hero Frank Tompkins and known to his troops as 'the pink-whiskered s.o.b.', went in at the gallop with pistols drawn, and the infantry completed the rout with a bayonet charge. By mid-morning the army which Villa had been building carefully for many months had ceased to exist. Again he had been broken by the American army and this time there was to be no comeback.

Though Villa again eluded his pursuers, small groups of his followers were hunted down by Mexican government troops, and early in November General Angeles was captured, brought to trial in Chihuahua City and sentenced to death. Though Britain and France urged Carranza to spare his life, Angeles was shot on 26 November. He refused to wear a blindfold and himself gave the signal for the execution squad to fire. It was a senseless waste of a brave and brilliant man. General Scott, the U.S. Chief of Staff, thought his death 'a great pity'. He considered Angeles 'the most cultivated and loyal gentleman I have known in the history of Mexico. He was Villa's candidate for president, and he was mine so far as I have a right to have any.'

The execution of Angeles had its sequel soon afterwards when Villa attacked a northbound train in Chihuahua. Two powerful bombs exploded under the engine, blowing it to pieces, and the military guard riding on the roofs of the carriages was soon wiped out. The mail carriage was looted and the passengers robbed of all their valuables. The two railway guards were hauled before Villa, who shot them through the heart; then he ordered that the passengers be lined up for execution. But as he was about to give the order to fire Villa changed his mind and, with tears in his eyes, told the trembling captives, 'Since the execution of my friend Felipe Angeles I have been thirsting for vengeance. That is why I blew up the train. Well, I have avenged his murder. Now, in memory of him I spare your lives. You may go.'

It was to be one of Villa's last acts of banditry.

The three years following the publication of the Constitution of 1917 were years of depression and disillusionment. Ernest Gruening wrote of this period, 'The bloody devastation of the Revolution had left the country in ruins, industry prostrate, a people in rags, diseased, despairing, dying. Every class suffered. . . . Agrarian reform was carried out so blunderingly and so dishonestly that the peasantry seldom benefited. Labour, which had supposedly broken its chains, was restive under the sky-rocketing cost of living.'

Inflation meant that the workers were earning even less than they had done in the days of Díaz. The financial situation had become so bad by 1919 that many civil servants received only half or three quarters of their pay. In some of the states schoolteachers had not been paid for five months and in Mexico City schools were forced to close because of lack of funds to pay the teachers. Yet in 1918 more than £12 million, two-thirds of the national budget, was assigned to the army. Nearly all of this went into the generals' pockets.

The world epidemic of influenza swept across Mexico, reducing an already diseased population by an estimated million. Mexico City's death rate during the Carranza régime was 42 per 1000, compared with 17·5 per 1000 in the main European cities.

An article in the *New York Sun* on 29 January 1918, reported: 'Mexico City is full of starving Indians, insufficiently clad and with no shelter to protect themselves at night to escape the icy winds. . . . They huddle together for warmth on recessed doorsteps, passing the bitter night in a physical state that must somewhat approach that of the hibernating bear and in the morning they crawl into a sunny place and slowly thaw into life again, resuming their pathetic quest for food. They mutely appeal with outstretched hands and wistful eyes to the passer-by, and there are legions of them.'

An American resident of Mexico City reported that 'beggars, always numerous, have multiplied tenfold'. Waiters had to be constantly on the alert to prevent starving Indians entering restaurants and begging scraps of food from the diners.

Venereal disease was so common in Mexico that to reach adult life without having contracted it was considered exceptional. One Mexican doctor explained, 'Venereal diseases are considered as trivial as measles or whooping cough, as illnesses to which every man must some time in his life pay tribute.' In 1919 the Department of Education's medical service reported that the majority of children attending school were afflicted with hereditary syphilis ... yet it was only the *better-off* children who were able to go to school.

The Mexico City newspaper *El Excelsior* revealed in December 1918 that 116,311 children in the Federal District around the capital were receiving no education at all. It commented, 'This figure ... is all the more significant—and discouraging—in that it relates to a section which is usually considered the most cultured of the Republic.' The article also pointed out that in 1910, under Díaz, there had been 419 schools in the Federal District. Eight years later the figure had fallen to 382.

The *Daily Mail* attempted to explain the incredible corruption to British readers in a leader page article written by 'An Englishman Just Returned from Mexico':

'The Mexican government has been increasing old taxes and inventing new ones ruthlessly; enormous sums have flowed into the government exchequer but they have not found their way into the public service. The taxes are tremendous; every user of the telephone or electric light pays a government tax proportionate to his bill; consumers of all kinds are similarly mulcted. ...

'Yet despite this colossal taxation the public services are shamefully neglected. For instance, public education is at a standstill. There are no funds to pay the professors and teachers. How the money goes is proved by the fact that half a dozen or more men have become millionaires in sterling from nothing within the last five years. One of them is a relation of Carranza.'

The writer then gave this illustration of army corruption 'within my own experience':

'There was until recently a small town near the coast held for Carranza by a general who claimed to command a force of 1000 men with 800 horses. For this number he regularly drew pay and money in lieu of rations. One day he disappeared. He had married and fled to Cuba with a huge fortune awaiting him there.

'When he had gone it was discovered that his force had never consisted of more than 300 men, that there had been no horses, that for a long time even the 300 men had received no pay and had, in addition, been obliged to forage for themselves. . . .'

Against all expectations, Carranza's government was not overthrown. Rather, it committed suicide. Carranza made his blunder in the autumn of 1919 when he attempted to interfere in the free election of his successor. Carranza had campaigned so long under Madero's banner of 'No re-election' that even he dared not violate it. But he sought to impose on the country an alternative to the obvious man, Obregón. His choice was the insignificant and little-known Ignacio Bonillas, Mexico's Ambassador to the United States, who had spent so little time in Mexico that he was called derisively 'Meester' Bonillas. Some Mexicans even thought he was a naturalised American.

Carranza maintained that, since peace had been re-established in Mexico, a military president would only cause more trouble among dissatisfied generals. Mainly, however, Bonillas was picked by Carranza as a politician who would allow the First Chief to retain behind-the-scenes control of Mexico. But he was such an obviously ludicrous choice that there was never any hope of his being elected. Apart from his mastery of English and an impeccable taste in clothes he was generally regarded, even by Carranza's government colleagues, as an amiable nonentity.

The presidential election was set for June, 1920. Exactly a year before, on 1 June 1919, Obregón had given up chick pea farming and announced his candidacy. He allied himself with no political party and, with typical frankness, made no pre-election promises. 'The people care nothing for programmes which, in the last analysis, are little better than rhymed prose,' he maintained in his election manifesto. 'What they lay stress on are deeds. . . .'

Obregón added that the political field was dominated by two political groups: the conservatives, who were intent on perpetuating those evils of the Díaz days which had survived, and the liberals who, while gazing upwards at lofty ideals, stumbled into mud-holes 'and took to belabouring each other there'.

In one bitter campaign speech in the autumn of 1919 Obregón lashed the corrupt Carranza administration: 'The penal colony is not large enough to hold poor men for stealing bread, while bandits drive through the streets in costly automobiles, the fruits of their systematic robberies. There will be no justice in Mexico while the schoolteachers live on charity while mistresses pass them, loaded with jewels.'

Obregón's attitude towards Carranza was less outspoken. His manifesto declared, 'The historic personality of the First Chief . . . is in danger, if, despite the unquestionable energy and dexterity with which he overcame the more formidable hindrances to success, his work should prove barren . . . if, in a word, the country should be bereft of the right to emancipate itself from the emancipators.'

General Pablo González, who had confidently expected to be Carranza's choice for the next president, refused to back Bonillas and instead announced his own candidacy. The nomination of Bonillas had been a poor joke from the first, but Carranza refused to back down. He had named Bonillas and intended to stand by him.

Obregón considered Bonillas 'a man who is serious, honest and hard-working. The world has lost a magnificent book-keeper. If I become president, I shall offer him the management of a bank.' More seriously, Luis Cabrera, Carranza's Finance Minister, was reported to have said that if González were elected he hoped he would not be shot, that if Obregón became president he hoped he would not be exiled and that if Bonillas were chosen he hoped he would not have to take a position in the government!

In typical Mexican fashion, the campaigning was rough and bloody. *El Monitor Republicano* reported on 23 September that General Guajardo, Zapata's assassin, had ordered two of his officers who supported Obregón to shout 'Viva Pablo González' and, when they refused, shot them, explaining that he had acted 'in defence of the social interests of the community'. The next day the same newspaper reported that several employees of the Municipality of Mexico City had been dismissed because they were Obregón supporters. Generals, too, were removed from command because they were known to be loyal to Obregón. Carranza was treading dangerous ground.

Though he insisted that he represented no party or its aims, Obregón allowed himself to be announced as the candidate of the Liberal Constitutional Party in July 1919 and soon afterwards the Labour Party and the whole labour movement swung behind him. In November Obregón reached Mexico City on his campaign tour and had an interview with Carranza. Afterwards he commented, 'I cannot hook up my car to the train of Señor Carranza.' The break was official; and from now on it was to widen into an abyss.

Bonillas arrived in Mexico City from Washington on 20 March 1920 to begin his election tour. He was welcomed in the capital by a crowd of 50,000 who were just as curious to see what he looked like as to hear what he had to say. They had little chance of either, since Obregón's supporters let off stink bombs in front of the speaking platform and police had to be called in to break up the fighting. Bonillas also ran into trouble on his campaign tour. His timetable of speeches was severely disrupted by mysterious delays to his train (the railwaymen supported Obregón), and his opponents spread the word that 'Meester' Bonillas was busy learning Spanish.

One theatre in Mexico City presented a revue lampooning all three candidates. Bonillas appeared dressed as a little shepherd called Tea Blossom; Obregón talked about his chick peas and his intention of taking over the presidency by blows of a club; and González, wearing military uniform, a huge moustache and a fierce frown, advanced towards the footlights, firing a cannon and growling 'I am a pacifist.'

All three were wasting their time campaigning. The election was destined never to take place.

It was the north-western state of Sonora, for a long time the revolutionary home of Carranza himself, which was instrumental in his downfall. The trouble started late in 1919 when the state governor, Adolfo de la Huerta, repudiated the First Chief's declaration that the Sonora River belonged to the nation. Next, de la Huerta accused Carranza of planning to renew a campaign against the state's wild Yaqui Indians. Any pretext, it seemed, would serve to promote the split with Carranza which the Sonora politicians were obviously seeking.

On 4 March 1920 Carranza gave them their opportunity when he attempted to send government troops into the state to break a railway workers' strike. De la Huerta accused Carranza of violating the sovereignty of the state (though states' sovereignty had, in fact, been ignored by every Mexican president who felt strong enough to do so), and Sonora withdrew its recognition of the Carranza régime. It was in this chaotic atmosphere that, on 2 April Obregón received a summons to appear in Mexico City as a witness at the trial of an Army officer, Colonel Roberto Cejudo, who was charged with treason. Suspecting a plot to involve Obregón and discredit him as a presidential candidate, his friends urged him to stay away from the capital but he told an election audience in Monterrey, 'I go protected by the armour of my conscience.' And when some of his audience cried, 'Death to Bonillas', Obregón pleaded with them to show 'proper respect for corpses'.

Obregón travelled to Mexico City, where he stayed at the home of a friend, Miguel Alessio Robles. The house was under constant observation and whenever Obregón left it he was followed by government agents on motorcycles.

Obregón made his first appearance at the trial of Cejudo, which was being held in the courtroom of Santiago Tlaltelolco military prison, on 11 April. The presiding judge, Pascual Morales y Molina, had been specially promoted to general so that he would not be outranked by Obregón, but according to one observer he was extremely nervous 'and once placed between his lips the burning end of a cigar he

was smoking'. The plan of the government to implicate
Obregón became immediately obvious when the prosecutor,
General Juan Barragán, Carranza's handsome, twenty-
seven-year-old Chief of Staff, famous for his dazzling array
of uniforms, produced a letter alleged to have been written
by Cejudo to Obregón but intercepted by the government.
When the trial was adjourned that day Obregón was
ordered to report to court again next morning; but he
decided instead to escape from Mexico City, since it was
now obvious that the trial had been rigged to discredit
him.

Early that evening he left the Robles house in a car
accompanied by three companions and followed by the
usual motorcycle escort. But Obregón fooled his shadowers
by changing hats with one of his fellow passengers and leap-
ing from the car as it was passing a public park.

Obregón made his way to the house of a railway worker
named Margarito Ramírez, where he borrowed a railwayman's hat and lantern. A coat was flung over his right
shoulder to make his missing arm less noticeable and that
night he was smuggled to Buenavista Station and aboard a
goods train, which left for the state of Guerrero at six the
next morning. When Obregón's escape was reported to
Carranza telegrams were sent to all state governors ordering his arrest. But Obregón found a friendly welcome in
Guerrero from a former comrade-in-arms, General For-
tunato Maycotte—and the new rebellion was on. When he
became president Obregón did not forget the railwayman
who had helped him to escape. Ramírez was appointed
Chief of Military Trains and eventually became governor of
the state of Jalisco.

On 20 April Obregón announced from the former Zapata
stronghold of Chilpancingo that he was abandoning his
presidential campaign and that arms would have to be used
to 'safeguard the virtues which the government is seeking by
arms to destroy'. Obregón's state of Sonora was already in
rebellion and on 23 April there was published the Plan of
Agua Prieta, which had been drawn up by de la Huerta,
Calles and another Obregónista, General Salvador Alvarado.
Though it was a sterile and pompous document which paid
little attention to the country's economic problems and

attacked instead Carranza's so-called 'assault on states' sovereignty', the plan attracted such quick allegiance from military groups all over the country that Luis Cabrera likened the switch of support to an 'army strike'. It was not so much a rebellion against Carranza as a wholesale desertion of a corrupt régime. Even General Jacinto B. Treviño, who had been the first man to sign Carranza's Plan of Guadalupe in 1913, joined Obregón.

As support for Obregón swelled, Pablo González, the presidential candidate and commander of the Republic's largest single force, 22,000 men garrisoning the Federal District, was in an agony of indecision. From the start of the uprising against Victoriano Huerta he had been a Carranza man and had owed his success since then to his adroit riding on the First Chief's coat tails.

At the end of April González compromised. He left Mexico City saying that his presidential campaign had exhausted him and he was going to the country for a rest. The country air and the frantic scramble to board the Obregón bandwagon soon helped González to make up his mind and he too declared against Carranza.

Fast running out of an army, Carranza decided to flee to Veracruz as he had done in 1914, and to make a stand against Obregón there. He commented bitterly, 'I cannot trust anyone. My closest friends, men whom I have made, have turned against me.' Before leaving, he contacted General Guadalupe Sánchez, commander of the Veracruz garrison, asking whether he still supported the government. Sánchez telegraphed back, 'President and Father, though everyone else betray you I shall not. If but one man remains loyal to you, I am that man.' Thus encouraged, Carranza prepared to leave Mexico City once again.

It was an exodus in the Biblical sense of the word. The departure was delayed for several days while Carranza and his hangers-on practically dismantled the capital. Mrs Moats wrote, 'You could not go two blocks without seeing a line of automobiles and carriages in front of some house, and into these cars were being loaded everything from old oak wardrobes to kitchen stoves. The whole city seemed to be moving ... Carranza might have escaped with his life if he hadn't been so greedy. His train stood waiting with steam

up for two or three days but there were always a few more
things to be taken away.... He even took the light fixtures
from the National Palace.'

When eventually the presidential 'Golden Train' pulled
out of Mexico City on 7 May it was accompanied by thirty
others, totalling more than eight miles of rolling stock and
carrying thousands of Carranza's government colleagues
and officials, relatives, friends, hangers-on and their wives
and mistresses, with mountains of valuables, belongings and
household goods. Some 10,000 people, half of them
women, took part in this weird evacuation which was distinguished, apart from its bizarre quality, by its complete
lack of organisation. Though they had remembered to bring
along the entire National Treasury and even the dies of the
government mint, nobody had given a thought to medical
supplies, or water for the engines and passengers.

As the vast horde chugged out of the capital, rebel troops
under Pablo González and Jacinto Treviño entered the city.
They managed to derail one of the trains and prevent about
half of Carranza's hangers-on getting further than the
suburbs. The remaining trains made desperately slow progress, having to halt frequently to seek water or repair torn-
up track. On 9 May, while Carranza's loyal guard was
beating off an attack on the trains at Aljibes in Puebla,
Obregón made a triumphant entry into the capital from
which he had fled in disguise less than a month earlier. And
on 15 May González formally withdrew from the presidential race, stating that he was 'sacrificing political interests
for those of the nation'.

In the meantime, Carranza's luck had finally deserted
him. As he struggled towards Veracruz he was told that
Guadalupe Sánchez, the general who had recently expressed his loyalty in such fulsome terms, had gone over to
Obregón. Now Carranza had nowhere to go. After further
heavy attacks had been made on the trains on 13 and 14
May the First Chief decided to abandon them and, accompanied by his closest friends and a small escort, set out on
horseback for the northern part of the state of Puebla,
where the local commander, General Francisco P. Mariel,
was known to be loyal. The First Chief's column of about
seventy men made their painful way along mountain trails

in heavy rain. 'It was appropriate weather for a bitter occasion,' wrote the American historian, John Dulles.

Fleeing with Carranza were his presidential candidate, Ignacio Bonillas, Luis Cabrera his Finance Minister and long-time friend, Manuel Aguirre Berlanga the Home Secretary, General Juan Barragán his Chief of Staff and the loyal General Francisco Murguía. The exhausted party received a friendly welcome from General Mariel, who left them in charge of a local bandit-turned-general, Rodolfo Herrero, while he went ahead of the presidential party to make arrangements for Carranza to stay in a town called Villa Juárez. Mariel's choice of Herrero as Carranza's guide was hardly a wise one. Herrero had, until the spring of 1920, been fighting in the mountains as an anti-Carrancista and had only surrendered to Mariel on the condition that his self-given rank of general would be recognised by the government.

On 20 May, in pouring rain, Herrero escorted the group towards Villa Juárez, and suggested that they make an overnight stop in a squalid village called San Antonio Tlaxcalantongo, which consisted of a ruined church and a few primitive huts of wood and thatch, huddled on a strip of land between a mountain and a ravine. Leading Carranza to one of the huts, Herrero told him, 'For now, señor, this will be the National Palace.' Carranza shared his one-room hut with his private secretary, Pedro Gil Farías, Home Secretary Aguirre Berlanga and two army officers.

The president bedded down for the last night of his life with a saddle for a pillow and a horse blanket as his only cover. Shortly before dawn a force of Herrero's men attacked the village; bullets were poured through the walls of the hut where Carranza was sleeping. The First Chief cried out, 'I cannot get up, my leg is broken,' and told the other occupants to save themselves. Then Herrero's men burst into the hut and finished him off. Three bullets struck him in the chest, one just missing the red initials V.C. embroidered on his vest over his heart. As a weeping aide tried to cover the body with a blanket, the assassins made off with Carranza's clothing and most of his belongings, including his spectacles, pistols, portable typewriter and watch.

Other members of the group had remarkable escapes. Luis Cabrera, stumbling out of his hut without his spectacles when the shooting started, fell into the ravine but lodged in a tree just below the edge, where he remained undetected. Ignacio Bonillas, whose hut was a little distance apart from the others, escaped the attack altogether and was guided by an Indian boy to Villa Juárez in the morning. Herrero rounded up about thirty prisoners, including Aguirre Berlanga, but released them after forcing them to sign a document saying that Carranza had committed suicide after being wounded in the leg.

On 22 May Carranza's body was taken to Villa Juárez, where it was embalmed and put on a train for Mexico City, guarded by Aguirre Berlanga, Bonillas, General Murgía and others who had survived the night of treachery at Tlaxcalantongo. The train was halted just outside the capital and Carranza's funeral escort were taken into custody. On 24 May Carranza was buried in Mexico City's Dolores Cemetery, the coffin being placed, in accordance with the First Chief's wishes, in a 'third-class grave where the poor people are buried'.

Rodolfo Herrero was never punished for the murder. In December 1920 Obregón ordered the arrest of Herrero and others held to be responsible for Carranza's death, and the new Minister of War, General Benjamín Hill, known as 'Obregón's lost right arm' prepared to prosecute. But on 14 December Hill died, apparently of poisoning after attending a banquet, and the judge at the trial freed Herrero. He returned to his ranch in Puebla, having lost nothing more than his title of general.

On the day Carranza was buried the Mexican legislature met to choose an interim president who would serve out the last six months of his term. Senators and Deputies balloted in secret, accompanied by a storm of noise from the public galleries, which were packed with Obregón supporters. There were four candidates: Adolfo de la Huerta, the Sonora governor and Obregón's own choice; General Pablo González, who had so recently renounced all presidential ambitions; Antonio I. Villareal, who had been president of the Convention of Aguascalientes, and Fernando Iglesias

Calderón. When the counting began cheers greeted every vote for de la Huerta and the presiding officer had to request the public to stop booing every vote for González. De la Huerta was voted into power overwhelmingly, gaining 224 votes to González's 29. Villareal and Calderón picked up one vote each.

On the afternoon of 1 June the thirty-nine-year-old de la Huerta rode in an open carriage from his modest lodgings at the Hotel Regis to the Chamber of Deputies, where he was officially sworn in as interim president. Next day he reviewed a massive parade of 25,000 Obregónista troops from the balcony of the National Palace. Thus Mexico was launched on one of the most enlightened six months in its history. De la Huerta, a former bank official, had become a member of the Sonora State legislature after Madero's overthrow of Díaz. He backed Carranza against Victoriano Huerta (to whom he was not related) and during Carranza's presidency he had spells as Home Secretary in the First Chief's cabinet and Mexican Consul General in New York before being appointed Governor of Sonora. De la Huerta particularly liked the New York appointment, since he had an excellent voice and his early ambition had been to sing for the Metropolitan Opera Company there.

De la Huerta's frankness, informality and honesty made a great impression on a nation that was sick of rebellions and even more sick of militarism. More was accomplished towards the pacification of the country during de la Huerta's six-month term than during the previous six years. His first move was to announce that all Mexicans living in exile because of the Revolution could return whenever they wished, whatever their past activities. Next he freed from prison Generals Murgía and Mariel and all the others who had remained loyal to Carranza until the end. Among them was the presidential candidate Ignacio Bonillas, who promptly availed himself of the opportunity to retire to the United States and renounce the hazards of Mexican politics.

Those supporters of Zapata who were still holding out in Morelos quickly agreed to lay down their arms when de la Huerta promised the peasants permanent possession of the land they had taken during the Revolution.

But de la Huerta's most spectacular feat was to negotiate the retirement of Pancho Villa. When the Plan of Agua Prieta was announced, Villa had offered his support against Carranza; but both Obregón and Calles opposed a pact with Villa, and it was not until de la Huerta took office that Villa's depredations were ended. On 26 July Villa's forces captured the town of Sabinas in Coahuila. Having taken the town, Villa proceeded to pull up miles of railway track on either side of it, making certain that he would not be disturbed or surprised for the next few days.

His privacy assured, Villa got in telegraphic touch with de la Huerta in Mexico City, offering to surrender his men and arms to the government in return for a *hacienda* and a small escort for his protection. When Obregón, who was on a political tour of Sinoloa, heard the news, he expressed strong disapproval, but de la Huerta ignored him and opened negotiations with Villa.

General Eugenio Martínez, de la Huerta's Head of Military Operations, travelled to Sabinas to confer with Villa and it was there, on 28 July 1920 that Villa, the man who had once boasted that he could march 100 miles without stopping, go 100 days without food, 100 nights without sleep and kill 100 men without remorse, signed the pact which made him a private citizen. The price (for the Government) was high but the guarantee of peace which went with it was well worth the cost. He was offered, and accepted, a 25,000 acre estate at Canutillo, near Parral, for which the government paid £60,000. The site had been carefully chosen by de la Huerta. It was in Durango, close to the state border with Villa's beloved Chihuahua but well isolated from both state capitals and also far from a railway line. He was also permitted to retain fifty *Dorados* as a bodyguard. These men were to be chosen by him but paid from Ministry of War funds. The rest of Villa's force, consisting of 239 officers and 511 men, were each given a year's pay and offered land wherever they wanted to settle. Those who wished to stay in the army were recruited into the government forces on the spot. After the pact was signed, Villa telephoned de la Huerta to express his satisfaction with the deal.

There were more triumphs of diplomacy for Mexico's

interim president. After Carranza's assassination, that small-voiced dissenter Félix Díaz, who had been in fitful rebellion in the state of Veracruz, contacted General Guadalupe Sánchez and asked to be taken prisoner 'as I do not want to appear as having surrendered', so that his sadly misman-aged career of uprisings might come to a peaceful end. Sánchez obliged Díaz by arresting him and, on the orders of General Calles, also prepared a military court to try and to execute him. But when de la Huerta became president he ordered that Díaz be given a safe conduct to the United States. Even this narrow escape did not teach Díaz a lesson. Two years later, from the safety of New Orleans, he issued an anti-Obregón manifesto in which he promised to erase the 'hodgepodge' Constitution of 1917.

The next one to get a de la Huerta reprieve and safe conduct was Pablo González who, with his old companion in treachery, Jesús Guajardo, had been making suspiciously anti-government noises in Monterrey.

Guajardo was arrested and, to the undisguised satisfac-tion of all those who remembered the way he had trapped and killed the proud Zapata, he was shot by order of the Nuevo León state government on 17 July. Soldiers who went to Gonzalez's home found him hiding in the cellar, which only served to add to the deep suspicion about his activities. González was tried for treason in a circus set-ting: a Monterrey theatre jammed with cheering and jeer-ing spectators.

González's lawyers insisted that the trial was improper because all of the army officers comprising the tribunal were of inferior rank to the accused man. So, by order of the government, each member of the tribunal was appointed Divisional General, the highest rank in the army, for the duration of the trial. (This sort of promotion was a com-mon thing in Mexico. It had happened when Obregón gave evidence at the Cejudo trial the previous April and it was to be used, in a slightly more chilling context, in a later uprising against the Obregón government when a lawyer accused of treason was condemned to death. When he pointed out that as a civilian he should not suffer the military penalty of execution, a notice was published in the

newspapers promoting the lawyer to general. Next day he
was shot.)

On 21 July the military tribunal found González guilty
and sentenced him to death. But de la Huerta agreed with
government officials who felt that it would be a political
mistake to shoot a man who had so recently been a presidential candidate. So González was freed and travelled to
the United States, from where, from time to time, he issued
meaningless pronouncements against the Obregón government.

Before his brief term expired de la Huerta also managed
to negotiate the peaceful settlement of other rebellions in
the outlying states of Baja California and Chiapas. A
general called Alberto Pineda O. had risen against the
government in Chiapas, threatening to shoot any emissaries
sent by de la Huerta to discuss peace. According to John
Dulles, one of Pineda's spies was caught in the presidential
offices in the capital and handed over to the authorities for
execution. But de la Huerta intervened, gave the man 1000
pesos, safe-conduct papers back to Chiapas and a key with
which to enter the presidential offices whenever he chose.
The spy's breathless account of his treatment at the hands
of de la Huerta brought about the quick pacification of
General Alberto Pineda O.

The presidential election, originally scheduled for June,
was set for 5 September 1920. Though both Bonillas and
González, his previous opponents, were now no longer con-
tenders, Obregón's election to the presidency was not un-
contested. The National Republican Party, the Catholic
Party and other small groups who opposed Obregón put
forward Alfredo Robles Domínguez as their candidate.
Though the priests, in defiance of the government ban on
their taking part in politics, wrote on Domínguez's ballot
boxes 'Here you vote for God', the election was a formality.
On 26 October Obregón was announced the winner with
1,131,751 votes to Domínguez's 47,442. In the states of
Tamaulipas and Tabasco Domínguez failed to gain a single
vote.

As Obregón prepared to take office as Mexico's next
president, the country was more pacified than it had been
for ten years, and more united than it had been for twice

that long. Now Mexico could begin to rebuild from the ruins of the Revolution.

Precisely at midnight between 30 November and 1 December in the Chamber of Deputies, Alvaro Obregón raised his one arm and was sworn into office. Mexico was launched on its era of reconstruction.

Villa, who was forty-three when he retired to Canutillo in 1920, devoted the liberal funds supplied by the government and his own volcanic energy to making it a model estate. He had forgiven the Americans sufficiently to buy their modern farm machinery, and with it he raised profitable crops of wheat, corn and potatoes. He also constructed a road from his ranch into the nearest town, Parral, and built a school at Canutillo for the children of his employees and bodyguards, ordering that the windows should be set high in the walls. This, he said, provided better ventilation and prevented the children looking out when they should be studying. Villa also paid for the sons of some of his *Dorados* to be educated at American military academies, and paid the expenses of eight sons of farm employees at a business school in El Paso.

Soon after retiring to the ranch Villa agreed to be interviewed by a group of American newspapermen. It was a short meeting. One of the first questions was whether he would ever take up arms again. Villa replied that he would do so if the Americans attacked Mexico or if Adolfo de la Huerta should ever need his help. But when a photographer asked him to perform some cowboy tricks Villa lost his temper and the group had to leave.

When Carl Beers, a farm machinery salesman from El Paso, visited him, Villa had so far forgiven the Americans that he insisted on Beers staying the night in his own bedroom. Beers recalled that it was a 'neatly furnished room, with heavy brass bed and dresser. The dresser was weighted down with bottles of perfume of many kinds. Most of the bottles were unopened'. Villa ordered a dozen ploughs from Beers, who asked if he might send a gift to the ranch school. 'Yes,' Villa told him. 'I would like to have a picture of your two great men, Washington and Lincoln, to hang in the school room.' And when Beers asked what he considered the solution to Mexico's problems, Villa replied 'Work and education.'

Villa began to acquire a taste for the fine life. He ordered his stationery from England, with his name embossed in dignified lettering, and he took to riding around in American cars more often than on horseback. Now, too, he weighed more than fifteen stone.

Wherever he went, Villa took bodyguards with him. And when he visited Parral, where he owned a hotel and where he had many enemies, Villa would carry with him two machine-guns which, he claimed, were a gift from his old enemy, Obregón. One attempt was made to assassinate him as he was loading hay at his ranch, but gradually the number of his bodyguards was reduced and, just as gradually, his own guard slipped. One day in 1923 when a Parral car dealer named Gabriel Chavez muttered as Villa drove past 'I wonder if anybody dare let him have it?' one of his companions offered to organise Villa's assassination for £5000.

The would-be assassin's name was Jesús Salas Barraza ('I *do* wish they would not call their murderers by a name so divine,' complained the author, Charlotte Cameron) and he was a member of the Durango State Legislature. Within a month, a 'Kill Villa' fund of £10,000 had been subscribed by relatives of those who had suffered at Villa's hands during the Revolution. Salas Barraza used the money to buy rifles and ammunition and to hire eight gunmen. He rented a house on a corner of a street where Villa always slowed down before turning onto a road which led to his ranch. By the beginning of July the gunmen were in position and all was ready.

On 10 July Villa passed the house twice but on both occasions the killers were frustrated. The first time children coming out of a near-by school were in the line of fire and on the second occasion Villa's Dodge car was travelling too quickly. On 19 July Villa travelled to attend the christening of the child of one of his former *Dorados*, taking with him only his secretary, Miguel Trillo, and four guards, since a heavy guard would have stretched the new father's meagre resources. He spent the night at his hotel in Parral, planning to travel back to his ranch next morning. This time the conspirators were ready. They hired a pumpkin-seed vendor to stand beside a tree at the corner of the street and shout 'Viva Villa' when the car appeared—once if Villa rode in the front seat, twice if he was in the back of the car.

Early on the morning of Friday 20 July 1923 the Dodge set off with Villa at the wheel, Trillo beside him and the four guards sitting in the back. As they approached the corner the pumpkin-seed seller stepped into the road and shouted 'Viva Villa.' As Pancho raised an arm in reply a torrent of gunfire poured from the house into the slowly-moving car, which swerved into a tree. Villa was struck seven times (his unlucky number) and Trillo was riddled by nine bullets. Both died instantly. Three of the bodyguards were also killed but the other managed to get away, one arm shattered and a gaping hole in his abdomen. The Dodge had more than forty bullet holes.

In preparation for the day of his death Villa had built himself an elaborate mausoleum in Chihuahua City and surrounded it with the graves of his dearest comrades. But he was buried instead in a simple grave in Parral. Even then Villa was not left in peace. In 1926 the grave was broken open and Villa's head stolen. It has never been recovered.

Villa's killers escaped but shortly afterwards Salas Barraza admitted organising the assassination. He was arrested and sentenced to twenty years' imprisonment but served only six months before being set free and made a colonel in the army, a rank he retained until his death in 1951. On his deathbed Salas Barraza claimed 'I'm not a murderer. I rid humanity of a monster.'

It was widely assumed that the assassination was political. Villa's widow Luz Corral still claims that her husband was killed on the orders of Obregón and Calles to prevent him carrying out his threat to mobilise in favour of Adolfo de la Huerta, who was opposing the election of Calles to the presidency in 1924. No evidence has ever been produced to link Obregón with the killing, though his leniency towards Salas Barraza shows that he was not exactly over-concerned at the removal of Villa.

Appendix 2: The Death of Obregón

Obregón, a born leader, proved just as successful a president as he had been a general. A complete realist, he understood the people's needs and did his best to cater to them, though without disrupting the Republic's frail economy. He refused, for instance, to make too deep and violent an inroad into the *hacienda* and private land ownership system, and during his four years in office he distributed three million acres among 624 villages—not a spectacular amount but seven times greater than Carranza's figure.

It was over the question of presidential succession that Obregón ran into trouble. There was never any doubt that Obregón would choose one of his Sonora group as his successor. After his highly successful six months as interim president, Adolfo de la Huerta was favoured by many to succeed Obregón, but the president plumped instead for his loyal lieutenant Plutarco Elías Calles. The succession question was raised by Obregón when the three men—known as the Sonora Triangle—were taking a car ride through Chapultepec Park in Mexico City. The president said, 'You and I, Plutarco, cannot leave politics because we would die of hunger; on the other hand Adolfo knows how to sing and give classes in voice and music. Under these circumstances who do you feel should follow me in the presidency?' Calles said nothing; eventually de la Huerta managed to force out 'Well, after you should come Plutarco.'

But the anti-Calles generals rallied behind de la Huerta who, after pledging his support to Calles, eventually gave way and allowed himself to be put forward as a rival presidential candidate. The election preliminaries followed the all-too-familiar Mexican pattern: bitterness, violence and—eventually—armed rebellion. On 4 December 1923, de la Huerta took the night train to Veracruz and from there declared himself in rebellion against the government, issuing the Plan of Veracruz and accusing Obregón of 'odious and intolerable violence of the sovereignty of the people' in attempting to install Calles as the next president.

The scales were finely balanced; 23,000 government troops went over to de la Huerta, while some 30,000 stayed loyal. Of the Mexican Army's 508 generals, 102 joined the rebellion. The rebels scored some initial successes but Obregón's organising genius and his popularity soon swayed the balance and by the summer of 1924 the revolt had been crushed, fifty-four new generals created to replace those who had paid with their lives for supporting de la Huerta, and the former interim president himself had fled to California, where he earned a living giving music lessons, as Obregón had predicted.

Calles was elected the next president without further dissension but in 1927, as the four-year term was drawing to a close, Obregón decided the nation's interests would best be served by his own re-election in 1928. Though this was in direct violation of one of the Revolution's most sacred precepts, the Obregonista majority in Congress forced through an amendment to the constitution to permit 'non-consecutive re-election' and increased the presidential term from four to six years. Two of Obregón's generals who had fancied themselves as presidential material, Arnulfo R. Gómez and Francisco R. Serrano, staged uprisings. Both rebellions were ruthlessly put down and Gómez and Serrano were shot.

After this there was little opposition to the election of Obregón on 1 July 1928. But he did not live long enough to be installed in office.

Though he had coped capably enough with the military uprising, Obregón was unprepared for the reaction of the country's religious fanatics whose lives had been so heavily restricted under his previous régime. Their plot was led by a woman known as Madre Conchita, who, in April 1928, had devised a spectacular way of poisoning Obregón. It had been planned that a girl should ask Obregón for a dance and, while they were waltzing, inject him with a hypodermic needle hidden in her bouquet. But the plot miscarried.

However, Madre Conchita soon found the ideal instrument for her plans—a twenty-six-year-old artist named José de León Toral, who wanted to give his life for Christ and who felt that Obregón's death would solve all Mexico's religious problems.

Toral borrowed a pistol and hung about Obregón's residence all day on 16 July without seeing the president-elect.

Next day Obregón was due to attend a political banquet in his honour at a restaurant called La Bombita (The Little Bomb) in San Angel, just outside Mexico City. Obregón overruled his aides' fears about attending the function and even joked about the restaurant's name.

Toral followed Obregón to San Angel by taxi and managed to get into the restaurant by showing a pad and pencil and pretending that he had been commissioned to sketch some of the notables at the gathering. Gradually Toral made his way towards the raised dais where Obregón sat at the table of honour.

Toral showed Obregón the sketches he had made and asked if he would pose for him. As Obregón turned and smiled towards the artist standing behind him, Toral shot him five times in the face.

Obregón died in his seat at The Little Bomb.

Acknowledgements

All the books and periodicals listed in the bibliography proved useful during my three years of research into the Mexican Revolution. However, some were particularly valuable, and I feel their authors deserve a special vote of thanks.

I am particularly grateful to Martín Luis Guzmán, who graciously consented to an interview during my visit to Mexico City in 1967, and whose excellent books, *Memorias de Pancho Villa* and *El Águila y La Serpiente* provided me with much material on the Revolution by a man who lived through those eventful years. I am also deeply indebted to Robert E. Quirk, managing editor of the Hispanic American Historical Review, of Indiana University, whose *The Mexican Revolution 1914–15* and *An Affair of Honour* are brilliant additions to the sparse library of authoritative English-language works on the Revolution and its side effects. *An Affair of Honour* filled a long-missing gap by telling the full, incredible story of the American invasion, and occupation, of Veracruz in 1914, and Professor Quirk's *Mexican Revolution* gives a superb description of the fateful Aguascalientes Convention of 1914 and the suffering which Mexico, and in particular Mexico City, endured the following year.

Professor Henry Bamford Parkes' splendid single-volume *History of Mexico* also contains an excellent, if necessarily brief, description of the days from Díaz to Obregón, and was a most useful reference source. I am also grateful to other authors for their learned works on particular aspects, or episodes, of the Revolution: to Col. Clarence C. Clendenen, for his self-explanatory *The United States and Pancho Villa*; to Barbara W. Tuchman, whose *The Zimmermann Telegram* is a superb account of a hitherto-ignored piece of dramatic history; to Charles C. Cumberland for *Mexican Revolution—Genesis Under Madero*, the rise and fall of Mexico's Redeemer; and to Richard O'Connor and Dr Haldeen Braddy whose books on the Pershing Expedition into Mexico which followed Pancho Villa's raid on Columbus, New Mexico, were indispensable.

I found, too, the personal reminiscences of people who lived through the Revolution a rich and vivid source of information. People like the Englishman Patrick O'Hea who went to Mexico in 1907 for his health and lived an exciting and full life until 1958 and whose description of the ragged *torero* who 'fought' the Federal shells at Torreón is, in my opinion, a minor masterpiece; Edward Bell, editor of an English-language newspaper in Mexico City during the dramatic days of Madero's arrival and overthrow; Timothy Turner, an El Paso newspaperman, who went into battle with the rebels at Ciudad Juárez; Dr Ira Jefferson Bush, who served as a revolutionary surgeon; Major Frank Tompkins, who fought Villa at Columbus and helped Pershing to hunt the bandit chief in Mexico; and, not least, those assiduous diary-keeping ladies, Edith O'Shaughnessy, Leone Moats and Rosa King, intrepid women who lived through the excitements and tribulations of the Revolution.

My brief, but nonetheless sincere thanks to the following people who willingly gave of their time and knowledge to assist my researches:

In Mexico: Luz Corral Villa, widow of Pancho, who showed me round her small museum in Chihuahua City and helped me to fill in some gaps in my file on her famous husband; Helia d'Acosta, who provided information on her uncle, Felipe Angeles; Yolanda de Casasola, who helped me to wade through her family's priceless collection of photographs of the Revolution; Doris Oakley Smith, whose knowledge of her adopted city and its history, and posting of much valuable material on the Revolution to Britain, were much appreciated; Professor Angel Metaca, for his hospitality and friendliness; Javier Rivas Garcia of the Consejo de Turismo and Shirley and Adolfo Fernandez, for their helpfulness.

In El Paso, Texas: Bill McGaw, editor of *The Southwesterner*, whose brains I picked unashamedly on the details of the Columbus Raid, and who got his revenge by driving me from El Paso to Columbus over fifty miles of desert trails; John Wayne Smith, director of the El Paso Public Library, and his wife Anita, good friends and wonderful hosts; Mrs Virginia P. Hoke, head of the El Paso Public Library's Southwest Reference Section; Mrs Emma

Evans, of the same library, who assisted in the selection of pictures from the Otis Aultman collection; Dr Haldeen Braddy, a Chaucer scholar at the University of Texas who proved just as knowledgeable on the Revolution; and Baxter Polk, the University Librarian.

In London: John Ford, the Mexican National Tourist Councillor, whose enthusiasm for my project, if anything, exceeded my own, and whose assistance was the major factor in my being able to travel to Mexico to complete my research; B.O.A.C., and in particular their Senior Press Officer, Douglas Ditton, who gave me much valuable advice and help; the courteous and efficient staff of the Reading Room at the British Museum; Tom Kelly, Deputy Librarian of the *Daily Mail*, and Jean Land, Ann Melsom, Sean Toolan and Sr Licenciado Don Hugo Gutierrez Vega, Cultural Attaché of the Mexican Embassy, who had the patience to read my manuscript and whose criticism and corrections I appreciate.

Reference Sources

General Sources

BOOKS, DOCUMENTS AND MANUSCRIPTS

Alba, Victor, *The Mexicans*, Pall Mall Press, London, 1967.

Alessio, Robles, Miguel, *Historia Política de la Revolución*, Ediciones Botas, Mexico City, 1938.

Baerlein, Henry, *Mexico, The Land of Unrest*, Simpkin, Marshall, Hamilton and Kent, 1914.

Baker, Ray Stannard, *Woodrow Wilson, Life and Letters*, Heinemann, 1932.

Barragán Rodríguez, Juan, *Historia del Ejército y la Revolución Constitucionalista*, Mexico City, 1946.

Barrera, Alberto Calzadiaz, *Villa Contra Todos*, Editores Mexicanos Unidos, S.A., Mexico City, 1965.

——, *Villa Contra Todo y Contra Todos*, Editores Mexicanos Unidos, 1963.

Beals, Carleton, *Porfirio Díaz, Dictator of Mexico*, J. B. Lippincott Co., New York, 1932.

Bell, Edward I., *The Political Shame of Mexico*, McBride, Nast and Co., New York, 1914.

Blasco Ibañez, Vicente, *Mexico in Revolution*, New York, 1920.

Braddy, Haldeen, *Cock of the Walk: The Legend of Pancho Villa*, University of New Mexico Press, Albuquerque, 1955.

——, *Pancho Villa at Columbus*, Southwestern Studies, Texas Western College Press, Spring, 1965.

——, *Pershing's Mission in Mexico*, Texas Western College Press, El Paso, 1966.

Brand, Donald D., *Mexico: Land of Sunshine and Shadow*, D. Van Nostrand Company Inc., New Jersey, 1966.

Brenner, Anita R., and George Leighton, *The Wind That Swept Mexico*, Harper, New York, 1943.

Bulnes, Francisco, *The Whole Truth About Mexico*, Bulnes Book Co., New York, 1916.

Bush, Dr Ira Jefferson, *Gringo Doctor*, The Caxton Printers Ltd., Caldwell, Ohio, 1939.

Calero, Manuel, *Un Decenio de Política Mexicana*, New York, 1920.

Callahan, James Norton, *American Foreign Policy in Mexican Relations*, New York, 1932.

Callcott, Wilfrid Hardy, *Liberalism in Mexico, 1857–1929*, Archon Books, Hamden, Conn., 1965.

Cameron, Charlotte, *Mexico in Revolution*, Seeley, Service, 1925.

Casasola, Miguel y Gustavo, *Historia Gráfica de la Revolución*, (4 vols.) Mexico City, 1960.

Clendenen, Clarence C., *The United States and Pancho Villa: A Study in Unconventional Diplomacy*, Cornell University Press, 1961.

Cline, Howard F., *The United States and Mexico*, Harvard University Press, 1963.

Clissold, Stephen, *Latin America: A Cultural Outline*, Hutchinson & Co., 1965.

Creel, George, *The People Next Door*, John Day Co., New York, 1926.

Creelman, James, *Díaz, Master of Mexico*, Appleton and Co., New York, 1911.

Cumberland, Charles Curtis, *Mexican Revolution—Genesis Under Madero*, University of Texas Press, 1952.

De la Huerta, Adolfo, *Memorias*, Ediciones Guzmán, Mexico City, 1957.

De Wetter, Mardee Belding, 'Revolutionary El Paso'. Series of articles in *Password*, issued by the El Paso Historical Society, 1958.

Dillon, Dr E. J., *Mexico on the Verge*, Hutchinson & Co., 1922.

——, *President Obregón—A World Reformer*, Hutchinson, 1922.

Dulles, John W. F., *Yesterday in Mexico*, University of Texas Press, 1961.

Dunn, H. H., *The Crimson Jester: Zapata of Mexico*, George Harrap & Co., 1934.

Estrada, Roque, *La Revolución y Francisco Madero*, Guadalajara, 1912.

Evans, Rosalie, *Letters from Mexico*. Arranged with comments by Daisy Caden Pettus, Bobbs-Merrill Co., Indianapolis, 1926.

Farrell, Cullom Holmes, *Incidents in the Life of General Pershing*, Rand, McNally and Co., New York, 1918.

Flandrau, Charles Macomb, *Viva Mexico*, Appleton and Co., New York, 1908.

Foix, Pere, *Pancho Villa*, Ediciones Xochitl, Mexico City, 1950.

Fornaro, Carlo de, *Carranza and Mexico*, Mitchell Kennerley, New York, 1915.

Fyfe, H. Hamilton, *The Real Mexico*, Heinemann, 1914.

Gibbon, Thomas Edward, *Mexico Under Carranza*, Doubleday, Page and Co., New York, 1919.

González Roa, Fernando, *Las Cuestiones Fundamentales de Actualidad en México*, Mexico City, 1927.

Grayson, Cary T., *Woodrow Wilson: An Intimate Memoir*, New York, 1960.

Gruening, Ernest, *Mexico and Its Heritage*, Stanley Paul 1928.

Guzmán, Martín Luis, *Memoirs of Pancho Villa* (translated by Virginia H. Taylor), University of Texas Press, 1965.

——, *The Eagle and the Serpent*, Doubleday, New York, 1965.

Harris, Larry A., *Pancho Villa and the Columbus Raid*, McMath Co. Inc., El Paso, 1949.

Hatch, Nelle Spilsbury, *Colonia Juárez: An Intimate Account of a Mormon Village*, Deseret Book Co., Salt Lake City, 1954.

Hendrick, Burton J., *Life and Letters of Walter H. Page*, Heinemann, 1924.

Herrera, Celia, *Francisco Villa, Ante La Historia*, Mexico City, 1964.

Horgan, Paul, *Great River: The Rio Grande in North American History*, Rinehart and Co. Inc., New York, 1954.

Hutton, Graham, *Mexican Images*, Faber and Faber, 1963.

Inman, Samuel Guy, *Intervention in Mexico*, New York, 1919.

Iturbide, Eduardo, *Mi Paso Por La Vida*, Mexico City, 1951.

Johnson, William Weber, *Mexico*, Life World Library, New York, 1961.

——, *Heroic Mexico*, Doubleday, New York, 1968.

King, Rosa E., *Tempest Over Mexico—A Personal Chronicle*, Methuen, 1936.

Lara Pardo, Luis, *De Porfirio Díaz á Francisco Madero*, New York, 1912.

——, *La Prostitución en México*, Mexico City, 1908.

Lord, Walter, *The Good Years: From 1900 to the First World War*, Longmans, 1960.

Márquez Sterling, Manuel, *Los Últimos Días del Presidente Madero*, Havana, 1917.

McNeely, John H., *The Railways of Mexico: A Study in Nationalisation*, Southwestern Studies, Texas Western College Press, Spring, 1964.

Moats, Leone B., *Thunder In Their Veins*, George Allen and Unwin, Ltd., 1933.

Molina Enriquez, Andres, *Los Grandes Problemas Nacionales*, Mexico City, 1909.

Muñoz, Rafael F., *Pancho Villa: Rayo y Azote*, Populibros La Prensa, Mexico City, 1955.

Nagel, *Travel Guide to Mexico*, Nagel Publishers, Switzerland, 1960.

Nicholson, Irene, *The X In Mexico: Growth Within Tradition*, Faber and Faber, 1965.

Obregón, Alvaro, *Ocho Mil Kilómetros en Campaña*, Librería Bouret, Mexico City, 1917.
O'Connor, Richard, *Ambrose Bierce*, Gollancz, 1968.
——, *Black Jack Pershing*, Doubleday and Co., New York, 1961.
O'Hea, Patrick, *Reminiscences of the Mexican Revolution*, Editorial Fournier, Mexico City, 1966.
O'Reilly, Edward S., *Roving and Fighting: Adventures Under Four Flags*, Century Co., New York, 1918.
O'Shaughnessy, Edith, *A Diplomat's Wife in Mexico*, Harper, New York, 1916.
——, *Intimate Pages of Mexican History*, George H. Doran Co., New York, 1920.
Pani, Alberto J., *Hygiene in Mexico*, New York, 1917.
Parkes, Henry Bamford, *A History of Mexico*, Eyre and Spottiswoode, 1962.
Pershing, General John J., *My Experiences in the World War*, Hodder and Stoughton, 1931.
Pinchon, Edgcumb, *Viva Villa! A Recovery of the Real Pancho Villa*, Cassell, 1933.
Prida, Ramón, *De la Dictadura á la Anarquía*, El Paso, 1914.
Puente, Ramón, *Vida de Francisco Villa, Contada por El Mismo*, Los Angeles, 1919.
——, *Villa En Pie*, Mexico City, 1937.
Quirk, Robert E., *The Mexican Revolution, 1914–1915*, Indiana University Press, 1960.
——, *An Affair of Honour: Woodrow Wilson and the Occupation of Veracruz*, Norton and Co. Inc., New York, 1967.
Reed, John Silas, *Insurgent Mexico*, Appleton and Co., New York, 1914.
Regler, Gustav, *A Land Bewitched*, Putnam, 1955.
Reyes, Victor, *Cabalgando Con Villa*, Populibros La Prensa, Mexico City, 1961.
Rippy, J. Fred, *The United States and Mexico*, Alfred A. Knopf, New York, 1926.
Romney, Thomas Cottam, *The Mormon Colonies in Mexico*, Deseret Book Company, Salt Lake City, 1938.
Schuster, Ernest Otto, *Pancho Villa's Shadow*, Exposition Press, New York, 1947.
Scott, Major General Hugh Lennox, *Some Memories of a Soldier*, Century Co., New York, 1928.
Seymour, Charles, *Intimate Papers of Colonel House*, Houghton Mifflin, Boston, 1926.
Simpson, Eyler Newton, *The Ejido—Mexico's Way Out*, University of North Carolina Press, 1937.

Simpson, Lesley Byrd, *Many Mexicos*, University of California Press, 1952.

Smart, Charles Allen, *Viva Juárez!*, Eyre and Spottiswoode, 1964.

Smith, Randolph Wellford, *Benighted Mexico*, John Lane Co., New York, 1916.

Steffens, Lincoln, *The Autobiography of Lincoln Steffens*, New York, 1931.

Stephenson, George M., *John Lind of Minnesota*, University of Minnesota Press, 1935.

Stevens, Louis, *Here Comes Pancho Villa*, Frederick A. Stokes, New York, 1930.

Stirrat, May, *The Francisco Villa Raid on Columbus, New Mexico*. Thesis submitted for degree of Master of Arts in History, University of New Mexico, 1935.

Strode, Hudson, *Timeless Mexico*, Harcourt, Brace and Co., New York, 1944.

Swarthout, Glendon, *They Came to Cordura*, Heinemann, 1958.

Tannenbaum, Frank, *Peace by Revolution*, Columbia University Press, 1933.

——, *Mexico: The Struggle for Peace and Bread*, Alfred A. Knopf, New York, 1950.

Taracena, Alfonso, *Madero, Vida del Hombre y del Político*, Ediciones Botas, Mexico City, 1937.

Thompson, Charles W., *Presidents I've Known and Two Near-Presidents*, Indianapolis, 1929.

Tompkins, Major Frank, *Chasing Villa*, Military Service Publishing Co., Harrisburg, Pa., 1935.

Toulmin, Col. H. A., *With Pershing in Mexico*, Military Service Publishing Co., Harrisburg, Pa., 1935.

t'Serstevens, A., *Mexico, Three-Storeyed Land*, Hutchinson and Co., 1959.

Tuchman, Barbara W., *The Zimmermann Telegram*, Constable, 1959.

Turner, John Kenneth, *Barbarous Mexico*, Cassell and Co., 1911.

Turner, Timothy G., *Bullets, Bottles and Gardenias*, South-West Press, Dallas, 1935.

Tweedie, Mrs Alec, *Mexico from Díaz to the Kaiser*, Hutchinson and Co., 1917.

——, *Porfirio Díaz*, Hurst and Blackett Ltd., 1906.

——, *Mexico As I Saw It*, Hurst and Blackett Ltd., 1902.

United States Foreign Relations Papers, 1911–1920, Library of Congress, Washington.

United States National Archives, Mexican Affairs, File No. 812.00, Library of Congress, Washington.

Urquizo, Francisco L., *Carranza*, Mexico City, 1954.
——, *México—Tlaxcalantongo*, Editorial Cultura, Mexico City, 1943.

NEWSPAPERS AND PERIODICALS

London
Daily Mail
The Times

United States of America
The New York Times
The New York Herald
Collier's Magazine
Literary Digest
Saturday Evening Post
Time
United States Cavalry Journal
El Paso Times
El Paso Herald Post

Mexico
El Imparcial
El Independiente
El Pais
La Patria
Nueva Era
The Mexican Herald

Detailed Sources

PART ONE: DÍAZ

Chapter 1: *Dancing on a Volcano*

The Dazzling month: Carleton Beals, Porfirio Díaz, Dictator of Mexico, pp. 421–2. 'A Thousand sweet blossoms': ibid., p. 421. Certain shabby ministers: George Creel, The People Next Door, p. 289. Germany's Kaiser: Mrs Alec Tweedie, Mexico from Díaz to the Kaiser, pp. 42–3. 'There were banquets': Henry Lane Wilson, Diplomatic Episodes in Mexico, Belgium and Chile, p. 189. Silver and gold plates: Hudson Strode, Timeless Mexico, p. 219. Rumbling warnings: Strode, p. 218. 'The scene and music': Leone B. Moats, Thunder in their Veins, p. 27. 'Doddering mummies': Manuel Calero, Un Decenio de Política Mexicana, p. 16. A government of old men: Frank Tannenbaum, Peace by Revolution, p. 132; Francisco Bulnes, The Whole Truth About Mexico, pp. 116–17; Beals, pp. 374–8. A new generation: Tannenbaum, Peace by Revolution, p. 132. A cholera epidemic: Strode, p. 199. Death of Juárez: Henry B. Parkes, A History of Mexico, p. 241. 'He set himself...': ibid., p. 243. 'Few governments have furnished...': Luis Lara Pardo, De Porfirio Díaz á Francisco Madero, p. 38. 'Not much of a manager...': Moats, p. 50. González made governor: John Kenneth Turner, Barbarous Mexico, p. 265.

Chapter 2: *'Poor Mexico...'*

Land of contrasts: Donald D. Brand, Mexico: Land of Sunshine and Shadow, pp. 7, 16. 'Poor Mexico...': Strode, p. 263. Crumpled paper: ibid., Preface xiv. Change in height and climate: Graham Hutton, Mexican Images. p. 27. Three-storeyed land: A. t'Serstevens, Mexico, Three-Storeyed Land, p. 11; Howard F. Cline, The United States and Mexico, pp. 18–19; Brand, p. 19. Patria chica: Cline, pp. 88–9. 30 per cent of the population: Brand, p. 26. Mestizos 'have inherited...': Hamilton Fyfe, The Real Mexico, p. 231. A dog with a bone...: Parkes, p. 244. 'The bands of wolves...': ibid., p. 244. Safer than Hyde Park: Edward I. Bell, The Political Shame of Mexico, p. 88. Rucales: John K. Turner, p. 149; Parkes, p. 251; Strode, p. 205; -Moats, p. 50. 'A law which allows...': Mrs Alec Tweedie, Mexico As I Saw It, p. 346. Journalists summoned: Randolph Wellford Smith, Benighted Mexico, p. 101. Press subsidised: Beals, pp. 231–2. Matador arrested: Beals, p. 293. Mi caballada: Lesley Byrd Simpson, Many Mexicos, p. 263. Puppet

Congress: Beals, pp. 289–90; Parkes, p. 250. 'The most perfect...': John K. Turner, p. 141. Church's influence, wealth: Tannenbaum, Peace by Revolution, pp. 42, 52. Foreign capital: Charles Curtis Cumberland, Mexican Revolution—Genesis Under Madero, p. 9. Petrol figures: Brand, p. 113. 5s an acre. Strode, p. 212. Cowdray projects: Desmond Young, Member for Mexico, p. 2. 'Cowdray would have owned Mexico...': ibid., p. 141. 75,000 Americans: Henry Lane Wilson, p. 260. Root's tribute: Simpson, p. 263. Tolstoy, Carnegie quotes: Beals, p. 24. Eulogy of eulogies: Marie Robinson Wright, Picturesque Mexico 'The prices I charged ...': Rosa E. King, Tempest Over Mexico, p. 24. Foreigners' treatment: Cumberland, p. 26. 'Lame, incompetent ...': Beals, p. 293. 'The mother of foreigners ...': Ernest Gruening, Mexico and Its Heritage, p. 60. 'Díaz was no less deceived ...': Bell, p. 22. 'What use was it ...' Gruening, p. 65.

Chapter 3: *The Feudal Estates*
Bewildered Indians: Cumberland, p. 19. Epoch of land grabbing: Nathaniel and Sylvia Weyl, The Reconquest of Mexico, p. 25. 17 families: Beals, p. 300. The Mexican hacienda: Tannenbaum, Peace by Revolution, p. 187. Guanajuato taxes: Strode, p. 208. Absentee ownership: Gruening, p. 135; Parkes, p. 261. Seduced his own niece: Beals, p. 373. Plantation system at its height: Tannenbaum, Peace by Revolution, p. 192. Visit to a hacienda: Tweedie, Mexico As I Saw It, pp. 337–42. Amors' lives saved: Edith O'Shaughnessy, Intimate Pages of Mexican History, p. 119. The peon's life: Tannenbaum, Peace by Revolution, pp. 188–9; Parkes, p. 262; Beals, pp. 305–7; Gruening, pp. 137–8; John Silas Reed, Insurgent Mexico, pp. 16–17, 31 (Reed, an American journalist, was also the author of the famous book on the Russian Revolution, Ten Days That Shook The World. He founded the U.S. Communist Labour Party in 1919 and, while under indictment for sedition, fled to Russia where he died of typhus. He is buried in the Kremlin). 'It is impossible to imagine ...': Reed, p. 31. 'Liquor and fiestas ...': Parkes, p. 262. 'No people whose diet...': Charles Macomb Flandrau, Viva Mexico, pp. 44, 119. 'At absolute rest': Alberto J. Pani, Hygiene in Mexico, p. 71. Intestinal ailments, Gruening: p. 542; Brand, p. 35. 'It would be interesting ...': Flandrau, p. 69. Yaquis land patent: John K. Turner, p. 34. A bonus for ears: Beals, p. 311. Navajoa hangings: John K. Turner, pp. 35–6. 'Those Indians wanted to cheat us ...': ibid., p. 36. Fluctuating wheat prices. Fernando González Roa, Las Cuestiones Fundamentales de Actualidad en Mexico, p. 159; Cumberland, pp. 14–15; Parkes, p.

262. Employers' paradise: Cumberland, p. 16. San Juan de Ulúa: Charlotte Cameron, Mexico in Revolution, pp. 24–5. The *científicos*: Cumberland, pp. 10–12; Parkes, pp. 255–6. The Full Car: Bell, p. 6. Limantour: Beals, p. 316; Strode, p. 210; Bell, p. 4; Henry Lane Wilson, p. 173; Parkes, pp. 353, 256. 'Those were the great days ...' Moats, pp. 21–2. Mexico City description: Patrick O'Hea, Reminiscences of the Mexican Revolution, p. 7: Juárez statue: Parkes, p. 259. Zuñiga y Miranda: ibid., Beals, pp. 318, 266. 'Don Porfirio will simply ...': Creel, p. 285. Reyes' salary: Gruening, p. 59. The Díaz biography: Beals, p. 350. Reyes kicked out: Parkes, pp. 265–6. 'Corral more closely resembled ...': Henry Lane Wilson, p. 173. 'Porfirio remembers me ...': Beals, p. 369. Díaz meets Taft: Paul Horgan, Great River: The Rio Grande in North American History, pp. 907–8. Japanese in Mexico: Barbara W. Tuchman, The Zimmermann Telegram, p. 34.

Chapter 4: *Rebellion by the book*
The Creelman interview. Anita R. Brenner, The Wind That Swept Mexico, p. 16; Beals, pp. 389–92; Parkes, p. 268; Cumberland pp. 47–8. 'Tell Bernardo ...': Beals, p. 398. Gradually coalescing opposition. Cumberland, pp. 28–9. Madero description and family history: Strode, p. 215; Cumberland, pp. 30–3; Beals, pp. 403–4. The Chocolate Fool: Wilfred Hardy Callcott, Liberalism In Mexico, 1857–1929, p. 196. Madero's book: Cumberland, pp. 55–8. Madero a candidate: George B. Winston, Mexico Past and Present, p. 171. Díaz–Madero interview: Moats, pp. 57–8; Parkes, p. 270; Cline, p. 119. Madero's arrest and escape: Cumberland, pp. 110–18. Plan of San Luis Potosí: ibid., pp. 121–3.

Chapter 5: *'Die on Your Feet'*
Aquiles Serdán: Revolución Mexicana, Cronica Illustrada, No. 3; Cumberland, p. 124. Madero crosses border: Beals, p. 423; Cumberland, p. 124. 'The political situation ...': *Daily Mail*, 25 November 1910. The North: Horgan, p. 911; Weyl, p. 28: Tannenbaum, Peace by Revolution, p. 137. Pascual Orozco: Dr Ira J. Bush, Gringo Doctor, p. 164; H. H. Dunn, The Crimson Jester, p. 129. Pancho Villa descriptions: Brand, p. 30; Gruening, p. 311; Horgan, pp. 922–3; Dr E. J. Dillon, President Obregón—a World Reformer, p. 61; Haldeen Braddy, Cock of the Walk: The Legend of Pancho Villa, pp. 11, 13, 16, 42. 'The conspiracy lacks coherence ...': U.S. Foreign Relations, 1911, p. 363. 'It is preposterous ...': James Creelman, Díaz, Master of

Mexico, pp. 426–7. Finances exhausted: Beals, p. 423; Cumberland, p. 125; Cline, p. 122; *The Times*, 25 November 1910. Margarita Neri: Dunn, pp. 58–9; Henry Baerlein, Mexico, The Land of Unrest, p. 271; Beals, p. 423. Zapata descriptions: Brenner, pp. 24, 41; Louis Stevens, Here Comes Pancho Villa, pp. 272–3. Zapata's background: Dunn, p. 7; Gruening, pp. 141–2. 'Of all the figures ...': Tannenbaum, Peace by Revolution, p. 176. 'Men of the south ...': Strode, p. 259. 'We have begged ...': Tannenbaum, Peace by Revolution, p. 176. 'The Army was honeycombed ...': Bell, p. 31. Lover conscripted: Beals, p. 233. 'This affair ...': Baerlein, p. 236. Casas Grandes defeat: Bush, pp. 189–90. U.S. troop movements: *Daily Mail*, 8 March 1911; Cumberland, pp. 132–3. The Limantour talks. Details of Limantour's visit to Europe, and his talks with the Madero family in New York are from Edward I. Bell's The Political Shame of Mexico, pp. 15–49. Agua Prieta battle: *Daily Mail*, 14 March 1911. Díaz statement: ibid., 13 March 1911. Out-of-date maps: Beals, p. 427; Strode, p. 223. Soldiers desert: Baerlein, p. 235; Grüening, pp. 94, 302. Díaz concessions: Beals, pp. 435–6; Bell, p. 70. Six-month volunteers: Tweedie, Díaz to the Kaiser, p. 66. Massacre of Chinese: Braddy, Cock of the Walk, p. 78; Baerlein, Preface xiii. Hon. Claud Stanhope: *Daily Mail*, 18, 19 May 1911. The Mormons: Nelle Spilsbury Hatch, Colonia Juárez, An Intimate Account of a Mormon Village, p. 181; Thomas Cottam Romney, The Mormon Colonies in Mexico, p. 157. 'Yelling and whooping ...': O'Hea, p. 46. 'Colourful, romantic ...': Timothy G. Turner, Bullets, Bottles and Gardenias, p. 23. Battle teas: *Daily Mail*, 17 March 1911. Agua Prieta: *Daily Mail*, 18, 19 April 1911; Cumberland, pp. 138–9; Collier's Magazine, 19 August 1916. Civil War cannon: Bush, pp. 182–8. 'Americans on the border ...': ibid., p. 167. Foreign Legion: Edward S. O'Reilly, Roving and Fighting, p. 274; Ernest Otto Schuster, Pancho Villa's Shadow, pp. 76–7; Braddy, Cock of the Walk, p. 97; Bush, p. 195; Timothy Turner, pp. 24–5. 'The disappointment of the public ...': *El Paso Times*, 6 February 1911. 'Madero too kindhearted ...': Timothy Turner, p. 53. Madero abandons siege: Cumberland, p. 140; Bush, p. 199. 'Shameful to retire ...': Martín Luís Guzmán, Memoirs of Pancho Villa, pp. 45–6. 'He was attended ...': Bell, p. 70. Díaz agrees to resign: *Daily Mail*, 9 and 10 May 1911. Battle for Juárez: *El Paso Times*, 9–12 May 1911; 8 May 1922; 17 May 1953; Timothy Turner, pp. 51–64; Bush, pp. 188, 200–10; Cumberland, pp. 140–1; Baerlein, pp. 236–42; Guzmán, Memoirs, pp. 46–8. Revolutionary spoons: Mardee Belding de Wetter, Revolutionary El Paso, p. 59. Navarro's escape: Timothy Turner, pp. 67–9. Orozco, Villa rebel:

Alfonso Taracena, -Madero: Vida del Hombre y del Político, pp. 417–18, 421–3; Beals, pp. 438–9. 'I greatly fear ...': Bush, p. 256.

Chapter 6: The Fall of Díaz

'Most pathetic ...': The Times, 18 May 1911. Abscessed tooth: Tweedie, Díaz to the Kaiser, pp. 75–6. Wilson visits Díaz: Henry Lane Wilson, pp. 214–15. Zócalo riot: Ramón Prida, De la Dictadura á la Anarquía, pp. 324–5; Bell, pp. 78–81; Beals, p. 443. Díaz resigns: Beals, pp. 444–5. Díaz flees: Tweedie, Díaz to the Kaiser, pp. 80–5. 'Today I believe ...': Cumberland, p. 150. 'Those venerable tears ...': O'Shaughnessy, Intimate Pages, p. 60. 'The greatest calamity ...': Tweedie, Díaz to the Kaiser, p. 2. 'Practically the king ...': Wellford Smith, p. 94. 'Undeviating personal honesty ...': Henry Lane Wilson, p. 228. 'He built a machine ...': John K. Turner, p. 275. 'My usual economy ...': O'Shaughnessy, Intimate Pages, p. 240. 'He rose early ...': Beals p. 454. Madero's train journey: Bell, pp. 107–8. The earthquake: Daily Mail, 8 June, 1911; Moats, p. 70; Tweedie, Díaz to the Kaiser, pp. 102–3.

PART TWO: MADERO

Chapter 1: The Plan of Ayala

De la Barra: Creel, p. 299. 'Very good tightrope walker ...': O'Shaughnessy, Intimate Pages, p. 113. 'Surely all the strength ...': King, pp. 68–9. Rebels in a minority: Tannenbaum, Peace by Revolution, pp. 151–2. Madero embraces Blanquet: Cumberland, p. 161. 'Madero has unleashed ...': ibid., p. 151. Zapata in rebellion: ibid., pp. 176–84. 'He allowed no laxness ...': King, p. 83. Huerta replaced: ibid., p. 86. Reyes returns: Cumberland, pp. 165–6. Madero elected: ibid., pp. 169–70; Bell, p. 119; Nueva Era, 24 October 1911. The oath taking: O'Shaughnessy, Intimate Pages, p. 137. The Plan of Ayala: Dunn, pp. 76–7; Cumberland, p. 183. 'A wild-looking ...': King, pp. 63–4. 'I for one ...': ibid., p. 74. The land problem: Gruening, p. 142; Strode, pp. 229–30; Cumberland, pp. 208–21. Gustavo Madero's payment: Creel, p. 301; Bell, pp. 90–3. Reyes uprising: Cumberland, pp. 187–9. Reyes surrenders: Daily Mail, 27 December 1911. Orozco rebellion: Bell, pp. 167–9. 'The well-groomed gentlemen ...': U.S. National Archives, 812.00/9484. Luis Terrazas: Larry A. Harris, Pancho Villa and the Columbus Raid, p. 33; Beals, p. 373; Stevens, pp. 157–9. Villa occupies Parral: Guzmán, Memoirs, pp. 58–9. Tom

Fountain's death: O'Reilly, p. 288. Orozco's telegram: U.S. Foreign Relations 1912, p. 790. Mormon victims: Romney, p. 176; De Wetter, pp. 112–13. Eleanor Wilson's 'lark': *Daily Mail*, 27 February 1912. The land torpedo: John H. McNeely, The Railways of Mexico, p. 22; O'Reilly, p. 287. Salas suicide: Mc-Neeley, p. 22. 'The Beginning of the End': *El Pais*, 26 March 1912. Huerta recalled: Parkes, p. 280; Creel, p. 305. Madero interview: Bell, p. 153. Rellano battle: ibid., p. 206. 'Huerta and his staff ...': Harris, p. 46. 'If his judgment ...': Guzmán, Memoirs, p. 69. 'Violent, undisciplined ...': O'Shaughnessy, A Diplomat's Wife, p. 159. Villa faces firing squad: Guzmán, Memoirs, pp. 73–5. 'I am no book-keeper': Bell, p. 212; Gruening, p. 302. Félix Díaz rebellion: Tweedie, Díaz to the Kaiser, pp. 113–14; Bell, pp. 231–2; Cumberland, pp. 202–4. Villa's escape from prison: Guzmán, Memoirs, pp. 76–90; Clarence C. Clendenen, The United States and Pancho Villa, pp. 25–6. 'Villa would not talk ...': *El Paso Times*, 13 January 1913.

Chapter 2: *Ten Tragic Days*

'The concrete net results ...': Eyler Newton Simpson, The Ejido—Mexico's Way Out, p. 49. 'Apathetic, ineffective ...': Henry Lane Wilson, p. 229. 'He had posted ...': Bell, pp. 248–9. 'Personal vendetta ...': Cline, p. 130. 'Unfortunate to the last degree ...': ibid., pp. 224–5. 'Mexico is seething ...': U.S. National Archives, 812.00/3048. 'Before returning here ...': Henry Lane Wilson, pp. 234–5. 'You have come at a bad time ...': Callcott, pp. 202–3. The plot against Madero: Bell, pp. 257–66. The uprising: Bell, pp. 268–79; Gruening, p. 304; Cumberland, pp. 233–4. 'A man of iron mould ...': Henry Lane Wilson, p. 295. 'Villian on an Elizabethan scale ...': Parkes, pp. 282–3. 'To destroy the appetite ...': Bell, p. 283. Belem prisoners released: Baerlein, p. 314. Madero in Cuernavaca: King, p. 107. Angeles court-martialled: Bell, p. 284. 'Many people killed ...': *Daily Mail*, 13 February 1911. Wilson's cables: U.S. National Archives, 812.00/6075. Sir Francis Stronge: Henry Lane Wilson, pp. 181–2; Baerlein, p. 314. The Minister's eggs: Moats, p. 99. The Japanese offer: Bell, p. 286. Wilson sees Madero: Henry Lane Wilson, pp. 256–8. 'Everything went beautifully ...': Moats, p. 91. Diplomatic corps meet: Gruening p. 567; Henry Lane Wilson, pp. 262–4. 'Huerta notifies me ...': U.S. National Archives, 812.00/6225. Simonds interview: *Daily Mail*, 18 February 1913. Blanquet arrests Madero: Bell, pp. 299–300; *Daily Mail*, 20 February 1913. Over-eager Wilson: Gruening, p. 567. Gustavo Madero arrested: Bell, p. 300; Gruening, p. 305.

Chapter 3: *Death of a President*

'Mexicans, brothers ...': Bell, p. 301. 'Without desiring ...': Henry Lane Wilson, p. 277. 'Mexico has been saved ...': Manuel Márquez Sterling, Los Últimos Días del Presidente Madero, pp. 471–2. 'To the Mexican people ...': Bell, p. 303. 'A wicked despotism ...': U.S. National Archives, 812.00/6277. Márquez Sterling and Madero: O'Shaughnessy, Intimate Pages, p. 181. Huerta's Cabinet: ibid., p. 213. Madero resigns: Henry Lane Wilson, p. 347. 'I swear to you ...': Ramón Prida, pp. 555–6. Lascuráin takes over, resigns: Callcott, p. 228; O'Shaughnessy, A Diplomat's Wife, pp. 18–19, Henry Lane Wilson, p. 291; *Daily Mail*, 21 February 1913. Gustavo Madero killed: Bell, p. 304; O'Shaughnessy, A Diplomat's Wife, p. 221. Train waits in vain: Cumberland, p. 240; Henry Lane Wilson, pp. 284–5. 'What was best ...': U.S. National Archives, 812.00/6271. Knox message: ibid. Mrs Madero sees Wilson: Interview between Mrs Madero and Robert Hammond Murray of the *New York World* on 15 August 1916 (quoted in Gruening, pp. 570–2); Henry Lane Wilson, pp. 283–4. Huerta manifesto: Bell, p. 316. 'Adiós, my general ...': King, p. 116. Madero's death: *Daily Mail*, 24, 25, 27 February 1913; Bell, p. 321; Moates, pp. 104–5. Cárdenas promoted: Creel, p. 321. Cárdenas suicide. John W. F. Dulles, Yesterday in Mexico, p. 92. 'In the absence ...': U.S. National Archives, 812.00/6353. 'This dark and sordid tragedy ...': *The Times*, 24 February 1913. 'I would suggest ...': Creel, p. 324. 'My most valuable moment ...': Henry Lane Wilson, p. 282. 'He was not a Strong Man ...': Strode, p. 237. 'The only fool ...': O'Shaughnessy, Intimate Pages, p. 157. 'A weak dreamer ...': Wellford Smith, p. 117. 'Considering all the factors ...': Cumberland, p. 258.

Chapter 1: *Mexico's Cromwell*

Huerta welcomed: Brenner, pp. 33–4. Carranza to Taft: Ray Stannard Baker, Woodrow Wilson: Life and Letters, p. 241. William Jennings Bryan: Tuchman, p. 40; Walter Lord, The Good Years, p. 295. Wilson's policy statement: Baker, p. 242. Carranza descriptions: Horgan, p. 916; Weyl, p. 33; Parkes, p. 290. Plan of Guadalupe: Robert E. Quirk, The Mexican Revolution 1914–15, p. 9. Obregón description: Hamilton Fyfe, article 'Ups and Downs in Mexico' in the *Daily Mail*, 23 October 1913; Young, p. 178; Dunn, p. 230. Obregón's early years: Dr E. J. Dillon, President Obregón—A World Reformer, pp. 31–48. 'The Maderist party ...': ibid., p. 59. Villa's telegram: Guzmán,

Memoirs, p. 95. Rabago's offer: Ramón Puente, Villa en Pie,
p. 74; Weyl, p. 37. Soldaderas Stevens, pp. 104–6; Reed, pp. 141,
187. Prisoners shot three deep: Guzmán, Memoirs, p. 97. 'I some-
times have to pause ...': Cary T. Grayson, Woodrow Wilson:
An Intimate Memoir, p. 30. The irony of fate: Baker, p. 237.
Laughlin and the Foreign Office: Burton J. Hendrick, Life and
Letters of Walter H. Page, pp. 180–1; Young, pp. 150–1. Britain
recognises Huerta: Charles Seymour, Intimate Papers of Colonel
House, p. 196; Callcott, p. 238. 'If the British government ...':
ibid., p. 196. 'Slow-minded, unimaginative ...': ibid., p. 215.
Henry Lane Wilson sacked: Baker, p. 254. William Bayard
Hale: Tuchman, p. 45; Baker, pp. 243, 253. Lind description:
O'Shaughnessy, A Diplomat's Wife, p. 3. 'To Whom It May
Concern ...': George M. Stephenson, John Lind of Minnesota,
p. 208. Lind's proposals: Hendrick, p. 193; Baker, pp. 266–8.
Wilson before Congress: Hendrick, p. 196; Baker, p. 274. 'About
five o'clock.': Stephenson, p. 225. Mondragón exiled: Bell,
p. 357. 'Huerta's Cabinet was made up ...': ibid., p. 358. El
Globo: Moats, p. 122; King, p. 124. 'That old Aztec ...': Moats,
p. 122. 'Acutely alcoholic ...': Brenner, p. 34. 'I arrest you ...':
O'Shaughnessy, A Diplomat's Wife, p. 24. Huerta's 'bookcase':
Daily Mail, 14 November 1913. The Fourth of July: Moats,
pp. 109–11.

Chapter 2: The Rise of Villa
  'He is a great man for little things ...': Dillon, Obregón, p. 80.
'We shall execute anybody ...': Fyfe, p. 14. 'As our eyes ...':
Reed, pp. 273–4. Tomás Urbina: Stevens, p. 86; Reed, p. 22.
Fausto Borunda: Reed, p. 65. Rodolfo Fierro: Stevens, pp. 87–
8; O'Hea, p. 69. 'When we entered ...': O'Reilly, p. 309. Villa's
fear of poisoning: Stevens, p. 109. Torreón description: O'Hea,
pp. 57–8. Villa elected commander: Guzmán, Memoirs, p. 102.
The torero of Torreón: O'Hea, pp. 122–4. Hospital train: Reed,
p. 144. 'Disgraced their cause': Review of Reviews, November
1913, p. 540. Dr Domínguez murdered: Gruening, p. 307. The
elections: Bell, p. 367; O'Shaughnessy, A Diplomat's Wife, p.
25; Stephenson, pp. 240–1; Baker, pp. 277–80; Callcott, p. 241.
'In saving the country ...': O'Shaughnessy, Intimate Pages, p.
218. 'Barrack Room President': Daily Mail, 22 November 1913.
'Mexico is like a snake ...': O'Shaughnessy, A Diplomat's Wife,
p. 130. 'If Huerta does not retire ...': Baker, p. 286. Letters to
Mrs Hulbert: ibid., pp. 273, 305. 'I should not worry ...':
Stephenson, p. 246. Lind criticises Britain: ibid., pp. 240, 244, 250.
'I cannot too strongly ...': Baker, p. 295. Tyrrell in Washing-
ton: Hendrick, p. 200. Carden recalled: ibid., p. 215.

Chapter 3: *To The Cannon's Mouth*

Financial chaos: Bell, pp. 372–3; O'Shaughnessy, Intimate Pages, pp. 264–5. Recruiting methods: O'Shaughnessy, A Diplomat's Wife, pp. 58, 66–7; Weyl, p. 53; Wellford Smith, pp. 143–4. Villa's women: Stevens, pp. 118, 200, 213–14; Braddy, Cock of the Walk, pp. 41, 46. Villa attacks Chihuahua City: Guzmán, Memoirs, pp. 109–11; The capture of Ciudad Juárez: ibid., pp. 111–14; Clendenen, p. 42; Puente, Vida de Francisca Villa, pp. 73–6. Black Cat Cafe: Schuster, pp. 119–22. General Castro accused: McNeely, p. 23. Firing squad story: De Wetter, pp. 116–17. Tierra Blanca: Guzmán, Memoirs, pp. 118–22; Clendenen, p. 45. 'Pathetic, worried figure': Reed, p. 8. Terrazas flees: Stevens, pp. 163–4. 'My valet was not there ...': De Wetter, p. 118. Luis Terrazas jr, ransom: *Daily Mail*, 7 March 1914; Stevens, pp. 165–7. Spaniards expelled: Reed, pp. 128–9. Villa re-equips: Harris, pp. 71–2. The Dorados: ibid., p. 68; Stevens, pp. 112–13; Reed, p. 141.

Chapter 4: *The Murdered Scotsman.*

Huerta's New Year's Eve speech: O'Shaughnessy, Intimate Pages, p. 254. Pre-Bastille France: Tuchman, p. 45. 'After the country is pacified ...': O'Shaughnessy, Intimate Pages, p. 262. Ojinaga falls: Reed, pp. 2–3, 9; Clendenen, pp. 57–8; Guzmán, Memoirs, p. 131. Fort Bliss cartoon; *Collier's Magazine*, 1 August 1914. Arms embargo lifted: Parkes, 294; O'Shaughnessy, Intimate Pages, p. 276. Von Hintze's offer: Tuchman, pp. 46–7. Cumbre Tunnel: *Daily Mail*, 19 February 1914; Schuster, pp. 140–1. Benton's death: Guzmán, Memoirs, pp. 133–7; Clendenen, pp. 66–70; Stevens, pp. 177–96; Baker, p. 308; *Daily Mail*, 23, 24, 25 February, 2 March 1914; *The Times*, 20, 21 February 1914; *Literary Digest*, XLVIII, 1914, pp. 481, 546; and information on the Benton family supplied by Mr Marcus K. Milne, City Librarian of the Aberdeen Public Library. General Scott meets Villa. Hugh L. Scott, Some Memories of a Soldier, pp. 500–2, 507, 516; Stevens, p. 131; Reed, pp. 142–3. Tuchman, p. 59. 'Villa threw me aside ...': O'Hea, pp. 200–1. 'You brute, you animal': Richard O'Connor, Black Jack Pershing, p. 109. 'If you should hear ...': Richard O'Connor, Ambrose Bierce, p. 299. Villa prints money: Reed, pp. 123–4; Guzmán, Memoirs, p. 143. Angeles joins Villa: Clendenen, p. 73. The medal ceremony: Reed, pp. 113–16. The Press wagon: Timothy Turner, pp. 176–7. 'I am a soldier ...': *Daily Mail*, 18 March 1914. Villa attends wedding: Quirk, Mexican Revolution, p. 20. Bermejillo falls: ibid., p. 20; Guzmán, Memoirs, p. 148. The telephone calls: Guzmán, Memoirs, p. 149. Attack on

Gómez Palacio: ibid., pp. 160–3; Quirk, Mexican Revolution, pp. 22–3. 'They were not viciously aggressive ...': O'Hea, p. 145. Vice-consul Cummins: ibid., pp. 148–9; Timothy Turner, pp. 192–3; *Daily Mail*, 11 April 1914. Torreón falls: Guzmán, Memoirs, pp. 172–6; Quirk, Mexican Revolution, pp. 23–4. Sorting horse manure: Timothy Turner, p. 194. 'Bacchanalian scenes ...': *Daily Mail*, 4 April 1914. 'The greatest leader ...': Reed, p. 140. Attack on San Pedro: Guzmán, Memoirs, pp. 186–7; Quirk, Mexican Revolution, pp. 25–6. 'Some of our horses ...': Guzmán, Memoirs, p. 185. Torreón Spaniards: Bell, p. 386; *New York Times*, 6 April 1914; Clendenen, p. 78; U.S. Foreign Relations, 1914, pp. 795–8. The first aircraft: Dulles, p. 7. The funeral salute: *Daily Mail*, 26 May 1914. Attack on Monterrey: Fyfe, pp. 46–7. Mexicans' bravery: ibid., p. 234. Tampico statistics: Brand, p. 113; Quirk, An Affair of Honour, p. 6. 'I am as proud ...': Young, p. 176.

Chapter 5: *A Question of Honour*

Lind's ludicrous plan: Stephenson, pp. 259–60, 'Lind leaves tonight ...': ibid., p. 261. 'Salutary equilibrium ...': Cline p. 155. U.S. Naval Strength: Quirk, Affair of Honour, pp. 8, 10–11. Arrest of whaleboat crew: ibid., pp. 20–3; Tuchman, p. 47. Admiral Mayo's attitude: Quirk, Affair of Honour, pp. 24–6. 'Mayo could not have done ...': U.S. National Archives, 812.00/11483. Esteva Ruiz: Quirk, Affair of Honour, p. 39. Wilson sees Lind: ibid., pp. 49–50. Atlantic Fleet for Tampico: *Daily Mail*, 16 April 1914. 'Is it a calamity?' Baker, p. 321. 'The old Indian ...': U.S. National Archives, 812.00/11514. Mail orderly's arrest: ibid., 812.00/11532; Cline, p. 156. 'Intolerable insults ...': *Daily Mail*, 16 April 1914. Huerta's proposal: O'Shaughnessy, A Diplomat's Wife, p. 259. Wilson's ultimatum: Baker, p. 322. Cabinet meeting: ibid., p. 322; Quirk, Affair of Honour, p. 70. Wilson's Press conference: Baker, p. 324. Wilson addresses Congress: ibid., p. 324; Quirk, Affair of Honour, pp. 74–6. The Pyjama Conference: Tuchman, pp. 49–50. 'If a man's house was on fire ...': Quirk, Affair of Honour, p. 77. The landing: ibid., pp. 85–97; Tuchman, p. 51; Tweedie, Díaz to the Kaiser, pp. 174–5. Naval Academy shelled: Tweedie, Díaz to the Kaiser, p. 189; O'Shaughnessy, A Diplomat's Wife, pp. 309, 316, 319–20. Huerta's statements: O'Shaughnessy, A Diplomat's Wife, p. 292, *Daily Mail*, 23 April 1914. Newspaper quotes: *El Imparcial*, 24 April; *La Patria*, 23 April; *El Independiente*, 23 April 1914, Carranza's comment: Baker, p. 321; Clendenen, p. 83. Obregón prepared to fight: Guzmán, Memoirs, p. 190; Quirk, Affair of Honour, p. 117. 'It is Huerta's bull ...';

Baker, p. 321. 'We could keep Veracruz ...': U.S. Foreign Relations, 1914, pp. 485–6. Anti-American riots: Moats, p. 141; O'Shaughnessy, A Diplomat's Wife, pp. 279, 304. Poisoning scare: Clendenen, p. 83. Girls smuggling cartridges: *Daily Mail*, 7 May 1914. O'Shaughnessys leave: O'Shaughnessy, A Diplomat's Wife, p. 295. 'We have done a great wrong ...': ibid., p. 316. 'The daily task ...': ibid., p. 355. Ypiranga unloads: Tuchman, p. 52, Cdr. Tweedie's rescue: Tweedie, Díaz to the Kaiser, pp. 189–93. The ABC Talks: Quirk, Affair of Honour, pp. 118–19; Baker, pp. 335, 345, 349; *Daily Mail*, 27, 28, 29, 30 April, 1, 2, 9 May, 10, 15 June 1914. 'An elaborate quadrille ...': Quirk, Affair of Honour, p. 118. 'My passion ...': Samuel G. Blythe, Mexico: The Record of a Conversation with President Wilson, *Saturday Evening Post*, 25 May 1914. 'Hesitation waltz ...': Quirk, Affair of Honour, p. 113. 'Merely give the order ...': ibid., p. 126.

Chapter 6: *Huerta's Last Glass*
Tampico falls: Bell, p. 401; *Daily Mail*, 27 April 1914. 'Well, we'll do it ... ': Juan Barragán Rodríguez, Historia del Ejército y de la Revolución Constitucionalista, p. 476. Paredón captured: Guzmán, Memoirs, pp. 196–7. Officers shot at lunch: ibid., pp. 198–9. Villa resigns command: ibid., pp. 213–14; Quirk, Mexican Revolution, p. 31. 'We do not accept ...': Guzmán, Memoirs, p. 220. The battle for Zacatecas: ibid., pp. 228–39. St. Clair Douglas: *The Times*, 6 July 1914; *New York Times*, 4, 7 July 1914. Coal supplies cut: Weyl, p. 43. Huerta resigns: Tuchman, p. 53; *Daily Mail*, 17 July 1914. 'Another Wilson Triumph': *New York Times*, 16 July 1914.

Chapter 1: *'Shoot This Traitor'*
Carranza's threat: Quirk, Mexican Revolution, p. 50. 'Nobody here doubts.': U.S. National Archives, 812.00/12614. 'A historical accident ...': Quirk, Mexican Revolution, p. 56. Iturbide in Teoloyucan: Eduardo Iturbide, Mi Paso Por La Vida, pp. 127–39; Wellford Smith, pp. 148–57. Obregón enters Mexico City: Quirk, Mexican Revolution, p. 59. Carranza arrives: ibid., pp. 61–4; Dulles, p. 7. Naco talks: Clendenen, p. 110. Nine-point plan: Guzmán, Memoirs, pp. 302–3. Villa's massive parade: ibid., pp. 314–15. Villa and Obregón argument: ibid., pp. 316–18; Dillon, President Obregón, pp. 109–13; Clendenen, pp. 115–16; Alvaro Obregón, Ocho Mil Kilometros en Campaña, p. 266. Villa withdraws recognition: Guzmán, Memoirs, p. 320. Obregón

brought back: Quirk, Mexican Revolution, p. 79. Obregón's escape: Dillon, President Obregón, pp. 116-20; Quirk, Mexican
Revolution, pp. 81-2; Guzmán, Memoirs, p. 321. 'His eyes were
dancing ...': U.S. National Archives, 812.00/13326. Herrera
rebels: Guzmán, Memoirs, p. 323. Suicide pact: ibid., p. 311.
Aguascalientes description: Dunn, p. 233; Tannenbaum, Peace
by Revolution, p. 158. 'I had only to take ...': Guzmán, The
Eagle and the Serpent, pp. 264, 267. Villa at the Convention:
Guzmán, Memoirs, p. 338; Tannenbaum, Peace by Revolution,
p. 158. Carranza stays away: Quirk, Mexican Revolution, p. 114.
The film show: Guzmán, Eagle and Serpent, p. 266; and conversation with Señor Guzmán in Mexico City, 18 May 1967. 'At the
age of thirty ...': Quirk, Mexican Revolution, p. 109. Díaz
Soto's speech: Guzmán, Eagle and Serpent, pp. 272-3; Quirk,
Mexican Revolution, pp. 109-10; U.S. National Archives,
812.00/13619. Carranza offers to resign: Quirk, Mexican Revolution, p. 115. 'I propose not only ...': Guzmán, Memoirs, p.
349. Gutiérrez chosen: Quirk, Mexican Revolution, p. 118. The
collapse of the Convention: ibid., pp. 120-8. The occupation of
Veracruz: Quirk, Affair of Honour, pp. 124-71.

Chapter 2: *A Suffering City*
    Zapatistas enter Mexico City: Strode, p. 246; Wellford Smith,
p. 283; Moats, p. 182. Villa meets Zapata: Guzmán, Memoirs,
pp. 378-9; Quirk, Mexican Revolution, pp. 135-9. 'The people
of the city ...': Guzmán, Memoirs, pp. 378-9. 'Soldiers afoot...':
Harper's Weekly, 16 January 1914. 'The supreme gamble ...'.
Weyl, p. 62. Puebla captured: Quirk, Mexican Revolution, p.
141. Iturbide's escape: O'Shaughnessy, A Diplomat's Wife, p.
240; Clendenen, pp. 137-8. 'What days those were ...': Guzmán,
Eagle and Serpent, p. 342. Berlanga's death: ibid., pp. 345-9;
Quirk, Mexican Revolution, pp. 144, 148. 150 people shot:
Quirk, Mexican Revolution, p. 145; Clendenen, p. 138. 'Killed by
mistake': O'Reilly, p. 237. Gutiérrez breaks with Villa, flees:
Quirk, Mexican Revolution, pp. 147-8, 166-7; Guzmán, Memoirs,
pp. 409, 421; Guzmán, Eagle and Serpent, pp. 354-6; Clendenen,
p. 144. González Garza elected: Quirk, Mexican Revolution, pp.
169-70. 'Milk tickets': Moats, p. 172. Naco: Major Frank
Tompkins, Chasing Villa, pp. 37-8; Scott, pp. 509-11; Clendenen,
pp. 141-3; Quirk, Mexican Revolution, pp. 158-64; *Collier's
Magazine*, 19 August 1916. Carranza's social programme: Weyl,
p. 47; Strode, p. 248. Obregón enters Mexico City and description of conditions in capital: Quirk, Mexican Revolution, pp.
180-96. Clendenen, p. 146. 'The situation grows worse....' U.S.
Foreign Relations, 1915, p. 650. 'Filth and pestilence.': Moats,

p. 171. 'In the last 100 years ...': Tannenbaum, Peace by Revolution, p. 65. 'From the moment ...': Dillon, President Obregón, p. 102. 'You will find yourselves ...': Quirk, Mexican Revolution, p. 214. Zapatistas come to tea: O'Shaughnessy, Intimate Pages, p. 120. McManus killed: Moats, p. 185; Wellford Smith, p. 283; Clendenen, p. 153. Homes wrecked: Dunn, pp. 244–5; Moats, p. 154.

Chapter 3: Obregón v. Villa
Villa–Garza conference: Guzmán, Memoirs, p. 423. 'Defeats also are battles ...': ibid., p. 430. 'Jingle of my spurs': ibid., p. 446. Battle of Celaya: Edgcumb Pinchon, Viva Villa! pp. 311–15; Barragán Rodríguez, p. 294; Dulles, pp. 11–12; Quirk, Mexican Revolution, pp. 221–5; Guzmán, Memoirs, pp. 454–69. 'I wanted everyone to understand ...': Guzmán, Memoirs, p. 471. 'I saw in his glance ...': ibid., p. 473. 'I will win by attacking tomorrow': ibid., p. 480. Obregón loses an arm: Dulles, pp. 12–13; Dillon, President Obregón, pp. 122–3. 'The best Mexican army ...': Dunn, p. 259. Urbina's death: Stevens, pp. 279–81; Pinchon, pp. 323–6. Hungry women invade Chamber: Quirk, Mexican Revolution, pp. 245–6, 249–50. Wilson's speeches: Tompkins, pp. 34–5; Clendenen, pp. 171–3; Mexican Revolution, pp. 256–7; U.S. Foreign Relations, 1915, pp. 697–708. Bryan resigns: Clendenen, p. 176. 'Any reasonable proposition ...': U.S. National Archives, 812.00/15490. Mexico City changes hands again: Quirk, Mexican Revolution, pp. 264–76; U.S. Foreign Relations, 1915, p. 274; Moats, p. 181; Cameron, p. 244. Huerta's return and arrest: Tuchman, pp. 66–82; Bush, p. 244; O'Shaughnessy, Intimate Pages, p. 341. Orozco's death: Bush, p. 245; Schuster, p. 196. Huerta at Fort Bliss: Tuchman, pp. 82–3; Stevens, pp. 266–8; O'Shaughnessy, Intimate Pages, p. 343. Huerta's death: Tuchman, pp. 91–2; O'Shaughnessy, Intimate Pages, p. 350. Villa's stolen cattle: Quirk, Mexican Revolution, p. 284. Washington conference: ibid., pp. 280–1; Cline, p. 173; U.S. Foreign Relations, 1915, pp. 734–66. Carranza recognised; newspaper quotes: Literary Digest, 23 October and 6 November 1915. General Scott's quote: Scott, p. 517. Rhoades comment: Clendenen, p. 207. Battle of Agua Prieta: ibid., pp. 209–11; Weyl, pp. 49–51; Pinchon, pp. 330–3; Collier's Magazine, 19 August 1916. American doctors imprisoned: Braddy, Cock of the Walk, p. 121. Mormons suffer: Romney, p. 241. Border violence. Clendenen, pp. 218–19, 223. Santa Ysabel massacre: ibid., pp. 225–6; Schuster, p. 200; Literary Digest, 22 January 1916. 'Villa did not know ...': Albuquerque Morning Journal, 23 January 1916, quoted in May Stirrat, The Francisco Villa Raid

on Columbus, master's thesis, University of New Mexico, 1935, p. 27. Rodríguez's body on display: Braddy, Cock of the Walk, p. 128. El Paso riot: O'Connor, Pershing, p. 113; de Wetter, p. 154. Newspaper comments: *Literary Digest*, 29 January 1916. 'Why do you celebrate ...?': Lincoln Steffens, The Autobiography of Lincoln Steffens, p. 735. 'I begin to understand ...': Fyfe, p. 22. 'The killing of Mexicans ...': Samuel Guy Inman, Intervention in Mexico, pp. 150-1.

Chapter 4: *The Pershing Expedition*

Columbus description: Tompkins, pp. 48-51; Stevens, p. 283; Harris, p. 84; Braddy, Pancho Villa at Columbus, p. 17; O'Connor, Pershing, p. 113 (this and all further references mentioned here are from Richard O'Connor's book, Black Jack Pershing). The garrison: Tompkins, pp. 44, 48; O'Connor, p. 113; Col. H. A. Toulmin, jr. With Pershing in Mexico, pp. 22-31. 'We rode stealthily ...': Col. S. A. Villanueva, *El Paso Herald Post*, 21 February 1962. McKinney, Corbett killed: Tompkins, pp. 61-2. The attack plan: Bill McGaw, interview at Columbus, May 1967. The Columbus Raid: Toulmin, pp. 31-8; Tompkins, pp. 48-59; Braddy, Pancho Villa, pp. 17-30. Carson Jackson: Toulmin, p. 37. 'Am sure Villa's attacks ...': Tuchman, p. 95. 'The most vigorous means ...': Horgan, p. 926. Orders to Funston: U.S. Foreign Relations, 1916, p. 483. Pershing: Haldeen Braddy, Pershing's Mission in Mexico, pp. 5-6 (all Braddy's references in this chapter are from the Pershing book) John's up against a lot: O'Connor, p. 118. 'Fourth-class skirmish': *Literary Digest*, 1 April 1916. Shortage of trucks: Scott, p. 531; Stirrat, p. 58. Expedition leaves: Tompkins, p. 74; O'Connor, p. 118. Conditions: Horgan, p. 930; Tompkins, pp. 113, 248; Braddy, pp. 20-1. Villa wounded: Braddy, p. 17. Dodd at Guerrero: Toulmin, pp. 52-3; Tompkins, pp. 87-8. 'Go find Villa ...' Tompkins, p. 110. The Parral incident: ibid., pp. 137-54; Toulmin, pp. 62-6; Braddy, pp. 32-4. Border talks: Scott, pp. 525-8; Clendenen, pp. 272-4. Von Bernstorff's quote: Horgan, p. 928. 'Damn fine fight': Toulmin, p. 85. Cárdenas killed: Tompkins, pp. 200-2; O'Connor, p. 134. Cervantes killed: Tompkins, p. 203; Braddy, pp. 42-3. Treviño's warning: O'Connor, pp. 134-5; Clendenen, p. 277. The Carrizal affair: Toulmin, pp. 71-8; Tompkins, pp. 208-12; O'Connor, pp. 135-6; Clendenen, pp. 278-81; Braddy, pp. 48-54. Uncle Sam cartoon: *Acción Mundial*, 6 July 1916. Peace commission: Scott, pp. 529-30; Horgan, p. 936; Clendenen, pp. 284-5. 'Through no fault of his own ...': *New York Herald*, 24 November 1916. 'Since General Pershing ...': *Kansas City Journal*, 1 July 1916. Villa captures Chihuahua City: *Daily*

Mail, 22 September 1916. Villa takes Torreón: Weyl, p. 54; O'Hea, pp. 206; Clendenen, p. 293. The Christmas storm': Tompkins, p. 214; Braddy, p. 61. 'Nobody got punished': Horgan, p. 936. 'Failure in every respect': Strode, p. 252. 'Hodge-podge of interference ...': Tompkins, p. 184. 'Record of barren futility': *Literary Digest*, 3 February 1917. Funston's death. O'Connor, p. 140.

Chapter 5: *Germany's blunder*
Carranza and von Eckhardt: Young, p. 180. Germans in Mexico: Tuchman, pp. 99, 103, 117. The Zimmermann Telegram and reactions: Tuchman, pp. 7, 116–95. Fletcher booed: Vicente Blasco Ibañez, Mexico In Revolution, pp. 68–9. 'The most corrupt administration ...': Letter from Plutarco Elías Calles to Adolfo de la Huerta, 1 February 1920, quoted in Gruening, p. 318. Carranza's régime: Parkes, pp. 304–5; Gibbon, p. 23. Obregón resigns: Dillon, President Obregón, pp. 150–1. 'They speculate with everything ...': Letter from Calles to de la Huerta, 1 February 1920. 'All of us are thieves ...': Strode, p. 272. 'I confess that ...': Dillon, President Obregón, p. 129. The new verb: Parkes, p. 305. 'The most important event ...': Tannenbaum, Peace by Revolution, pp. 166–7. The Constitution of 1917: Parkes, pp. 306–8; Strode, pp. 254–8; Gruening, pp. 100–1, 214–15; Cline, pp. 166–71. 'The history of Mexico ...': Parkes, p. 308. Land distribution figures: Weyl, p. 59; Brand, p. 89. Carranza's relations with labour: Weyl, p. 60; Parkes, p. 308. A.B.C. comment: Thomas Edward Gibbon, Mexico Under Carranza, pp. 189–93. Blanquet's rebellion: O'Shaughnessy, Intimate Pages, p. 177.

Chapter 6: *The Death of Zapata*
Countryside ravaged: Tannenbaum, Peace by Revolution, pp. 176–9. 'There was only devastation ...': King, p. 206. Zapata's tortures: Dunn, pp. 31–2, 38, 153. Death of Zapata: Parkes, p. 309; Gruening, pp. 310–11. Avenue of Hanging Men: Information supplied to the author during visit to Chihuahua City, May 1967. Knotts kidnapped: Braddy, Cock of the Walk, p. 83. 'Most people feel ...': Romney, p. 246. Parral captured: Braddy, Cock of the Walk, p. 147; Clendenen, pp. 309–10. Villa attacks Juárez: Clendenen, pp. 310–12; *Daily Mail*, 17 June 1919. Angeles executed: King, p. 308; Scott, pp. 504, 507. Villa attacks train: Dillon, Mexico on the Verge, p. 18. 'The bloody devastation ...': Gruening, p. 105. Health: Callcott, p. 261; Gibbon, pp. 11–12. V.D.: Pardo, La Prostitución en Mexico, pp. 179, 181. 'This figure ...': *El Excelsior*, 21 December 1918. *Daily Mail* article: *Daily Mail*, 12 May 1920. Bonillas chosen: Gruening,

p. 106; Dulles, pp. 19–20, 22; Dillon, President Obregón, p. 178; Creel, p. 349. Obregón a candidate: Dillon, President Obregón, pp. 171–3. 'The penal colony ...': Creel, p. 348. Obregón and Cabrera quotes on Bonillas: Dulles, pp. 22–3. *El Monitor* quotes: Dillon, President Obregón, p. 179. 'I cannot hook up ...': Dulles, p. 20. Bonillas arrives: ibid., pp. 22–3; Dillon, President Obregón, pp. 185–6. Mexico City revue: Vicente Blasco Ibañez, El Militarismo Mejicano, quoted in Dulles, p. 24.

Chapter 7: *Murder in the Mountains*
Sonora troubles: Dulles, p. 23; Weyl, p. 61. Cejudo trial and Obregón's escape: Dulles, pp. 25, 27–31; Dillon, President Obregón, pp. 187–91, 195. Rebellion begins: Dulles, pp. 31–4; Weyl, p. 61 'I cannot trust anyone ...': Dillon, President Obregón, pp. 201–2. 'President and Father ...': Gruening, p. 319. 'You could not go ...': Moats, p. 231. Carranza's trains: Dillon, President Obregón, pp. 202–3; Creel, p. 352; Stevens, p. 276; Dulles, pp. 36, 38. Carranza's flight and death: Dulles, pp. 41–8. Carranza's burial: ibid., p. 59. De la Huerta elected: ibid., pp. 59, 63–5. Zapatistas pacified: Parkes, p. 311. Villa retires: Lansford, p. 262; Dulles, pp. 68–70. González and Guajardo: Dulles, pp. 73–4. Pineda O.: Adolfo de la Huerta, Memorias, pp. 165–8. 'Here you vote for God ...': Gruening, p. 212. Obregón elected: Dulles, pp. 84–6; Cline, p. 439.

Appendix 1: *The Death of Pancho Villa*
Villa at Canutillo: Braddy, Cock of the Walk, pp. 153, 156; Dulles, pp. 177–8; Stevens, pp. 295–8. Carl Beers quotes: *El Paso Herald Post*, 30 July 1959. Villa's assassination: Schuster, p. 305; Gruening, p. 313; Cameron, p. 260; Pinchon, pp. 371–6; *Daily Mail*, 24 July 1923; *El Paso Herald Post*, 21 July 1923; *Time Magazine*, 4 June 1951. 'I'm not a murderer ...': *Time*, 4 June 1951.

Appendix 2: *The Death of Obregón*
'You and I, Plutarco ...': Jorge Prieto Laurens, *El Universal*, 15 January 1958, quoted in Dulles, pp. 173–4. De la Huerta rebellion: Dulles, pp. 188–263. Plots against Obregón: ibid., pp. 362–3. Death of Obregón: ibid., pp. 364–9.

Index

Index

Note: The significant part of many Mexican names is the penultimate one, therefore Francisco Vázquez Gómez, for instance, will be found indexed under Vázquez Gómez, Francisco and not under Gómez, Francisco Vázquez. The names of states appear in brackets after the names of cities and towns.

Urbina, Tómas, 165–6, 167, 168,
243, 263, 279–80

Vázquez Gómez, Emilio, 111
Vázquez Gómez, Francisco, 63,
74–5, 105, 107, 111
Velasco, General José Refugio,
201–2, 203–4
Vera Estañol, Jorge, 138, 161
Veracruz, City of, 24, 32, 49, 94,
119, 140, 161, 172, 191, 210–
25, 227, 253–5, 266
Villa, Pancho (Francisco)
(Doroteo Arango): description, 67–8, 199; wives, 101,
180; character, 196–7; opposition to Díaz, 68; hatred of
Chinese, 78–9; triggers off
assault on Juárez, 84; loyalty
to Madero, 90; opposes
Orozco, 113–17; relationship
with Huerta, 117; sentenced
to death but escapes, 118–21;
returns to Mexico, 153; fights
Colorados at Casas Grandes,
155; recognises Carranza,
155; relationship with supporters, 166–7; leader of
Division of the North, 168;
takes Torreón, 170; attacks
Chihuahua City, 181–2; captures Juárez, 182–3; routs
Federals, 185–6; takes Chihuahua, 186; forms Dorados,
188; takes Ojinaga, 186;
Castillo incident, 191; death
of W. S. Benton, 191–5;
meeting with Scott, 195–6;
treatment of prisoners, 196,
205, 206–7, 228, 231; Pershing
on, 197; prints currency, 198;
decorated by Angeles, 199;
takes Bermejillo, 201–2; takes
Gómez Palacio, 202–4; takes
Torreón, 204–5; and Verz-
cruz incident, 220; captures

Saltillo, 227–8; resigns, 229;
takes Zacatecas, 230; meetings with Obregón, 240–4;
repudiates Carranza, 244; and
Convention of Aguascali-
entes, 247–50; appointed
commander of Army of Con-
vention, 252; meets Zapata,
257–9; fighting in Naco, 264;
attacks Guadalajara, 274;
defeated by Obregón at
Celaya, 275–7, and at León,
278–9; sympathy for, 289;
reaction to U.S. recognition
of Carranza, 290; defeated at
Agua Prieta, 291–2; besieges
Hermosillo, 293; implicated
in Santa Ysabel massacre,
294–6; the 'Columbus Raid',
300–5; hounded by Pershing
Expedition, 306–7; wounded
at Guerrero, 309; raids Chihuahua City, 317, and Torreón, 317–18; reappears and
raids Chihuahua and other
northern towns, 331, 332, 333;
defeat by U.S. forces in
Juárez, 334; negotiates retirement with de la Huerta, 348;
in retirement, 353; murdered,
355
Villar, General Lauro, 127,
128
Villareal, Antonio I., 127, 246,
250, 262, 275, 346

Wilson, Henry Lane, 18, 34, 36,
54, 68, 92–3, 95, 107, 111,
122–5, 129, 131–2, 133, 134,
137, 138, 141–2, 144–6, 149,
150, 157, 159
Wilson, Woodrow, 33, 115,
124–5, 149–50, 155–60, 174,
210, 213–17, 219, 222, 224,
227, 233, 254, 269–70, 281,
320–5